24.99

Contemporary Learning Disability Practice

Contemporary Learning Disability Practice

edited by
Mark Jukes and Martin Bollard

Quay Books
MA Healthcare Limited

Quay Books Division, MA Healthcare Limited, Jesses Farm, Snow Hill, Dinton,
Salisbury, Wiltshire, SP3 5HN

British Library Cataloguing-in-Publication Data
A catalogue record is available for this book

Printed in the UK by Bath Press, Bath

Contents

List of contributors

John Aldridge is Senior Lecturer in Nursing (learning disabilities), University College Northampton, Park Campus, Boughton Green Road, Northampton NN2 7AZ

Mark Alison is Senior Practitioner, St David's Hospital, Carmarthen, Pembrokeshire and Derwen NHS Trust

Janet C Bailey is Senior Lecturer (learning disabilities), University College Worcester, Henwick Grove, Worcester, WR2 6AJ

Sue Bickerton is Community Nurse (learning disabilities) — specialist practitioner, Smallwood House, Church Green West, Redditch, Worcester

Martin Bollard is Senior Lecturer (learning disability nursing), School of Nursing and Midwifery, De Montfort University, Charles Frears Campus, Leicester

Sandra Brickley is Community Nurse (learning disabilities), New Burton House, Burton Bank Lane, Moss Pit, Stafford ST17 9JW, South Staffordshire Health Care NHS Trust

Rosemary Brown is Continuing Care Liaison Officer, Cannock Chase Primary Care Trust, Block D, Beecroft Court, Cannock, Staffordshire WS11 IJP

Jane Bullock is Community Nurse (learning disabilities) — specialist practitioner, Droitwich Health Center, Droitwich, Worcestershire Mental Health Partnership NHS Trust

Catherine C Doherty is Epilepsy Liaison Nurse, St Stephen's Centre, Birmingham, South Birmingham PCT NHS Trust, Learning Disabilities Directorate

David Elliott is Community Nurse (learning disabilities), New Burton House Community Unit, Stafford, South Staffordshire Health Care Trust

Noel Fagan is Lecturer in Nursing, University of Manchester, School of Nursing and Midwifery, Gateway House, Piccadilly South, Manchester M60 7LP

Elaine Harris is Community Nurse (learning disabilities) — specialist practitioner, Smallwood House, Church Green West, Redditch, Worcestershire, Worcestershire Mental Health Partnership NHS Trust

Andy Howe is Community Nurse/Behaviour Therapist, Joint Community Learning Disability Team, 40 Tan Bank, Wellington, Telford, Shropshire TF1 1HW

Veronica R Jackson is Lecturer Practitioner, School of Health, University of Wolverhampton, Walsall Campus, Gorway Road, Walsall, WS1 3BD

Mark Jukes is Senior Lecturer (learning disabilities) School of Primary Health Care, Faculty of Health and Community Care, University of Central England, Birmingham

Sharon Mackenzie is Community Nurse (learning disabilities) — specialist practitioner, St Stephen's Centre, Handsworth, Heart of Birmingham, South Birmingham Primary Care Trust

Steve McNally is Lecturer Practitioner, Oxford Brookes University, Oxfordshire Learning Disability NHS Trust, School of Health and Social Care, Oxford Brookes University, ISIS Education Centre, Warneford Lane, Headington, Oxon OX3 7JX

Bernard Natale is Clinical Nurse Specialist, Joint Commissioning Team for People with Learning Disabilities, Fenham, 5 Moorfield Road, West Didsbury, Manchester M20 2VZ

Ruth Northway is Professor of Learning Disability Nursing, Unit for Development in Intellectual Disabilities, School of Care Sciences, University of Glamorgan, Pontypridd, Wales, CF37 1DL

Neville Parkes is Lecturer Practitioner (focusing on sexual issues with regard to people with learning disabilities), North Warwickshire NHS Trust, PCT and University of Wolverhampton

Tim Plant is Community Nurse (learning disabilities), Salford Primary Care Trust, New Directions, White Moss House, Bracken Avenue, Walkden, Manchester M28 3SS

Penny Pritchard is Clinical Coordinator, Community Teams, South Staffordshire Healthcare NHS Trust, New Burton House, Burton Bank Lane, Moss Pit, Stafford ST17 9JW

Rachael Skinner is Lecturer Practitioner (sensory and learning disability), North Warwickshire Primary Care Trust and School of Health, University of Wolverhampton

Caron Thomas is Nurse Consultant (learning disabilities), South Staffordshire NHS Trust, St George's Hospital, Stonefield House, Corporation Street, Stafford

Foreword

Within the wider disabled people's rights movement, the campaign for greater recognition of the rights and dignity of people with learning disabilities has often struggled to keep up. The Government's White Paper, *Valuing People: A New Strategy for Learning Disability for the 21st Century* was a very welcome step forward, but published as it was in 2001, it was not before time. People with learning disabilities face particular challenges in having their voices heard by the wider community, and the barriers they face are not always as immediately obvious to policy makers as the ones that present people with physical and sensory disabilities.

The Government's White Paper outlines four important principles that are further explored in this book: civil rights, inclusion, independence and choice. This is a far cry from the medical model that dominated care for people with learning disabilities in the twentieth century. The books' contributors do not shy away from the inherently political nature of this new approach and, as such, politicians as well as healthcare professionals should read it.

Earlier this year, I launched a report in the European Parliament by the Mental Disability Advocacy Centre about the widespread use of cage beds for people with learning disabilities in the Czech Republic, Slovenia, Slovakia and Hungary. In the United Kingdom we have thankfully moved on from such practices long ago. The challenge is now to lead by example.

Liz Lynne MEP
Vice Chair of the European Parliament's All Party Disability Intergroup
and a member of the Committee for Employment and Social Affairs.
Rapporteur for the European Year of Disabled People 2003
October, 2003

Introduction

This book is about celebrating the diverse contemporary learning disability practices of registered learning disability nurses (RNLDs), across a broad spectrum of health and social services.

It has long been our ambition to create a comprehensive text which provides an academic and professional debut of the value RNLDs have in contributing towards the quality of life for people with learning disabilities.

This book also encourages 'closure' upon debates which endorse scepticism, cynicism and doubts over what an RNLD has to offer people with learning disabilities who live and interact within a variety of settings.

Although the vision has been in our minds for some time, the actual development of this book has taken just two years. This has mainly been due to the overwhelming desire and motivation from a rich array of specialist practitioners, who wish to put their knowledge, skills, interventions and innovations into the public domain.

We are confident that from these chapters, you will discover that these specialist areas of practice are written with an underlying passion, empathy, warmth, confidence and competence, when engaging in meaningful relationships with people with learning disabilities. The text clearly demonstrates the broad spectrum of services within which this practice takes place.

For us as editors, it has been most rewarding in seeing first, second, third and in some cases fourth and fifth drafts of chapters unravelling into a true reflection of the practitioner's 'art' of contemporary learning disability practice.

A number of contributors collectively formed a 'Writers Guild', from which not only peer support assisted in the formulation of individual chapters, but also personal and critical reflection. When creating our vision for this text, it has always been the intention to capture the essence of particular domains of practice, while not restricting individual contributors with a prescribed chapter structure. Presenting contributors with a loose, but focused structure, gave new emergent authors a framework in which to attach their thinking.

It has been important from our own professional networking to know those specialist practitioners who are able to produce work and keep to deadlines. We acknowledge the many competing demands that people have within the hectic professional practice world and that writing about professional practice often becomes a low priority. We are immensely indebted to those practitioners who have sacrificed their time in helping us to achieve a most comprehensive account of specialist practice across the field of learning disability.

We would like to thank Liz Lynne for agreeing to write the foreword to this book, and to acknowledge her lifelong personal and political crusade in support of human rights for all people who are subjected to marginalisation across the field of disability. Also, to Binkie Mais, publisher at Quay Books, MA Healthcare Ltd, for her unparalleled passion, enthusiasm and support in developing *Contemporary Learning Disability Practice*.

Summary of chapters

The book is divided into five sections: foundations for specialist practice; primary health care; person-centred perspectives, specialist services; and further dimensions of learning disability nursing practice.

Section I (foundations for specialist practice)

Chapter 1: Mark Jukes provides a lucid account of what constitutes specialist practice for people with learning disabilities. The chapter is grounded in an optimism that specialist learning disability practice can move away from the incessant practice insecurities that have historically dogged this area. Strategies are given that can assist in the narrowing of the theory-practice gap.

Chapter 2: Martin Bollard highlights the relevance, importance and challenges in achieving effective inter-professional working. Certain approaches are offered as a way in which workers in the field can develop meaningful collaboration, not only with people with learning disabilities, but also with other professional groups.

Section II (primary health care)

Chapter 3: Jane Bullock and Sharon McKenzie cite the menopause as one of the many examples where the health needs of women with learning disabilities have been overlooked. The authors share their own work and a tool to offer guidance for others wishing to pursue work in this important area.

Chapter 4: Penny Pritchard clearly demonstrates how a specialist practitioner has grounded her work in the relevant evidence base on health surveillance. She shares her case work and health screening process in a reflective manner.

Chapter 5: Sandra Brickley skilfully shares her research and work with parents who have a learning disability. The chapter offers guidance to others who may be working in this highly skilled and sensitive area of practice, pinpointing the implications and impact upon parents, children and professionals when parents with learning disabilities are denied the right to parent.

Chapter 6: If readers ever need a good example of where nurses are able to demonstrate a level of professional introspection and reflection, they need look no further than this chapter. How specialist practitioners demonstrate leadership skills, affect change and underpin their practice with a health promotion model are highlighted in this chapter on being a learning disability nurse board member of a primary care group.

Chapter 7: This chapter builds on a seminal paper by Martin Bollard and Mark Jukes (published in 1999), which described a primary care model for people with learning disabilities. Grounded in the social exclusion debate, it offers clear signposts for practitioners, managers and commissioners to grasp this timely opportunity to meet the primary health care needs of people with learning disabilities.

Section III (engagement with a person-centred perspective)

Chapter 8: John Aldridge explains this widely used model of health assessment. This explicit and versatile example of an holistic model should be immensely useful for all students, practitioners and academics associated with the field.

Chapter 9: Restates the significance and impact that loss and bereavement has on people with learning disabilities. David Elliott ably and sensitively outlines a process of bereavement support that is underpinned by two clear conceptual frameworks.

Chapter 10: Steve McNally revisits the ubiquitous topics of advocacy and empowerment. Through the dissemination of primary research data, he urges practitioners, in particular, to ground their work in the experience of people with learning disabilities, utilising group work as a tool to promote client advocacy.

Chapter 11: Neville Parkes demonstrates, quite powerfully at times, the skilled interventions required when working with people with learning disabilities who have been sexually abused. The chapter explicitly applies appropriate models of care to help readers understand the level of competence and humility needed, when working with case examples of this nature.

Chapter 12: Ruth Northway is an active proponent of participatory research, and through this chapter gives an overview of this process, exploring some of the practical implications when adopting such a research design, where the ethos is about a real partnership with people with a learning disability.

Section IV (specialist services)

Chapter 13: Janet C Bailey and Veronica R Jackson offer more clarity to the often misunderstood notions of mental health in learning disabilities, with particular reference to recognition and assessment of mental health and models of care.

Chapter 14: Andy Howe illustrates the necessity for skilled intervention when working with people with challenging behaviour in the community. He not only flags up different assessment tools that should be of use to all workers involved with people with challenging behaviour, but also discusses conflicts surrounding the role of a community nurse as behaviour therapist within joint teams.

Chapter 15: Bernard Natale gives a unique insight into the unchartered waters of commissioning specialist forensic services, and the value of applying learning disability nursing skills to a forensic commissioning role. Apart from providing an interesting account of a commissioning role, he identifies the transferability of specialist nursing skills within a merged health and social services team.

Chapter 16: Mark Alison demonstrates the ability of a practitioner with generic skills, adapting effectively to working with people with forensic needs. Learning disability nurses can make a significant contribution to a very new and specialised area of practice.

Chapter 17: Rachael Skinner discusses the needs of people with multi-sensory impairment, crystallising an integrated approach to meeting multi-sensory needs: useful guidance for all those involved with this group of people.

Chapter 18: Catherine C Doherty gives a lucid description of the specialist epilepsy nurse's role. The 'Epilepsy Health Record', presented for the first time in print, (*Appendix IV*), should be of particular interest to all workers, both nursing and medical, working in partnership with people with epilepsy.

Section V (further dimensions of learning disability nursing practice)

Chapter 19: Rosemary Brown gives an insight into how practitioners have developed reflective practice through the clinical supervision process. The chapter demonstrates how self-awareness, critical reflection and problem solving can be enhanced through the use of 'home-grown' reflective tools.

Chapter 20: Caron Thomas provides a well-balanced discussion of the role of the nurse consultant in relation to clinical governance. This chapter not only debates some of the core functions of the nurse consultant, but also delivers an intriguing insight into this new and emerging role from the perspective of the nurses themselves.

Chapter 21: Noel Fagan and Tim Plant discuss the value of joint practitioners in health and social care. The topic of joint training is not a new one, however, this chapter relocates the debate in recent policy initiatives and states the changing needs of people with learning disabilities, which requires practitioners with a heterogeneous knowledge base.

Mark Jukes
Senior Lecturer in Learning Disabilities
School of Primary Health Care
University of Central England, Birmingham

Martin Bollard
Senior Lecturer in Learning Disabilities
School of Nursing
De Montfort University, Leicester
September 2003

Section I:
Foundations for specialist practice

I

Towards practice development in contemporary learning disability nursing

Mark Jukes

This chapter will identify the present policy context in the justification for promoting specialist nursing practices within learning disability services. Themes pursued are specialist nursing practice development, creating a culture for practice development where a strategic approach is proposed in an attempt to narrow the theory-practice gap. A case study will follow to illustrate how this process may be applied. Emphasis on these perspectives are regarded as essential building blocks to assist in furthering specialist knowledge in pursuance of an authoritative practice base within learning disability nursing.

Historically, learning disability nursing has had a somewhat fractured evolution and development in the midst of policies which have ranged from the support of the colony/hospital institutional era, community care reforms and now within the context of individualised care, supported living and person-centred planning.

A study by Alaszewski *et al* (2000) has focused upon the development of learning disability nursing, and found that through the influence of various evolving policies and changes in societal attitudes, that these have directly impacted upon the learning disability nurse's role.

The report identified that existing reforms and influences across the health and social care sectors were placing more emphasis on the learning disability nurse as manager, who is also experiencing a dissonance associated with the demand and expectation for a greater diversity of roles and skills in the support of people with learning disabilities and their families. The implication being, that many nurses found their amount of client contact was being eroded or compromised by the demand for managerial and leadership responsibilities.

This study also identified that some nurses found that by specialising in areas such as behaviour therapy and community nursing were ways of ensuring direct client contact.

Greig (1999), also supports the harnessing of clinical skills by specialist learning disability nurses to ensure that appropriate skills are redirected at people with a learning disability. This ensures the best use of professional resources as opposed to nurses being forced down a quasi-care management route, as experienced by some transferred to social service teams, where the learning disability nurse is devalued by social service managers in what skills they have to offer (Messant and Caan, 2001).

The present policy context offers no new comforts for the learning disability nursing profession, particularly at pre-registration level. New threats have arisen, such as the Peach Report (Peach, 1999) on the future of the nursing branches, and the possibility of resurrecting the proposal for the learning disability nursing branch to be dropped and relegated to a post-registration specialty, as was proposed ten years ago (Department of health [DoH], 1993) as a result of the Concensus Conference on the future of learning disability nursing.

Justification for a specialist practitioner

A key priority for the future learning disability workforce training agenda is to consider a balance in the preparation of key professionals who work in the generic, primary healthcare services, and those in specialist services, coupled with the move towards interprofessional training and shared learning.

It is with these considerations in mind that the Government, Nursing and Midwifery Council (NMC) and other interested professional bodies and agencies need to acknowledge that through support and election of a generic model for nurse education, this will potentially lead to a repetition of what has been witnessed and experienced in Australia.

Here, people with an intellectual disability were inappropriately and inadequately supported by professionals through the direct de-registering of the mental retardation nurse in 1993 (Davis *et al*, 2001); and, being no longer in receipt of services from this specialist nurse, a significant loss of opportunities for people with an intellectual disability has occurred.

The report which was commissioned by the Scottish Executive to underpin *Promoting Health, Supporting Inclusion* (2002) states:

> *It is important to retain a group of 'Registered Professionals' with expertise in the skills required to meet the higher than average health, mental health, challenging behaviour and developmental needs of people with an intellectual disability...* [The report goes on to say] *If Scotland makes the decision to no longer have learning disability nurses, then a new disability profession should be established to ensure that the gaps in service delivery experienced in Victoria do not occur.*

As Mitchell (2003) comments on the idea of generiscism, 'The strength of the specialism (learning disability nursing), is that it is the only professional preparation in health and social care that concentrates solely on work with people with learning disabilities.'

Scotland has incorporated lessons learnt from the Australian experience into their own learning disability reforms (Scottish Executive, 2002) where a valued and strategic inclusion of the learning disability nurse is proposed through the recommendation of a tiered approach to health care. In *Valuing People* (DoH, 2001), learning disability nurses are granted a cursory mention as appropriate professionals who can take on the role of a health facilitator.

Also, in *Valuing People* (2001), it is recognised that 75% of the workforce is unqualified, so it is important that the Government and other bodies do not rely solely upon the Learning Disability Awards Framework (LDAF) for providing an all inclusive workforce. Many providers are grappling with the workforce issue of putting all care support staff through LDAF, where the minimum standard acquisition of level two competency for all care workers is expected as part of non-vocational qualifications (NVQ) training. At this level of performance, a mere snapshot is only indicative of where the care worker is currently at; in reality, giving an assessment which shows a minimum level of performance is achieved without having to demonstrate higher levels of knowledge or learning.

In contrast to this form of training, there are specialist nurses in learning disability who are professional, academic and practice-focused and are a valuable and essential asset. The breadth and extent of the spectrum of learning disability (as illustrated within the following chapters), is confirmation and further endorsement of their worth and contribution towards an evolving evidence base, making a difference in the quality of life for people with a learning disability.

It is important for the development of nursing in this specialist field not to return to the debates and controversy generated in the 1970s and 1980s as to whether or not nurses are a relevant profession to be involved with people with a learning disability. The Briggs (1972) recommendation 74 was that a new caring profession should emerge and the Jay Committee (1979), through its enquiry, was to facilitate this with an increased emphasis on social aspects of care. The debates since have been polarised on whether people with a learning disability constitute as a 'social', 'medical', 'psychological' or 'educational' concern, leading to various proposals and attempts at different models of educational preparation for professionals from within both nursing and social work.

Nurses in learning disability focus upon the holistic dimensions of the human, irrespective of what social constructs are perceived as fashionable at any given time.

They are entering into the twenty-first century with a renewed sense of purpose, devoid of confusion and ambiguity associated with the legacies of the past. Nevertheless, across the United Kingdom, this still appears not to be a shared perspective in some areas and the contemporary role of some specialist nurses is an arduous journey (Messant and Caan, 2001), when nurses come under the auspices of social services. Their endeavours within such arrangements can create conflict in their attempts to case manage as opposed to care manage people with a learning disability and their families. The goal is to work in partnerships with the generic, specialist and social care sectors to assist in empowering people to receive appropriate services. This means an ability to discriminate and celebrate the specialist skills that various professionals have to offer, including those of specialist learning disability nurses.

Specialist learning disability practice

Continuing the Commitment (DoH, 1995) was an important publication and milestone in the support for the learning disability nursing profession. It served as a public and Government recognition that nursing, as a qualification within learning disability, was significant in the care of people with a learning disability, and an important dimension among many other disciplines' involvement and contribution.

This report highlighted eight key areas which emphasised and provided a long-awaited attempt and illustration of the scope of practice by the learning disability nurse (*Box 1.1*). This is clearly referred to, revisited and elaborated upon by individual contributions to this book.

> **Box 1.1: Eight key areas of the learning disability nurse (DoH, 1995: 18–35)**
>
> * Assessment of need
> * Health surveillance and health promotion
> * Developing personal competence
> * Using enhanced therapeutic skills
> * Managing and leading teams of staff
> * Enhancing the quality of support
> * Enabling and empowerment and coordinating services.

What can be derived and observed from *Continuing the Commitment* — or rather absent from it — was a lack in pursuance and application of rigorous academic and practice developments. A missed opportunity within the report for nurses to support their interventions based upon a sound integration of theory and practice.

This book assists to redress the theory/practice gap by presenting a sound, academic account of what is involved in specialist learning disability practice.

Specialist practitioners who articulate their current areas of specialism are demonstrating specialist practice which effectively means that:

Specialist health care and specialist client requirements call for additional education for safe and effective practice... and where... practitioners... exercise higher levels of clinical decision making and will be able to monitor and improve standards of care through supervision of practice, clinical audit, the provision of skilled professional leadership and the development of practice through research, teaching and the support of professional colleagues.

United Kingdom Central Council for Nursing
Midwifery and Health Visiting (UKCC), 1994: 9;
English National Board (ENB), 1995: 22

People with a learning disability within the UK are exposed to a variety of service models from a myriad of service providers and it is within this culture and context that, 'Clients and their carers have the right to expect appropriately qualified professionals to realise their total needs' (Clifton *et al*, 1993).

Indeed, specialist practitioner programmes have, prior to the formation of the Nursing and Midwifery Council (2002), focused upon the following four main areas, which have enabled practitioners through specialist educational programmes to meet the demands of specialist practice (UKCC, 1994,1998; ENB,1995). These are:

Clinical nursing practice: embraces and pursues the specific knowledge and skills necessary for meeting the needs of specialist practice and specialist needs of clients.

Care and programme management: The ability to address the needs of individual clients and family within the community and the environment of care. The practitioner develops skills in bringing together the necessary agencies, professionals and other allied workers to meet the need.

Clinical practice development: The quality and audit agenda whereby practice development can be enriched through research and setting of standards relative to the specialist area of practice.

Clinical practice leadership: To be able to pursue management of change processes through effective leadership strategies in order to develop sensitive services relative to consumer need, and able to influence and teach others in this process.

The object and essence of such programmes are for specialist practitioners to relate theory to practice within their specialist area, justifying practice-based interventions which contribute towards client and service development. Practice development means the support of those strategies which underpin the basis for our interventions within learning disability nursing practice, and reflects the ethos behind quality and clinical governance in contributing towards contemporary health and social care evaluation.

Quality and evaluation in learning disability services

Recent Government legislation over the last five years has particularly been concerned with quality and service effectiveness across the health and social care sectors (DoH, 1998, 2000).

This policy development and concern for quality has largely been through the need to monitor and measure quality within social and health services, and as a result from the growth in influence of the consumer and advocacy movements.

Following on from the hospital closure programme over the last two decades, and the subsequent diversity in providers of learning disability services, quality and evaluation has been associated with those services who give 'Best Value'.

Attempts in evaluation of services have largely focused upon people living in 'staffed homes', where the emphasis is on supporting people to live valued lives within such environments within the community. O'Brien's (1987) five accomplishments provide an evaluative approach which gives details about the lifestyles enjoyed by people with a learning disability.

There are a plethora of evaluation tools available and directories that provide a wide range for appropriate selection, eg. Raynes (1988) on quality of life measures and service user led outcomes (Quality Network, 2000).

According to Perry and Felce (1995), the quality of life of service users has been proposed as the ultimate criterion for the assessment of the effectiveness of social care delivery, where the focus is on such areas as; quality of housing, social and community integration, social interactions, development, activity and autonomy and choice.

Service user led outcomes are what people with learning disabilities see as their needs and priorities, which are achieved by researchers exploring their feelings and perceptions about the service they receive, and then translated into outcomes for measuring people's lifestyles. Such initiatives have identified that the needs and priorities of those within an inclusive society, such as; 'feeling part of the community', 'having personal relationships', and 'making choices' are in fact no different to anyone else's needs and priorities.

The significance is that not only do people with a learning disability have similarities in their needs and priorities for living as with other people, but also that they can be related to and transferred to healthcare concerns demonstrated from research. An example being research by the Picker Institute. This specialises in measuring patient's experiences of health care, based on twelve years of research and more than 450,000 interviews. Patients identified eight 'dimensions of care' (*Box 1.2*) which reflect their most important concerns.

Dimensions identified, such as concerns regarding respect, communications and access, reverberate with those findings from research which have impacted upon people with a learning disability (PWLD) (*Box 1.3*).

> **Box 1.2: Eight dimensions of care**
>
> ⌘ Respecting a patient's values, preferences and expressed needs
> ⌘ Access to care
> ⌘ Emotional support
> ⌘ Information, communciation and education
> ⌘ Coordination of care
> ⌘ Physical comfort
> ⌘ Involvement of family and friends
> ⌘ Continuity and transition
>
> Source: The Picker Institute, Boston

Box 1.3: Findings from primary and secondary health care for PWLDs

* Rigorous evidence indicates that PWLDs have generally higher health needs than the general population which are ignored (Mencap, 1997)
* Communication with the health provision and actually getting to the service remain significant problems (NHSE, 1999)
* Most PWLDs do not receive good quality health services. Evidence from research in primary and secondary health service provision often finds people and their carers dissatisfied with the care provided (Hart, 1998; Kerr *et al*, 1996; Mencap, 1997).
* Research shows that the health needs of PWLDs are too often unreported or undetected (Beangue *et al*, 1995; Cumella *et al*, 1992; Howells, 1986; Martin *et al*, 1997; Meehan *et al*, 1995; Wells *et al*, 1997; Wilson and Haire, 1990).
* When asked PWLDs do voice dissatisfaction with services (Hart, 1998).

These findings illustrate quite clearly that if quality is to be aimed directly at the individual consumer, there needs to be a rigor and accountability by individual practitioners; and practice development within the context of clinical governance needs to be, 'The main vehicle for continuously improving the quality of client/patient care' (Scally and Donaldson, 1998). This, in addition to the evidence of what people with learning disabilities themselves say about general hospitals, nurses and GPs is growing. There can be no better judgements about the quality of health care than those who receive the service.

Clinical governance is the core framework within *A First Class Service* (DoH, 1998) as part of the modernisation agenda, and has been formally defined as:

A framework through which NHS organisations are accountable for continually improving the quality of their services and safeguarding high standards of care by **creating an environment in which excellence in clinical care will flourish** *[author's emphasis].*

Donaldson and Gray, 1998

Practice development in learning disability nursing

This emphasis is on 'creating an environment in which excellence in clinical care will flourish...'; where specialist practice in learning disabilities means acquiring specialist knowledge; where the relationship between theory and practice is of utmost concern; and where health trusts become and provide a learning environment so as to sustain effective and evidence-based practices.

Both Rafferty *et al* (1996) and Thompson (1995) have reviewed the extent of the theory-practice gap in nursing and health and social welfare, and agree that practice devoid of theory is an erroneous position to take, and that practitioners need to evaluate consistently the evidence by continuously exploring those theories of practice through the experiential application within practice.

It is through this continuous interplay between theory and practice that the essence and nature of contemporary specialist practice can be developed. It is important to emphasise that as specialist practitioners there is a need to examine practice-based interventions and theories in the context of where practice is located (the environment), as well as the influences of culture, the social and political world in which we live and work. The development of theory and practice is continuously in a state of flux, consistently fluid and never static.

Thompson (1995) explores narrowing the theory practice gap in the adoption of a strategic approach which consists of nine dimensions in an effort to narrow the gap, and which have been adopted and adapted here to assist in facilitating an integration between learning disability theory and practice so as to promote excellence, and in this case to promote contemporary effective and evidence-based learning disability nursing practice.

Box 1.4 illustrates the components for a strategic approach to narrowing the theory practice gap. The bracketed headings are my substituted terms: an attempt to place additional emphasis and engagement by the practitioner on the process.

Box 1.4: Strategies for narrowing the gap

Cycles of learning	Beyond practice wisdom	Beyond theoryless practice
(lubricating practice)	(challenging existing practice)	(search beyond your assumptions)
Beyond common sense	Research-minded practice	Beyond elitism and anti-intellectualism
(unsetting the glue)	(a liberation for all)	(balancing the scales)
Critical incident technique	Developing a group approach	Continuous professional development
(unravelling the journey)	(a common goal shared)	(promoting self-growth)

Source: Thompson, 1995

Cycles of learning (lubricating practice)

Kolb and Fry (1975) were early instigators in the area of developing an experiential learning cycle, where to engage into a cycle of learning reinforces that learning and applying theory to practice are both part of an active cyclical process and the nurse's engagement with this process is a valuable tool for learning from reflection.

Learning, however, needs to be tested out by applying what has been learnt and transferred into new situations if the theory/practice relationship is to be integrated.

For example, use a model for assessment in one area and test it out in another for comparison of its usefulness and efficacy in identifying clients' needs.

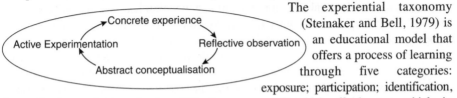

The experiential taxonomy (Steinaker and Bell, 1979) is an educational model that offers a process of learning through five categories: exposure; participation; identification, internalisation and dissemination. This forms a gestalt which affords as a vehicle in facilitation of evidence-based practice, critical thinking, reflection, problem solving, decision-making and towards innovation in practice. Here the practitioner can move through an experience from exposure to dissemination, entering an experience at a different level, being determined by previous learning or experience and facilitated by an experienced supervisor.

Beyond practice wisdom (challenging existing practices)

For many observers into the practice of learning disability nursing as an art, it has often been difficult to capture or define it in terms of demonstrable skills which are derived from theory. It has largely become over the years subsumed under either the technology of behaviour therapy, or under the umbrella of global theory such as normalisation (Wolfensburger, 1972, 1983).

Over recent years, the physical environment has been a predominant focus for services and professionals in the provision of an ordinary life for people with learning disabilities. This emphasis on the physical location of where people live, has detracted away from perhaps an additional consideration into an identification of a repertoire of skilled interventions also necessary for enhancing the quality of life for people with learning disabilities.

The theory base of practice is required to be custom tailored so as to fit the needs of the individual, and not globally applied as if one theory fits all individuals and situations. We, as professional nurses, need to review consistently our practices relative to their theoretical origins in our relationships with people with a learning disability and their families.

To challenge existing everyday practice is to be consistently vigilant as to how assumptions are formed about what interventions based on theory are to be appropriately employed.

The term practice wisdom is used to invest in those theories and strategies which do not quite fit the individual's needs — a bit like going to a major chain store and buying a piece of fashion clothing which does not quite fit, but will pass for the situation intended.

In theory and practice terms, this could be in the area of assessment where a conventional format such as 'Pathways to Independence' (Jeffree and Cheseldine, 1982), is applied to generate a planned series of teaching goals, but where a more holistic assessment, such as through holistic nursing theory, will generate a more meaningful psychological/social needs agenda which the person would benefit from relative to their overall development. This focus could elucidate areas such as stress reduction, improving self-image or esteem. Needless to say, a variety of theoretical sources are crucial to acknowledge and apply in any individual case, but the point here is that a narrow application of theory in the form of practice wisdom is often applied due to a parochial appreciation into theory and practice.

A case in point could be the adoption of cognitive behaviour therapy across all situations and all individuals. Predominant ideology within learning disability such as normalisation has also significantly influenced what practitioners think about what is appropriate for people with learning disabilities; that is, all individuals will be part of an integrational service where O'Brien's (1987) five accomplishments of community presence, choice, competence, respect and community participation have become the homogenised 'gold-star' criteria for measuring services and that the community is perceived as a panacea for all needs. Consideration of the individual's personal traits and cultural origins, such as world views, customs, beliefs, behaviour patterns, interests or desires are essential constructs to consider when attempting to assess individual needs. Conscious efforts need to be made to go beyond existing practice wisdom within learning disability services and practices — to be complacent in relation to everyday practice is an invitation to become constrained by narrow thinking and action.

Beyond theoryless practice (search beyond your assumptions)

It has been identified that many practitioners find it difficult to link theory with practice or to acknowledge the importance of any theoretical framework (Dalrymple and Burke, 1995), and that no element of practice should be devoid of theory.

In terms of learning disability nursing practice, this can be illustrated within a small scale study into the comparative practice between qualified and unqualified community nurses and their practice (Jukes, 1994), where the adoption of theory was demonstrated. In this study, unqualified community learning disability nurses tended to adopt their own practice wisdom in the form of trial and error approaches or from the predominant application of psychological functional assessments in response to individual/family needs.

Those qualified community learning disability nurses in the study, however, purposely pursued counselling and holistic nursing theory to be applied to the situation when assessing the needs of parents and people with a learning disability. Owen (1995) adopts such holistic theory in her work as a community nurse in the care of a young lady with Down's syndrome.

Beyond theoryless practice is essentially knowing what is out there in terms of theory, and applying it through testing out its concepts, and reflecting back on its value and efficacy with a competent supervisor, as well as identifying gaps in theory.

Beyond common sense (or unsetting the glue)

Common sense in health and nursing care is essentially short hand for the expression and demonstration of dominant cultural values, the dominant ideology which pervades across professional services or sets of ideologies which we are socialised into from an early age or the 'glue' which holds us together both individually and professionally. The 'glue' relates to our individual experiences of culture, our customs, influence of genetics, our behaviours and our beliefs in mysticism or in spirituality.

We need to recognise our own personal, individual and professional histories and what that brings to how our beliefs and assumptions contribute to any assessment or analysis of a person and situation within the home or learning disability service.

Common sense is also a means of expression in preventing any critical reflection and as a means of closing debates or discussion, rather than opening them.

A reliance on not questioning theory acts as a stumbling block to the integration of theory and practice; maintaining a critical perspective is crucial.

In application terms, this means a critical appraisal of all theories and systems that impact on the lives of people with a learning disability, such as supported living which reflects the ethos of living autonomously in the community: a common sense panacea for all people with a learning disability to experience.What potentially does this mean for the broad spectrum of people who have a learning disability in terms of psychological effects, social and economic consequences — who does and does it not benefit as a system? What are the pitfalls? Only through analysis and evaluation and a subjective and participative approach with people directly will we be able to appraise objectively.

Research-minded practice (a liberation for all)

In learning disability practice we need to examine what theory works for the practitioner, and what positive effects it has upon the person with a learning disability. We need to understand more about the lived experiences of people with learning disabilities through our planned interventions, and this can best be achieved by having a participative approach and partnership.This leads to a more informed and research-minded approach towards the application of theory where an effective combination of research enquiry coupled with practical application is achieved (see *Chapter 12* where Ruth Northway pursues this participative dimension).

Self-awareness and knowledge is also an important attribute to the qualities of being research-minded and attempts at understanding the individual's perspective — a liberating inclusive position for all, based on partnership and inclusion rather than distant paternalism — and demystifies the research agenda and practice, ie. brings together practitioners and people with a learning disability.

Beyond elitism and anti-intellectualism (balancing the scales)

In this context, elitism refers to the academic and research culture where theory and ideology is perceived as superior, or more important, than the real world of learning disability practice.

Anti-intellectualism attaches little or no significance or value to the role of theory and is seen as not only irrelevant but a barrier to existing practice. By some managers in learning disability, the specialist practitioner degree can also be seen as a non-essential criteria for the domains of community learning disability nursing practice (Jukes, 2001).

In this era of collaborations and coalitions, both academics and practitioners have a part to play to develop a shared and balanced value-base within the triad of user, the service and educator with a responsibility for breaking down these barriers.

In essence, enabling the development of theory and knowledge to be more accessible to practitioners and applicable to practice.

An example of this could be university lecturers/joint-practitioners working together on the development of a model for assessment and practice. (*Chapter 8* is the result of consistent working together in formulating and applying the ecological model for practice in Northamptonshire.)

The critical incident technique (unravelling the journey)

Reflective practice represents a move towards successfully blending theory with practice. Promotion of reflective practice can be achieved through the critical incident technique which can be used in team or staff meetings or in discussion as part of a supervisory relationship. Wolverson (2000) has identified that reflective practice is critical within the field of learning disability nursing as many emotive and challenging areas of practice are experienced which require skilled and critical reflective processes of engagement.

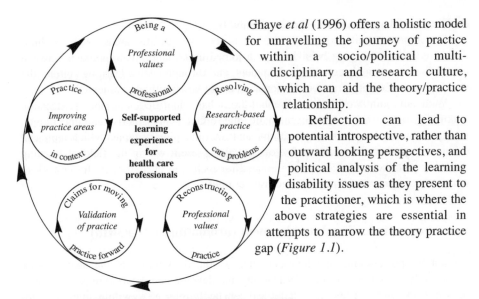

Ghaye *et al* (1996) offers a holistic model for unravelling the journey of practice within a socio/political multi-disciplinary and research culture, which can aid the theory/practice relationship.

Reflection can lead to potential introspective, rather than outward looking perspectives, and political analysis of the learning disability issues as they present to the practitioner, which is where the above strategies are essential in attempts to narrow the theory practice gap (*Figure 1.1*).

Figure 1.1: A holistic reflective cycle (Ghaye *et al*, 1996)

Developing a group approach (a common goal shared)

Valuing People (DoH, 2001) promotes partnerships across health, social care, education, built environment and leisure, and therefore specialist practitioners need to capitalise upon developing alliances and networks across these sectors in partnership with people with a learning disability.

In development and pursuance of theory and practice a natural extension would be to develop 'learning sets' which are essentially a group of professionals specifically set up to promote learning and develop a better understanding of a particular issue or set of issues in order to assist in narrowing the theory practice gap.

A specific example within a triad of psychiatrist, pharmacologist and nurse practitioner would be the introduction of supplementary prescribing, where potential nurse prescribers in learning disability would within a series of meetings share individual perceptions and experiences/dilemmas in order to maximise their opportunities for learning within this evolving role.

Other methods which would involve wider membership would be the establishment of practice research networks in areas such as dual-diagnosis, challenging behaviour, epilepsy or autistic–spectrum disorder provision.

Communities of practice could be developed where partnerships between research- and practice-based communities which are organised either locally or on a consortium-based level could strengthen the links between universities, trusts, local authorities and the private sector. The core basis of such initiatives is to make theory and practice malleable.

To promote evidence-based practice, multi-disciplinary focus groups could provide a vehicle for sharing knowledge, research findings or operate as local 'Think-Tanks', review evidence and provide an overview of recent research and findings.

Multi-disciplinary journal clubs as proposed by Topham and Hunt (2002), could also foster an early and focused attempt on research-minded collaboration to enhance evidence-based approaches in learning disability.

Development units could also be established in specific areas, such as dual-diagnosis and challenging behaviour, as a joined up collaborative approach between universities, trusts and research development, and through such a learning culture, the development of theory/practice relationships could be effectively harnessed.

With any joint-working, as Webb (2002) has identified, attempts at decision making in social work can be problematic, due to factors such as risk and uncertainty, multiple criteria, long-term implications, and interdisciplinary inputs which represent different vested interests. These factors are also present within the field of learning disability practice, which supports the need for inclusion of a strategic framework to pursue theory/practice dimensions across the field.

Continuous professional development (promoting self-growth)

Continuous professional development refers to the recognition of the need to seek consistently those opportunities for learning and development beyond registration as a nurse (also known as lifelong learning and constantly referred to within all policies for reform and service development). Three elements are pursued here:

⌘ Lifelong learning: where involvement in professional development education and training enhances the relationship between ideas and action.
⌘ Reflective practice and clinical supervision: where the scope and extent of professional practices are reviewed and which explores the heart of theory development and practice interventions and the subsequent evaluation of both.
⌘ Appraisal: where professional development is reviewed in context to actual practice; that is, ensuring that professional development is in harmony with the requirements for practice.

Without such an emphasis, there is a distinct possibility that practitioners will practice in an uncritical and routine manner all too familiar within learning disability services, and will lose sight of the values and knowledge base that underpins practice.

According to Thompson (1995), the nine strategies (*page 9*) can begin to offer a substantial contribution to initiate or continue the process of integration of theory and practice, where reflective practice is an underlying and common theme throughout, and from which specialist practitioners within this text make constant reference to in the development and sustainment of their practice.

As part of the framework for clinical governance these nine strategies for developing a sound integration of theory and practice for practice development must not be perceived as a singular and uni-disciplinary activity.

Indeed, practice development can be nurtured and developed within the context of a multi-disciplinary and inter-agency culture by moving practitioners into learning sets within a more challenging culture, where there is more active learning across boundaries, and where questions and methods of working are articulated in the true spirit of a learning and development culture.

The following case-study provides an illustration of how a strategic approach can be of value when internalised and adopted by a learning disability nurse practitioner.

Case study

Rajinder is a twenty-seven-year-old Asian lady with a mild learning disability who attends an integrated day service. Although she enjoys the company of Jonathan, who is of a similar age and from a different culture, she has difficulty and conflict in pursuing and forming a relationship with him.

It must be emphasised that Rajinder's parents had difficulty in accepting this day placement, as they preferred their daughter to attend a female only resource and do not approve of integrated services, but that no such service was being considered at this time). Studies such as Azmi *et al* (1996) have identified that Asian users and families will access services if they accommodate their specific needs.

Rajindor's family also object to their daughter establishing a relationship, and consistently convey this message strongly to their daughter in both overt and covert ways. The result is that Rajinder has increased aggression and disruptive behaviour, which includes self-harm and aggression to others.

The referral is made to the community learning disability nursing team, who consist of predominately 'white' professionals.

This case-study is challenging as it confronts many professionals' assumptions in the assessment, care and interventions underlying predominate ideology which pervades across the field of learning disability service provision.

Firstly, normalisation or social role valorisation (Wolfensberger, 1972, 1983) is challenged as it is eurocentric in origin and assumes that everyone who has a learning disability 'fits' the integrational perspective and that the 'ordinary living' model suits everyone's personal agenda. A functional versus an individual empowerment dimension (Chappell, 1992).

Secondly, traditional and predominant psychological assessment and intervention models offer a traditional and again eurocentric origin (Jukes and O'Shea, 1998), which fails to identify cultural difference in identification of world views from both Rajinder's and her families perspective.

Finally, it is the consequence of referral and response of the 'white' community learning disability team to examine team philosophy, methods of assessment and interventions appropriate for multi-cultural 'competency', and to act and work within an anti-discriminatory and anti-oppressive framework. The criteria and strategic approach in examining the theory/practice gap is quite clearly of value in this instance.

Conclusion

This chapter has examined the contextual issues and professional concerns in the justification and identification of what constitutes specialist learning disability nursing practice.

Quality and evaluation perspectives have been pursued in the recognition of what constitutes practice development for learning disability nurses where a strategic approach has been offered and appraised in how the theory/practice gap in learning disability nursing can be narrowed.

A case-study has been presented to assist in consolidating such an approach.

Table 1.1: Narrowing the gap: a transcultural focus and challenge

Criteria for narrowing the gap	Strategic approaches towards narrowing the gap
Cycles of learning or (lubricating professional practice)	What have you experienced previously in terms of exposure towards cultural diversity. Through exposure what does this case highlight in terms of 'need to know' theory and practice perspectives. What are the issues for further enquiry and development of knowledge. What is already 'out there' in this area that can benefit from further analysis. As a starting point review *Ethnicity and Learning Difficulties Report* (DoH, 2001).
Beyond practice wisdom or (transcending parochial knowledge)	In relating to professional practice, what would be applied normally in such a case relative to diagnosis and ranges of assessment and intervention strategies? Are these adequate, and do they address cultural issues, eg. through traditional adoption of assessment and counselling theories.
Beyond theoryless practice or (search beyond your assumptions)	The influence of informal theory, ie. trial and error approaches by practitioners — what has worked in the past will they work in this situation. Search beyond what appears obvious, ie. ask questions like, 'why is this young lady self-harming?' 'what internal and external conflicts are influencing her world?'
Beyond common sense or (unsetting the glue)	Get outside of your glue. See further than your existing mindset relative to your beliefs, assumptions and values. How does this young woman feel, think and believe in response to her emotions? What does her religion and family reflect in terms of values and beliefs, ie. how can you attempt to understand this lady? Assessment methodology which reflects worldview considerations and cultural competency, eg. ACCESS model by Narayanasamy (2002).
Research-minded practice or (liberation for all)	A self-aware practitioner would search beyond what is observable; a desire to search further meaning behind what is experienced. Analysis behind the presenting issues coupled with practical engagement of theory and practice. A participative research approach, futher consideration and engagement with people representative within the Asian community.
Beyond elitism and anti-intellectualism or (balancing the scales of practice)	Forge relationships with local research/practice development unit/university links to promote further investigative work in practice development within transcultural services and, in particular, furtherance of assessment and intervention strategies within multi-cultural environments.
The critical incident technique or (unravelling the journey of practice)	Use this case as a discussion forum within a team meeting on transcultural issues in learning disability. Reflective journal writing and analysis.
Developing a group approach or (a common goal shared)	Promote further enquiry and help to initiate and set up a learning set across disciplines to focus specifically on transcultural issues across the field of learning disability. Aim to share experiences and maximise opportunities for learning. Forge links with the local university. Develop practice development and research links and influence curriculum design.
Continuing professional development or (promoting self-growth)	Through appraisal, identify opportunities for continuing education seminars, conferences, become a member of the Transcultural Nursing Association promoting initiatives within learning disability. Active reflective practice and clinical supervision.

At the time of writing the Nursing and Midwifery Council's President, Jonathan Asbridge, announced proposals that a new Register for Specialist Practitioners, including the recording of learning disability nurses,will be created (Scott, 2003).

This, in effect, will mean that if these proposals are passed it will be illegal for nurses to call themselves specialists unless their qualification is recorded.

For nurses in learning disability who have pursued specialist educational programmes this will be a long overdue recognition of their specialist skills and knowledge.

Reflective points

⌘ What methods do you use in assessing the relevance of theory with practice issues?

⌘ Relate this criteria and strategic approach to areas of your professional practice such as dual-diagnosis, autistic-spectrum disorder, self-injurious behaviour, challenging behaviour, community nursing, dispersed housing and supported living.

⌘ What about the concept of person-centred planning and those strategies proposed which support professional decision-making?

⌘ How may we encourage others in this process?

References

Alaszewski A, Gates B, Ayer S *et al* (2000) Education for diversity and change: final report of the ENB-funded project on educational preparation for learning disability nursing. University of Hull, UK

Azmi S, Hatton C, Caine A, Emerson E (1996) *Improving Services for Asian People with Learning Disabilities: The Views of Users and Carers*. Hester Adrian Research Centre/Mental Health Foundation, Manchester

Beangue H, McElduff A, Baker W (1995) Medical disorders of adults with mental retardation: a population study. *Am J Mental Retard* **99**: 595–604

Briggs Report (1972) *Report of the Committee on Nursing*. HMSO, London

Chappell A (1992) Towards a sociological critique of the normalisation principle. *Disabil Handicap and Society* **7**(1): 35–52

Clifton M, Brown J, Shaw I (1993) *Learning Disabilities and the Specialist Nurse*. SPSW Publishing,York

Cumella S, Corbett J, Clark D *et al* (1992) Primary health care for people with a learning disability. *Ment Handicap* **2**: 23–125

Dalrymple J, Burke B (1995) *Anti-oppressive practice social care and the law*. Open University Press, Buckingham

Davis R, Phillips A, Nankervis K (2001) *Service delivery to people with an intellectual disability in Victoria and Australia*. A report to the Scottish National Review of the Contribution of Nurses to the Care and Support of People with a Learning Disability

Department of Health (1993) *New Direction for Nursing People with Learning Disabilities*. Statement from Multi-Disciplinary Consensus Conference (press release). DoH, London.

Department of Health (1995) *Continuing the Commitment. The Report of the Learning Disability Nursing Project*. DoH, London

Department of Health (1998) *A First Class Service — quality in the new NHS*. HMSO, Leeds

Department of Health (2000) *A Quality Strategy for Social Care*. HMSO, London

Department of Health (2001) *Valuing People: A New Strategy for Learning Disability for the 21st Century*. HMSO, London

Donaldson LG, Gray JAM (1998) Clinical Governance: A quality duty for health organisations. *Qual Health Care* **7**(Suppl): 537–44

English National Board (1995) *Creating Lifelong Learners: guidelines for the implementation of the UKCC's Standards for Education and Practice following Registration*. ENB, London

Ghazala M, Noon A, Ahmed V, Jones L (2001) *Learning Difficulties and Ethnicity. A Report to the Department of Health*. DoH, London

Ghaye T, Cuthbert S, Danai K, Dennis D (1996) *Learning through Critical Reflective Practice: Self-supported learning experience for healthcare professionals*. Pentaxion Ltd, Newcastle upon Tyne

Greig R (1999) *Beyond the Community Learning Disability Team? A Discussion Paper by the Community Care Development Centre*. King's College, London

Hart SL (1998) Learning-disabled people's experience of general hospitals. *Br J Nurs* **7**(8): 470–7

Howells G (1986) Are the health needs of mentally handicapped adults being met? *J Roy Coll Gen Practitioners* **36**: 449–53

Jay P (1979) *Report of the Committee of Enquiry into Mental Handicap Nursing and Care*. HMSO, London

Jeffree D, Cheseldine S (1982) *Pathways to Independence. Checklists of self-help and social skills*. Hodder and Stoughton, Kent

Jukes M (1994) Development of the community learning disability nurse (2). *Br J Nurs* **13**(16): 848–53

Jukes M (2001) Learning disability nursing needs theory practice experience. *Br J Nurs* **10**(3): 164

Jukes M, O'Shea K (1998) Transcultural therapy 2: Mental health and learning disabilities. *Br J Nurs* **7**(20): 1268–72

Kerr M, Fraser D, Felce D (1996) Primary health care for people with a learning disability; a keynote review. *Br J Learning Disabilities* **24**: 2–8

Kolb D, Fry R(1975) Towards an applied theory of experiential learning. In: Cooper G, ed. *Theories of Group Processes*. Wiley and Sons, Chichester

Martin DM *et al* (1997) Health gain through screening — users' and carers' perspectives in health care. *J Intellectual and Developmental Disability* **22**(4): 241–9

Meehan S, Moore G, Barr O (1995) Specialist services for people with learning disabilities. *Nurs Times* **91**(13): 33–5

Mencap (1997) *Prescription for change* (summary). Mencap Research, London

Messant P, Caan W (2001) Community learning disability nurses must stay linked to the NHS. *Br J Nurs* **9**(19): 2062

Mitchell D (2003) Threat of the generic nurse. *Learning Disability Practice* **6**(1): 34

Narayanasamy A (2002) The ACCESS model: A transcultural nursing practice framework. *Br J Nurs* **11**(9): 643–50

NHS Executive (1999) *Once a Day*. HMSO, London

Nursing Midwifery Council (2002) *Code of Professional Conduct*. NMC. London

O'Brien J (1987) A guide to lifestyle planning. In: Wilcox B, Bellamy GT, eds. *Comprehensive Guide to the Activities Catalog*. Paul H Brookes, Baltimore

Owen M (1995) Care of a woman with Down's syndrome using the Neuman Systems Model. *Br J Nurs* **4**(13): 752–8

Perry J, Felce D (1995) Objective assessments of quality of life: How much do they agree with each other? *J Community Appl Soc Psychol* **5**:1–19

Peach L (1999) *Fitness for Practice*. UKCC, London

Picker Institute Suite 100, 1295 Boylston Street, Boston, MA 02128. Available on line at: http://www.picker.org

Quality Network (2000) Introduction to the Quality Network. On line: http://www.qualitynetwork.org.uk

Rafferty AM, Allcock N, Lathlean J (1996) 'The Theory/Practice "Gap": Taking issue with the issue'. *J Adv Nurs* **23**(4): 685–91

Raynes N (1988) *Annotated directory of measures of environmental quality for use in residential services for people with a mental handicap*. Department of Social Policy and Social Work, University of Manchester

Scally G, Donaldson LJ (1998) Looking forward: Clinical governance and the drive for quality improvement in the new NHS in England. *Br Med J* **317**(7150): 61–5

Scottish Executive (2002) *The National Review of the Contribution of Nurses to the Care and Support of People with Learning Disabilities*. Scottish Executive

Scott H (2003) Specialist nurses are to be assessed and regulated. *Br J Nurs* **12**(6): 340

Steinaker N, Bell R(1979) *The Experiential Taxonomy. A new approach to teaching and learning*. Academic Press, London

Thompson N (1995) *Theory and Practice in Health and Social Welfare*. Open University Press, Buckingham

Topham L, Hunt C (2002) Setting up a multidisciplinary journal club in learning disability. *Br J Nurs* **11**(10): 688–93

United Kingdom Central Council for Nursing, Midwifery and Health Visiting (1994) *The Future of Professional Practice: The council's standards for education and practice following registration*. UKCC, London

United Kingdom Central Council for Nursing, Midwifery and Health Visiting (1998) *Standards for Specialist Education and Practice*. UKCC, London

Webb S (2002) Evidence-based practice and decision analysis in social work. An implementation model. *J Social Work* **2**(1): 45–63

Wells M, Turner S, Martin D, Roy A (1997) Health gain through screening — coronary heart disease and stroke: developing primary health care services for people with intellectual disability. *J Intellectual and Developmental Disability* **22**(4): 251–63

Wilson DN, Haire A (1990) Health screening for people with a mental handicap living in the community. *Br Med J* **301**: 1379–81

Wolfensberger W (1972) *The Principle of Normalisation in Human Services*. National Institute on Mental Retardation,Toronto

Wolfensberger W (1983) Social role valorisation: a proposed new term for the principle of normalisation. *Ment Retardation* **21**(6): 234–9

Wolverson M (2000) On reflection. *Learning Disability Practice* **3**(2): 24–7

2

Inter-professional working: Its relevance and importance to learning disability practice

Martin Bollard

Inter-professional working (IPW) cannot occur without genuine collaboration between workers in health and welfare settings. It usually refers to relations between different professional groups, such as; medicine, nursing, professions allied to medicine, social workers, probation, and teaching. Recently, with the horrors surrounding the Victoria Climbié case (DoH, 2003) and the Bristol Inquiry (DoH, 2002), the necessity for effective interprofessional working, has been starkly brought into focus.

The promotion of inter-professional working in the delivery of health, welfare and educational services has been perceived for a long time by service planners, policy makers and practitioners as a worthy end to pursue (Irvine, 2002). Debate covering this topic is extensive (Øvretveit, 1993; Leathard, 1994; Soothill *et al*, 1995; Barr, 2002). However, sound empirical evidence that demonstrates whether IPW improves the quality outcomes of patient/client care is still scant (Zwarenstein *et al*, 2002). Relationships within health and welfare services, where frontline practitioners operate, are still characterised by conflict and mutual suspicion (Loxley, 1997).

The diverse nature of learning disability practice and the complexity of needs that people with learning disabilities have, determines the need for inter-professional working.

This chapter describes the definitions surrounding the terms inter-professional working, highlighting where the need for collaboration and IPW has come from and why, despite the challenges involved in achieving IPW, it is perceived by many as a relevant and important endeavour to realise. Inter-professional education (IPE) is explored as a possible starting point for relevant workers to achieve the necessary pre-requisites for effective IPW. The chapter focuses upon the learning disability field: given the wide and complex needs that people with learning disability have, achieving effective IPW is relevant and important, although challenging. Finally, some approaches are advocated that can assist workers in the field to think about the way in which they collaborate and interact with others. The co-existing terms of partnership and collaboration are specifically highlighted.

Defining inter-professional work and its associated terminology

Within the terminology surrounding inter-professional work, there are a number of prefixes to certain terms that are used interchangeably, such as: **inter**, **multi** and **trans**.

Multidisciplinary is identified as 'involving a number of different academic disciplines or methods'. Inter-professional or inter-disciplinary denotes mutuality or 'involving two or more disciplines or methods of study'.

The distinction between the latter terms are that multidisciplinary is composed of many who may not necessarily interact and inter-professional, which implies interaction between the disciplines. When such terminology is transferred into the health and welfare sectors, such distinctions seem imprecise (McCallin, 2001).

Leathard (1994) grouped problematic terms such as, collaboration, trans-professional, interagency, partnership and inter-disciplinary according to concepts, generic issues or processes. This on the surface was a useful exercise although delicate differences that were associated with context and service, altered the understanding of such terms again. Sorrell-Jones (1997) aimed to clarify this situation stating:

Multidisciplinary refers to a team or collaborative process where members of different disciplines assess or treat clients independently and then share the information with each other... . Interdisciplinary/inter-professional describes a deeper level of collaboration in which processes such as evaluation or development of a plan of care is done jointly, with professionals of different disciplines pooling their knowledge in an independent manner.

The key difference with this understanding of the two terms is that multidisciplinary focuses upon the tasks identified with an individual's professional work, whereas inter-professional emphasises collective action and process-orientation (Sorrell-Jones, 1997). Collective action implies at least some kind of teamwork and it would be remiss to discuss inter-professional work without considering the term, teamwork.

Øvretveit (1996) who has studied inter-professional work for a number of years, suggests that IPW is much broader than teamwork. Teamwork or achieving effective teamwork is apparently in the literature rarely realised (Freeman *et al*, 2000). Øvretveit (1997) describes teams in accordance with the level of integration and collective responsibility that they are able to achieve. Øvretveit (1997) classifies teams in four key ways: integration; membership; client pathway and decision making and management.

Collaboration is another term that is frequently associated with inter-professional working. Although the confusion over the term has prevented its usefulness as a variable in studies that have tried to evaluate its effectiveness (Henneman and Lee, 1995), the term, for two key reasons, has relevance to those working in the learning disability field. Initially, practitioners strive hard to work in partnership with people with learning disabilities. Building a relationship and collaborating with people with learning disabilities, often on a one-to-one basis is viewed by many practitioners as fundamental to their practice (see *Chapter 11*).

The second reason is that practitioners in this field, due to the complexity of need surrounding this client group, have become accustomed to seeking out, forming networks and understanding that other professionals have an equal role to play in the provision of care, particularly in aspects of assessment (Mathias *et al*, 1997).

There are many definitions and associated attributes of collaboration. The one which, in principle, if not always in practice reflects learning disability practice, is when it is seen as 'a co-operative venture based upon shared power and authority... it is non-hierarchical in nature, assuming power based on knowledge or expertise as opposed to role or function' (Kraus, 1980).

Perhaps it is because collaborative interactions among different professionals are rarely studied (Cott, 1997) that a firmer understanding of inter-professional working and its associated terminology has not yet crystallised. Hudson (1999) warns of a tendency to 'over-collaborate' where situations can become over-complex and over-costly, raising unrealistic expectations which are not matched with the eventual outcomes.

Origins of inter-professional work

Changes in the health sector over the last two decades have been driven by an increasing emphasis on measurable outcomes, best practice, continuity of care and cost containment. In welfare services, similar emphasis can be seen with the adoption of 'Best Value' (Cambridge and McCarty, 2001) and shrinking social service budgets. This, in turn, has led to the call for greater adoption of clinical pathways and for inter-professional models of care to replace traditional models of healthcare delivery, based around a single medical practitioner (Irvine *et al*, 2002).

A shift in practice ideology towards seeing the client as a whole in the form of holistic practice, originating in the 1970s has provided a catalyst to reconsider the relationship between the plethora of medical specialists and allied technologies and the professions.

It has been acknowledged for some time and is particularly relevant within the learning disability field, that clients present with multi-faceted difficulties that one profession alone cannot solve. Patients and clients may present with needs that can be defined as both medical (health) and social, therefore requiring a 'broad' form of care. Yet defining needs in terms of health and social terms has for some time provided a tension between different professional groups at a practice level. Little research has focused upon the difficulties surrounding the development of inter-professional relationships between such professional groups.

Contrary to this and from a political standpoint, many policy and statutory obligations have firmly focused upon the necessity for partnership working between agencies (DoH, 1999; DoH, 2000; DoH, 2001). Hudson (2002) argues that the assumption is made that if interagency partnerships, processes and structures are established, then inter-professional working among professional groups will naturally follow. This assumption is contrary to the sociological evidence that exists which presents the inherent challenges involved when self-interested professional groups try to work together.

Challenges to inter-professional working

Why is achieving inter-professional working such a challenge for professional groups? Carrier and Kendall (1995: 18) believe it is not surprising as inter-professional working implies:

> *The sharing of knowledge; the respect for the individual autonomy of different professional groups and administrators; the surrender of professional territory where necessary; and a shared set of values concerning appropriate response to shared definitions of need... professions are likely to find this an ambitious and demanding agenda.*

Such barriers are deep rooted in professional cultures that make realising inter-professional collaboration a challenge. Loxley (1997) claims such conflict is interwoven into the social differences in the division of labour, which have developed over the last 200 years of health and welfare services.

Traditionally, decision-making power and authority has been dominated by the discipline of medicine. Medicine is a long established, large professional organisation whose members are drawn from a predominantly well-educated body who can command high income and high status (Navarro, 1976). This has meant that for most of the twentieth century the health division of labour has been organised and hierarchically structured around the dominant profession of medicine (Freidson, 1970). More recent critiques have claimed that the dominance of medicine is being challenged with the intensifying hierarchies within medicine itself and the expanding role of other disciplines, namely nursing (Annandale, 1998).

Increases in different specialist roles within health care is one of the key causes of tension within the inter-professional debate (Irvine, 2002). The professional and functional specialisation has fragmented knowledge and expertise and contributed to the growth in a complex social and technical distribution of knowledge and work in health care. The possible dangers for learning disability practice are that an already marginalised field continues to specialise in too many fragmented areas, at the expense of developing a core recognised generic skill base. Over the years, professional status and identity have been difficult for learning disability practitioners to ascertain. Indeed, inter-professional education itself arose as an attempt to overcome ignorance and prejudice among health and social care professions (Barr, 2002), which can exaggerate such professional rivalries.

Inter-professional education

There are clearly areas in which the roles of individual professional groups overlap. As professional bodies recognise extended roles and healthcare providers seek to implement multi-skilling initiatives, such common learning will become increasingly relevant (Miller *et al*, 1998). This, coupled with such a strong emphasis that the present Government places upon collaboration within public services (DoH, 2000), lays the platform for the extension of inter-professional education (IPE).

Overview of inter-professional education

Inter-professional education is not a new phenomena. Attempts in the 1970s to facilitate this way of working have been attempted in a number of different settings (Barr *et al*, 1999).

The intention behind IPE is that by bringing students from different professional backgrounds together would increase their understanding of respective roles and responsibilities, generate mutual trust and relinquish stereotypes (Barr, 1999). This, in turn, would enhance the potential for collaborative practice. It has to be stated that attempts to evaluate such claims have up until now been inconclusive (Barr, 1998). A systematic review conducted by Zwarenstein *et al* (2002) for the Cochrane database revealed that despite a large body of literature on the evaluation of IPE, the studies lacked the methodological rigour needed to begin to understand the impact IPE has on professional practice and patient outcomes.

Some studies of IPE have highlighted positive benefits. A study by Carpenter (1995), who examined the stereotypes that doctors and nurses had on each other, revealed that through 'shared learning' the overall attitudes towards each respective profession had improved. Hammick (1998) attempts to reveal a clearer understanding of the application of IPE as a concept. Drawing on a broad body of knowledge, Hammick (1998) identifies a number of key benefits of IPE:

⌘　Inter-professional collaboration in the last decade has emerged as one way for providing effective health and social care (Pietroni, 1994).

⌘　Students who share such learning experiences, in an inter-professional manner, emerge with skills to promote effective working in multi-professional teams (Davison and Lucas, 1995).

⌘　The early organisation of knowledge can be described in terms of 'singular discourses'. By bringing together the different regions of knowledge that are represented by different disciplines, new discourses that integrate different types of knowledge can be enhanced.

In the learning disability field there is a growing literature that describes a number of universities providing pre-registration courses in learning disability nursing and social work. *Chapter 21* highlights a potential strength of such programmes in developing a willingness to question traditional practices and to explore professional knowledge from a range of sources. Such behaviour is seen as intrinsic to being able to work in an inter-professional manner. Actively seeking collaboration with other agencies and workers should be part of every day practice for all health professionals (McGray and Carter, 2002). Davis *et al* (1999) claim such joint training initiatives ground practitioners with a holistic model and a value base that enables them to prioritise both health and social care needs. Whether such initiatives will provide practitioners with a distinct and valued role within services will be down to employers, workforce planners and validating bodies (Parry and Renouf, 2003).

Difficulties in achieving inter-professional education

Interprofessional-education is as much about facilitating new ways of learning as it is about learning a new way of working. Clearly it is not perhaps as straightforward as this. Historical and current patterns of higher education provision for healthcare professions vary considerably. These differences throw obstacles in the way of inter-professional initiatives on a number of levels, including organisation, logistics of time-tabling, group size, timing and the appropriateness for students (Miller *et al*, 1998).

Interprofessional-education does not provide the panacea to establishing effective inter-professional working. The practice setting must support students by creating a culture that allows the development of collaborative practice. In the busy acute sector, organisational policies and the quick throughput of patients complicates the practical development of collaborative practices. Within the community setting the different cultural and philosophical bases that underpin different disciplines make it difficult for effective cross-agency working. Community learning disability teams, as an example, in the main have found it difficult over the last twenty years to establish and sustain an effective and cohesive working relationship, that can clearly demonstrate improvements in client care and intervention outcomes that can be directly attributed to IPW. Learning disability practitioners have demonstrated that they have the potential ability and are equipped with some of the necessary attributes to realise IPW with and on behalf of people with learning disabilities.

It is hoped that pre- and post-registration learning disability programmes within higher education create more opportunities for 'shared learning'. New graduate and postgraduate programmes which aim to develop competence in assessment and collaborative practice skills, could lead to the emergence of a hybrid worker. Such a worker, equipped with generic skills and a dynamic knowledge base should be well placed to conduct health and social care assessments themselves, thereby theoretically removing the ubiquitous conflict that surrounds the care management process. These programmes should be in addition to those aimed at developing practitioners who can facilitate access to mainstream health services through the promotion of health interventions.

Inter-professional working in learning disabilities

The following section will explore how partnership, as a concept, is intrinsically linked to IPW and why partnership is and has been crucial to the nurse client relationship within learning disability practice.

Depicting the sequence of interactions that make up a partnership between a practitioner and a person with learning disabilities is difficult. Yet, every day practice for many professions, not just nurses within the field, will rely upon some form of partnership to facilitate their work. As people with learning disabilities often have complex needs this in the reality of practice, requires that partnerships are not only formed with people with learning disabilities but also with other professional groups. Given the pressures of work, the necessary skills needed to maintain collaborative relationships are often overlooked and it is not until relationships break down that their absence is noticed (Hornby and Atkins, 2000).

Collaboration and partnership with people with learning disabilities

Gallant *et al* (2002) state that the idea of a nurse client relationship has intuitive appeal, yet the current literature is unclear about the elements and processes in such a relationship. A number of examples within this text relate the necessity for learning disability practitioners to form relationships with individuals as a basis for their work. Neville Parkes (*Chapter 11*) identifies a trust, almost a bond, that is involved with work with a male survivor of sexual abuse. He is able to articulate how the partnership is developed between practitioner and the person with learning disabilities, based upon counselling theories and a nursing model.

The relevance of such partnership building with people with learning disabilities as a bedrock of learning disability practice should not be underestimated. Sines (1995) reaffirms this, claiming that much of the knowledge acquired by learning disability nurses has been acquired from the intimacy of their relationship with their clients over a considerable period of time. This level of intimacy demands that nurses adhere to various codes of ethics for professional practice (NMC, 2002), incorporating respect for patient autonomy as a moral and ethical obligation (Gallant *et al*, 2002). Matched to the importance of having a code of ethics for practitioners, is demonstrating a level of introspection and reflective skills (Schon, 1983).

A number of prerequisites or antecedents have been identified that can determine a partnership. These, in principle, delineate a set of values, beliefs and assumptions that the nurse and the client wherever possible should hold about people and relationships. Patterson (1998) argues that partners must subscribe to the democratic value that each individual, regardless of social class (and perhaps age, condition, culture and ethnicity), is a worthwhile human being with unique needs. These humanistic principles underwrite the strong philosophy of humanism, that have been associated with learning disability practice for some time, coupled with the emphasis on empowerment. Both concepts are still perceived as crucial for practitioners to uphold, in order to be able to collaborate effectively with people with learning disabilities.

Approaches to assist collaboration

As stated previously, the complexity of needs that people with learning disabilities have, brings the learning disability practitioner into contact with many different professionals. The following approaches are highlighted to help workers in the field think about the way in which collaboration can be undertaken on different levels and a code of ethical principles that may govern inter-professional work.

Primary, secondary and participatory collaboration

Hornby and Atkins (2000) identify three types of collaboration where the individual is able to be supported to make some decisions and carry certain activities to the extent where they can be perceived as 'self-helpers'.

Primary collaboration begins when the individual and the practitioner start to explore together the issue or problem that has arisen. This may be at the beginning of a programme of care or following an incident that requires some form of therapeutic work.

Secondary collaboration describes the relationship between a number of workers, working together on behalf of the individual. This may refer to a small team of staff within the same unit or a psychiatrist, nurse and social worker assessing and monitoring individuals within a community setting.

Participatory collaboration refers to the complexity of individual and group relationships that occur when the user is present and taking part to whatever extent. This incidence may be during a formal review process or a GP appointment when carer, individual and practitioner are present.

Social network approach

This theoretical perspective is described by Cott (1997) as a series of interactions that takes place in teams, that are not concerned with professional status but more the patterns of relationships that occur within teams. Cott (1997) argues that the informal relationships that develop among workers affects the pattern of work itself. This is in relation to how much work there is, the division of that work and the emergence of a hierarchy to that work, which is not frequently recognised by management structures.

The foundation to this approach is proximity:

⌘ **Physical proximity**, where people are more likely to interact if they are situated close to one another, for example, in community teams where different professional disciplines are 'housed together'.

⌘ **Professional proximity**, where people of similar backgrounds are more likely to interact informally than people with different professional backgrounds.

⌘ **Task proximity**, people working on the same tasks or type of work are more likely to interact informally than people working on different tasks.

⌘ **Social proximity**, is where people who have social contact with one another are more likely to interact formally with regards to their work.

⌘ **Formal organisation-created proximity**, refers to people who are in the same organisational unit.

Readers of this chapter can no doubt identify with this general approach and locate their own understanding in relation to their particular professional experience.

Code of ethics for health and social care practitioners

Berwick *et al* (2001) suggests a code of ethics or principles to which all health and social care professionals can adhere:

⌘ Rights: people have a right to health and health care (all workers in the field should consider how, within the capacity of their role, they can support or promote this right).

⌘ Balance: care of individual people is central, but the health of the population is also our concern (a person-centred approach is useful but the broad needs of the learning disability population should not be overlooked).

⌘ Co-operation: health care succeeds only if we co-operate with those we serve, each other and those in other sectors/agencies (underpins the importance of effective inter-professional working).

⌘ Safety: do no harm (this reinforces a basic professional and ethical code that whatever aspect of a practitioner's work is undertaken, it should not in any way harm the individual).

⌘ Openness: being open, honest and trustworthy is vital (this is an undisputed requirement for professional practice but has additional relevance and importance when working with vulnerable groups).

⌘ Team working and networking: theoretical perspectives have been introduced into inter-professional education to inform the understanding of collaborative practice (both aspects have tacit relevance to the field, but are seen as essential for inter-professional working to be effective).

Conclusion

This chapter has attempted to grapple with the topic of inter-professional working and demonstrate its importance and relevance to learning disability practice. Many terms have been associated with inter-professional working; namely, partnership and collaboration which have become to a degree clichés within modern health and social care practice. Team work has been a term linked with inter-professional working, yet as a concept is rarely realised. Moving beyond such semantics, what is clear is that the processes that depict the way in which workers interact with other workers and relate to people with learning disabilities will always be important, if perhaps not truly ever understood and demonstrated.

It is clear that the political emphasis that has been placed upon inter-professional working, outweighs the existence of any empirical evidence that helps develop an understanding of the processes involved in collaborative practice. Decreasing resources and changes in practice ideology from specialisation to holism, have kept inter-professional working on the agenda. The assumption made mainly by politicians, is that by developing the structures and partnerships necessary for inter-professional working, then inter-professional practice will naturally follow. This clearly overlooks the barriers that can exist within different professional cultures, with different professional identities and status.

Inter-professional education (IPE) has been highlighted as an endeavour to bring together different professional groups to increase the awareness of different roles, responsibilities, relinquishing stereotypes to enhance the potential for collaborative practice. Some evidence demonstrates that by bringing different professional groups together in different educational initiatives, the awareness and understanding of respective roles does increase and integrated knowledge can be enhanced. However, evidence that   this collaboration improves patient/client care and outcomes has not yet been revealed.

Joint training initiatives between learning disability nursing and social work have offered some direction for the potential development of practitioners who can overcome the health and social care divide in an holistic manner. Whether this leads to the development of a hybrid worker will be down to local workforce planners, employees and higher education institutions. This chapter has highlighted that IPE will not be the panacea for developing effective inter-professional working. The practice setting, the way in which practitioners continue to develop, or are allowed to develop and the way in which they respond to client need, will also be important factors.

The final part of the chapter has discussed some of the skills and the consideration necessary to work in partnership with people with learning disabilities: factors that are often overlooked. The ability to develop a rapport and to collaborate effectively with individuals and their carers is highly relevant to most workers in the field. Hornby and Atkins (2000) provide different types of collaboration that can help workers understand and promote an empowering form of interaction. Understanding the pattern of relationships with other professional workers can be assisted by types of proximity (Cott, 1997). Overarching these latter approaches is a set of principles (Berwick *et al*, 2001) that can underpin any form of inter-professional work on an individual client basis or with other professionals.

It is clear that the landscape of provision for people with learning disabilities is going to change over the next two to three years. With single assessment processes and single points of access into specialist provision emerging, the relevance and importance of effective inter-professional working will be crystallised. Achieving genuine inter-professional working could measurably improve the journey in and out of services that people with learning disabilities and their carers have. Establishing evidence that this journey is an effective and positive one, for both people with learning disabilities, their carers and the professionals involved, is the real challenge.

Reflective points

⌘ Given the complexity of needs that people with learning disabilities have, inter-professional working is an integral part of contemporary learning disability practice.

⌘ Achieving effective inter-professional working is a challenge for most professional groups.

⌘ Inter-professional education can offer the opportunity to raise awareness of different professional roles.

⌘ Inter-professional training initiatives can offer the opportunity to develop practitioners that can prioritise the health and social care needs of people with learning disabilities.

⌘ Partnership building with people with learning disabilities still needs to be based upon humanistic principles.

References

Annandale E (1998) *The Sociology of Health and Medicine. A Critical Introduction.* Polity Press, Cambridge

Barr H (1998) Competent to collaborate: towards a competency-based model for interprofessional education. *J Interprofessional Care* **12**(2): 1814

Barr H, Hammick M, Koppel I, Reeves S (1999) Evaluating Interprofessional Education: Two systematic reviews from health and social care. *British Educational Research Journal* **25**(4): 533–44

Barr H (2002) *Interprofessional Education. Today, Yesterday and Tomorrow. A review Occasional Paper 1.* Learning and Teaching Support Network

Berwick D, Davidoff F, Hiatt H, Smith R (2001) Refining and implementing the tavistock principles for everybody in health care. *Br J Med* **323**(7313): 616–27

Cambridge P, McCarty M (2001) User focus groups and best value in services for people with learning disabilities. *Health and Social Care in the Community* **9**(6): 476–89

Carrier J, Kendal I (1995) Professionalism and interprofessionalism in health and community care: Some theoretical issues. In: Owens P, Carrier J, Horder, J, eds. *Interprofessional Issues in the Community and Primary Health Care Setting.* Macmillan, London

Carpenter J (1995) Doctors and nurses: Stereotypes and stereotype changes in inter-professional education. *J Interprofessional Care* **9**(12): 151–61

Cott C (1997) 'We decide, you carry it out'. A social network analysis of multi-disciplinary long-term care teams. *Soc Sci Med* **45**(9): 1411–21

Davidson L, Lucas J (1995) Multi-professional education in the undergraduate health professions curriculum: observations from Adelaide, Linkoping and Salford. *J Inter-professional Care* **9**(2): 163–76

Davis J, Rendel P, Sims D (1999) The joint practitioner — a new concept in professional training. *J Inter-professional Care* **13**(4): 395–404

Department of Health (1999) *Partnerships in Action.* HMSO, London

Department of Health (2000) *The National Plan. The NHS for all.* DoH, London

Department for Health (2001) *Valuing People: A Strategy for People with Learning Disabilities in the 21st Century.* DoH, London

Department of Health (2002) *Learning from Bristol. The Department of Health response to the Bristol Inquiry.* DoH, London

Department of Health (2003) The Victoria Climbié Inquiry. The report by Lord Laming. DoH, London

Freeman C, Miller C, Ross N (2001) The impact of individual philosophies of teamwork on multi-professional practice and the implications for education. *J Inter-professional Care* **14**(3): 237–47

Freidson E (1970) *Professions of Medicine*. Dodd Mead and Company, New York

Gallant MH, Beaulieu MC, Carnvale FC (2002) Partnership: an analysis of the concept within the nurse-client relationship. *J Adv Nurs* **40**(2): 149–157

Hammick M (1998) Interprofessional education: concept, theory and application. *J Inter-professional Care* **12**(3): 323–33

Henneman EA, Lee JL (1995) Collaboration: a concept analysis. *J Adv Nurs* **21**: 103–9

Hornby S, Atkins J (2000) *Collaborative Care: Interprofessional, interagency and interpersonal*. 2nd edn. Blackwell Science, Oxford

Hudson B (2002) Interprofessionality in health and social care: the Achilles' heel of partnership. *J Interprofessional Care* **16**(1): 7–17

Irvine R, Kerkridge I, Mc Phee, Freeman S (2002) Interprofessionalism and ethics: consensus or clash of cultures? *J Interprofessional Care* **16**(3): 199–210

Kraus WA (1980) *'Collaboration and Organisations': An alternative to hierarchy*. Human Sciences Press, New York

Leathard A (1994) *Going Interprofessional — Working Together for Health and Welfare*. Routledge, London

Loxley A (1997) *Collaboration in Health and Welfare. Working with Difference*. Jessica Kingsley, London

Mathias P, Prime R, Thompson T (1997) Preparation for interprofessional work: trends in education, training and the structure of qualifications in the UK. In: Øvretveit J *et al*, eds. *Interprofessional Working for Health and Social Care*. Macmillan, Basingstoke

McCallin A (2001) Interdisciplinary practice — a matter of teamwork: an integrated literature review. *J Clinical Nurs* **10**: 419–28

McGray J, Carter S (2002) A study to determine the qualities of a learning disability practitioner. *Br J Nur* **11**(21): 1380–8

Miller C, Ross N, Freeman M (1999) *Shared Learning and Clinical Teamwork: New directions in education for multiprofessional practice*. Research report series for the English National Board, London

Nursing and Midwifery Council (2002) *Code of Professional Conduct*. NMC, London

Navarro V (1978) *Class Struggle, the State of Medicine: an historian and contemporary analysis of the medical sector in Great Britain*. Martin Robinson, London

Øvretveit J (1993) *Co-ordinating Community Care. Multi disciplinary teams and Care Management*. Open University Press, Milton Keynes

Øvretveit J (1996) Five ways to describe a multi-disciplinary team. *J Interprofessional Care* **10**(2): 163–1171

Øvretveit J (1997) *Interprofessional Working for Health and Social Care*. Macmillan, London

Parry R, Renouf C (2003) Education and training. In: Gates B, eds. *Learning Disabilities. Towards Inclusion*. 4th edn. Churchill Livingstone, Edinburgh

Patterson B (1998) Partnership in nursing education: a vision or a fantasy? *Nurs Outlook* **46**: 284–9

Pietroni P (1994) Inter-professional work: its history and development in hospitals, general practice and community care (UK). In: Leathard A, ed. *Going Interprofessional: working together for health and welfare*. Routledge, London

Schon D (1983) *The Reflective Practitioner: How professionals think in action*. Basic Books, New York

Sines D (1995) Impaired Autonomy — the challenge for caring. *J Clinical Nurs* **4**: 109–15

Soothill K, Mackay L, Webb C, eds. *Interprofessional Relations in Health Care*. Arnold, London

Sorrell-Jones J (1997) The challenge of making it real: interdisciplinary practice in a seamless organisation. *Nursing Administration Quarterly* **21**(2): 20–30

Zwarenstein M, Reeves S, Barr H, Hammick M, Koppel I, Atkins J (2002) *Interprofessional Education: Effects on professional practice and health care outcomes*. The Cochrane Library, Issue 3, Oxford

Section II:
Primary health care

3

The menopause

Jane Bullock, Sharon Mackenzie

Over the last twenty-five years or more there has been a significant increase in women becoming more self-aware of their own specific health needs and actively taking responsibility for seeking advice and treatment. Contrary to most of the literature, women with learning disabilities have the same scope of life experiences that women in the general population encounter. For example, issues around low self-esteem, relationships, abuse and self-acceptance, to name but a few (Corbett, 1996).

There is a conflict within the primary healthcare arena and specialist services in women's health phenomenas. Women with learning disabilities risk being doubly discriminated against, by being perceived by their disability status and being excluded from having their primary healthcare needs identified and met effectively. This subsequently excludes them from further investigation, which would provide evidence to support not only a diagnosis, but also treatment appropriate to their symptoms.

Over the last decade there has been an abundance of evidence to support the claim that people with learning disabilities have undiagnosed and unmanaged primary healthcare needs (Howells, 1986; Wilson and Haire, 1990; Kerr 1998; Bollard, 1997).

The menopause is a naturally occurring significant life event that all women experience, generally between the ages of forty-five and fifty-five years. Women with learning disabilities tend to experience the menopause earlier by comparison to the general population.

The menopause is known commonly as 'The Change'. Signs and symptoms fall into two distinct categories with two distinct outcomes in relation to mental health and/or physical health. 'Menopause' is when the ovaries have ceased to function, marking the end of a woman's reproductive cycle (Gould 1990).

It is important that we, as nurses, understand the physiology of how the female hormones function and change with age (*Table 3.1*).

The hypothalamus secretes a hormone, which stimulates the pituitary gland, situated in the base of the brain to release the follicle stimulating hormone (FSH) and the luteinizing hormone (LH).

The two female sex hormones are progesterone and oestrogen. Progesterone is mainly released on the fourteenth to the twenty-eighth day within a woman's menstrual cycle. Its function is to prepare for pregnancy. Oestrogen, the predominant hormone, is produced continually and is responsible for physical characteristics changing at puberty and maintaining the functional state of the reproductive system until menopause (Gould, 1990).

Follicle stimulating hormone stimulates the follicles containing eggs to open, this occurs in the first fourteen days of a woman's cycle; ovulation occurs when the ovum is released. Ovulation is initiated by LH. After ovulation has taken place the empty follicle folds in on itself, which is known as the corpus luteum (lies on the surface of the ovary). It is this corpus luteum that produces progesterone. Together, these two hormones act on the hypothalamus and pituitary gland in a negative way and levels of FSH and LH fall (Anderson, 1991).

Table 3.1: An overview of how the female hormones function and change with age

Oestrogen also relates muscle walls of blood vessels and contributes to retaining calcium in bones. Its presence is also influential in maintaining the psychological well being of the woman (Bevis 1991).

Progesterone contributes to the retention of some water and salt in the body. It also stimulates alveoli glands in the breasts. In the second half of the menstrual flow it contributes psychologically resulting in premenstrual syndrome.

In the menopause, it is the winding down of the above hormones that signals that the reproductive episode in a woman's life is ending. A sequence of events occur:

> Egg cells diminish
> Fail to respond to FSH
> Decline in production of oestrogen
> Increase in FSH and LH levels

Adapted from Anderson, 1991

The endometrium is stimulated during the first half of the cycle by oestrogen. During the second half of the cycle the endometrium is influenced by progesterone: preparing a nourishing environment for the fertilized egg.

If fertilisation does not occur, then the levels of oestrogen and progesterone decrease; consequently, sustaining the endometrium becomes unviable and it sheds itself. It is this shedding that results in the menstrual flow and the process of menstruating.

As a result of the reduction in oestrogen and progesterone, not only does the menstrual cycle cease but women also suffer from other symptoms.

Discussion

Women who have learning disabilities are doubly discriminated against. Jones (1994) reports greater numbers of women are diagnosed as needing psychiatric help. She found that this may be due to general practitioners (GPs) readiness to classify them as emotional and unstable.

Recent research studies have identified that people with learning disabilities have unmet, unmanaged primary healthcare needs (Kerr, 1998; Howells, 1986). Interestingly though, Butler (1998) argues that, 'women with intellectual disabilities have the same health needs as all other women' and that the onset of menopause is between forty-five and fifty-five years of age.

Hormone replacement therapy (HRT) should be considered to relieve short-term symptoms and long-term risks such as osteoporosis. The risks of HRT may outweigh the advantages, but each woman needs to be assessed individually (DoH, 2002).

Sutcliffe (1999) states that osteoporosis affects one in three women and one in twelve men. Brockie's (1999) study found that women can expect to live forty per cent of their lives after the menopause. Hormone replacement therapy offers relief from menopausal symptoms with the long-term benefits of possible prevention of cardio-vascular disease, osteoporosis, Alzheimer's disease and colon cancer. Many women only take HRT short term and are missing out on long-term benefits.

Women may choose to initiate, reinstate or discontinue HRT at any time beyond the postmenopausal period. Keller *et al*'s (1998) study further endorses HRT but also recommends exercise, nutrition and its potential as primary and secondary preventatives therapies against coronary heart disease, osteoporosis, breast and genital cancer and the maintenance of cognitive function among older, post-menopausal women. Hormone replacement therapy, as a treatment, acts dually in alienating symptoms and as a preventative measure for a number of significant illnesses.

Posthuma *et al*'s study (1994) reported the reduced relative risk for cardiovascular disease in post-menopausal women taking HRT (35–40% in risk) and further suggests that HRT has been recommended for all post-menopausal women to prevent cardio-vascular disease and that further analysis of the results showed a reduced risk of cancer in women taking HRT.

McPherson (1993) states that epidemiological studies have confirmed that oestrogen prevents cardiovascular disease; a reduction of between 30–40%. Osteoporosis is reduced as HRT preserves bone density, preventing fractures. McPherson further suggests that depression is common at the time of menopause. Many factors requiring careful assessment (eg. significant life events) should be considered, as anti-depressant drugs may be the first line of treatment.

Gould (1990) suggests menopause often coincides with changes in lifestyle and family structure, which may be unwelcome.

Although Furecki and Tidyman (1994) endorse the above, they stress that women should be fully informed of the risks of HRT and that it should only be prescribed after careful assessment and consideration.

Bevis (1991) also endorses the benefits of HRT and the preventative aspect of reducing the risk of developing osteoporosis and cardiovascular disease.

Anderson (1991) asks if treatment is always necessary, as symptoms are self-limiting. However, she recognises the preventative element of HRT and the reduction in cardiovascular disease and osteoporosis.

Reshidk (1998) suggests that we should consider the interplay between older adults' activities and the environment. Neurological, muscular skeletal and cardiovascular changes as well as others associated with ageing are important considerations, identifying and reducing risk. Chandler (1993) endorses this by recommending health assessments and management of underlying illness and deficits.

Butler (1998) states that menstrual suppression may result in lower circulating oestrogen levels: this, in turn, may lead to an increased long-term risk of osteoporosis. Therefore, women with a disability have a relatively higher rate of hysterectomy than the non-disabled population: a procedure that has been used for menstrual management and contraception.

Clinical experience has shown that ladies who have menopausal syndrome increasingly suffer from difficult to manage behaviour that has correlated each month with their menstrual cycle.

Duncan's (1997) study of epilepsy, fertility, contraception and pregnancy concluded that changes in hormones, especially noted in the follicular phase (oestrogen is high), correlated with increase in seizures. However, up to fifty per cent of women reported that their epilepsy was better controlled during pregnancy, possibly because of the avoidance of fatigue, better compliance and hormonal change.

Carr and Hollins' study (1995) of menopause in women with learning disabilities consisted of 171 women, forty-five of whom had Down's syndrome. The results suggested that, compared to data on 'normal' women, the menopause may occur earlier in women with learning disabilities and even earlier still in women with Down's syndrome. Interestingly, the role of the thyroid should be considered as thyroid deficiency is found in ten to twenty-two per cent of adults with Down's syndrome. Martin *et al* (2001) endorses this by saying that thyroid dysfunction can also affect menopause and that this condition is also prevalent in people with Down's syndrome. This suggests that the implications of endocrinological irregularities should ideally form part of any future enquiry into early menopause in women with learning disabilties.

Confusion is also a reported symptom of the menopause by women, and can be mistaken by professionals as an indicator and onset of dementia (espectially for women with Down's syndrome) (McCarthy, 2002).

McCarthy's study (2000) focuses on the phenomenon of women with learning disabilities and menopause, stressing the importance of specialist and generic services providing equality in accessing appropriate services and being given a choice in therapies; together with information about the menopause for women with learning disabilities and their carers.

Martin *et al* (2001) recognises how menopause, affecting women with learning disabilities is a neglected area of research. They assert that clear information on this subject would empower women with learning disabilities, as well as benefiting carers and specialist service providers by raising awareness. Clear accurate information 'distinguishing between symptoms that are the result of loss of ovarian function and symptoms that arise from the ageing process' (*Table 3.2*).

McCarthy's (2002) study reflects, once

Table 3.2: Issues supporting the need for assessment in women with learning disabilities

❖ Higher rates of hysterectomy:
  ● management of menstrual cycle
  ● contraception
❖ Increase in challenging behaviour
❖ Increase in seizures
❖ Menopause occurring earlier, earlier still within the Down's syndrome population
❖ Endrocrinological irregularities due to premature ageing

again, the lack of recognition and advice available to women with learning disabilities who are, or may be, menopausal. General practitioners report that when a woman with learning disabilities goes to see them, it is usually one of three problems; hot flushes, followed by problems with menstruation and changes in mood or behaviour. Sixty per cent of GPs had never treated a woman with learning disabilities regarding menopause. Several doctors commented that menopause was not an issue, which they or their colleagues had considered seriously in relation to women with learning disabilities. This highlights the importance of collaborative practices and the ongoing need for education and awareness of the menopause. More research is needed in this area, together with an assessment for and access to appropriate treatment.

The Department of Health (2002a) released an urgent message regarding 'the risks and benefits of HRT' based on the results of an American study. The results confirmed what is already known about the long-term risks of HRT, including breast cancer and venous thromboembolism, and that combination HRT is only indicated for the treatment of menopausal symptoms and prevention of osteoporosis.

HRT has not been proven to be beneficial in preventing coronary heart disease. Coronary heart disease increased from thirty to thirty-eight cases per 10,000 women. Stroke increased from twenty-one to twenty-nine cases per 10,000 women. Breast cancer also increased from thirty to thirty-eight cases per 10,000 women.

The benefits were a reduction in colorectal cancer from sixteen to ten cases per 10,000 women, and hip fractures from fifteen to ten cases per 10,000 women. The study did not look at short-term risk/benefits from HRT. for the relief of menopausal symptoms. It was especially designed to establish long-term risks and benefits. Women who were included in the trial were not suffering from menopausal symptoms and were significantly older than the majority of women who use HRT in the UK. A clear message was given to GPs for regular check ups. Women should have regular mammograms and cervical screening appropriate to their age.

More studies are needed in this area concerning earlier onset of menopause with women who have learning disabilities. Evidence of hormonal change and the impact it has on difficult to manage behaviours; increase in epileptic seizures during pregnancy and earlier onset of, not only menopause, but premature ageing with women who have Down's syndrome is a positive indicator. Given this need and the available evidence, it adds further justification for the assessment to be implemented on all women aged thirty-five and over who have a learning disability.

The equitable inclusion of people with a learning disability alongside the mainstream population into a primary healthcare framework, presents as an important challenge for providers (Kerr *et al*, 1996). It is widely acknowledged that those with a learning disability should have access to the same general health services as everyone else; including health promotion, education, surveillance and maintenance and be able to access primary, secondary and additional support as required to meet individual needs (DoH, 1995). This process has been further endorsed through the publication of *Valuing People* (DoH, 2001), where inclusion underpins the strategies for targets for change.

'Change' in today's NHS and social care cultures means that service developments and expectations are continually evolving and this, in itself, prompts changes required in professional work practices.

A philosophy that underpins community learning disability nursing is one of primary healthcare (WHO, 1978), which includes holistic assessment, equitable partnerships, autonomy, independence and respect and where a recognition that individuals with a learning disability have unmet and additional unmanaged healthcare needs often associated with their learning disability. For community specialist nurse practitioners this means an agenda which includes working towards tackling social exclusion.

Clinical governance promotes raising standards, which encompasses individual practitioners and organisations taking more ownership and responsibility for developing and maintaining individual professional standards via clinical audit, clinical effectiveness, quality assurance, risk management and staff development (DoH, 1997, 1998).

The menopausal assessment/screening tool proposed and introduced in this chapter aims to achieve this. It is necessary to appraise the process and structure in order for this assessment tool to be proven clinically effective and subsequently valid in its clinical relevance and credibility. The three-part assessment aims to identify women who are menopausal, providing an evidence-based recommendation for the management of signs and symptoms of the menopause.

The assessment tool was developed through a literature review and clearly reflects a process towards providing an evidence base in this area. It positively reflects health promotion, education and surveillance, linking theory to practice, exploring also one of the domains of a community learning disability nurse.

The specialist practitioner higher award in nursing is acknowledged and embellished by way of synthesising theory to practice.

This development in assessment is also driven as a direct result of clinical experiences and the occurrence of unidentified mismanagement of the menopause in women with learning disabilities. The Bullock Indicator Scale is a three-part assessment providing due diligence within the primary healthcare arena, where after analysis of the current evidence available the tool was designed with a clear inference on the appropriate management of the menopause depending on the score (*Appendix 1*). Guidance notes accompany the assessment tool to aid the practitioner in completion.

The aims of the assessment are that the risks of mismanagement are reduced and that women who are menopausal are identified and appropriate treatment is recommended.

The assessment is to be used in conjunction with the practitioner guidance notes and a primary healthcare screening assessment. All women with learning disabilities aged between thirty and fifty-five years of age will automatically be screened. The screening will be part of their initial and ongoing assessment and act as a provider of baselines as well as regularly monitoring for relief of signs and symptoms of the menopause.

The screening will be completed by a community learning disability nurse. The involvement of primary carers and significant others along with the individual being screened is also recommended to provide clarity of responses and to assist in overcoming possible communication barriers, which have so often been identified in the literature.

The assessment is done in collaboration with the primary healthcare team, involving GPs, practice nurses and acute services as necessary. Collaborating involves educating and creating an awareness of the clinical needs of women who have learning disabilities and, subsequently, aims to extend our current knowledge base by sharing and acting upon the available evidence in order to discriminate positively for women who are menopausal.

Findings

The indicator scale provides an ongoing, evolving practical approach by way of a checklist for screening women with a learning disability for the menopause. It has presented as both challenging and informative to individuals, allied health professionals, community disability nurses, and specialist practitioners.

The pilot project screened twenty-eight women with a learning disability aged thirty-five and upwards after a generic health screening checklist was completed. The mean age of this small study was 39.3 years. The results were:

- 17.86% of women screened were identified as menopausal
- 7.14% of women have commenced on HRT for a trial period
- 28.57% of the ladies screened also had Down's syndrome
- 25% of the women screened scored high enough on the indicator scale to be re-assessed for specific mental health problems
- 10.71% of women are now in the process of accessing further gynaecological investigations as a result of the initial screening using the tool

- 60.71% of the women will continue to be monitored and reviewed within an elected timescale of three, six and twelve months
- 100% of the baseline assessments will be used for outcome measures when undertaking clinical audits.

The Bullock Indicator Scale is not only a baseline assessment but appears at this stage to identify positively menopausal women recommending alternative interventions at three levels. The checklist is easily adapted to uphold clinical governance, enabling community learning disability nurses to identify outcome measures. Clinical effectiveness can perhaps be demonstrated by the therapeutic benefits of any prescribed medication against the baseline checklist findings as the checklist is evidence-based.

As with any pilot project, amendments to the indicator scale are required and reviewed as more feedback is received and changes are being made accordingly. We are also in the process of developing a practitioner's guide/booklet to accompany the checklist.

Conclusions

The community learning disability nurse and the specialist practitioner not only provide specialist functionalised roles to people within the learning disability profession, but also positively contribute to the nursing evidence base, extending credibility and developing the domains of nursing practice and informing allied professionals.

The Bullock Indicator Scale aspires to inform practice but, more importantly, to facilitate positive health gains for women with learning disabilities.

Recommendations

- ⌘ To continue the pilot project for the next twelve months.
- ⌘ To review/analyse the evidence at the end of this period to assess how consistent findings are.
- ⌘ To consider comparing findings to those in the general population.
- ⌘ That practitioner guidelines to completing the checklist be made available along with the indicator scale.
- ⌘ That all women entering the learning disability service over the age of 35 are offered the screening as a matter of course.
- ⌘ Continue to educate and promote the use of the tool within the learning disability field but also, where appropriate, to our primary healthcare colleagues.
- ⌘ Continue to gather evidence and research in this particular subject area.

References

Anderson (1991) *The Menopause*. Faber and Faber Limited, London: 16

Baumen *et al* (1999) cites Forceia *et al* (1996); Reshidk (1998); Chandler (1993) in: Defying gravity and fear. The prevention of falls in community dwelling older adults. *Clinical Effectiveness for Nurse Practitioners* 3(5): 254

Bevis R (1991) *Caring for Women: Obstetric and gynaecological nursing.* 4th edn. Baillière Tindall, Edinburgh: 304, 307

Bollard M (1997) *The Coventry Primary Health Care and Learning Disability Project Report.* Coventry Healthcare NHS Trust, Coventry

Brockie J (1999) Using Serums for Treating Post-menopausal Symptoms. Community Nurse, January: 30–1

Carr J, Hollins S (1995) Menopause in Women with Learning Disability. *J Intellectual Disability Res* **39**(Part 2): 137–9

Corbett A, Cotti S, Morris S (1996) *Witnessing, Nurturing and Protecting. Therapeutic Responses to Sexual Abuse of People with Learning Disabilities.* David Fulton Publishers, London

Department of Health (1995) *The Health of the Nation: A Strategy for People with a Learning Disability.* HMSO, London

Department of Health (1997) *The New NHS — modern, dependable.* HMSO, London

Department of Health (1998) *A First Class Service: Quality in the new NHS.* HMSO, London

Department of Health (2002a) *Public Health Link: Risks and Benefits of HRT.* DoH, London

Department of Health (2002b) *Valuing People: A New Strategy for Learning Disability for the 21st Century.* HMSO, London

Duncan J (1997) *Epilepsy 97 from Science to Patient – Lecture Notes.* Novartis, chap 40: 293

Furecki A, Tidyman M (1994) *Women's Health Guide.* British Library Cataloguing Public Data: 264, 271

Gould D (1990) *Nursing Care of Women.* Prentice Hall International (UK) Limited: 225

Howells G (1986) Are medical needs of the mentally handicapped adults being met? *J R Coll Gen Practitioners*, October 1986: 449–53

Jones L (1994) *The Social Context of Health and Health Work.* MacMillan Press Limited, London: 254

Keller C (1998) Fullerton J, Flavry J (1998) Primary & secondary prevention strategies among older post menopausal women. *J Nurse/Midwifery* **43**(4): 262–72

Kerr M (1998) Innovations in health care for peple with intellectual disabilties. Cited: Butler J, Tracy J *Women's Health.* Glaxo Welcome: 67–79

Kerr M, Fraser W, Felce D (1996) Primary Healthcare for People with a Learning Disability. A Keynote Review. *Br J Learning Disabilities* **24**: 2–8

McCarthy (2000) Change in life, the menopause and women with intellectual disabilities. *J Intellectual Disability Res* **44**(3.4): 384

McCarthy M (2002) Responses to women with learning disabilities as they go through the menopause. *Tizard Learning Disability Review* **7**(1): 4–12

McPherson A (1993) *Women's Problems in General Practice.* Oxford University Press, Oxford: 198

Martin D, Cassidy G, Ahmad S, Martin M (2001) Women with learning disabilities and the menopause. *J Learning Disabilities* **5**(2): 121–31

Posthuma W *et al* (1994) Cardioprotective effect of hormone replacement therapy in postmenopausal women: Is the evidence based? *Br Med J* **308**: 1268–9

Sutcliffe A (1999) A regional nurse-led osteoporosis clinic. *Nurs Standard* **13**(37): 46–47

Wilson DN, Hair A (1990) Health care screening for people with a mental handicap living in the community. *Br Med J* **301**: 1379–81

Whitehead *et al* (1996) Assessing general practitioner care of adult patients with a learning disability: case control study. *Qual Healthcare* **5**: 31–5

World Health Organization (1978) Alma Ata Primary Health Care. Who, Geneva

4

Health screening and health surveillance

Penny Pritchard

Research has indicated that the healthcare needs of people with learning disabilities are not being met (Howells, 1986; Lawrie, 1995; Meehan *et al*, 1995); and the impact of an absence of health promotion strategies has been graphically identified through the findings of Barr *et al* (1999) and Cumella and Martin (2000).

Services for people with learning disabilities within South Staffordshire Healthcare NHS Trust recognise that in order to meet their healthcare needs, clients may need additional help to keep well. A health screening project was undertaken to identify unmet healthcare needs and structure a health promotion strategy to meet these needs in the future.

This chapter gives an overview of the research undertaken, and shows the health screening process being utilised with a service user. It demonstrates the health gains achieved for that person, and gives account of the changes in clinical practice as a result of the research.

It highlights the outcomes of developing and maintaining a health promotion strategy for service users living within the South Staffordshire Healthcare NHS Trust. The health needs of this population, present major challenges to the primary health care services (Cumella *et al*, 1992). It is hoped that by working in partnership with primary healthcare teams, that these challenges will be significantly reduced in the best interests of people with learning disabilities.

In the past twenty-two years there have been significant changes in the care of people with learning disabilities. The impact of long-term Government initiatives has brought about fundamental changes in the way this minority group have been cared for. The NHS Community Care Act (1990) brought about changes, not only in the way in which care was perceived, but also in how the professionals were required to respond to the individual health needs of people with learning disabilities. The transition from institutions to community living has been a complicating factor for people with learning disabilities attempting to gain access to primary and secondary health care.

Government White Papers spanning a period of five years; *Caring for People* (DoH, 1989b), *Promoting Better Health* (DoH, 1987), *Working for Patients* (1989a), *The Health of the Nation* (DoH, 1992); and the *Strategy for people with learning disabilities* (DoH, 1995), have all contributed to, and reflected considerable changes in organisational structures and responsibilities. These developments at national level have had a profound impact on local agendas.

It was as a response to these initiatives, that it was proposed to develop a health promotion strategy. This was achieved by devising a health screening process to meet the healthcare needs of people with learning disabilities living in south Staffordshire.

The research proposal for this work was acknowledged by the West Midlands Regional Health Authority (NHSE) in an 'Innovation in Practice' Award 1995/96.

Roy (1992) stated the importance of 'assessment' in gaining a fuller understanding of the health of people with learning disabilities; and stressed how health needs can be underestimated due to communication difficulties and problems being wrongly attributed to the learning disability itself. Many research initiatives have given valuable observations and data regarding the health status of people with learning disabilities, and provide evidence to confirm this. Studies by Cole (1986), Minihan and Dean (1990), Wilson and Haire (1990) all identified significant health needs, which were not being met. Meehan *et al* (1995) highlighted that needs were not being addressed and that there was evidence to suggest differences in health status according to age. This indicates a rise in healthcare needs as a person ages, and reinforces that health promotion strategies should take place at an early age to prevent ill health and/or deterioration in later life.

The research process is a systematic and structured enquiry. For the purpose of this study; a descriptive survey appeared to be the most appropriate way of collecting data. The data generated by this methodology was both quantitative and qualitative in nature. The overall aim of the study was to identify unmet health needs, and structure a health promotion strategy in order to meet those needs in the future.

A research study involving participants with learning disabilities is not without its challenges and, as Kay (1994) points out, ' ... can be a minefield of ethical and moral dilemmas'. Reference to the then UKCC's *Guidelines for Professional Practice* (1996) assisted the nurses involved in this project in the safe and ethical conduct of the research.

Process

The starting point was to conduct a literature search, looking for evidence in relation to the meeting of the health needs of people with learning disabilities. To gain access to the sampling frame the initial letter, consent form, questionnaire, letter to GP, screening form and criteria, were sent to the Ethics Committee for approval and discussed at a GP forum.

Using existing data available on the special needs register, a representative sample of adults with learning disabilities between the ages of nineteen to thirty-five years were identified. To enable greater accuracy the population was stratified according to the criterion of gender and equal numbers of males and females selected randomly to take part. Using estimated population figures of 1 per 1,000 population as having some degree of learning disabilities, the mean number of people to be screened was thirty, ten from each of the three locality team areas.

A letter outlining the purpose of the project and consent to participate form was sent with an initial questionnaire to those chosen to participate. A stamped addressed envelope was included for reply and reminders sent out to clients who had not responded by the stated date in an effort to encourage the best response. Clients who did not wish to take part, were asked to complete the initial questionnaire so that this data could be utilised even if screening was not carried out. If clients were unable to complete the questionnaire, a relative/carer or advocate would be asked to do so on their behalf. Once initial information and consent was obtained the participant's GP was informed of the purpose of the project and that their patient had consented to take part.

Each respondent was invited to attend a clinic nearest their home at an appropriate time. If clients experienced difficulties with attending, a home visit was arranged.

Using the screening form and criteria developed by the strategy group, screening was carried out by qualified learning disabilities nurses. Care was taken to ensure that the client and, if necessary, their relatives/carers, fully understood the process and the reason for participation before screening began. When screening was completed the participant's GP was informed of all results of the health screen and any action needed was taken, eg. referral to speech therapist, bereavement counsellor, etc. Areas of concern were highlighted, ie. high blood pressure; and the client was encouraged to make a doctor's appointment to discuss these issues further.

Results

Raw data was collated following completion of the screening. Statistical analyses were carried out in the form of percentages; enabling the readers to see which health needs were most apparent.

The data collected showed that health needs were not being met, and that there was evidence that some people were not accessing services, which could meet their needs (*Figure 4.1*).

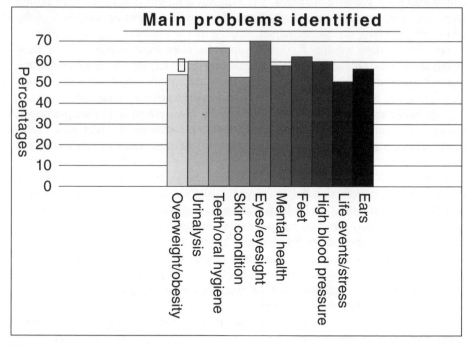

Figure 4.1: Main problems identified

Using the criteria for assessment, evidence showed that 54% of the respondents screened were overweight or obese, and that 60% had high blood pressure, giving cause for concern. The screening process identified that 60% of respondents had identified problems when urinalysis was carried out, and further investigations were required. A significant number had poor oral hygiene, 67% required dental treatment. There was also a significant number found to have problems with the condition of their ears, skin and feet. In contrast, 80% of respondents had good condition of the eyes, scalp and hair.

Of all respondents completing the initial questionnaire, 59% were taking prescribed medication; of these, 32% were suffering from epilepsy. The results indicated that 91% of respondents did not have access to a neurologist. Half of the clients surveyed had a physical disability, although only 9% received help from a physiotherapist. It was also identified that only 22% of respondents were receiving help from the community learning disabilities nursing service; and an even smaller percentage had access to occupational and speech and language therapies.

General practitioners who had agreed to their patient taking part in the project, were informed of all findings, and a follow-up questionnaire was sent to participants asking whether they had seen their GP since the screening was carried out. They were also asked to indicate whether the GP had addressed the health issues raised from the screening process. In 90% of cases, the GP had not been seen to have taken any action.

Discussion

To improve the health of people with learning disabilities calls for a strategic, collaborative and cohesive approach. The evidence from this project validated results from previous research; and highlighted how health screening carried out by community learning disabilities nurses alone is not the answer. Accessing primary health care services requires facilitation on a far more interactional level. Bollard (1997) shows how GPs and the primary healthcare teams require information regarding learning disabilities *per se*; and that awareness of the specific healthcare needs of this client group and the role that specialist services can play, needs to be raised.

The health screening project identified that the development of a health promotion strategy is essential to enable people with learning disabilities to meet their health needs. Through providing an accurate picture of the prevalence of conditions and disorders, community teams can provide a pro-active model of service to ensure increased health status of the individual and early detection and treatment of conditions. Health promotion through screening enables health surveillance for people with learning disabilities. The health promotion strategy adopted following this project has also led to healthy lifestyles group activities, and individual interventions, enabling the client to take responsibility for their own health care needs.

Through education, collaboration, and facilitation with primary care services, community learning disabilities nurses can influence the provision of viable services, which will benefit the individual with learning disabilities by promoting health, well being and enabling autonomy on the basis of informed choice.

The Government's commitment to the health needs of people with learning disabilities has been demonstrated further through *Signposts for Success* (DoH, 1998) and *Once a Day* (DoH, 1999). The introduction of the most recent White Paper, *Valuing People: A New Strategy for Learning Disability for the 21st Century* (DoH, 2001), addresses good health as one of its key objectives. Its challenge to services is:

To enable people with learning disabilities to access a health service designed around their individual needs, with fast and convenient care delivered to a consistently high standard, and with additional support where required.

The White Paper sets three challenges:

⌘ That health facilitators may be more appropriately located from community learning disability teams, to support people with learning disabilities to access the health care they need.
⌘ All people with learning disabilities will be registered with a GP.
⌘ All people with learning disabilities will have their own health action plan.

The health screening tool developed for use through the research project in South Staffordshire goes some way to addressing these challenges. Through health facilitation it has enabled the person with learning disabilities to develop their own health action plan, and be supported to get the health care they need.

The following case study shows how health screening enabled one service user to take responsibility for her own health care, and promote her independence in community life. (Names and details have been changed to maintain anonymity.)

Case history

Jane has been known to our service following a number of referrals, over the past twenty years. At the time of the referral she was living at home with her parents, who, during the authors involvement with the family, sadly died within six months of one another. Jane has one brother who is married and lives in the local area. Jane was seen on a regular basis by the consultant psychiatrist and supported by the community nursing service in relation to her anxiety, anger and difficult behaviours; which impacted very much on the family dynamics at that time.

Jane saw her father as the focus for her anger, and blamed him for her feelings and subsequent behaviours. She had a poor self-image, saw herself as useless and would frequently say everyone would be better off without her around. Jane had previously had several admissions to hospital, to address her mental health problems and behaviour. She would repeatedly say that she wanted to go back to hospital, and would gain attention from this and display challenging behaviour towards her parents.

It was at the time of our health screening project that Jane had been re-referred to our service. It seemed an ideal opportunity to offer her a health screen and enable her to take a positive interest in herself. Jane had weight problems, and had been going to a slimming club for years with no success. The health screening project was explained to Jane and her mother and she decided that she would like to participate.

A letter of consent was given and explained to Jane and she signed to agree to the health screen. A letter was also sent to Jane's GP, giving a detailed explanation of the process.

Using the health screening tool developed as part of the project (*Appendix II*) the following areas were addressed:
- scalp and hair condition
- life events/stress
- sleeping
- eyes and eyesight

- medication
- nutritional and dietetic screen
- condition of hands and finger nails
- continence promotion
- epilepsy
- condition of feet and toe nails
- female and male sexuality
- urine analysis
- skin condition
- circulation and breathing
- teeth and oral hygiene
- communication
- ears and hearing
- mental health.

The main objective of using the tool was to provide Jane with a balanced view of her health status by recognising:

- what she was doing well
- areas which she needed to consider improvement
- areas which needed action to be taken.

As part of the project a dietician was employed one day a week and her expertise was utilised, not only in the development of a nutritional screen as part of the health screening tool; but also in developing individual nutrition care plans for clients.

Using the criteria developed for the project, the health screen was carried out by the author with Jane in her own home. The areas in which Jane was doing well were then discussed with her.

Jane's personal hygiene was very good, and she took a keen interest in ensuring that she dressed and presented herself well. Jane visited her GP regularly and took responsibility for ensuring that she collected her prescriptions on time and took her medication regularly. She was also committed to wanting to lose weight, even though she had tried various methods over the years with little sustained success. Jane's ability to communicate effectively enabled her to give and receive information, which would allow her to take more responsibility for her own health.

Health needs were identified with Jane as part of her personal health record (*Box 4.1*), and discussed and agreed with her as being areas to consider improving on.

The results of the health screen were sent to Jane's GP and she was encouraged to visit her doctor to discuss the findings. Her GP was asked to refer formally to the dietician, who, together

---

Box 4.1: Personal health record

- ⌘ To have a healthy eating plan.
- ⌘ To develop a more active lifestyle.
- ⌘ To reduce oily scalp and improve hair care.
- ⌘ To improve oral hygiene and visit dentist regularly.
- ⌘ To attend for eye test.
- ⌘ To improve skin care of hands and feet.
- ⌘ To consult with psychiatrist and community nurse in relation to sleep problems and emotional needs.
- ⌘ To improve self-esteem.
- ⌘ To attend for a cervical smear/breast check.

with the community learning disabilities nurse; gathered more information from Jane about her eating habits in the form of a daily food diary. An individual nutrition care plan was set up with Jane and a regular appointment with the practice nurse for advice and weight recording was arranged. The community learning disabilities nurse supported Jane with her healthy eating plan, and discussed with Jane and her mother ways of enabling Jane to have a more active lifestyle. This initiated Jane and her mother to start swimming and walking together, and Jane was encouraged to participate in gardening activities. She also liked keep fit videos and was keen to watch and join in with the exercises.

Jane's healthy eating plan and healthier lifestyle enabled her to start to lose weight and be more active. Jane has continued to lose weight steadily over the past few years, and is now some six stones lighter than before. The consultant psychiatrist has regularly reviewed Jane's medication and this, in turn, has been a contributing factor to her weight loss. As a result, Jane's self-confidence and esteem has increased considerably. The *Health of the Nation* document (DoH, 1992; 1995) identifies that obesity, in particular, is significant in the prevalence of coronary heart disease and stroke. Intervention with Jane has drastically reduced these risks to her health.

Following the initial screening, Jane was given advice regarding hair and skin care. She refused the offer of referral for chiropody; so a mutually agreed care plan was put in place to help her care for her feet. Jane's GP prescribed a skin softening cream and she was encouraged to care for her feet in a better way. Instruction on how to apply cream, remove hard skin, cut nails and choose appropriate footwear were given. Appointments at the dentist, and for an eye test were made. Jane visited the optician with her mother; but asked for support from the community learning disabilities nurse when attending her dental appointment. Jane has continued to have regular check ups and has successfully received dental treatment, including two extractions and regular dental hygiene. The support given has enabled her to build confidence and reduce anxiety about visiting the dentist. She now makes and keeps regular appointments on her own, and is aware of the importance of good oral hygiene.

The community learning disability nurse also supported Jane in visiting the practice nurse for cervical and breast screening. This was particularly important to Jane as her mother had died from a related cancer, and she wished to ensure her own health remained good.

Jane has been supported by the community learning disabilities service throughout a very difficult period in her life. The loss of her parents and the desire to remain living independently in the community have at times proved very stressful for her. Jane was helped to adjust to, and move on with life, by facilitation through the grief process. Using Worden's (1991) model of grief counselling, Jane has been helped to come to terms with the death of her parents.

The ongoing review of her health needs has enabled the appropriate support needs to be addressed. 'Health is a dynamic entity that encompasses an individual's physical, mental, social and spiritual well being' (Kiger, 1995). Certainly this is true for Jane, who has benefited enormously from the opportunity to address her health needs in all of these areas of her well being.

Reflection

Evidence produced from using the health screening tool validated results from previous studies, which had shown that the health care needs of people with learning disabilities were not being met. Subsequent studies have added to the overwhelming evidence that regular health checks can identify and treat problems and conditions (Whitfield *et al*, 1996; Martin *et al*, 1997; Barr *et al*, 1999; Webb and Rogers, 1999; Cassidy *et al*, 2002).

Community learning disabilities nurses alone cannot achieve improvement in health care for people with learning disabilities.

Involvement in the health screening project raised awareness of the need to facilitate access to the primary healthcare services on a far more interactional level.

Since this health screening project was carried out, various assessment tools have been developed by professionals for use with people with learning disabilities. One of the most well known being the 'OK' health check (Matthews, 1996). However, the community learning disabilities service in the author's NHS Trust decided to continue with the use of the health screen developed from the health screening project. It was preferred as it provides the service user with their own personal health record, giving opportunity to celebrate what the person is doing well in respect to their health.

As a result of the health screening project, this user-friendly tool was adopted for use as part of the overall client assessment process. The purpose was to identify not only whether that person had health needs that were not being addressed, but whether there were unrecognised health needs that were having a major impact on their lives. The author recalls a case whereby a client referred to her died from breast cancer, yet the referral was for assistance with challenging behaviour. This lady was being seen regularly by her GP and the consultant psychiatrist, however, with the challenging behaviour as the focus for 'treatment' her primary health need was not identified. Had the health screening tool been part of the initial assessment process at that time, this condition may well have been detected much sooner and treatment could have been offered.

Through the health screening project and ongoing clinical practice in this area, it has been possible to provide a pro-active model of intervention to ensure increased health status of the individual. Learning disabilities nurses have been encouraged to develop their skills in the areas of health promotion and health surveillance, and build meaningful links with GP practices. One of the key aims being to educate the primary care team about the specific needs of people with learning disabilities, and raise awareness of the specialist services. It has then been possible to work collaboratively to ensure that there is equal access to services for all.

Conclusion

The White Paper *Valuing People: A New Strategy for Learning Disability for the 21st Century* (DoH, 2001) emphasises the importance of rights, independence, choice and inclusion. It must be recognised that this is a vulnerable group of people who require assistance and support to enter into the use of health services. To empower people with learning disabilities calls for specialist services to develop their role as educators and facilitators of primary health care. People with learning disabilities may have the same or additional health needs as others, but it is crucial that assistance is given in a way that values the individual by maximising choice, autonomy and decision making in the person (DoH, 1995). The development of the personal health record has given people with learning disabilities this assistance, and enables health professionals in whatever field of clinical practice to work in true partnership with them.

Through the development of a health promotion strategy, people with learning disabilities in South Staffordshire have been able to address their health needs more effectively; to access the health services available to everyone else and receive specialist services, if appropriate, to facilitate the process.

The project enabled learning disabilities nurses to develop their clinical governance agenda by maintaining and improving standards, developing services and involving service users in their care. It provided the opportunity for a development post in health promotion, which enabled an approach, whereby the meeting of health needs was seen as a long-term proactive process addressing health awareness and quality of life issues, as opposed to short-term outcomes.

The people who have gained most from the health screening project and subsequent strategy have been people with learning disabilities, their relatives and carers. As one person with learning disabilities points out, 'If you don't know what to ask for how can you get help?' (DoH, 1998). The service users receiving health screening, health surveillance and health promotion are now being given the opportunity to ensure that their health care needs are being met. The challenge is to ensure that this is the case for all people with learning disabilities, not only those who are referred to our services.

I would like to thank the following people who enabled this project to take place: Caron Thomas, Nurse Consultant in Learning Disabilities, South Staffordshire Healthcare NHS Trust; Christopher Dale, Community Nurse Manager, South Staffordshire Healthcare NHS Trust; David Elliott, Community Nurse, South Staffordshire Healthcare NHS Trust; Mark Jukes, Senior Lecturer in Learning Disability Nursing, UCE Birmingham; John McKenzie, formerly from Health Promotion Department, First Community Health Trust.

References

Bollard M (1997) Promoting the health care needs of people with learning disabilities. *Br J Community Health Nurs* **2**(1): 46–50

Barr O, Gilgunn J, Kane T, Moore G (1999) Health screening for people with learning disabilities by a community learning disability nursing service in Northern Ireland. *J Adv Nurs* **29**(6): 1482–91

Cassidy, G, Martin DM, Martin GHB, Roy A (2002) Health checks for people with learning disabilities — addressing needs through psychiatrists and nurses in community learning disability teams working together with general practitioners and primary health care teams. *J Learning Disabilities* **6**(2): 123–6

Cumella S, Corbett JA, Clarke D, Smith B (1992) Primary health care for people with a learning disability. *Ment Handicap* **20**: 123

Cumella S, Martin DM (2000) *Secondary care for people with learning disabilities*. Report completed for the Department of Health: June

Cole O (1986) Medical screening of adults at social education centres Whose responsibility? *Ment Handicap* **14**(6(): 54–6

Department of Health (1987) *Promoting Better Health*. HMSO, London

Department of Health (1989a) *Working for Patients*. HMSO, London

Department of Health (1989b) *Caring for People; Community care in the next decade and beyond*. HMSO, London

Department of Health (1990) *Community Care; Agenda for Action*. HMSO, London

Department of Health (1992) *Health of the Nation: A Strategy for Health in England*. HMSO, London

Department of Health (1995) *Health of the Nation: A Strategy for People with Learning Disabilities*. HSMO, London

Department of Health (1998) *Signposts for Success in Commissioning and Providing Health Services for People with Learning Disabilities*. NHS Executive, London

Department of Health (1999) *Once a Day*. NHS Executive, London

Department of Health (2001) *Valuing People: A New Strategy for Learning Disability for the 21st Century*. Department of Health, London

Howells G (1996) Are the medical needs of mentally handicapped adults being met? *J R Coll Gen Pract* **36**: 449–53

Lawrie K (1995) Better health care for people with learning disabilities. *Nurs Times* **91**(19): 32–4

Kay B (1994) People with learning difficulties. In: Tschudin V *Ethics, Nursing People with Special Needs, Part II*. Scutari Press, London

Kiger A (1995) *Teaching for Health*. 2nd edn. Churchill Livingstone, New York

Martin DM, Roy A, Wells MB (1997) Health gain through health checks: improving access to primary healthcare for people with intellectual disability. *J Intellectual Disabil Res* **41**(5): 401–8

Matthews DR (1996) *The 'OK' Health Check for assessing and planning the Health Care Needs of People with Learning Disabilities*. Fairfield Publications, Preston

Meehan S, Moore G, Barr O (1995) Specialist services for people with learning disabilities. *Nurs Times* **13**: 33–5

Minihan PM, Dean DH (1990) Meeting the needs for health services of persons with mental retardation living in the community. *Am J Public Health* **80**: 1043–8

Roy A (1992) *Health Assessment in Learning Disability*. British Institute of Mental Handicap Seminar Papers, Kidderminster

United Kingdom Central Council for Nursing, Midwifery and Health Visiting (1996) *Guidelines for Professional Practice*. UKCC, London

Webb O, Rogers L (1999) Health screening for people with intellectual disability: the New Zealand experience. *J Intellectual Disabil Res* **43**(6): 497–503

Whitfield M, Langan J, Russell O (1996) Assessing general practitioners' care of adult patients with learning disability: case controlled study. *Qual Health Care* **5**(1): 31–5ß

Wilson D, Haire A (1990) Health care screening for people with mental handicap living in the community. *Br Med J* 15 Dec: 1379–81

Worden WJ (1991) *Grief Counselling and Grief Therapy*. Routledge, London

5

Working with parents who have a learning disability and their children

Sandra Brickley

We went to see her in the hospital to say goodbye, they had been and took her.
I've always had an instinct to be a mum.
Help would have been better than criticism.

This chapter aims to give the reader an insight into working with parents who have a learning disability. It looks at research that has been carried out on the topic area, and how prevalence and attitudes have contributed to the experiences of parents with learning disabilities. The author will then look at research into parental competence and how legislation has affected the way in which services have been provided and are to be provided in the future. A case study has been chosen to give some insight into the effectiveness of learning disability services and how working with other professionals can lead to positive outcomes for parents and their children.

The components that led to the positive outcomes being achieved and the implications this has for services, parents, professionals and children are explored.

Theoretical overview

The opening quotes come from a piece of local qualitative research carried out by the author in 1998. This research was aimed at looking at the lived experiences of parents with learning disabilities. The participants gave accounts of their experiences that ranged from happy memories to traumatic events. These experiences are by no means unique to the parents in the author's research

Many researchers around the United Kingdom are carrying out research around parents with learning disabilities and, as a consequence, are developing their services in order to meet individual needs. This is a growing area of importance to professionals as the rates of referrals to services increase. Historically, research has tried to estimate the prevalence of parents with learning disabilities (Johnson and Wright, 1985; English, 2000). The research around parenting is not contained to the UK. In Germany, a nation-wide survey found that there were 969 people with intellectual disabilities who had parented 1366 children (Kettner, 1998). Prevalence research has been made difficult and its reliability questioned through differing definitions of learning disability and response rates.

There are many factors that may have contributed to the increase of referrals to services alongside the growing numbers of parents with learning disabilities. The Community Care Act (1990) contributed to the closure of long-stay hospitals, increasing opportunities for people with learning disabilities. Booth and Booth (1993) and McGaw (1998) attributed the increasing prevalence to these closures alongside changes in societal attitude and the concept of social role valorisation. The concept of social role valorisation was influential in the construction of the rights of people with learning disabilities to have sexual relationships, marriage and families (Wolfensberger, 1972, 1983). Hence, people with learning disabilities were given the 'same rights, responsibilities and opportunities as are available to others' (Perrin and Nirje, 1985). These rights are upheld today in The Human Rights Act (1998) and the Disability Discrimination Act (1996).

The rise in numbers of parents with learning disabilities led to research into the parental competence of those parents. This research focused on mainly negative aspects. Some areas of concern were highlighted as:

⌘ Abuse and neglect (Whitman and Accardo, 1990). This study found that 45% of children studied had been removed from their family due to neglect, sexual abuse, and unsafe living conditions.

⌘ Lack of maternal stimulation of the child (Feldman, 1986). Research found that mothers with a learning disability were less likely to play with their children and failed to praise them.

⌘ Significant harm (*Re M* (a minor) [Wardship] 1989, *Re H* (a minor) (Section 37 Direction [1993]). Court proceedings have removed children from their parents on the grounds of the 'likelihood' of harm at that time or in the future.

⌘ Social and economic factors (Booth and Booth, 1994; McGaw, 1993). When looking at parental experiences it was identified that many lived in poverty and poor conditions. In 1999 a parenting support group in Newcastle-upon-Tyne, found their participants were socially isolated and had difficulty attending mainstream parenting group (Wills, 1999).

In the 1990s, research looked more at positive outcomes being achieved by parents and the need to support parents and examine services (Cross and Marks, 1996; Maternity Alliance, 1997; Booth and Booth, 1993, 1994; Edmonds, 2000; Welsh, 1998).

The Children Act (1989) states that its general purpose is to safeguard and promote the child's welfare in their own families as far as possible. It saw prevention as an important part of all agencies practice. Part three of the Children Act (1989), relates to the support provided for families and children by local authorities. This support had two roles:

1. To provide family support to help parents to bring up their children (schedule 2, part 1, para 8, 9, 10).

2. To prevent court proceedings unless they were felt to be in the child's best interests (schedule 2, part 1, para 7).

This support could be crucial for parents with learning disabilities to keep their children in the family. Gibbons (1992), points out that this support has a role of 'buffing' the effects of stress on the family (*Messages from Research*, 1995: 3). This support reflects that children are in need of services (The Children Act 1989, section 17) and does not necessarily point to section 47 investigations under the act where children are at risk.

There had been an assumption that The Children Act (1989) would reflect the ethos of the National Health Service and Community Care Act (1990) services for adults. For example, there were many discrepancies and the two pieces of legislation led to confusion when looking at the recipients of community care facilities for parents with learning disabilities and the Children Act's (1989) provision for their children.

A *Jigsaw of Services* (DoH, 2000) was a social services inspection of services providing support to disabled adults who were parents. This research included parents with learning disabilities. Concerns were raised about interventions and decision making being made by staff untrained to work with the individual group. McGaw (2002) states that 'these findings fuel apprehension and anxiety for families and services that try to support them'. In context, this is that forty to sixty per cent of children of parents with a learning disability are removed from the family.

The White Paper, *Valuing People: A New Strategy for Learning Disability for the 21st Century* (2001), focuses on individual needs and has four key principles; choice, inclusion, rights, and independence. This paper emphasises the need for services to work jointly as regards parents with learning disabilities:

Social services departments have a duty to safeguard the welfare of children, and in some circumstances a parent with a learning disabilities will not be able to meet their child's needs ... this should not be the result of agencies not arranging for appropriate and timely support.

(DoH, 2001: 81)

This is supported in the *Framework for the Assessment of Children in Need and their Families* (DoH *et al*, 2000). Here, it is stated that people with learning disabilities have the same rights, expectations and choices as non-disabled people. Also, that they could benefit from support to enable them to care for their children.

Legislation and attitudes are changing to address and meet the needs of parents with learning disabilities. In order to utilise the information, services need to be trained and skilled in working with parents with learning disabilities and their children.

Case study

Personal information has been changed in order to respect the privacy and confidentiality of those involved.

This case study was before the *Framework for the Assessment of Children in Need and Their Families* (DoH, 2000). It has been chosen as it demonstrated the need to assess all parents on individual need and work in partnership with all agencies and the parent. It also highlights that past parenting failure does not necessarily reflect future parenting.

The community nursing team had received a referral for a mother with learning disabilities who was six months into her fifth pregnancy. The referral asked our service to contribute to a parenting assessment and to provide interventions as appropriate. There had been considerable concerns over the unborn child and it was felt that there might be a need to place the unborn child's name on the Child Protection register.

Previous to this, the mother had had two children removed from her care as a result of physical abuse and neglect. At present in the family there was a daughter aged seven years who attended a local mainstream school and there was also a four-year-old daughter who had a diagnosis of autism and challenging behaviour. The mother and her partner had a relationship that led to domestic violence upon her and the children. There was also a member of the paternal family who had a conviction for sexual offences to children.

The situation at the time was that the father had died tragically and the mother was now alone to care for her two children and the unborn child. She had no appropriate social networks and had moved to our area recently.

Assessment

There were many concerns and a holistic assessment was required. The assessment needed to be thorough and provide baseline recordings to measure future progress. It was acknowledged that some parts of the assessment would take place following the child's birth. It was felt that despite the childcare history, many historical concerns had been removed following the death of her partner. A decision was made to remove the four-year-old to a foster placement. This was due to concerns that the child was injuring herself when exhibiting behavioural difficulties and that the mother was at this time unable to manage the situation. At this time there was no definite tool available for the author to assess parenting ability. Hence, the service utilised the Comprehensive Assessment Framework from social services alongside research developed by Feldman (2000) and resources adapted from child health professionals. The assessment aimed to:

1. Identify areas of parenting that already existed and were acceptable.
2. Identify areas of need and risk for the mother and children.
3. To highlight intervention strategies that could be employed to enhance skills and knowledge.
4. To gather information on the mother's feelings and wishes.

Prior to commencing, a core meeting was held where professionals identified roles and expectations were explored.

The assessment was conducted using a semi-structured interview to assess knowledge and direct observation of current parenting. Resources were not readily available for use with people with learning disabilities so adaptations were made from existing materials. The mother was also supported to attend childcare groups. However, this assessment could only assess knowledge regarding the parenting of a newborn child. The areas assessed were:

⌘ Physical care, eg. washing, dressing, meal preparation, shopping, budgeting.
⌘ Security, eg. warmth, protection, consistency in care, consistent environment, establishing routines.
⌘ Stimulation/play, eg. play, appropriate use of language and communication.
⌘ Emotional well being, eg. attachment, praise, positive interaction, physical contact, awareness of children's emotional needs.
⌘ Use of appropriate discipline and behaviour management, eg. acknowledging appropriate ways of managing behaviour, recognising stress levels.
⌘ Encouraging age appropriate independence.
⌘ Safety, eg. in the home, in community, personal safety, recognition of 'grooming' behaviour.

Questions were asked using open questions as opposed to closed questions, for example:

⌘ What would you do if your child swore at you?
⌘ Do you think it is important to talk to a baby?
⌘ Look at the picture of the park, what things can you see that might be dangerous to children?
⌘ You have left the bleach in the bathroom. Will this be safe? Where do you think it should be kept?
⌘ What would you do if one of your children started to choke?
⌘ At what age would you allow your children to make a hot drink?

Alongside the assessments of social services, community learning disability nursing and the health visitor, an assessment was commissioned from psychology. This was to determine the mother's ability to understand the processes, give consent, and identify her own emotional needs and anxieties and to help professionals pitch the intervention at the correct level. The mother spoke about missing her partner and, on occasion, became tearful and unable to accept her loss. Professionals acknowledged that she was grieving and bereavement support was given.

Planning

From those assessments, all professionals met and shared outcomes and identified the areas of need and set goals. These goals needed to be realistic and achievable. They also needed to be presented to the mother so that she could identify what she was being asked to achieve, in order to parent her children. However, the main focus of community learning disability nursing was upon the unborn child. Resources were identified and a plan was devised for visiting and teaching after the child was born (*Figure 5.1*). These resources needed to be very visual and devised from baseline observations. A record of contact notes were devised, this was to be kept with the mother so that all professionals and the mother were aware of progress.

At this point a case conference was convened under area child protection guidelines for the unborn child. The decision was made that at birth the child would be placed with foster carers and daily contact would be arranged. This contact provided quality time for mother, baby and the sibling. The quality of interaction between the baby and mother was crucial at an early stage to ensure positive attachment. It also meant that teaching and further observations could be carried out in various situations. The areas taught were in line with needs identified from the areas of assessment, for example, under the heading 'physical care' the mother continued to be taught bathing skills which were observed to ensure that she was able to demonstrate that earning had taken place. The support package was very specific and demonstrated working in partnership with the mother.

This is an example of the visits that would have taken place over a week. In addition, unplanned visits would occur by the social worker. These visits were gradually decreased when they were thought to be unnecessary. No names have been used but, in practice, first names were used. Pictures were not necessary for all aspects as the mother had a good reading ability. Photographs and drawings can be used if the parent is unable to read. These can also be put onto a clock face to enable the parent to associate the time with the activity.

Monday Date	9.00 am Health visitor, weight 11.00 am Community nurse, bathing and child care issues	4.00 pm Social worker, observe interaction and feeding
Tuesday Date	10.00 am Mums and toddlers group	3.00 pm Support worker, observe child care, interaction and feeding
Wednesday date	9.00 am Bathing and teaching on child development and interaction	3.00 pm Support worker Observe child care and feeding
Thursday Date	11.00 am Core group meeting at home	6.00 pm Evening visit, look at night routines for children
Friday Date	8.00 am Support worker Observe morning routines breakfast, school (for older child) and care of baby	4.00 pm Community nurse Observe feeding and inter- actions, look at plan for weekend activities for the family
Saturday Date	No service visits 10.30 am Swimming lesson (older child)	
Sunday Date	No service visits	

Figure 5.1: Planned visits

Intervention

Following the birth of a healthy baby boy, assessment was commenced and teaching carried out alongside this. It is important to acknowledge that when you commence any intervention you are always assessing progress to allow for changes to be made. Initially, there was a need to use visual aids to prompt skills, eg. sterilising bottles. However, there was a good correlation between the assessed knowledge of the mother and her skills. The objectives that had been set were being met and a core group meeting identified the need to move forward. A return home was planned on a gradual level so that stress levels and coping strategies could be observed. The needs of the baby were changing and the mother was coping with the increasing demands placed upon her. However during this time she identified that she could not manage to look after the seven-year-old daughter and her son if her four-year-old daughter was returned home. Arrangements were made for long-term foster placement for this child with regular contact.

During the intervention, generalisation and maintenance were taught by using a variety of settings and multiple examples. At parent groups the mother was able to start making relationships and developing support that was free of professionals.

Evaluation

The progress was reviewed at each core meeting and areas of need still existed. These areas did not put the children at significant risk of harm but it was felt that long-term support would be necessary by the local authority. Support from professionals was withdrawn gradually until the child's name was removed from the child protection register. Support was given in line with Section 17 of the Children Act 1989.

This depicts a parent who may have had her fifth child removed on the basis of historical information. However, professionals felt that circumstances had altered and that measures could be put in place to assess parental competence without putting the child at risk. As a result, the mother was able to look after her two children with minimal support. This support may have been costly to services initially but, in the long term, was less costly than placing a child in the care system. There would have also been implications for health as this loss would have been another emotional strain, possibly leading to mental health problems.

Relevance to other practice areas

Good practice within this case study reflected positive outcomes and enabled the family to remain together. The areas of good practice were; working together, partnership and participation with the mother, shared objectives and consistency in providing information and teaching to the mother.

The initial assessment was a significant factor in the successful outcome. Both psychological and cognitive assessment had been carried out alongside functional assessments. Assessment needs to look at historical factors that may have contributed to present thinking and functioning, eg. parental upbringing, vulnerability, socio-economic influences, etc. Holistic assessment also enables professionals to look at other factors influencing parenting capacity, eg. domestic violence, mental illness, drug and alcohol misuse. These may impair the parent child relationship and effect positive attachments. Parents with learning disabilities may be influenced by such factors and need to be supported by skilled professionals.

The lack of teaching resources for parents with learning disabilities does not have to be an obstacle. Parentcraft materials can be adapted. Working alongside other professionals, eg. occupational therapy and speech and language therapists, can be beneficial when devising materials specific for individual parents. Professionals need to be creative when working with parents.

Implications for parents, children and professionals

Parenting capacity and what constitutes 'good enough parenting' cannot, due to its vastness, be highlighted in a list. Jones (2001: 258) stated that, 'parenting capacities and behaviour are therefore complex, and subject to influences within the family and from outside'. The *Framework for the Assessment of Children in Need and Their Families* (DoH, 2000) can be applied to parents with learning disabilities as it is a systematic way of looking at children's developmental needs alongside parental capacity, the family, and environmental factors. Children can suffer unnecessarily when removed from their families (McConnell and Llewellyn, 2000). Booth and Booth (2000) stated that the support parents received had an impact on the experiences children had while growing up: competence was not solely attributed to the parents. Their research showed that there were more factors than parenting that affected child outcomes, eg. social exclusion and family support. While professionals analyse and assess the three aspects within the assessment framework they can look at these wider influences, while safeguarding the child.

When working with parents with learning disabilities we cannot lose sight that, 'the objective must always be to safeguard and promote the welfare of the child' (DoH, 2000). Despite the *Framework for the Assessment of Children in Need and Their Families* (DoH, 2000) considering the needs of parents with learning disabilities, if parental capacity is not sufficient to meet the needs of the child, then professionals need to highlight these concerns. However, parents should not be judged on stricter thresholds than non-disabled parents as suggested in research (Czukar, 1983; Booth, 2001).

There are implications for services to train staff in a number of skills, eg. childcare practices, legislation and models of working with people with learning disabilities. Booth (2001) found that it was to the disadvantage of parents when professionals lacked experience in working with people with learning disabilities, eg. child protection workers. Multi-agency training can help professionals work together and share knowledge and skills. Professionals need to be aware of each other's areas of expertise and use these skills. To enable parents, professionals cannot work in isolation. Services need to audit the local need and look to developing services that can provide a long-term commitment to parents with learning disabilities and their children. At present, many services cannot provide long-term support due to demands on the service. This raises the question: 'should a specialist parenting service be established on a national level'?

Legislation introduced by the Blair administration (eg. *Valuing People* [DoH, 2001]) is now including the needs of people and parents with learning disabilities, and local policies need to reflect this. There should be a national framework within learning disability services that looks at the whole concept of parenting with a learning disability and provides a pathway from referral to discharge.

Community learning disability teams have the skills to help meet the needs of parents and their children. Learning disability services need to raise awareness of our skills and effectiveness in working with other agencies to help maintain children in their families. Reactive working is not as effective as working proactively. This implies that education is needed at an earlier stage, eg. health education in schools. Learning disability services also have a role in working with parents whose children are removed from the family and in supporting parents through statutory proceedings and in enabling them to access advocacy services.

Conclusion

On reflection, the experience of working with this family informed my working practice immensely. Within my practice I have seen negative outcomes for some parents with learning disabilities. This has been for a variety of reasons, eg. inability to parent, or lack of coordination between services to support and teach. My experience with this parent demonstrated that effective outcomes are possible. This parent had experienced negativity in her life which had led to the removal of some children. This did not prevent her from working alongside professionals to ensure that the children remained in her care. The mother was subject to vigorous observations and intense teaching. She was able to take up all the challenges. This led me to believe that people with learning disabilities have the ability to change and achieve despite their social histories. In order to do this, incentives need to be present alongside support networks.

The role of being a parent is valued in society, but there are times when concerns raise questions about parenting capacity and child welfare. These concerns do not necessarily mean that children should be removed from the family; they may highlight that support is needed. If positive outcomes are to be achieved with families then services and professionals need to:

- work in partnership with parents and children
- ensure professionals have training and supervision
- be aware of the needs of parents with learning disabilities
- refer to learning disability services at an early stage of need so pro-active working can take place
- make assessments which should be holistic and pertinent to the individual
- take into account the needs of the child alongside parental skills, deficits and ability
- make interventions based on the information obtained in the assessment. They should be devised at levels the parent understands
- build generalisations into any intervention. By this, professionals can ensure that knowledge and skills are learnt in a variety of settings which can then be utilised by the parent
- evaluate and assess need continually throughout the intervention.

There are undoubtedly a number of parents who cannot meet the needs of their children and put them at risk. However, there are many parents with learning disabilities who with the appropriate support will be able to bring up their children in the family. Professionals need to ensure that they are in no doubt that they have provided this to the best of their ability before making decisions that lead to children being removed from the family.

References

Booth T, Booth W (1993) Power to parents. *Nurs Times* **89**(35): 61–3

Booth T, Booth W (1994) *Parenting under Pressure: Mothers and fathers with learning difficulties.* Open University Press, Buckingham

Booth T, Booth W (2000) Against the odds: Growing up with parents who have learning difficulties. *Mental Retardation* **38**(1): 1–14

Booth T (2001) Barriers to justice facing parents with learning difficulties. *Disability, Pregnancy and Parenthood International* **36**: 6–7

Cross G, Marks B (1996) Special families, special needs. *Nurs Times* **92**(13)

Czukar G (1983) Legal aspects of parenthood for mentally retarded persons. *Can J Community Mental Handicap* **2**: 57–69

Department of Health (1989) *The Children Act.* HMSO, London

Department of Health (1990) *The National Health Service and Community Care Act.* HMSO, London

Department of Health (1995) *Child Protection: Messages from research.* HMSO, London

Department of Health (1995) *Disability Discrimination Act* (1995). HMSO, London

Department of Health, Department for Education and Employment and Home Office (2000) *Framework for Assessment of Children in Need and their Families.* HMSO, London

Department of Health (2000) *A jigsaw of services, inspection of services to support disabled adults in their parenting role.* HMSO, London

Department of Health (2001) *Valuing People: A New Strategy for Learning Disability for the 21st Century.* HMSO, London

Edmonds J (2000) *On Being a Mother: A positive identity in the face of adversity.* British Institute of Learning Disabilities, Kidderminster

English S (2000) Parents in Partnership. *Learning Disability Practice* **3**(2): 14–18

Feldman MA (1986) Research of parenting by mentally retarded persons. *Psychiatr Clin North Am* **9**: 777–96

Feldman MA (2001) Parenting with Learning Disabilities. Spring seminar, 10 May 2001. Medical Institute, Stoke-on-Trent

Human Rights Act (1998) HMSO, London

Johnson D (1985) Parents with learning disabilities: A study of the reasons for the referral of parents with a learning disability and an estimation of their number in the Sunderland population. Unpublished report from the Department of Clinical Psychology, Sunderland

Jones D (2001) The assessment of parental capacity. In: Horwath J, ed. *The Child's World.* Kingsley, London

Kettner UP (1998) *Parents with Intellectual Disability in Germany: Results of a nation-wide study.* British Institute of Learning Disabilities Bulletin, Kidderminster

Maternity Alliance (1997) *Action on Disability and Maternity.* Maternity Alliance Publication, London

McConnell D, Llewellyn G (2000) Disability and discrimination in child protection proceedings. *Disabil Soc* **15**(6): 883–95

McGaw S (1993) Working with parents on parenting skills. In: Craft A (1993) *Parents with Learning Disabilities.* British Institute of Learning Disabilities, Kidderminster

McGaw S (1998) Services for parents with learning disabilities. *Tizard Learning Disability Review* **1**: 1

McGaw S (2002) *Rights for parents with learning disabilities*. British Institute of Learning Disabilities Bulletin, Kidderminster

Perrin B, Nirje B (1985) Setting the record straight a critique of some frequent misconceptions of the normalisation principle. *Austr N Z J Developmental Disabilities* **11**: 64–74

Re M (a minor) (Wardship) 1989. FLR; 443–452

Welsh K (1998) *The Development of a service for Parents with Learning Disabilities*. British Institute of Learning Disabilities, Kidderminster

Whitman B, Accardo PJ (1990) *When a Parent is Mentally Retarded*. Brookes, Baltimore

Wills C (1999) *Learning to be a parent*. Royal College of Speech and Language Therapists, London

Wolfensberger W (1972) *The principles of normalisation in human services*. National Institute of Mental Retardation, Toronto

Wolfensberger W (1983) Social role valorisation; a proposed new term for the term 'normalisation'. *Mental Retardation*, December: 234–9

6

Primary care groups and the learning disability nurse member

Sue Bickerton, Elaine Harris

The first part of this chapter aims to demonstrate through reflection the experience of a learning disability nurse in her role as board member to a primary care group (PCG).

The introduction will lay out the background to PCGs and the rationale behind their development. Using models of reflection the main text will account for the changes and challenges within the individual undertaking the role and emphasise the key points underpinning the modernisation programme. The chapter highlights the benefits to the learning disabled client group and services that evolved through this process.

The conclusion summarises the key points and makes recommendations to the learning disability nursing profession for their future within a primary care setting.

Introduction

The first of May 1997 brought about the end of the eighteen-year-long Conservative government. Labour was elected into government. Health care under the Conservative government had seen the introduction of GP fundholding. This had led to a divisive internal market system and inequity across the country. The new Labour government, in looking at healthcare provision wanted to keep what had previously worked: separation between planning of hospital care and its provision; the important role of primary care in the NHS; and decentralised responsibility for operational management. The new Government wanted to abolish the internal market and, by so doing, discard what had failed: fragmentation, unfairness, distortion, inefficiency, bureaucracy, instability and secrecy (DoH, 1997).

In order to achieve the above the Government introduced a white paper, *The New NHS — modern, dependable*.

In a foreword statement to the White Paper, Tony Blair, stated that:

> *Creating the new NHS was the greatest single act of modernisation ever achieved by a Labour government. It banished the fear of becoming ill that had for years blighted the lives of millions of people. But I know that one of the main reasons people elected a new Government on May 1st was their concern renewed that the NHS was failing them and their families.*

> (DoH, 1997)

With the White Paper, *The New NHS — modern, dependable* (DoH, 1997), a ten-year modernisation programme was launched. There are six key guiding principles to the White Paper, namely:

⌘ Renew the NHS as a genuinely **national** service
⌘ Make the delivery of healthcare against these new national standards a matter of **local** responsibility
⌘ Get the NHS to work in **partnership**
⌘ Improve **efficiency** so that every £in the NHS is spent to maximise the care for patients
⌘ Shift the focus on to the quality of care, and development of centres of **excellence** where quality becomes more of a guarantee for all patients to experience
⌘ Re-build **public confidence** in the NHS

The White Paper sets out three areas for action.

National standards and guidelines through:

❖ New evidence-based **National Service Frameworks** (NSFs) to help ensure consistent access to services and quality of care right across the country.
❖ A new **National Institute for Clinical Excellence** (NICE) to give a strong lead on clinical and cost effectiveness, drawing the new guidelines on the latest scientific evidence.

A local drive for quality through:

❖ **Teams of local GPs and community nurses** working together in new primary care groups to shape services for patients, concentrating on the things which really count.
❖ **Explicit quality standards in the long-term services agreement** that will replace the annual contracts between health authorities, primary care groups and NHS Trusts.
❖ A new system of **clinical governance** in NHS trusts and primary care to ensure that clinical standards are met and there are processes to ensure continuous improvements, backed by a new strategy duty for quality in NHS Trusts.

A new organisation to tackle shortcomings:

❖ A new **Commission for Health Improvement** (CHImp) will support and oversee the quality of clinical services locally, and will tackle shortcomings. It will be able to intervene by invitation or on the Secretary of State's direction, where a problem has not been gripped.

A retrospective look at the formation of primary care groups

One of the major developments from the White Paper is the development of primary care groups. The aim of primary care groups is to bring together GPs and community nurses in a given area that will take responsibility for commissioning services for their local community.

In doing so, it replaces GP fund holding, ending the internal market. Primary care groups will work closely with social services.

The development of primary care groups posed new challenges and opportunities to the nursing profession. This was the first time that nurses would have a direct involvement in shaping the delivery of health care. In particular, it provided an opportunity for learning disability nurses to be involved.

The Royal College of Nursing stated that it was essential for nurses to have a passion for health, community development and the knowledge of public health. In addition to this they would need knowledge and involvement in public health assessments (RCN, 1998).

The author, believing that the learning disability discipline was grounded in the above and having a strong commitment to influence the delivery of healthcare, applied for one of the nursing board appointments.

The process was nomination, election and selection. The author's confidence was knocked at the election stage on realising that votes could only be made for your own primary care group area. Being one member of a team of two learning disabilities community nurses the author was unsure of securing other votes.

Following a successful interview, the author clarified the election and learned that coming from a small discipline had highlighted a flaw in the process that had not previously been anticipated and therefore the votes were not taken into account.

Following appointments to all the board positions of the primary care group the board became operational in shadow form in October 1998. The board comprised: chief executive; chairman (GP); six general practitioners; two nurses (one learning disability, and one district nurse), social services representative (joint commissioning manager learning disability); lay person; health authority non-executive member. The board was reflective of the proposed structure, as shown below:

> **PCG board structure as per guidelines:**
> Four to seven GPs
> One to two nurses
> Social services representative
> Lay member
> Health authority representative
> Chief officer

Four differing levels of responsibility could be adopted by a PCG. The choice of which is dependent on the degree to which the PCG and the health authority feel that the PCG is able to take on responsibility.

Level 4

Established as freestanding bodies accountable to the health authority for commissioning care, and with added responsibility for the provision of community services.

Level 3

Established as freestanding bodies accountable to the health authority for commissioning care.

Level 2

Take a devolved responsibility for managing the budget for health care in their area, acting as part of the health authority.

Level 1

At a minimum, act in support of the health authority in commissioning care for its population, acting in an advisory capacity.

(PHD, Solutions for Primary Care, 1998)

The journey into the new world of primary care groups had begun.

The subtle way in which changes occurred for me were not immediately apparent as my term of office as a board member developed. It was only when colleagues brought to my attention that both my behaviour and language in my role as a board member, for them, had become incomprehensible, that I realised that changes had, indeed, begun to take place.

In an attempt to demonstrate some of the changes a SWOT analysis is provided to account for personal/professional reflection at the start of the journey.

Strengths	Weaknesses
● eight years community experience	● no prior experience working at a strategic level
● ability to work across different disciplines	● lack of confidence in abilities
● commitment to change	● clarity of what was expected
Opportunities	**Threats**
● being on the first 'wave' of board nurses (therefore starting at the same point as others)	● not knowing what I did not know!
● to provide a learning disability focus to primary care issues	● time element influencing the following: ⌘ impact on team ⌘ impact on clinical practice
● to enable other disciplines to gain a greater insight into learning disability nursing skills, increasing the LD profile	
● to make a contribution to the evolving world of primary care	

Role development

In considering the role development of specialist practitioners, Chatterjee (2002), acknowledged the framework of Hamric and Taylor as being one that best allows a description of the emerging role into specialist practitioner. Similarly, this model allows a clear demonstration to the developing role as nurse board member, as depicted in the *Table 6.1*.

Table 6.1: Descriptions of role development (Hamric and Taylor, 1989)			
V Baker (1989)	**M Kramer (1974)**	**D Cola (1977)**	**Characteristics**
Orientation	Honeymoon	Role identification	New board nurse, optimistic anxious, eager to prove self, make change, clarifying role to self and setting. To develop as a team
Frustration	Shock		Depression and frustration in the face of overwhelming problems; fast speed of change and expectation to deliver. The need to learn new skills
Implementation	Recovery	Role transition	Good communication skills, ability to work across different agencies and different levels. Consumer involvement. Awareness of self. Involvement in specific projects
Reassessment	Resolution	Role confirmation	Acceptance and rein-forcement in role definition. Sense of pride in achievement and acknowledgement of discipline. Insecurity and frustration role and non-inclusion of LD

The role of a board nurse

The job description of a primary care group board nursing member (Wychavon, 1999) summarises four key points:

⌘ To be a member of the primary care group board, sharing responsibility for the corporate governments of the primary care group and the delivery of primary care group commitments.

⌘ To bring an overall nursing and therapy perspective to board decisions and decision taking.

⌘ To ensure effective two-way communications between the board and the nursing and therapy professions within the primary care group.

⌘ To be in line with the board's communications strategy, to act as an ambassador for the board in external communications.

From this summary, it is evident that there are two key themes emerging: communication and leadership.

Communication

An essential part of the board nurse's role was to provide two-way communication from the nurses and therapists within the PCG area to the board and back again. For this to occur a nurse therapy forum was established. This group comprised of all disciplines within primary care and met regularly. The group was chaired by the nurse board members. Issues discussed within this group were reflective of developments around the board table. Holding this regular forum allowed for feedback to the board, based on comments made within the forum, allowing inclusion to its optimum ability of all primary care professionals. In addition, a newsletter was produced from the PCG, which was circulated on a monthly basis to all stakeholders.

The communication and management model (Open University Business School, 2000) cites Bill Quirke (1997) as showing the five key objectives of communication as:

- raising awareness
- achieving understanding
- gaining support
- generating involvement
- earning commitments.

The nurse therapy forum was the vehicle through which these objectives were met.

Communication *per se* was a challenge within this new world of primary care groups. As board members, a new language had to be learnt. For example: service and financial frameworks; joint investment plans; health improvement programmes and many more. Abbreviations were common and the three mentioned above were known as SAFFs, JIPs, HiMPs. This is the language of primary care groups which proved a challenge in ensuring that what was being spoken was being understood. The board meetings were held in public so consideration had to be given that not only board members understood but, most importantly, the general public understood (see points i–iii below).

It was essential to follow the communication process to ensure optimum benefit to all involved.

Any communication involves a transmission of the message by the sender and the receiving and understanding of it by the recipient. The process can fail at each of these stages — transmission, reception and understanding.

i. **Transmission** — is about how you shape and send the message. It may be necessary to consider different approaches for different people.
ii. **Reception** — the people who are supposed to receive the message have many choices about how they do this. The message needs to be in a form that is acceptable to the person who is to receive it.
iii. **Understanding** — the fact that the message has been received does not necessarily mean that it has been fully understood. The receiver may want to ask questions to ensure their understanding.

Many communication problems could be avoided or at least minimised by:

- recognising and responding to the needs of the other people concerned, whether they are the senders or the receivers of a message
- using appropriate language
- choosing an appropriate time

- taking time to communicate the message
- choosing an appropriate place
- checking for understanding
- asking for clarification
- encouraging or giving feedback (The Open University Business School, 2000).

Leadership

There is a difference between leadership and management. Leadership is of spirit, compounded of personality and vision; its practice is an art. Management is of the mind, a matter of accurate calculation; its practice is a science. Managers are necessary; leaders are essential.

(Field Marshal Lord Slim, when Governor General of Australia,
quoted by John Van Maurik,
Discovering the Leader in You, 1994)

The Government puts nurse leadership at the forefront of modernising healthcare. In July 1999 they published *Making a Difference: strengthening the nursing, midwifery and health visiting contribution to health and healthcare* (DoH, 1999). In addition to this, in 2000 the *NHS plan* states that, 'clinical leadership must be strong at all levels of nursing and midwifery because strong leadership leads to innovation'. It continues by saying, 'leadership is not about position or job title— it is a skill which is needed at every level of the NHS'.

In this paper they say, 'more nurses, midwives and health visitors need better leadership skills.'

At a conference in 2000, Jean Faugier, who was the national lead for the strengthening leadership chapter in *Making a Difference*, offered the following:

The concept of transformational leadership underpinned by 'emotional intelligence' as the nature of leadership required.

Transformational leadership was explained as requiring attention to the 'four I's':

- ❖ Idealised attributes: the leader can be counted on to do the right thing, demonstrate high levels of ethical and moral conduct, avoiding power for personal gain.
- ❖ Inspirational motivation: ability to motivate those around them by providing meaning.
- ❖ Intellectual stimulation: questioning assumptions and refraining problems.
- ❖ Individualised consideration: special attention to the individual's need for growth.

Jean explained emotional intelligence as referring to the kind of thinking characteristic of many nurses, which is informed by the experience of working closely with patients and clients. It implies an understanding of an individual's care and life trajectories; essential if services and interventions are to provide real added quality to people's lives (Conference summary *Making a Difference in Primary Care*, 2000).

In 2000, Mansell carried out a small study, which looked at the relevance and prevalence of leadership in the new NHS. The study indicated that leadership does exist within PCGs, however, like the wider NHS, these new organisations are thought to be dominated by management. While acknowledging that this was a small study it did appear to reinforce Kotter's (1990) suggestion that most organisations are over managed and under led (Mansell, 2000)

As the nurse board members, the author and colleague were acting as nurse leaders. The author was most unfamiliar with this role and it took time to develop and to have confidence in it. Ensuring the dissemination of nursing strategies and Government guidelines was part of this role. Local interpretation of such guidelines would then occur using the nurse therapy forum and any conclusion or feedback would be taken back to the board.

Conclusion

On reflection of the author's experience as a PCG board nurse, the SWOT analysis (*page 71*) is proposed as a summary of the overall experience. In 'grey' is the early SWOT and in 'black' the latter one.

This analysis not only summarises the author's experiences as a nurse board member but, also, highlights some thoughts for the future for learning disability nursing within a primary care setting. In comparing the initial SWOT (in grey) to the latter (in black), it is evident that movement has taken place. Some early weaknesses ended as strengths; equally, the early opportunities, 'providing a learning disability focus and developing awareness of LD to others' ended as a strength.

It would not be possible to conclude this chapter without comment on a personal level as to how the author perceived this journey.

From the start I was filled with a mixture of emotions. These were; excitement, pride, disbelief and a sense of panic and fear. Following time away getting to know colleagues, these fears started to subside when I began to develop confidence in my own abilities. In April 1999 we became 'live' as a PCG and operational. At this time the reality hit home. The sheer volume of work seemed immense and unmanageable, particularly at a time when this new language had to be learnt. (Memories of the book 1984 and the concept of 'newspeak' suddenly seemed a reality!)

When specific jobs were allocated to individual board members, based on experience and interest, I was allocated to the accident prevention framework of the health improvement programme (HImP). This group was led by the health promotion manager and it was a role with which I was comfortable as it meant working as part of a multi-agency team in formulating a strategy to reduce accidents within our area. My nursing colleagues' role was working with a team developing an intermediate care strategy, which allowed for early discharge from the acute hospital along with prevention of admission. Equally, with a district nursing background, this was a role with which she was comfortable. The two of us recognised how our individual skills complemented each other's, and how well we worked together in our roles on the board. I also was the nurse member of the complex case team, which met monthly to consider high cost treatments and those not covered within contract. This role I continue to do.

During the time spent on the board I frequently felt proud of what I had achieved in highlighting the profile of learning disabilities. This was sometimes in a subtle way, but it was good to realise that my presence had allowed for inclusion of our sometimes disadvantaged client group.

The time serving as a board member was a huge learning curve but an enjoyable one. That is not to say that there were times when there was friction but dealing with conflict was very much a part of the position.

The excellent skills of both the chairman and the chief executive played a major part in the overall experience as board nurse, being both enjoyable and educational. Both of these people nurtured and developed the board members and enabled us to all work as part of a team. There was never a time when I considered myself to be or was made to feel any less equal to the others. I am sorry that my time has ended due to the development of primary care trusts. I have, however, maintained links with the PCT that should allow for some inclusion of our client group to remain.

On the termination of the three-year experience, the author had requested specific feedback from the chief executive on any skills that she had considered were brought to the board table by the learning disability nurse. The reply was skills of negotiation and acting as a communicator and the supplying of a holistic perspective to health. Other learning disability nurses can learn from the experience shared within this chapter, and have confidence in their own skills and what they can contribute to the future of health care for our client group.

Primary care groups and the learning disability nurse member

The second part of this chapter provides a commentary on the role of the nurse board member linked in with how learning disability practitioners can develop a broad health promotion role within primary care.

Relationship with generic services

Chambers (1998) confirmed what has been known within the field of learning disabilities for many years: that learning disability nurses assess, intervene more holistically than other nursing disciplines and are in a stronger position to identify the barriers to service users accessing primary care. Many of these barriers were outlined in a study carried out by Rimmer and Whitfield (1996), which highlighted poor understanding of the needs of this client group in terms of actual health issues and also accessibility of primary care as a core feature of poor uptake of health care. Only with universal recognition of these barriers can services become fully inclusive and enhance service delivery. The findings identified poor communication between primary care and specialist services as a reoccurring core feature, concluding that while examples of good practice do exist, access to primary care can be patchy and joint working does not always happen.

Strengths	Weaknesses
• eight years community experience	• no prior experience working at a strategic level
• ability to work across different disciplines	• lack of confidence in abilities
• commitment to change	• clarity of what was expected
• an understanding of White papers	
• level of skills learned	• as a PCG nurse time factor in juggling board priorities/clinical priorities
• experience working at a strategic level	
• comprehension of primary care language	• possible loss of communication across primary care clinical areas/learning disability clinical areas now at board level
• learning disability had dominant focus	
• developing awareness of peers on PCG board of learning disability issues/skills	

Opportunities	Threats
• being on the first 'wave' of board nurses (therefore starting at the same point as others)	• not knowing what I did not know!
	• time element influencing the following:
	⌘ impact on team
• to provide a learning disability focus to primary care issues	⌘ impact on clinical practice
• to enable other disciplines to gain a greater insight into learning disability nursing skills, increasing the LD profile	
• to make a contribution to the evolving world of primary care	
• to maintain and continue to develop links with primary care trust	• loss of vision towards learning disabilities from PCT level
• to advocate learning disability issues within PCT	• segregation of services
• implementation of Government-led strategies, for example, *Valuing People*	• professional isolation from primary care colleagues
• the development of leadership skills	

The opportunity to have a learning disability nurse as a board nurse in the Redditch Primary Care Group was a way of addressing some of the above; providing an avenue for communication between the purchaser and the provider. It is understood that the representation of this specific client group was not the primary function of the role, however, it at last created an avenue for effective communication. Recent Government policy (DoH, 1995, 1997, 1998, 1999, 2001) has introduced a health promotion programme for adults with learning disabilities, the intention primarily to be planned and implemented by community learning disability nurses (CLDNs). It is useful, to consider briefly the CLDN in the wider context of primary healthcare. In retrospect, the *Health of the Nation* (1995) provided a strategy to meet the needs of learning disabled people, urging commissioners to address the particular needs of those with a learning disability within the policies priority areas. The Government reflected this commitment in the *New NHS —modern, dependable* (1997), which stresses the need to modernise current service delivery, promoting effective, equitable and efficient utilisation of resources. Equitable inclusion of people with learning disabilities into a primary healthcare framework presents a challenge for service providers (Kerr *et al*, 1996). While it is widely acknowledged that those with a learning disability should gain the same access to generic services as everyone else, there are still inequalities in access for the learning disabled population (Kerr, 1998; Bollard, 1999). Individuals are not being included in current health improvement initiatives offered to the general public, for example, routine health screening ('Well men's clinics'). While acknowledging how marginalised learning-disabled people can be from mainstream services, any practitioner progress in overcoming this exclusion, is based on pockets of good practice by a few professionals' innovative work

Learning disability nurses have long acknowledged their skill base overlaps with other multidisciplinary team members, and maximised this potential in developing more effective networking. However, they must continue to exalt their specialist input, vital for proactive advantages for clients (Turnbull, 1993; DoH, 1993). This should include, as a key component of the role; giving advice, guidance and teaching others, and creating a partnership to achieve the agreed objectives. These factors supported the view that a community learning disability nurse was not only well placed but also suitably skilled to take on such a role as a board nurse.

Creating a change

The appointment of a learning disability nurse onto the primary care group panel created a real opportunity for developing open communication into the culture. By utilising good professional practice, evidence-based practice and a wealth of experience to consider issues of service delivery for atypical scenarios, created the ability to champion the cause of not just the learning disabled population but also other marginalised groups affected by similar issues. To be effective in this role it was necessary to consider the barriers to change, in particular, create a shift in knowledge and attitude toward those in society whose healthcare needs may require some specialist attention or thought prior to delivery. In this instance, as a board nurse, the author became the main change agent. The function is summed up by Broome (1998) as:

Someone who identifies major problem areas, identifies the opportunity for change, builds readiness and commitment, builds reviewing systems through creating a climate, and establishes internal capacity to sustain the change effort, evaluate and review it.

Sue, as the change agent, has been able to operate from an 'inside position' (Haffer, 1986) and become very much part of the system under alteration. Ottaway (1976) described the importance of the inclusion of all team members, and while maintaining professional status the change agent is able to motivate others. In fact, it becomes imperative to the success of implementation if there is to be significant long-term change.

Specialist health practitioners for people with learning disabilities endeavour to ensure that health promotion activities are, 'accessible to people with learning disabilities and geared to their needs' (DoH, 1997). *Valuing People* (DoH, 2001) highlights this priority area by stipulating that the role of the healthcare worker is imperative in the improvement of standards 'by encouraging an evidence-based approach to service provision and practice'. It is essential that community learning disability nurses be at the forefront in developing health promotion initiatives, by ensuring that the needs of this client group are met. Community learning disability nurses are growing in confidence in identifying and defining their scope of professional practice, particularly in the area of health (Dale and Elliot, 1999; Bollard, 1999; Bickerton and Thomas, 1999). Specialist learning disability nurses are well placed to become health promoters and, consequently, to help facilitate equal access to healthcare as a core function.

How primary care board nurses impacted on the community nursing team

The position of board nurse was initially perceived as a commitment of one day per week. Interestingly, funding was made available to back fill this absence from first contract with four and a half hours on a lower grade. While this led to the development for a post for a trained nurse to enter into the world of community nursing, in real terms it no where near met the shortfall of the amount of absences required by the primary care group (PCG). No appreciation of fundamental issues, such as the travelling time to meeting venues or the amount of background research and reading to consider accurately board business, appears to be considered to replace accurately the hours lost to the PCG. The effect on the community learning disability nursing team in Redditch was, for the first time ever, a waiting list. While a period of reflection to reconsider current working practices, access criterias for both taking on new work and closing current cases was undertaken, little impact could be made on the waiting list due to the decision to re-grade the back fill post (meaning initial assessments could not be done by this staff member) and the restriction of working four and a half hours per week. This situation was compounded during the second year when it became apparent that the PCG role actually required a commitment of two working days per week.

Benefits for the team

For Sue Bickerton, the board nurse representative, being projected within the team as the perceived 'expert' regarding the client group, when periodically feeling like the 'novice' in terms of the newness of the role, induced a vast and rapid learning curve. Steinaker and Bell's (1979) 'Experiential Taxonomy' gives rise to the opportunity to examine the learning that has taken place, for both individuals and the team as a whole, and developed understanding in many areas pertinent to the learning disabled population in the Redditch area. This model, widely adopted within nurse education, offers a good progressive model for the 'learner' to develop from novice to expert (Benner, 1988), giving a framework in which to measure knowledge learnt. It is important to recognise that the term 'learner' in this instance can be applied to the individual team members and also to the PCG as a whole

Working within this partnership ensured that clients'/patients' health and educational needs are shared effectively with other relevant healthcare workers, enhancing inter-professional relationships. An important consideration of the true skill of leadership is to have good interpersonal skills with others. These skills include genuineness, empathy and unconditional positive regard (Rogers, 1967). These skills are the 'bedrock' of all effective human relationships. This primarily will assist the change agent to be more connected to identify early signs of conflict to change

This level of effective leadership within learning disabilities is still rare, but very necessary for services to move forward in terms of inclusive services for the learning disabled population. Greig (1999) observed that often teams, as in this instance, could become synonymous purely with meetings. To avoid this scenario, working collaboratively with all members to improve relationships and support and encourage widespread innovative practice, should ensure that in the future this broader perspective is taken forward and becomes engendered into the culture. Teasdale (1992) purports the necessity for:

> ... *groups to be an equitable democratic group to truly maximize the potential of a group, which could be an issue as, generally, learning disability nurses have frequently been made to feel like the poor relations, working within a 'Cinderella' service.*

A key example of the most notable benefit from this improved visibility and understanding of the community learning disability nursing team and the learning disabled population was the invitation to apply for funding from the Regional Cervical Screening Quality Assurance Project Fund. The regional quality assurance co-ordinator had been made aware of the concerns raised by Sue regarding learning-disabled women's lack of participation in screening programmes. This gave rise to a project specifically aimed at women with learning disabilities in Redditch; targeting one of the national health improvement issues, namely, cervical screening.

A bid was submitted and accepted and a small amount of money was given to consider why the uptake for learning disabled women into the cervical screening programme has been so poor. This was an ideal opportunity to work closely with primary care members highlighting the areas of concern and jointly formulating a way forward within a broad health promotion framework. A steering group was established with representatives from the primary care board and primary care team, specialist learning disability nurses and quality advice. This led the way into more effective exchange regarding issues pertinent to the learning-disabled population's health.

Benefits for client group

The overall aim of the project is to devise and deliver a programme of education on women's health issues, namely cervical screening and breast awareness. This assisted women in making an informed choice when invited for screening. The project provided the necessary information around what is healthy? What is screening? Why it is important? And, what can happen post screening. It also incorporated information around risk factors and signs and symptoms of any potential problems.

This process empowered primary care team members to examine their professional knowledge regarding this group of women's health and accept the many barriers and limitations for women to achieve cervical screening. It highlighted the fact that most learning-disabled women locally had been omitted from the cervical screening programme; some purely as a direct result of their label 'learning-disability'. It became apparent that these women were stereotyped and thought not to be at risk from cervical cancer as it had been assumed that they were not sexually active. The long-standing issue of gaining informed consent from women that may have issues of impaired communication or understanding, leading to incidents of non-compliance or the lack of verbalisation, had been enough to exclude them from cervical screening. And, lastly, being able to offer appropriate time and support for these women to be able to make an informed choice regarding the procedure itself had not previously been given much thought by the smear takers, generally practice nurses.

The audit undertaken throughout the project shows conclusively the positive shift in knowledge around this subject with the learning-disabled women who received further information in an appropriate format around cervical screening. This has had a resolute effect on these women's confidence in feeling ready to attend screening. Unfortunately, the audit tool was not designed to gather the same information from primary care nurses, but this shift in knowledge has arguably had the most positive effect on this small sample group. The smear takers, now have resources available to explain the procedure more fully, have a better understanding of the client group but, most importantly, to consider issues of risk to each woman individually. As a direct result, the majority of the women in Redditch have been returned to the cervical screening programme.

There is a much better understanding of where our respective role can complement one another's to the benefit of clients, when pieces of work can be designed to combine skills, joint work and at what point to collaborate. The impact of this greater understanding has gone far wider than specifically cervical cytology but spread to all areas of health need.

Role development

Out of this an opportunity has arisen to become an integral part of the teaching team: to educate smear takers and dispel some of the myths that surround this client group, in particular, regarding lifestyles, risk and consent issues. Candidates for the smear takers course now have an awareness of not only the real issues which may inhibit women with learning disabilities to attend and participate in the screening process, but of how specialist services currently offer assistance and practical support to individuals.

Invitations to attend and present at practice meetings highlighting the needs of learning disabled clients, and the role of the community learning disability nurse have been extended successfully to a number of surgeries.

This project work has raised the profile on how successful a consultancy role is when liaising with primary care. It is paramount that people with learning disabilities are not disenfranchised in their right to use primary care. The emphasis must still be for specialist services to advocate for their inclusion to primary care. The consultancy role can have many positive facets to optimising this position, from advice regarding developing appropriate material and communicational tools to continuing to raise the awareness, by remaining clinically informed of current health issues that may be pertinent to this client group.

There is a real need to work effectively among agencies within the learning disability multidisciplinary team to develop and pilot resources that are user friendly. An example is to collaborate with specialist speech and language services.

Working in partnership with other agencies may require the specialist nurse to become primarily the co-ordinator and facilitator of joint initiatives with clients.

The future

Valuing People: The New Strategy for Learning Disability for the 21st Century (2001), can be viewed as an accumulation of all the recommendations for people with learning disabilities of the last thirty years; in fact, since the White Paper, *Better Services for the Mentally Handicapped* (1971). It offers a vehicle to steer change for the service users by underpinning four key principles: legal and civil rights; independence; choice; and inclusion. The strategy has highlighted the newly titled role of the 'Health facilitator' to assist with the development of individualised health improvement plans, and help clients with learning disabilities to navigate the mainstream health system successfully.

Valuing People focuses on promoting holistic services for people with learning disabilities through effective partnership working between all relevant local agencies in the commissioning and delivery of services, sighting effective partnerships are the very key to inclusion. It will be the role of partnership boards to review community learning disability teams' working practices, ensuring that professional staff become more accountable and create structures that actively encourage inclusive working.

Summary

Since the devolution of primary care boards and the advent of primary care trusts, the link of the board nurse has ceased. The main concern is that, in time, all progress reported in this chapter will be lost

The benefits of having a community learning disability nurse as a primary care board nurse have been numerous, directly affecting the health needs of individuals and also promoting specialist community services. This has been demonstrated effectively in a specific project for learning disabled women in Redditch within the health need area of cervical screening. Given the barriers for people with learning disabilities and other minority groups to access primary care, these health gains appear to be as a result of this link within the primary care group. The advent of *Valuing People* (2001) promotes the continuation of this kind of work. Unfortunately, a specialist role has not as yet been advocated within the structure of the primary care trust. The concern is that the excellent links forged throughout the three-year term of the primary care group board member may be lost if the alliances made are not built upon.

References

Benner P (1988) *Novice to Expert: Excellence and power in clinical nursing practice*. 3rd edn. Addison-Wesley, Menlo Park

Bickerton S, Thomas R (1999) The challenge of change. *Learning Disability Practice* **2**(2): 24–5

Bollard M (1999) Promoting the healthcare needs of people with learning disabilities. *Br J Community Nurs* **2**: 46–51

Broome A (1998) *Managing Change*. 2nd edn. Macmillan Press Ltd, London

Chambers S (1998) Nursing diagnosis in learning disabilities. *Br J Learning Disabilities* **7**: 19

Chatterjee A (2002) *Reflexive Account of Professional Development*. Unpublished

Conference Summary (2000) *Making a Difference in Primary Care*. Brocklehurst N, Unpublished PhD, University of Birmingham

Dale C, Elliot D (1999) The health wheel: a tool for assessing carer's health needs. *Nurs Times* **95**(11): 52–3

Department of Health (1971) *Better Services for the Mentally Handicapped: Government white paper*. HMSO, London

Department of Health (1993) *Opportunities for Change*. HMSO, London

Department of Health (1995) *The Health of the nation: A strategy for people with learning disabilities*. HMSO, London

Department of Health (1997) *The New NHS — modern, dependable*. HMSO, London

Department of Health (1998) *Signposts for Success: Good practice document*. HMSO, London

Department of Health (1999) *Once a Day*. NHSE, London

Department of Health (1999) *Making a Difference*. HMSO, London

Department of Health (2000) *The NHS Plan*. DoH, London

Department of Health (2001) *Essence of Care*. HMSO, London

Department of Health (2001) *Valuing People: A New Strategy for Learning Disabilities for the 21st Century*. HMSO, London

Gregg R (1999) *Beyond the Community Learning Disability Team*. Community Care Development Centre, King's College, London

Haffer A (1986) Facilitating change. *J Nurs Administration* **16**(4): 18–22

Hamric AB, Taylor JW (1989) Role development of the CNS. In: Hamric AB, Spross JA, eds. *The Clinical Nurse Specialist in Theory and Practice*. 2nd edn. WB Saunders, Philadelphia: 41–82

Kerr M, Frazer W, Felce D (1996) Primary healthcare for people with learning disabilities: a keynote review. *Br J Learning Disabilities* **24**: 2–8

Kerr M (1998) Primary healthcare gains for people with learning disabilities. *Tizard Learning Disability Review* **3**(4)

Kotter JP (1990) *A Force for Change: How leadership differs from management*. The Free Press, New York

Mansell J (2000) *Too Much Management and Not Enough Leadership*. Unpublished

Maurick JV (1994) *Discovering the Leader in You*. London, McGraw-Hill

Open University Business School (2000) *Managing in Health and Social Care*. Open University Business School, Milton Keynes

Ottaway R (1976) A change strategy to implement new norms, new styles and a new environment in the work organisation. *Personal Reviews* **5**(winter): 1

Rimmer JW, Whitfield M (1996) *Can PHGS and CLDTs collaborate and provide preventative health care for patients with learning disabilities?* Bristol Medical Advisory Group, Bristol

Rogers CR (1967) *Freedom to Learn*. Merrill, Columbus, Ohio

Royal College of Nursing (1998) *Primary Care Groups*. An internal paper, Lynn Young and Sue Antrobus. Royal College of Nursing, London: March

Simple Guide to PCGs (1998) *Solutions for Primary Care*. PhD

Steinaker N, Bell M (1976) *The Experiential Taxonomy: A new approach to teaching and learning*. Academic Press, New York

Teasdale K (1992) *Managing the Change of Healthcare*. Wolfe Publishing, London
Turnbull J (1993) Dead End Street. *Nurs Times* **89**: 26
Wychavon PCG (1999) Board Nurse Job Description

Websites

A First Class Service; Quality In The New NHS (1998) www.doh.gov.uk/newnhs/quality.htm
Making a Difference (1999) www.doh.gov/nurstrat.htm
Mental Health National Service Framework www.doh.gov.ik/nsf/mentalhealth.htm
NHS Plan (2000) www.nhs.uk/nationalplan
Our Healthier Nation (1998) www.doh.gov.uk/ohn.htm
Redditch and Bromsgrove PCT *www.randb-pct.nhs.uk*
Valuing People (2001) www.doh.gov.uk/vpst
Your Guide to the NHS www.nhs.uk/nhsguide

7

Developing a model for primary care in learning disabilities

Martin Bollard, Mark Jukes

The arguments for the development of an effective model of primary care will be based upon previous work by the authors (Bollard and Jukes, 1999). The rationale for pursuing such a model is driven by the necessity to overcome the social exclusion that people with learning disabilities experience.

Achieving equitable access to health and social care for all vulnerable groups has been a driving ambition for the present administration, a goal that has been pursued through most of its health policy (DoH, 1998, 1999). Despite this aim, the rationing of health care to disabled people is one of the most persistent and perplexing problems facing contemporary societies, regardless of their geographical location, political orientation, cultural values, or level of economic development (Albrecht, 2001). In England, this Government's drive for central control and the development of more infra-structures at a local level, is considered to stifle the practice of the community agents that could assist the Government in realising the aspiration of social inclusion. Documents such as *Realising the Potential* (Welsh Assembly Government, 2002) and *Promoting Health — Supporting Inclusion* (Scottish Executive, 2002) place more emphasis upon the potential of the role of the learning disability nurse to improve the health of people with learning disabilities and, as such, present a more strategic review of the learning disability nurse in comparison with *Valuing People* (DoH, 2001).

Social exclusion

Since community care was seriously gaining momentum in the 1980s, people with learning disabilities have had difficulty in accessing mainstream generic services.

Recent research has identified that health, social services, education and housing have failed to work together resulting in uncoordinated services and a postcode lottery exists in terms of access to services (DoH, 1999).

Children's rights to good health care and education are also being contravened and explicit exclusion of children with a disability from mainstream childcare, play and leisure services has also occurred.

Parents have had to search relentlessly and seek out available, but segregated services, which are also inappropriate, an example being hospice services (Rowntree, 1999).

Valuing People (DoH, 2001), in its ambitious agenda is attempting to tackle social exclusion in its targets for both children and adults with a learning disability. However, as reported by the Social Exclusion Unit (2002), 'One of the things which has marked this country out in comparison with the rest of Europe is its high level of social exclusion'.

There are many definitions of what constitutes social exclusion and the following offers a comprehensive definition from the European Commission:

Social exclusion refers to the multiple and changing factors resulting in people being excluded from the normal exchanges, practices and rights of modern society. Poverty is one of the most obvious factors, but social exclusion also refers to inadequate rights in housing, education, health and access to services. It affects individuals and groups, particularly in urban and rural areas, who are in some way subject to discrimination or segregation; and it emphasises the weakness in the social infrastructure and the risk of allowing a two-tier society to become established by default. The Commission believes that a fatalistic acceptance of social exclusion must be rejected and that all community citizens have a right to the respect of human dignity.

(Commission of the European Communities, 1993: 1)

This way in which exclusion is defined implies that structures, boundaries and the power and weight of Government policies, institutions and organisations are the causative and accepted factors through which exclusion operates.

This is partly the case, but people within society are also supportive of these boundaries and policies, and are members of the same political parties, institutions and organisations.

People are responsible for discriminatory and oppressive practices and represent a value which negatively perceive individuals and populations on the margins of society.

Exclusion is also exercised in the form of behaviour against people, by people who are exclusivist by nature.

Pierpoint (2002) cites an example of a senior Government official's response when asked, 'What should we do about those who aren't in the mainstream?' his reply (apparently partly in jest, partly in frustration), 'We train the best and shoot the rest'.

As practitioners we need to be aware and prepared to challenge both public and professionals' exclusivist attitudes and demonstration of exclusion.

Since the mid-1990s, clear examples of discrimination and exclusion have been cited particularly relating to GPs striking off their lists people with disabilities (Brindle, 1994; Singh, 1997).

Prior to setting up the Social Exclusion Unit in 1997 by the UK Government, both Oliver (1990) and Young (1990) have offered respective frameworks relative to consequences and oppression due to being disabled as they have impacted upon their lived experiences within the community *(Box 7.1)*.

Box 7.1: Consequences of disability and experiences of oppression

• Denial of social and human rights	• Exploitation
• Rejection of the disabled person's view with the imposition of medical definitions of needs	• Marginalisation
• Client's experience and perception of poverty	• Cultural imperialism (PWLDs are viewed negatively against dominant social norms)
• Dependency	• Violence (people with learning disability)
• Powerlessness	do experience violence and abuse
Source: Oliver, 1990	Source: Young, 1990

Percy-Smith (2002) offers an analytical framework which takes account of key dimensions and indicators as they relate to the analysis and impact of social exclusion. These indicators have been extracted from the originally cited indicators to emphasise the focus on the lives of people with a learning disability as they live in the community *(Box 7.2)*.

Box 7.2: Dimensions of social exclusion (as they impact on PWLDs)

Dimension	Indicators
Economic	Income, poverty, long-term unemployment, difficulty finding or sustaining employment or meaningful occupation. Decreased opportunities for earning capacity
Social	Limited social interaction or engagements. Subject to influence in committing crime, drug/substance abuse
Political	Disempowerment, low levels of community activity and engagement
Neighbourhood	Collapse of support networks. Environmental degradation. Conditions of housing
Individual	Mental and physical health. Loss of self-esteem/confidence. Educational underachievement or support in transition
Spatial	Concentration and marginalisation — where people live
Group	Concentration of above characteristics, in particular, the elderly, disabled and ethnic minorities

These indicators identified in *Box 7.2* form a 'snapshot' basis into examining which groups or individuals are at risk from social exclusion. These become necessary to establish baselines against which progress towards inclusion can be effectively measured. In this case, and for the purposes of this chapter, the 'individual' dimension identified in *Box 7.2* will become the focus in attempts to improve the physical and mental health access in the form of effective health facilitation. A role which, from a strategic perspective, requires positive action from practitioners who are prepared to tackle exclusivists and social exclusion for the optimum participation and inclusion of people with a learning disability into mainstream services.

Overview of practice development in primary care

To date, developments in learning disability within primary health care have been introduced and carried out by a growing number of practitioners.

Elements of work may not initially be perceived as primary care work, but considered to encompass the broad work that can be associated with such terms as health facilitation.

Andrew Beck, a project facilitator working within a large, busy primary health care Team (PHCT) in Tipton, West Midlands, conducted over 120 health checks with practice nurses. He operated clearly within the organisational level, identifying comprehensive practice registers and meeting highlighted need by linking in with specialist services.

Susan Brady, a project nurse, worked with a number of PHCTs in socially deprived areas of Birmingham. She conducted health checks and educational initiatives. Her work can be conceptualised at an organisational and strategic level.

Sue Denny's work in Barnet, London, was more concerned with developing vital information to educate PHCTs and acute hospitals. Operating at a strategic level, she was also able to ensure that the health needs of people with learning disabilities were identified on health improvement programmes, joint investment plans and other relevant documentation.

Judith Thorley's work in North Staffordshire General, culminated in developing health protocols for the medical and surgical directorates, in addition to offering training and developing educational materials for the hospital staff. She clearly operated at an organisational and strategic level.

Martin Bollard's work involved conducting health checks across fourteen PHCTs in Coventry, educating practice nurses and GPs and suggesting improvements within primary care to the Local Health Authority and Department of Health. In addition, individual interventions were conducted with people with learning disabilities from the practice registers. This work can be conceptualised at a strategic, organisational and individual level.

Conflict

All the previously cited work by the practitioners involved working across professional boundaries in primary and acute areas. This type of work is still considered a new domain of practice for the learning disability nurse, although the introduction of the role of 'health facilitator' has highlighted the necessity for workers in the field to work more proactively with or within primary care

Dealing with conflict at whatever level, has been a feature of such practice development. If primary care for people with learning disabilities is to develop, then those workers operating with and for this group of people will be required to embrace conflict skilfully and sensitively.

Wicks (1998) understands conflict through the three following dimensions; conflict with self, conflict between nurses and other health professionals, and conflict between nurses and doctors.

Workers taking on the different levels suggested within this chapter (*Figure 7.1c*) will require high levels of reflection and personal introspection. Such insight will be called upon when dealing with conflicts of self, where your own professional beliefs and value base may be challenged by, not only other professionals within the PHCT, but also the restraining organisation by whom you may be employed.

Workers may find themselves in situations where other health professionals are driven by the necessity to comply with a scientific focus upon health and illness. Such an outlook may well be in conflict with a subjective view of vulnerable groups of people. A perspective that does not stray from demonstrating emotion and different patterns of caring, while aiming to promote health and well being, is more aligned to learning disability practice.

Working with general practitioners (GP) within a primary care setting, on occasions will demand workers to deal directly with conflict. For historic and educational reasons, the GP has not been supported to develop a model of good primary care for people with learning disabilities. The aim of developing a workable model of primary care for people with learning disabilities, should provide a focus and rationale for working sensitively with medical colleagues. Adopting an approach that offers the GP advice, support, information in a pragmatic and useful way should be valued and seen as a way of promoting access for all people with learning disabilities.

Team building

The development of a model for practice within primary care work is built upon the author's previous work (Bollard and Jukes,1999; *Figure 7.1a*).

This work articulates that, in particular, the learning disability nurse's role must be realised within the structure of the PHCT. Locating a new professional member into a team, that is already overburdened with different professionals (Elston and Holloway, 2001) will involve, among other things, team building. For such a model to be achieved the endeavours by practitioners must be supported by service and commissioning managers. The following list offers basic considerations for managers pursuing such developments (Payne, 2000).

⌘ **Tasks:** these are defined in terms of the presenting client need. This will require an accurate practice profile which can then determine the level of intervention.
⌘ **Systems:** These are set up within a team to facilitate professional judgement that is based upon the client group identified. They should consider the health needs, degrees of vulnerability, potential crisis and risk. Adopting a health promotion approach that embraces partnership with clients and carers to prevent the escalation of identified need would be useful here. The systems can work if all members of the team are clear about their work in relation to each other, allowing for the integration of working practices.
⌘ **Priorities:** An accurate practice profile will allow workers and managers to determine the present and future workload. In establishing work patterns that may come about through a priority list, it is important to be aware of any perceptions of low status work. The team should be aiming for collective responsibility, where each member is aware and takes on his own tasks and responsibilities.
⌘ **Framework for organising work:** It is important to utilise any priority list sensitively, being conscious of any work that may be perceived as low status. Some initial conflict may be avoided if the community practitioners are of equal status, for example all G grade nurses or equivalent. Within the core team a flattened hierarchy is preferred. It is worth remembering that there will be an implicit hierarchy within the existing PHC structure, with senior GP partners at the top. Adding an additional infrastructure is likely to stifle the development.
⌘ **Management:** The management of the team could come from a team leader who sits within the PHC structure and is employed by the PCT. The Tile Hill Model (Taggart and O'Brien, 1998) provided an opportunity for different professional groups to work together within a primary care framework. There is potential for the practitioner to be isolated, particularly if the specialist services in the given locality are rooted in secondary care provision. Employment and contracting arrangements would require careful consideration.

Discussion

In order to embrace and realise the model of primary care work suggested in this chapter, a number of considerations will need to be acknowledged, prior to any attempts to employ such an approach and where strategic, organisational and individual levels are employed (*Figure 7.1c*).

⌘ Understand the historic culture that exists within health and social service provision in your locality. This could affect the development of primary care for people with learning disabilities. Think about the changes that have occurred, how they have been managed, the impact this has had upon relationships between primary and secondary care. The learning that has taken place from this that can offer pointers to progress, or pitfalls to avoid. What perception of people with learning disabilities has this experience left? Consider this within and outside of specialist services. Reflecting upon your own professional background will assist this process, whether you are a manager or a practitioner.

⌘ What is achieveable with the workforce within your area? Is there a case for re-educating people, or is there enough expertise and skill locally to take on this model?

⌘ Take stock of practice development to date. For some services realising that this development may not be that far away, for others there may be a lot of preparation and profiling required. What lessons have be learned from the multi-disciplinary approach taken in your area? Do all key stakeholders believe in inter-professional work? What levels of autonomy have your community workers really been exposed to? How much team building will be needed? Will commissioners of services see the benefit of this model? How can they be persuaded, will they encourage creative developments?

⌘ Involve people with learning disabilities from the outset, establishing what kind of primary health care they would wish for and level of representation that they feel is necessary within primary care, for them to achieve good health.

What is achieveable within current partnership arrangements

Local specialist learning disability services are charged with the responsibility of establishing Partnership Boards (DoH, 2001) to cover the broad and ambitious *Valuing People* agenda. Over the last two years, services have been avidly organising subgroups that are attempting to operationalise the key *Valuing People* objectives

This part of the discussion will focus upon and make recommendations with particular reference to aspects that are and will impact upon primary care development.

Tasks:

⌘ Identifying practice profiles that are based on primary care data, not solely drawn from special needs registers. Tools that are used to trigger primary care based data will need to be accurate and sensitive to avoid the potential of 'unwanted labels'. Look to use existing primary care systems and develop new ones that primary care can own.

⌘ Following national targets to identify need can be helpful, however, the morbidity and mortality of people with learning disabilities may differ from national targets and needs may be localised — a sound evidence base is not there yet.

⌘ The needs of people from diverse ethnic communities needs to be acknowledged and taken responsibility for.

⌘ Presentation of need within a GP practice may be different or understood differently to that which is presented in a specialist clinic.

⌘ Practitioners operating in primary care must look to providing interventions that meet need, not just supporting or facilitating health. Contemporary learning disability practice in primary care will only be sustained if interventions are conducted and quality outcomes to such interventions, established, disseminated and justified. A Health Action Plan (HAP), is only the start of meaningful work in this area. The co-ordination of needs as a result of a HAP, may require an ongoing health checking process for an individual. This may lead onto a practitioner carrying out interventions within the GP practice — a practitioner-led clinic on an individual or group consultation level.

Systems:

⌘ In order to implement such a model will require systems that strike a balance between embracing professional autonomy, while still adhering to the belief in genuine inter-professional working. Client-led teams that clearly identify needs and then take responsibility for those needs could help. The health facilitator situated in primary care could take the lead role in assessing, co-ordinating and carrying out specific interventions that are directly related to the identified need or highlighted in a HAP. The pathway from referral point to the completion of an intervention would require a sensitive outcome measure. Only then would it be possible to identify whether any health improvement has occurred and what specifically has led to the health improvement. Such a system would require an electronic recording process within a primary care database, maybe a template to match the planning and intervention processes involved. Given the client's and GP's permission, this could be connected and mapped to data elsewhere, thereby compiling a more comprehensive database.

Priorities:

⌘ Mutually agreed priorities would need to be established. The practice profile should indicate the type and level of localised need. This understanding could shape patterns of work. A significant prevalence of continuing health needs may lead onto annual screening across a number of practices in a PC or a larger than average practice. This type of work should involve service user groups to assist in the process of prioritising to build in the capacity to sustain developments that arise around the prioritising process.

Framework for organising work:

⌘ Given that there is no clearly defined structure of a primary care team, the organisation of work is likely to vary from one area to another. The health facilitator or learning disability practitioner will need quickly to gain credibility within the primary care structure to allow professional autonomy to flourish. The key components of a health professional's work are still likely to apply, focusing upon identifying need, co-ordinating and planning for those needs and conducting interventions that can be measured. The right time and energy will be required to build in organisational structures that can be sustained and stand up to the next NHS reconfiguration.

Management:

⌘ The management of the practitioners again will differ depending on how well local services are established, the way in which models of health facilitation may have emerged and the way in which community practitioners in this field have been allowed to expand their practice. The way in which such practitioners have conceptualised their own roles will also be important. Clinical leads in health facilitation are emerging across the country, with nurse consultants in primary care (learning disabilities) being asked to lead and take such practice developments forward. Much will depend upon the professional leadership capabilities of such nurse consultants, if the primary care needs of people with learning disabilities are to be met and new practice models established and sustained.

Leadership styles

Intrinsic to the drive for better health care in the UK over the last five years, has been the desire for leadership within health and social services. The preponderance of leadership courses on offer to, for example, nurses, can be seen as the State's attempt to skill up the workforce and hand over the responsibility of leading health care to front line workers. If only it was as simple as that, for the organisational cultures that the workers are expected to operate within are often constrained by hierarchical structures, poorly managed, with tight budgets, and forever changing central dictates, that even the strongest nurse leaders find it difficult to make progress.

Any worker being integrated into the changing primary care arena will need to see themselves as a change agent, who can clearly adopt an appropriate leadership style (Jukes, 2002). This cannot be left to chance, for working effectively across the professional boundaries that straddle the primary, secondary and acute interface for a vulnerable group of people, will require the worker to see themselves as a leader.

There are many theories of leadership, as identified by Marriner-Tomey (1996), and practitioners are required to select from these an appropriate style which will be dependent upon the situation and range of professionals involved.

Within contemporary health and social care transformational leadership (Bass, 1998) is perceived as an appropriate theory and visionary style to be adopted, particularly within renewing structures and organisations. However, in less mature or underdeveloped teams, situational leadership (Hersey and Blanchard, 1988) may be more appropriate where the practitioner within this new model of primary care should have qualities such as delegation, selling tasks across teams, as well as being acutely political (see Jukes, 2002: 698).

It is due to these challenges that the CALECT model was developed to support the strategic and individual role of a health facilitator. CALECT being a mnemonic for change agent/manager, advocate, leader, empowerment agent, collaborator and teacher (*Figure 7.1b*; Jukes, 2002).

Essentially, these roles encapsulate the many complexities that a health facilitator needs to embrace to tackle health inequalities, access and exclusion factors, which impact upon people with a learning disability.

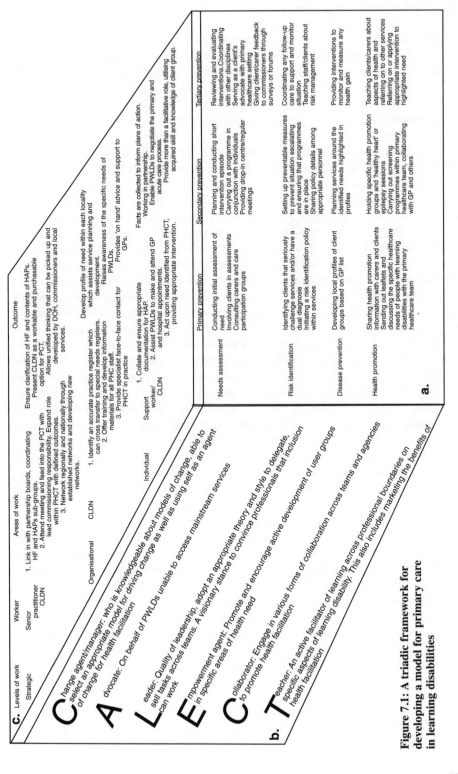

Figure 7.1: A triadic framework for developing a model for primary care in learning disabilities

All team leaders and managers must embrace such community workers, supporting them to nurture the coalitions necessary to realise good primary care for people with learning disabilities. This can take time and must be conceptualised as a genuine opportunity for practice development, while more importantly gaining contact with an often undiscovered learning disability population with unmet needs.

Conclusion

This chapter has considered the political and contextual issues involved in the development of a model for primary health care to support people with learning disabilities to access mainstream services.

Social exclusion has been briefly reviewed in terms of the complexities and potential difficulties for practitioners to engage across both health and social care agencies. Professionals, themselves, may demonstrate exclusivist behaviours and values which mitigate against the interests of people with learning disabilities.

A model for primary health care has been proposed which considers an in-depth analysis into how learning disability nurse practitioners may influence primary care work. This model provides a more integrative and interprofessional strategy, moving towards the inclusion of people with learning disabilities into mainstream services.

The new and emerging role of the health facilitator provides a tremendous opportunity for workers to improve the access to mainstream health services for and with people with learning disabilities. However, in focusing upon supporting and facilitating health, it is important to remember not to overlook the need to conduct specific interventions, that can enhance the well being of people with learning disabilities. Given the varied, specific and continuing health needs that this group of people has, the demand for skilled intervention will always exist. Contemporary learning disability practitioners, as this text demonstrates, are well placed to take on those specific interventions. Genuine professional work in this area will strive to establish outcome measures that can stand up as evidence for the particular chosen intervention. With the support of sensitive management and creative lead commissioners, this model could quite feasibly be realised. Leadership has arisen as a crucial factor within this chapter. An understanding and a recognition of the need to adopt different leadership styles, while individual practitioners simultaneously acknowledge the possession of, or deficit of leadership capabilities, is crucial to the progression of practice in this area. Significantly improving access to health care for a marginalised group of people, by an often marginalised professional group, is a challenge. The meaningful development of primary care work for people with learning disabilities, presents a genuine opportunity to assist skilfully a vulnerable group of people, as well as mark out a new era of professional learning disability practice.

References

Albrecht GL (2001) Rationing health care to disabled people. *Sociology of Health and Illness* **23**(5): 654–77

Bass BM (1998) *Transformational Leadership: Industry, military and educational impact*. Lawrence Erlbaum, Mahwah, NJ

Bollard M, Jukes MJD (1999) Specialist practitioner within community learning disability nursing and the primary health care team. *J Learning Disabilities, Health and Social Care* **3**(1): 11–19

Brindle D (1994) GPs rid lists. *The Guardian* 11 July: 6

Commission of the European Communities (1993) *Background Report: Social Exclusion — Poverty and other Social Problems in the European Community, ISEC/B11/93*. Office for Official Publications of the European Communities, Luxembourg

Department of Health (1998) *Signposts for Success: a commissioning guide*. HMSO, London

Department of Health (1999) *Facing the Facts. Services for People with Learning Disabilities: A policy impact study of social care and health services*. HMSO, London

Department of Health (2001) *Valuing People: A Strategy for People with Learning Disabilities for the 21st Century*. HMSO, London

Elston S, Holloway I (2001) The impact of recent primary care reforms in the UK on interprofessional working in primary care centres. *J Interprof Care* **15**(1): 19–27

Hersey P, Blanchard KH (1988) *Management of Organizational Behaviour; utilising human resources*. 5th edn. Prentice-Hall, Englewood Cliffs, New Jersey

Joseph Rowntree Organisation (1999) *Supporting Disabled Children and their Families*. Available online at: http//www.jrf.org.uk

Jukes M (2002) Health facilitation in learning disability: a new specialist role. *Br J Nurs* **11**(10): 694–8

Marriner-Tomey A (1996) *Nursing Management and Leadership*. 5th edn. Mosby, St.Louis

Oliver M (1990) *The Politics of Disablement*. Macmillan, Basingstoke

Payne M (2000) *Teamwork in Multi-professional Care*. Macmillan, Basingstoke

Percy-Smith J (2002) *Policy Responses to Social Exclusion. Towards Inclusion?* Open University Press, Buckingham

Pierpoint J (2002) *Inclusion vs Exclusion. Society is at a turning point*. Inclusion Press, Inclusion Network, Toronto, Ontario, Canada (www.inclusion.com)

Scottish Executive (2002) *Promoting Health — Supporting Inclusion*. Scottish Executive Department

Singh D (1997) *Prescription for Change*. Mencap, London

Social Exclusion Unit (1997) *Social Exclusion Unit: Purpose, work priorities and working methods*. HMSO, London

Taggart C, O'Brien P (1998) *A Report on a New Model of Primary Care*. Coventry Health Care Trust, Coventry

Welsh Assembly Government (2002) *Inclusion, Partnership and Innovation. A framework for realising the potential of learning disability nursing in Wales*. Welsh Assembly Government, Cardiff

Wicks D (1998) *Nurses and Doctors: Rethinking professional boundaries*. Open University Press, Buckingham

Young IM (1990) *Justice and the Politics of Difference*. Princeton University Press, Princeton

8

The ecology of health model

John Aldridge

The model has been developed in response to practitioners' need for a model of nursing which specifically addresses the health care needs of people who have learning disabilities within the current context of learning disability practice and the principles of person-centred planning (PCP). *Valuing People* (DoH, 2001a) notes that:

> *A person-centred approach to planning means that planning should start with the individual (not with services), and take account of their wishes and aspirations. Person-centred planning is a mechanism for reflecting the needs and preferences of a person with a learning disability and covers such issues as housing, education, employment and leisure.*

We might argue that PCP should also include health and well being and that well being includes satisfaction with all of the aspects included in the Department of Health definition. The National Electronic Library for Health (2002) notes that, 'Person-centred planning is a way of helping every person with a learning disability to work out what they want and how to get it'. Again, we might argue that 'what people want' may include health and well being.

An holistic nursing assessment need not be incompatible with person-centred planning, but may be used as the nurse's contribution to an overall plan directed by the client. What is important is not so much the kind of assessment used, as the way in which the assessment is carried out — an emphasis on a collaborative process as much as outcome. The nursing *Code of Professional Conduct* (Nursing and Midwifery Council [NMC], 2002) frequently emphasises the need to recognise clients as partners in all aspects of the delivery of health care and underpins for nurses the use of a collaborative partnership in assessment and care planning decision-making. This person-centred approach is implicit in all stages of assessment, planning, implementation and evaluation using the ecology of health model.

Valuing People (DoH, 2001a) indicates that, 'inequalities in health cannot be tackled without dealing with the fundamental causes'. A truly holistic model that acknowledges the influence of social and environmental factors is needed if we are to change many of the issues that underpin the health and ill health of people with learning disabilities. Further, the same document (DoH, 2001a) suggests that learning disability nurses might be well placed to fulfil the role of health facilitator. However, the nurse will need a suitable tool to enable him/her to identify health need and the causes of health need. A comprehensive nursing assessment could additionally be used as the basis for developing with the individual a health action plan. What follows is an outline of the ecology of health model and an example of its use in practice.

The model's theoretical basis and how the model works

In the context of this model, the person may be seen as having physical and psychological elements, which overlap to form the self and which exist within a social environment. The social environment is not part of the person, but a supportive environment necessary to optimum physical and psychological functioning. The person relates to their environment through interactive processes, termed 'healthy behaviours and relationships'. It may be seen that each of the elements of the model affects all the others in a reciprocal manner. The dynamics and inter-relationships of all these elements form an 'ecological system' — the ecology of health.

The model is inspired, at least in part, by the work of Bronfenbrenner (1977, 1979) whose concepts of human development and interaction in an ecological framework provided the basis for an assessment and care planning approach which would encompass all of the possible elements that might contribute to an individual's health, to see the person and their world in their entirety and to attempt to describe some of the interactions between those elements.

Further, Lipowski, (cited in Christie and Mellett, 1986) in discussing psychosomatic medicine, uses a definition which reflects an ecological conception of the person:

Psychosomatic is a term referring to or relating to the inseparability and interdependence of psychosocial and biological (physiological, somatic) aspects of man. (This connotation may be called 'holistic', as it implies the view of man as a whole, a mind-body complex embedded in a social environment.)

This ecological viewpoint informs the model's explanation of health, which may be defined here as, 'A dynamic and ever-changing state of individually-defined optimal functioning and well-being which is determined by the interplay between the individual's internal physiology and psychology, and their external environment'.

The elements of the model

The model may be conceptualised as a three-dimensional figure representing the person, surrounded in two dimensions by a number of concentric layers.

1. The person is composed of four overlapping domains, collectively called personal systems for health, which are seen as central for a number of reasons:

❆ They provide a person-centred perspective, from which we attempt to understand the individual's experience of the world, their health and behaviour.
❆ They contain the core internal processes, the 'internal environment', which may contribute significantly to an individual's health.
❆ They contain four sub-domains, each of which may affect the others:
   a) physical processes (or the physical self)
   b) cognitive processes (the thinking and knowing self)
   c) affective processes (the feeling self)
   d) self-concept (literally the core of the individual, the essence of the person).

Section III:

Engagement with a person-centred perspective

With caution, it may be helpful at times to think of people who have learning disabilities as 'developmentally young'. This is far from saying that they are like children, should be thought of as children, or treated as children, but implies that, like everyone, they are developing and growing individuals with a capacity to learn and to change. A learning disability and associated impairments may, however, affect the speed at which the individual matures and the specific difficulties that they may experience. If we have an understanding of the cognitive and emotional characteristics of each person (we might call these developmental characteristics), we are in a better position to help them to experience the world in a way that makes sense to them. If we ignore developmental aspects we risk either over- or under-estimating peoples' understanding and we may unwittingly compound their learning difficulty. It is, however, very challenging to balance the two elements of chronological age and 'developmental age' in a way that addresses age-appropriateness.

Learning disability, especially severe or profound and multiple learning disability may affect the individual in a number of ways, which will differ considerably from person to person. For example:

⌘ Physical impairments and physical health: damage to the brain and other bodily systems may result in frail physical health, a susceptibility to physical illness and disordered functioning of bodily systems, including the physical aspects of communication.

⌘ Cognitive impairments (or intellectual youth): literally a learning disability, which may affect thought processes, the ability of the individual to know and understand the world, their ability to think and learn. These may influence behaviours, interactions, and in some cases mental health.

⌘ Affective impairments (or emotional youth): people who have learning disabilities may have difficulty in recognising, labelling, managing and expressing emotions. Their feelings are the same as anyone else's, but they may be expressed in unusual ways. The individual may express their feelings more openly, more strongly and with less inhibition. In some cases, this might be labelled 'challenging behaviour'. An individual who has feelings that they have extreme difficulty in managing and expressing may possibly become distressed, dysfunctional or mentally ill.

⌘ Self-concept may be affected by the above three elements and may be negative, positive or incomplete. We need to consider the degree to which the person knows himself or herself: both their physical and mental self. The degree to which they feel happy and comfortable with themselves. Self-concept develops and matures as we grow and develop. As adults, we usually have a more complex and complete understanding of ourselves than we did as children. Self-esteem is affected by our life experience, but may also affect the ways in which we interact with others and with our environment.

2. Surrounding the person is a further domain, the social environment of health, which represents the physical, political, social and cultural environment of the person. The social environment of health encloses all of the other domains; our personal lives, our behaviour and immediate relationships are played out within a number of 'environments':

⌘ Our family environment: people in our family and the relationships and inter-actions that we have within them.

⌘ Our neighbourhood environment: this includes the nature and quality of housing and the neighbourhood, availability of local resources, accessibility and integration.

⌘ Our cultural environment: our religion and our ethnic background may have considerable influence on our life patterns and beliefs and the readiness of others to accept us and value us.

⌘ Our socio-economic environment: this encompasses 'social class' (which might also be included in culture) and financial status. People who have learning disabilities are themselves likely to be relatively poor and because of this to have limited access to valued activities and lifestyles.

⌘ The formal and informal supportive environment includes the existence (or otherwise) of professional support systems such as social worker or community nurse, and informal supports such as friends, self-help groups or neighbours who will help out.

⌘ The legal environment: the influence and constraints of the law on individuals or groups.

3. Between the person and the social environment of health lies the domain called healthy behaviours and relationships, which represents the individual's relationships and interactions with all aspects of their environment. We might think of this as an interface between the internal and external environment. These healthy behaviours and relationships are broadly equivalent to activities of daily living and may be listed as:

- eating and drinking
- moving and mobilising
- maintaining personal hygiene
- sleeping, resting and being comfortable
- dressing and grooming
- ensuring own and others' safety
- perceiving and responding
- knowing, learning and developing
- making and maintaining relationships
- expressing self and sexuality
- communicating and self-determining
- enjoying leisure
- working and occupation
- promoting health and well being.

'Healthy behaviours and relationships' represent the 'meeting point' between inner and environmental processes. These behaviours and relationships are supported by personal systems for health, which enable the individual to carry out the activities that are listed under this heading. At the same time, the environments in which they take place influence the behaviours and relationships. In many ways, healthy behaviours and relationships are the reason why we need good health. Health exists to enable us to do these things, to maintain our independence and to interact with our environment. If an individual has difficulty with eating and drinking, for instance, we need to consider why this might be. Is competence and independence in this activity affected by physical, cognitive or affective factors? What part does the environment have to play?

4. The third dimension, the temporal dimension, runs throughout all the preceding domains and represents the passage of time:

⌘ The past: people, their health and behaviour do not exist in a vacuum; each has a history and a future as well as a present. We often need to know how long situations and behaviours have existed and whether there are events that might be linked with this. It may be that the past contains 'secrets' of which no one is aware except the individual. It may appear foolhardy to dig around in an individual's past because we don't know what we might uncover, but the 'secrets' are there nonetheless, we don't create them. In uncovering events, ideas or feelings we offer the possibility of dealing with them and offering therapy. The essential issue here is the sensitivity with which we approach potentially difficult topics.

⌘ The present: the present contains the situation as it is now; this may be the same, or different to the situation in the immediate or distant past, and may be subject to change in the future. We may be able to discern patterns or themes emerging over time. The present contains actual health needs and health problems which we have to deal with now.

⌘ The future: everyone has a future, although it may be brighter for some than for others. The future may be a source for optimism, something to look forward to; or it may be a source of dread, something to be avoided or fought against. For some individuals the future may represent 'more of the same', and this may involve more boredom, more abuse or more confusion. It may be that for some individuals the future is empty, they cannot predict what might happen and this in itself may be disturbing. A more optimistic view would be that nurses could help to influence the future in a positive way, to offer help, therapy and support. It is important that we make some attempt to look into the future, to think about the implications of past and present and to consider what options we might offer the individual and their family. The future contains potential health needs and health problems, which we may be able to prevent or minimise, or we may need to be aware that this need will require attention at some point in the near or distant future.

Much of the inspiration for the temporal dimension is derived from life story work (Frost and Taylor, 1986; Ryan and Walker, 1993; Hussain and Racza, 1997) and this may provide a useful means of attempting both assessment and therapy. Although life story work has not been widely used in a therapeutic context in learning disability, its origins in fostering and adoption do contain strong therapeutic elements and principles which may usefully be adopted when working with people who have learning disabilities. Some useful discussion on the topic of working with sensitive issues is covered in Brigham (1998), McCarthy (1998) and Rolph (1998).

Each of these domains interacts with the others in a complex and dynamic manner. The relationships and interactions are not static or unchanging, but develop and evolve over time. Even seemingly unchanging elements (such as the 'frozen family', or a person with a long history of behaviour which challenges) may become more habitual and difficult to change as time goes by, and this in itself forms a dynamic. The interactions may take on a different form in different settings or circumstances, or when different people are involved. At different times each component of the domains will have greater or lesser influence over the overall dynamics.

For a diagrammatic representation of the model and its inter-relationships, see *Figure 8.1*. We might think of the figure as being somewhat like a stick of seaside rock. What we see is only a cross-section — a slice across the rock. The addition of the temporal dimension reminds us that in order to understand a client we need to see the whole of the person's life story — the whole length of the stick of rock.

Using the ecology of health model

1. The ecology of health model is deliberately structured to encourage an analytical approach to assessment. It is recommended that assessment is begun by using the healthy behaviours and relationships as a basis for assessment in much the same way that activities of daily living might be used in other nursing models.

2. Once this level of assessment has been completed and needs identified, we next need to ask why these needs exist. For instance, a person may be overweight and this may be due to a range of factors that might include:

   - the individual's understanding of the way in which food relates to body weight
   - the individual's emotional need to eat as a source of pleasure or comfort
   - the way they see themself as over or underweight
   - the opportunities they have for making healthy choices about what they eat.

The personal systems for health and the social environment of health act as a reminder of the range of possible factors that may influence an individual's health. We need to use our professional expertise to choose which of these factors to assess in order to find explanations for the individual's health needs. It is not intended that all of the factors under personal systems for health and the social environment of health should be slavishly assessed — this is very time-consuming and unnecessary. These factors need to be used as a kind of 'shopping list' for assessment. In the example assessment given, you will see how these domains have been used to provide further depth and analysis to the assessment.

3. The extra information gained in stage two can be used to enhance our understanding of the ecology of relevant healthy behaviours and relationships, so that a list of problems and difficulties may be drawn up and the team can make appropriate plans about how these might best be addressed. The word 'problem' has deliberately been used in preference to 'need' in spite of the fact that 'problem' may have negative connotations. The problem is not necessarily the client's problem but could be due to a range of ecological factors. The word 'need' has been avoided because it represents the second, rather than the first stage in the problem-solving process. Unless we know what the problem is, it is likely that we won't know how

to fix it and won't know when we have fixed it. The 'problems list' is balanced by a strengths list that is intended to emphasise the positive aspects of the client's life. *Figure 8.2* shows how the problem-solving process needs to work.

Assessment and care planning in practice

The following section is an example assessment and care plan carried out using the ecology of health model with a young woman called Valerie. The process of developing and analysing the assessment information would have been carried out as a team process, involving Valerie, her parents and those members of the multidisciplinary team who are involved with her. At the very minimum, a nursing assessment and subsequent care plan should be carried out with the involvement of the client (as far as possible), family members and/or the client's independent advocate. If there are disagreements about the accuracy of assessment data, the importance of identified difficulties or the ways in which difficulties might be overcome, these should be resolved through a process of discussion. It is more likely in this case that, once disagreements have been resolved, there will be joint ownership of an approach and greater enthusiasm for carrying out any care plans.

Because there are twenty-six identified problems and difficulties identified with Valerie (there could be even more if one looks carefully), it would be impossible within likely resource constraints to meet them all. In order to aid the reader's understanding, the problems and difficulties have been presented in probable rank order of impact. The principles of person-centred planning indicate that the choice of which issues to work on should rest primarily with the client. The complexity of Valerie's difficulties will influence the number that can be worked on at any one time and the availability of skilled help and resources will certainly influence the degree to which progress can be made. In the interests of conciseness, one example of a care plan that the nurse may write without joint work with multidisciplinary team members is given here.

Some of the other issues are dealt with by referral to other professionals and would be included in the current overall care programme.

In order to maintain care planning within realistic limits it may be useful to think of it as a three-layer process:

1. Identify the most important problems and difficulties. It is likely that we would expect to change these as quickly as possible and therefore we need to develop active care plans around these. Again, being realistic, it is not recommended that more than three of these be implemented at any one time.
2. There may be some problems and difficulties that require careful intervention but there is not the expectation of change in the near future. An example of this is the support needed by Valerie at mealtimes.
3. The remaining problems and difficulties may be written up as a care summary. This is useful as a means of giving an overview of a person's care and may be used to 'signpost' support staff to specific care plans. A copy of Valerie's care summary is given to indicate how non-urgent matters can be managed in an efficient but effective way without recourse to a confusing multiplicity of care plans.

Cognitive processes
- Cognitive developmental maturity
- Problem solving
- Learning, attention and consciousness
- Memory
- Moral reasoning
- Knowledge and understanding
- Effects of medication on cognitive processes

The social environment of health
- Family membership, dynamics and processes
- Neighbourhood, housing, living conditions and circumstances
- Religion, culture and ethnicity
- Socio-economic status
- Formal and informal support networks
- Legal and policy issues

Affective processes
- Emotional maturity
- Pleasure and gratification
- Motivation
- Mood
- Anxiety and confidence
- Giving and receiving affection
- Effects of medication on affective processes

A schematic diagram of the ecology of health model

Temporal dimension
- The past
- The present
- The future

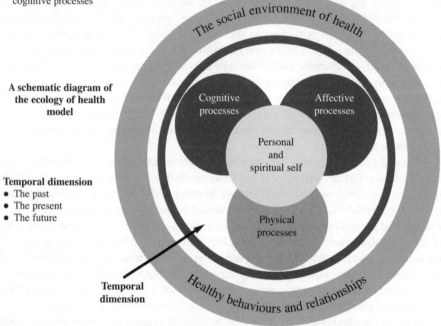

Physical processes
- Physical growth and maturity
- Gastrointestinal system
- Musculoskeletal system
- Neurological system
- Endocrine system
- Body equilibrium system
- Sensory systems
- Excretory systems
- Reproductive system
- Breathing system
- Circulatory system
- Skin and integumentary system
- Effects of medication on physical systems

Healthy behaviours and relation-ships
- Eating and drinking
- Moving and mobilising
- Maintaining personal hygiene
- Sleeping, resting and being comfortable
- Dressing and grooming
- Ensuring own and others' safety
- Perceiving and responding
- Knowing, learning and developing
- Making and maintaining relationships
- Expressing self and sexuality
- Communicating and self-determining
- Enjoying leisure
- Working and occupation
- Promoting health and well being

Personal and spiritual self
- Language and self-expression
- Attachment, separation and loss
- Self-concept and self-perception
- Locus of control and self-empowerment
- Self-esteem and self-regard
- Religious, cultural and ethnic self
- Personal continuity and coherence

Figure 8.1: A schematic diagram of the ecology of health model

Problem	Need	Objective setting	Means of achieving outcome	Attempt to achieve outcome	Comparison with original problem
Assess	Requirement	Outcome	Plan	Implement	Evaluate
What's the problem?	A need to have the problem 'fixed'	What does it look like when the problem is fixed?	How shall we fix it? Who might be involved?	Let's do it	Have we fixed the problem?
eg. contractures (that is restricted movement)	eg. a need for physical therapy	eg. greater movement	eg. use of passive exercises	eg. implement programme daily	eg. does the client have greater movement?

Figure 8.2: The problem-solving process

Introducing Valerie Bradley and the context of her life

Valerie is aged thirty-five and has spastic quadruplegic cerebral palsy. Her mother, Joan, is aged sixty and her father, Arthur, is aged sixty-two, both living at home with Valerie. Her brother, Edward, aged thirty-eight, is married and living ninety miles away.

Valerie is well loved within the family and they try their best to include her in all activities. Valerie's mother and father work together as a team and try to share her care equally, although Mrs Bradley does most of the caring and has not worked consistently since Valerie's birth. Her parents prefer to be independent and self-sufficient wherever possible and do not ask for help from others unless it is absolutely necessary.

For the last three years Valerie has spent one week every three months at Sandpiper Lodge, the local health trust short-term care facility. There has been an opportunity to use a greater number of nights, but Valerie's parents have declined, saying that they prefer to have her at home as much as possible, as it is their duty as parents to care for her. She says that she doesn't like being away from home.

The family live in a tied cottage, which comes with Mr Bradley's job as a farm worker. The house is a semi-detached three-bedroomed house standing in farm grounds to one side of Sandley village. The house is not really suitable for Valerie's needs or her parents' in caring for her. It has not been adapted in any way as the landowner is unwilling for work to be carried out that might, in his opinion, 'spoil' the house. Valerie's bedroom and the bathroom are upstairs, although there is a downstairs toilet. Consequently, her parents have to carry her upstairs and down several times per day. Both Joan and Arthur were born in the village in which they presently live and both came from farming families. They are well known in the village and have a highly developed feeling of 'belonging' to the area and its relatively uncomplicated lifestyle. Their friends and other villagers seem always to have accepted Valerie as a member of the community and will often help out in a minor way. Within the last few months, Arthur has been complaining of chest pains and has been diagnosed as having minor coronary heart disease. He has been told that he must not take on heavy manual work and on no account must he carry Valerie upstairs. They have therefore been forced to accept that Valerie needs to move into full-time accommodation and an offer has been made for her to take up a place in a house, managed by the local health trust, in a nearby town. However, this has not been finally decided upon, either by Valerie or her parents.

Healthy behaviours and relationships: *Eating and drinking*

Valerie has a poor appetite and eats very slowly. She needs complete help with eating and drinking and has great difficulties with meal times. It usually takes more than an hour to give her an adequate meal. A polycarbonate spoon is used to prevent damage to teeth and gums. Mouthfuls need to be given to her in small amounts, as she may otherwise choke easily and foods are currently mashed to a creamy consistency to remove lumps, which may also trigger a choking episode. She is able to drink from a spouted cup, but great care is needed, as she tends to spill a great deal. She does not enjoy meal times very much, but does have a preference for sweet foods and for hot drinks containing sugar. She has a tendency to constipation and this has largely been prevented by the use of dietary fibre with plenty of fluid and fresh fruits (mashed) given as a dessert.

⌘ Second level analysis

Physical maturity and growth
Height: 1.6 mtr; weight: 31.8 kg; BMI: 12.4. Valerie is slightly shorter than the average height for a woman of her age, but is considerably underweight at a BMI of 12.4. She has a lifetime history of delayed growth and development, associated with her diagnosis of quadruplegic cerebral palsy.

Gastrointestinal system
Valerie has a high arched hard palate and experiences the following:
- bite reflex (marked)
- tongue thrust (marked)
- dysphagia (severe)
- poor lip closure (mild).

There appear to be no anomalies in her gastrointestinal tract. There is a risk of choking, and her underweight is likely to be at least partially due to insufficient food intake.

Musculoskeletal system
Valerie is only slightly shorter than the mean for her age and sex. Valerie has spastic quadruplegic cerebral palsy; hypertonia is present for most of the time, though she does relax while in hydrotherapy. Due to her cerebral palsy, her muscular development is poor, with not a great deal of power. She has some difficulty in maintaining body posture in midline, especially when sitting. Oral spasm and poor muscular control lead to unwanted and uncomfortable mouth and throat movements, especially when eating and drinking.

Healthy behaviours and relationships: *Moving and mobilising*

Valerie has spastic cerebral palsy, which affects the whole of her body. Her natural muscle tone is normally relatively high, and her range of movements is limited. Due to a shortage of physiotherapists in the area, she is beginning to become quite twisted and her posture is poor.

Valerie has had difficulty with fine motor skills but she is beginning to be able to hold large objects to her body with both forearms, and is beginning to develop palmar grasp.

She uses a wheelchair for general mobility (fitted with a rubber air cushion to prevent sores) which needs to be pushed by a helper. When out of her wheelchair she is able to use 'rolling and swimming' movements to move around and can move quite a distance.

While at home, Valerie has great difficulty in mobilising due to the restrictions of her home environment.

⌘ **Second level analysis**

Musculoskeletal system

Valerie is only slightly shorter than the mean for her age and sex. Valerie has spastic quadruplegic cerebral palsy; hypertonia is present for most of the time, though she does relax while in hydrotherapy. Due to her cerebral palsy, her muscular development is poor, with not a great deal of power. She has some difficulty in maintaining body posture in midline, especially when sitting. Whole body spasm causes her considerable discomfort at times, especially at night or when she has not changed position for some time. There is some evidence of contractures: elbows will extend to an angle of 135 degrees, knees to an angle of 120 degrees. There is no evidence of windsweeping as yet. A degree of cogwheel rigidity causes impairment of free movement.

There is risk of further development of contractures, with other associated health problems.

Oral spasm and poor muscular control lead to unwanted and uncomfortable mouth and throat movements, especially when eating and drinking.

Neurological system

Valerie's cerebral palsy appears to affect mainly her motor centres, with possible involvement in hearing and visual centre. There may be some impairment of intelligence, though this is by no means certain. She experiences tonic-clonic epilepsy, averaging four seizures per month: this has been stable for at least the past ten years.

Healthy behaviours and relationships: *Maintaining personal hygiene*

Valerie is incontinent of both urine and faeces and appears not to have control of bowel or bladder. She wears a disposable incontinence pad and asks for this to be changed when it is wet or soiled. Constipation is a problem about twice weekly, and on these occasions, a micro-enema is given. She occasionally develops a urinary tract infection, which can cause discomfort.

Valerie enjoys a bath and relaxes considerably in the warm water. She needs full help with all aspects of personal hygiene, and is given a twice-daily bath (morning and evening) due to her incontinence. Her parents have been seeking to have an adapted bath fitted, as it is very difficult to lift Valerie into and out of their ordinary one.

Dental and mouth care is difficult as this may trigger her bite reflex and causes her some discomfort.

Valerie menstruates irregularly but the flow may be heavy and she sometimes experiences abdominal pain at this time.

⌘ Second level analysis

Excretory systems

Urinary system appears to function normally, though there does not appear to be any control of bladder sphincter.

Peristalsis of the gut and colon is slow, leading to constipation which becomes problematic about twice per week. Anal sphincter control not developed.

Reproductive system

Full development of sexual function and secondary sexual characteristics. Menstruation irregular and flow sometimes heavy. Valerie frequently experiences abdominal pain at menstruation.

Skin and integumentary system

Skin generally healthy. No pressure sores have developed yet though reddened areas on sacrum are common and risk factors for pressure sores are very high (Waterlow score 21).

Healthy behaviours and relationships: *Dressing and grooming*

Valerie needs full support in dressing and grooming, although she does have clear preferences in clothing, hairstyle and so on. She will select articles of clothing by eye-pointing if these are held up, or pointed out. Her spastic cerebral palsy and contractures make dressing a slow and uncomfortable process for her, and therefore style and suitability of clothes is a consideration when shopping. Valerie's parents help her to shop for clothes and enable her to choose clothing appropriate to her age.

Although she does have some difficulties with communication, she has a fairly highly developed sense of self-image. She is keen to explore the use of cosmetics and ways of dressing her long hair.

⌘ Second level analysis

Musculoskeletal system

Valerie has spastic quadruplegic cerebral palsy; hypertonia is present for most of the time. There is some evidence of contractures: elbows will extend to an angle of 135°, knees to an angle of 120°. There is no evidence of windsweeping as yet. Cogwheel rigidity make dressing and undressing difficult.

Language and self-expression

Valerie is unable to speak or to use signs other than in a broad gestural way. She recognises twenty-five words of social sight vocabulary and is beginning to recognise words in books. She will make sounds to gain attention and then uses eye-pointing to communicate, looking up and to the right for 'yes' and down for 'no'. She is learning to use a computer and has managed simple word processing, though this is slow because of her difficulty with fine motor control and the delay in finding appropriate switching. She appears able to understand most of what is said to her and responds appropriately; though, in practice, most of this is confined to concrete and immediate issues (eg. 'do you want?').

Self-concept and self-perception

Valerie is able to recognise herself in a mirror and in photos. She is able to point to parts of her own and others' bodies appropriately. She takes an interest in her appearance and enjoys looking attractive.

Locus of control
Valerie enjoys such limited independence and appears to recognise that she is necessarily dependent on others for most of her needs.

Healthy behaviours and relationships: *Sleeping and resting*

Valerie sleeps at home in an ordinary bed, to which a low rail has been added. She goes to bed between 10.00 pm and 10.30 pm, but sometimes takes a while to settle; her parents think that this may be due to discomfort caused by spasm. Valerie says that she doesn't find her bed comfortable. During the week, she needs to get up by 6.30 am to catch the bus to the day centre. She is not always awake at this time and is often drowsy until after her morning bath.

⌘ Second level analysis

Musculoskeletal system
Due to Valerie's spastic quadruplegic cerebral palsy; hypertonia is present for most of the time, though she does relax while in hydrotherapy. Whole body spasm causes her considerable discomfort at times, especially at night or when she has not changed position for some time. Valerie has difficulty changing her own position in bed due to poor muscle control and hypertonia.

Neighbourhood, housing, living conditions
The family live in a tied cottage, with the bedroom upstairs. The landowner is unwilling to have adaptations made to the house. Valerie has to be carried upstairs by her parents to go to bed.

Healthy behaviours and relationships: *Ensuring own and others' safety*

it is not known whether Valerie understands about dangers, but due to her limited mobility, she is unable to protect herself from physical dangers. She is at risk of choking at mealtimes and of aspiration pneumonia from food particles. She is also at risk of pressure sores.

⌘ Second level analysis

Musculoskeletal system
Valerie is unable to protect herself from assault or environmental dangers due to her limited mobility. She is at risk of choking and aspiration pneumonia due to her difficulty in coordinating chewing and swallowing movements. Her poor mobility increases pressure sore risk.

Skin and integumentary system
Valerie's pressure sore risk is increased by her low BMI and wet skin due to her incontinence.

Moral reasoning
Given her communicative difficulties, Valerie shows some understanding of right and wrong and is clearly upset when she thinks that others are behaving badly, even when she is not directly involved.

Healthy behaviours and relationships: *Perceiving and responding*

Valerie has difficulty with vision; she wears spectacles to help with this. She sometimes has difficulty in locating objects on a table in front of her and needs to be positioned carefully to see the television or a computer screen.

She has some difficulty in hearing. She wears bilateral aids although she sometimes finds them annoying and it is now many years since her last hearing assessment. She can hear a person's voice, provided that they are reasonably close, that they speak clearly and there is not a high level of background noise.

Valerie's senses of touch, smell and taste are probably unaffected.

⌘ Second level analysis

Neurological system
Valerie's cerebral palsy appears to affect mainly her motor centres, with possible involvement in hearing and visual centres.

Sensory system
Sight: Long sighted, spectacles worn. Left-sided internal squint. Possible lower field defect.
Hearing: Mild bilateral hearing loss (30dB), bilateral aids worn since age nine. Possible high frequency loss — this needs testing. Other senses probably unaffected.

Musculoskeletal system
Tracking of visual and auditory stimuli may be limited by difficulties in head control

---

Healthy behaviours and relationships: *Knowing, learning and developing*

Valerie attended Woodlands Special School (now closed) to age sixteen. Valerie is generally alert and able to interact with enthusiasm. She is limited by her communicative and motor abilities but, given the right means, is able to learn quite fast.

Valerie now attends Shakespeare Road Centre on a full-time basis and takes part in a number of activities during the week.

⌘ Second level analysis

Cognitive developmental maturity
Very difficult to assess due to Valerie's communication impairment. She does appear to be operating at least at the pre-operational stage in that she is able to use some symbols for communication and to use basic rules for problem solving. Valerie's intelligence and cognitive functioning appear not to have been formally assessed recently, and it is by no means certain that she has an intellectual impairment to any real degree. Her parents are convinced that she is of normal intelligence.

Learning, attention and consciousness
Valerie is able to concentrate on, for instance, a computer-mediated task for up to an hour.

Problem solving

Valerie is able to solve problems in computer mediated tasks up to a seven-year level, but further development in 'real life' is difficult to test due to difficulties with switching and this is a new area of learning for her.

Memory

Valerie's memory appears good when she is able to communicate this. She can remember things from one day to the next, through to events that happened in her childhood (tested with photographs).

Knowledge and understanding

Difficult to evaluate. Certainly able to indicate concrete knowledge, using flashcards (show me the ...) though abstracts (such as time) she finds difficult. Generally, parents and helpers feel that Valerie understands most of what she experiences and seems more limited by her ability to communicate her ideas and understanding.

Effects of medication on cognitive processes

Valerie has been taking Sodium Valproate for the last fifteen years. There may be some dulling of alertness, though this seems very minor and other side-effects have not become evident.

Healthy behaviours and relationships: *Making and maintaining relationships*

Generally, Valerie is a friendly and outgoing individual, who appears limited most by her physical disability. She enjoys the company of others and has a number of friends at the day centre with whom she relates well. She enjoys affection from people that she knows and becomes distressed when others are unhappy, upset or hurt,

Valerie has a number of friends who attend the day centre and she meets some of them at the Gateway Club on Wednesday evenings. However, she has no friends who do not have a learning disability and is reliant on others to take her to places where she can meet others. Her communication difficulties provide an added barrier to meeting others and interacting independently with them. She says that she would like to get out more often.

Her social network appears to be comprised mainly of family and professional people.

⌘ Second level analysis

Giving and receiving affection

Valerie enjoys affection from those that she knows well and is able to return this appropriately. She is rather more reserved with strangers or those that she doesn't like.

Attachment, separation and loss

Valerie has always lived with her parents in the same house and has spent little time away from them. Her brother lives away from home and visits about one a month. There are also members of the extended family living in the surrounding area. She is very close to her parents and is loved dearly by them in return. She has had the same keyworker, Anne, at the day centre for the last five years and they are very fond of one another. Valerie has a number of friends both at the centre and within the village where she lives, though there do not seem to be any special attachments or friendships. Her parents are beginning to find caring for her at home too difficult and it is likely that she will need to move into supported accommodation in the very near future. Although well supported at the moment, there is potential for loss if/when she moves into full-time accommodation.

Religious, ethnic and cultural self
Valerie and her parents are churchgoers, but religion does not otherwise appear to play a great part in their lives. They are country people who identify with their locality and the countryside. She has probably internalised much of this.

Personal continuity and coherence
Valerie's life so far has had a high degree of continuity and coherence, with few changes in recent years. Potentially, there is likely to be some break in this when she leaves home. It is hoped that accommodation will be found locally so that her parents can visit frequently and she can continue at Shakespeare Road Centre.

Family membership, dynamics and processes
Mother, Joan, aged sixty. Father, Arthur, aged sixty-two. Both living at home with Valerie. Brother, Edward, aged thirty-eight, married and living ninety miles away.

Neighbourhood, housing, living conditions and circumstances
Valerie and her family live in quite an isolated village, with relatively few opportunities for social activities.

Religion, culture and ethnicity of the family/individual
Valerie's parents do not express any strong religious belief, but regard themselves as 'C of E'. The family attend Sunday and other services at the village church on occasions when they are held there.

Formal and informal support environment
Although members of the extended family live in the locality, Valerie's parents rarely call on them for help, only in cases of need. There are good relationships with neighbours and other villagers, but they are not made use of for anything other than occasional emotional support.
Key worker (Anne) at day centre; occupational therapist; physiotherapist (sporadic contact); speech and language therapy (occasional); community nurse (recent); short-term care at Sandpiper Lodge (health), one week every three months.

Healthy behaviours and relationships: *Expressing self and sexuality*

Physically, Valerie is fully developed as a woman; she is pretty and likes to present herself in a feminine manner by choosing clothes, hairstyles and makeup which enhance her attractiveness. She says that she would like a boyfriend, but has no especially close friendship with any of her friends or much opportunity to develop a close relationship.

⌘   **Second level analysis**

Physical maturity and growth
Valerie is fully developed as a woman, with all secondary sexual characteristics and began menstruating at the age of fourteen.

Musculoskeletal system
Valerie is dependent on others for her personal mobility and has little opportunity to spend intimate time with another person.

Reproductive system
Full development of sexual function and secondary sexual characteristics. Menstruation irregular and flow sometimes heavy. Valerie frequently experiences abdominal pain at menstruation.

Pleasure and gratification
Valerie finds it difficult to control her own sources of pleasure. She likes to be fashionably dressed and well groomed. She enjoys the company of friends and especially enjoys live and recorded music (mostly jazz, folk and classical).

Giving and receiving affection
Valerie enjoys affection from those that she knows well and is able to return this appropriately. She is rather more reserved with strangers or those that she doesn't like.

Self-concept and self-perception
Valerie is able to recognise herself in a mirror and in photos. She is able to point to parts of her own and others' bodies appropriately. She takes an interest in her appearance and enjoys looking attractive.

Self-esteem
Again, difficult to test. At times Valerie seems quite happy with herself, but at others to be frustrated and self-conscious of her limitations.

Neighbourhood, housing, living conditions and circumstances
Valerie lives in a remote area and has little opportunity outside the day centre to develop a sexual relationship.

Healthy behaviours and relationships: *Communication and self-determination*

Valerie has not developed verbal communication; she does have a good receptive verbal understanding. Since her early childhood, she has been able to communicate by eye-pointing, looking up and to the right for 'yes' and down for 'no'. Communication is therefore possible, but sometimes a laborious process of asking questions and eliminating negatives. Her parents are adept at reading her facial expressions and using the context of situations to make 'educated guesses', and for them, the process is often faster than with others she knows, though there is an acknowledged danger that they may be placing their own interpretation on what she wants.
Due to her communication difficulties, it is often very difficult to know how Valerie may be feeling

or what she may be thinking, without going through a process of elimination, using eye-pointing for 'yes' or 'no'. Valerie is generally very even-tempered, but does become frustrated when she is unable to communicate her needs.

Valerie has some difficulty in hearing quiet speech or other sounds and doesn't always respond to peoples' voices because she doesn't seem to hear them.

⌘ Second level analysis

Musculoskeletal system
Due to Valerie's motor impairments she has difficulty in making speech sounds or signing.

Sensory system
Sight: Long sighted, spectacles worn. Left-sided internal squint. Possible lower field defect.
Hearing: Mild bilateral hearing loss (30dB), bilateral aids worn. Possible high frequency loss — this needs testing. Other senses probably unaffected.

Cognitive developmental maturity
Very difficult to assess due to Valerie's communication impairment. She does appear to be operating at least at the pre-operational stage in that she is able to use some symbols for communication and to use basic rules for problem solving. Valerie's intelligence and cognitive functioning appear not to have been formally assessed recently, and it is by no means certain that she has an intellectual impairment to any real degree. Her parents are convinced that she is of normal intelligence.

Knowledge and understanding
Difficult to evaluate. Certainly able to indicate concrete knowledge, using flashcards (show me the ...) though abstracts (such as time) she finds difficult. Generally, parents and helpers feel that Valerie understands most of what she experiences and seems more limited by her ability to communicate her ideas and understanding.

Language and self-expression
Valerie is unable to speak or to use signs other than in a broad gestural way. She recognises twenty-five words of social sight vocabulary and is beginning to recognise words in books. She will make sounds to gain attention and then uses eye-pointing to communicate, looking up and to the right for 'yes' and down for 'no'. She is learning to use a computer and has managed simple word processing, though this is slow because of her difficulty with fine motor control and the delay in finding appropriate switching. She appears able to understand most of what is said to her and responds appropriately, though, in practice, most of this is confined to concrete and immediate issues (eg. 'do you want?').

Formal and informal support networks
A speech and language therapist visits Valerie at the Centre about every six months.

Healthy behaviours and relationships: *Enjoying leisure*

Valerie's friends are almost exclusively drawn from people that she meets at the day centre and at the Gateway Club, which owns a minibus for the transport of its members. Her parents do not drive and find it almost impossible to take her to social activities that are more than a short walk away. Valerie enjoys almost any kind of social activity, including music, cinema and the theatre. Her keyworker at the centre sings and plays guitar and will sometimes play for Valerie, who says that this is one of her favourite times at the Centre.

⌘ Second level analysis

Musculoskeletal system
Valerie's opportunities to use leisure time are limited by her dependence on others for mobility.

Pleasure and gratification
Valerie finds it difficult to control her own sources of pleasure. She likes to be fashionably dressed and well groomed. She enjoys the company of friends and especially enjoys live and recorded music (mostly jazz, folk and classical).

Motivation
Valerie is strongly motivated to do the things that she enjoys and will make great physical and mental effort to overcome her disabilities.

Mood
Valerie is generally happy and contented, although she sometimes seems down or irritable, especially when menstruating.

Anxiety and confidence
Valerie is generally quite confident and keen to try new experiences.

Socioeconomic status, financial status and stability
Valerie's father is a farm worker, earning relatively low wages and they live in a small village in a tied cottage. Mrs Bradley does not work although she did, unsuccessfully, try some part-time work a number of years ago. The family does not have much disposable income to pay for leisure activities. Valerie claims Disability Living Allowance, which goes some way toward offsetting travel and extra living costs.

Healthy behaviours and relationships: *Working and occupation*

Valerie attends Shakespeare Road Centre every day and travels by social services transport. Staff say that activities at the centre tend to be rather passive because of her physical disability, but she likes to take part in craft and music activities and anything which involves being in a group, and will do her best to complete activities to the best of her ability. Valerie says that she likes going to the Centre but sometimes gets bored. Her intellectual disability has never been satisfactorily assessed and her parents are convinced that she understands far more than she is able to express. The centre has a number of computers, which Valerie may find more intellectually stimulating, but there has been difficulty in finding a switching system which gives her sufficient control over their functions.

✻ Second level analysis

Musculoskeletal system

Valerie's ability to take part in activities and to use equipment in sessions at the Centre is limited by her cerebral palsy and consequent mobility difficulties. There is not much adapted equipment available that Valerie can use.

Language and self-expression

Valerie is able to use signs in a broad gestural way. She recognises twenty-five words of social sight vocabulary and is beginning to recognise words in books. She will make sounds to gain attention and then uses eye-pointing to communicate, looking up and to the right for 'yes' and down for 'no'. She is learning to use a computer and has managed simple word processing, though this is slow because of her difficulty with fine motor control and the delay in finding appropriate switching. She appears able to understand most of what is said to her and responds appropriately, though, in practice, most of this is confined to concrete and immediate issues (eg. 'do you want?').

Motivation

Valerie is strongly motivated to do the things that she enjoys and will make great physical and mental effort to overcome her disabilities.

Mood

Valerie is generally happy and contented, though she sometimes seems down or irritable, especially when menstruating.

Anxiety and confidence

Valerie is generally quite confident and keen to try new experiences.

Cognitive developmental maturity

Valerie appears to be operating at least at the pre-operational stage in that she is able to use some symbols for communication and to use basic rules for problem solving.

Learning, attention and consciousness

Valerie is generally alert and able to interact with enthusiasm. She is limited by her communicative and motor abilities but, given the right means, is able to learn quite fast. She is able to concentrate on, for instance, a computer-mediated task for up to an hour.

Problem solving

Valerie is able to solve problems in computer-mediated tasks up to a seven-year level, but further development in 'real life' is difficult to test due to difficulties with switching and this is a new area of learning for her.

Memory

Valerie's memory appears good when she is able to communicate this.

Healthy behaviours and relationships: *Maintaining bodily health and equilibrium*

Valerie's main bodily health issues are:

- She has tonic-clonic epilepsy and has an average of four seizures per month, usually in early morning. Her epilepsy appears to be well-controlled by Sodium Valproate and by the prevention of constipation.
- In winter time, Valerie can readily develop chest infections, which are treated by the use of antibiotics.
- Valerie appears very thin: this has been usual since childhood and seems to be accepted by her parents as 'just the way she is'.
- Valerie's impaired movement and contractures are becoming steadily worse. These and her spasm cause her increasing discomfort.
- Valerie easily develops inflamed areas on her sacrum.

⌘   Second level analysis

Physical maturity and growth
Height: 1.6 Mtr; weight: 31.8 Kg; BMI: 12.4; aged thirty-five
A lifetime history of delayed growth and development associated with her diagnosis of quadruplegic cerebral palsy. Fully developed as a woman, with all secondary sexual characteristics and began menstruating at the age of fourteen.

Gastrointestinal system
Valerie has a high arched hard palate and experiences bite reflex (marked), tongue thrust (marked), dysphagia (severe), poor lip closure (mild).

Musculoskeletal system
Quadruplegic cerebral palsy with onset of contractures and cogwheel rigidity. Limited ability to change body position.

Neurological system
Valerie experiences tonic-clonic epilepsy, averaging four seizures per month: this has been stable for at least the past ten years.

Endocrine system
No known abnormalities.

Reproductive system
Menstruation irregular and flow sometimes heavy. Valerie frequently experiences abdominal pain at menstruation.

Breathing system
Breathing rate irregular, due to spasm. Volume of breathing shallow (difficult to measure accurately). There is a history of frequent chest infection and high risk of further infections due to hypostasis or inhalation of food particles.

Circulatory system

Normal resting pulse: 70; Normal resting BP: 130/80. Heart sounds appear healthy. Peripheral circulation a little poor — Valerie often has cold extremities and appears to feel the cold. Blood cells are normal but should be checked regularly in case of side-effect from medication.

Systems for body equilibrium

All appear stable, though chest infections can develop rapidly. Possible difficulty in maintaining body temperature.

Skin and integumentary system

Skin generally healthy. No pressure sores have developed yet though reddened areas on sacrum are common and risk factors for pressure sores are very high (Waterlow score 21 = high risk). (For a more complete explanation of the Waterlow assessment see Waterlow, 1991 and 1994.)

Effects of medication on physical processes

Currently receives Sodium Valproate 200mg X 3 daily. Potential side-effects on GI and blood: none currently observed. Antibiotics prescribed only in response to chest infection. No known allergies or sensitivities.

Difficulties and problems

Name: Valerie Bradley   **Date:**

	What is the difficulty (long-term goal)	Planned outcome	Action to be taken plan	Type of care achieved	Date
1	Valerie is underweight (BMI 12.4) (BMI 12.4)	V will achieve a weight of 76 kg	Liaise with dietitian to develop a suitable weight gain diet. Ensure that adequate time and effort is taken to provide intake	Health promotion	
2	Valerie is at risk of choking during mealtimes, due to dysphagia	V will develop functional swallowing	Liaise with speech and language therapist to develop a care plan to develop functional swallowing	Developmental	
		V will be free from choking at mealtimes	Use appropriate techniques to prevent choking	Maintenance	
3	Valerie's parents are finding it too difficult to care for her at home and the house is unsuitable	V will be housed in acceptable alternative accommodation	Liaise with care manager to investigate options for accommodation	Exploration	
4	Valerie experiences bite reflex, tongue thrust and poor lip closure	V will be free from bite reflex and tongue-thrust, and achieve lip closure	Liaise with speech and language therapist to devise exercises to decrease dysfunction and promote orthofunction	Developmental	
5	Valerie experiences discomfort due to whole body spasm	V will be free from discomfort due to body spasm	Refer to GP for possible medication. Develop a care plan to promote bodily relaxation	Referral Therapeutic	
6	Valerie has some contractures. Elbows extend to 135 and knees to 120	V will extend her elbows to at least least 160 amd knees to at least 145	Liaise with physiotherapist to develop an exercise programme aimed at promoting extension of limbs	Health promotion	
7	Valerie has shallow and irregular breathing, with high risk of chest infections	V will breathe deeply for at least five minutes every day	Liaise with physiotherapist to develop breathing exercises aimed at promoting deep breathing	Health promotion	
8	Valerie is at high risk of pressure sores (Waterlow 21)	V will be free from pressure sores	Reduce risk factors by: promoting movement and change of position; attention to hygiene; physical health	Maintenance	
9	Valerie has difficulty in balance, maintaining midline sitting	V will achieve balanced midline sitting	Liaise with physiotherapist and occupational therapist to investigate better seating and positioning	Exploration	
10	Valerie is incontinent of urine and faeces	Investigations will be made into better ways to manage V's incontinence	Liaise with incontinence advisor re. possible aids	Exploration	
			Investigate possibilities of continence training	Exploration	
11	Valerie's communication skills are limited by her physical disability	V will achieve an effective means of communication	Liaise with speech and language therapist re. possible communication aids	Referral/Exploration	

115

Difficulties and problems cont.

	What is the difficulty (long-term goal)	Planned outcome	Action to be taken plan	Type of care achieved	Date
12	Valerie requires full help with personal hygiene	V will be able to help with personal hygiene	Investigate ways in which V could be more involved in her personal hygiene	Exploration	
13	Valerie finds it difficult to control her own sources of pleasure	V will be able to control at least one source of pleasure	Liaise with key worker and V to investigate how she might use more choice and control	Exploration	
14	Valerie finds it difficult to express her emotions	V will be able to express her emotions	Liaise with speech and language therapist to investigate how V might develop more emotion-related signs or symbols	Referral/ exploration	
15	Valerie has difficulty hearing quiet speech and other sounds	Speech and important sounds will be presented so that V can hear them	Liaise with speech and language therapist to develop a strategy for more effective communication with V	Care summary	
16	Valerie requires full help with dressing and grooming	V will be able to help with dressing and grooming	Investigate ways in which V could be more involved with dressing and grooming	Exploration	
17	Valerie experiences constipation	V will be free from constipation	Use a combination of dietary, pharmacological and exercise strategies to promote colonic mobility	Maintenance	
18	Valerie has 4 tonic-clonic seizures per month	V will have less than 4 seizures per month	Investigate trigger factors with a view to preventing them	Exploration	
19	Valerie is unable to protect herself from physical dangers	V's safety will be maintained	Ensure that V is not placed in positions of risk and that positioning and seating are always safe	Care summary	
20	Valerie has a possible lower visual field defect	Objective data will be gained regarding V's visual field	Refer to opthalmologist for testing	Referral	
21	Valerie has a possible high frequency hearing loss	Objective data will be gained regarding V's current hearing status	Refer to hearing clinic for audiometry	Referral	
22	Valerie has a limited social life outside day centre activities	V will be able to access a social activity of her choice at least once per week	Liaise with V, parents and key worker to choose an accessible activity Investigate leisure link volunteer	Exploration	
23	Valerie's development status (intellectual impairment) is under question	Objective data will be gained regarding V's degree of intellectual impairment	Refer to psychologist for developmental testing	Referral	
24	Valerie experiences abdominal pain during menstruation	V will be free from abdominal pain during menstruation	Liaise with GP to investigate possible medication Investigate massage and aromatherapy	Referral\ Exploration	
25	Little is known about Valerie's self-esteem and level of satisfaction with her life	V will have means of communicating her degree of satisfaction with herself and her life	Liaise with V, her parents and key worker to develop life story work, in which she can be encouraged to express these issues	Exploration	
26	Valerie occasionally experiences UTIs	V will be free from UTIs	Prevent UTIs by attention to personal hygiene	Care summary	

Strengths

Name: Valerie Bradley   **Date:**

Physical resources

- Valerie is learning to use switches to control a computer
- Valerie is able to move about on the floor
- Valerie is able to relax when in a warm environment, such as hydrotherapy or bath

Cognitive resources

- Valerie is able to use symbols and eye pointing for communication. She recognises twenty-five words of social sight vocabulary and is learning to recognise words in books
- Valerie is alert and able to interact with enthusiasm, motivation often strong
- Valerie is able to concentrate on a task for up to an hour
- Valerie's memory is good
- Valerie has understanding of right and wrong

Emotional resources

- Valerie enjoys the company of others and enjoys live and recorded music
- Valerie is able to give and receive affection

Self as a resource

- Valerie appears to have a good sense of self-awareness, takes interest in her appearance and likes to be fashionably dressed and to use make-up
- Valerie is generally happy and contented

Social resources

- Valerie has a strong relationship with both parents
- Valerie has a number of friends, both in her village and at her day centre

Care summary

Client's name: Valerie Bradley

Eating and drinking

- Valerie has great difficulty with eating and drinking, see care plans for 1. weight gain, 2. swallowing and 3. bite reflex, etc
- Care needs to be taken that Valerie does not choke at mealtimes (see maintenance care plan)
- Eating and drinking take a long time and need to be persisted with gently
- Valerie prefers sweet foods
- Valerie is underweight. If she has not had a good meal, a food supplement may be offered

Moving and mobilising

- Valerie is a wheelchair user and has spastic cerebral palsy. She has some degree of contractures and cogwheel rigidity. Care needs to be taken not to over-extend limbs when dressing and undressing. The cogwheel effect can be overcome by extending her limbs in gentle stages, rather than in one go
- Valerie has difficulty in maintaining balance when sitting and needs wedges to help with positioning
- Valerie needs plenty of opportunity to move around out of her wheelchair to help her maintain mobility, prevent constipation and prevent pressure sores. She should be given the opportunity to get out of her wheelchair at least three times during the day
- See exercise care plan

Maintaining personal hygiene

- At the moment, Valerie needs full help with personal hygiene, but can be encouraged to do what she feels able to. She is doubly incontinent and therefore special care is needed with cleanliness in this area
- Valerie has some problems with constipation. She is able to indicate if she is feeling uncomfortable and at this point a micro-enema is usually given

Dressing and grooming

- At the moment, Valerie needs full help with dressing and grooming but is able to indicate her preferences. She will tell you what she wants to wear and how she wants her hair and can be encouraged to help with dressing and grooming as much as she feels able to
- Due to Valerie's contractures and cogwheel rigidity, care needs to be taken when putting limbs into garments. Straighten her arms and legs slowly — do not force them

Sleeping and resting

- Valerie finds it difficult to get comfortable and settle at night. She does not sleep in any particular position but will tell you when she is comfortable
- Ensure that the bed rail is raised once Valerie is in bed

Care summary cont

Ensuring own and others' safety

- Valerie is not able to protect herself from dangers and therefore is vulnerable
- Valerie is at risk of choking at mealtimes (see care plan)
- When seating Valerie in her wheelchair ensure that her lap belt is secured
- Valerie has epilepsy and has been known to have seizures in the bath and swimming pool

Perceiving and responding

- Valerie is longsighted, wears spectacles and has a squint. Careful positioning of objects is needed so that she can see them properly. It is thought that she may also have difficulty in seeing objects where she needs to look down
- Valerie also has some hearing loss in both ears. She can hear provided that the sound is nearby and reasonably loud (about the level of a slightly raised voice). It is possible that she may not hear high-pitched sounds as clearly as low-pitched sounds. Valerie wears aids in both ears. When fitting them in the morning check that they are functioning properly and that they are comfortably and properly located in the correct ear.

Making and maintaining relationships

- Valerie enjoys peoples' company and knows quite a number of people at the day centre and in her village. She appreciates opportunities to spend time with her friends
- When Valerie moves into full-time care it will be especially important that she will be able to keep up her friendships and family relationships

Expressing self and sexuality

- Valerie is aware of her sexuality and likes to look attractive
- She would like a boyfriend but does not have much opportunity at the moment

Communicating and self-determining

- Valerie is able to communicate by eye pointing and will make sounds to gain your attention. She looks up and to the right ('one o'clock position') for 'yes' and down ('six o'clock position) for 'no'. She can hear what you say, provided that you speak clearly, slowly and with a slightly raised voice. There is no need to shout
- You should assume that Valerie understands everything that you say, unless she appears puzzled
- Valerie needs the opportunity to use a variety of communication skills. She can read some words in the social sight vocabulary and is learning to use a computer keyboard
- Valerie is able to express choices and should be offered alternatives at all times

Enjoying leisure

- Valerie enjoys social activities, music, theatre and cinema on a full-time basis
- She especially enjoys modern jazz and likes to listen to music when she is relaxing. She will tell you which CD to play

---

Care summary cont

Working and occupation

- Valerie attends Shakespeare Road day centre on a full-time basis
- Most of her activities are developmental rather than work-oriented at this stage

Maintaining bodily health and equilibrium

- Valerie has about 4 tonic-clonic seizures per month. Care needs to be taken that she will not be in danger if she has a seizure
- Valerie's breathing is shallow and she can develop chest infections very quickly in winter. If she appears wheezy her GP should be called (see care plan for breathing exercises)
- Valerie's body mass index is very low. Weight should be recorded on the first of every month. Care and gentle persistence is needed for her to gain weight
- Valerie experiences discomfort because of her contractures and spasm. Gentle massage helps her to relax (see care plan)
- Valerie is at high risk of pressure sores. She needs great care with personal hygiene and the opportunity to move about and to get out of her wheelchair. Make sure that she is able to change her position frequently

---

Maintenance care plan

Client's name: Valerie Bradley   **Date set:**

Client difficulty or problem   **Evaluation date:**
Valerie is at risk of choking at mealtimes due to dysphagia

The outcome for this care plan
Valerie will be free from choking at mealtimes

How to meet this difficulty or problem

- Valerie usually has her meals sitting in her wheelchair. Ensure that she is sitting upright, with her bottom well back and knees as close to a right angle as possible
- Solid foods should be mashed to the consistency of 'grain or wheat', but not liquidised
- Use a small polycarbonate spoon for both main course and dessert
- Hot meals are placed in a heated dish, as they may go cold during the meal. Meals may be reheated once only in the microwave oven
- When helping Valerie with meals, sit at her level, facing her. She likes people to chat to her during mealtimes as it helps her to relax. Give her time to reply, rather than rushing ahead with the meal. Valerie's meals may take more than an hour and it is important that she persists, so that she gains sufficient nutrition. Give her time to swallow and then check if she would like more
- Valerie is best able to swallow if she is looking ahead and with her head at an approximate right angle. You may need to help her to correct this by gently supporting the top of her head with the palm of your hand

Maintenance care plan cont

- Offer Valerie a drink before her meal (usually she likes a few sips). If she says 'yes' by eye pointing, find out what kind of drink she would like and give her a small amount of her drink from a spouted cup. Give her time to swallow and then check if she would like more
- Ask Valerie is she is ready to take her meal. If she answers 'yes' by eye-pointing give her a small mouthful at a time, placing the spoonful towards the back of her tongue and pressing gently downwards
- Withdraw the spoon carefully and help Valerie to maintain her head in the correct position
- Allow Valerie to swallow each mouthful before offering the next
- Offer frequent sips of liquid to help her to clear her mouth

If Valerie chokes

1. If minor help her to keep her head up
2. If still choking, try a firm pat on the back
3. If the above fails summon assistance, flex her waist to position her head below her knees and repeat stage 2. You may need to remove her from her wheelchair to do this. Check with your fingers to see if there is food that may be removed from the back of her throat
4. If the above fails use Heimlich manoeuvre and/or suction. Summon qualified help or on-call

Evidence or rationale for the method

Correct positioning and pacing of mouthfuls obviates the majority of problems with dysphagia. Sources:

- advice from speech and language therapist
- 'Swallowing problems' — how to help'. Accessed from http://dementia.ion.ucl.ac.uk

Conclusion

Valerie's case example demonstrates how a detailed picture of a person's difficulties can be built up using a systematic approach. Using this information we can then build up a system of support around the individual that centres on the person and uses their network of support in a co-ordinated way. Valerie's needs are extensive and complex and at times it is difficult to differentiate between her needs and those of her mother and father. Valerie does have the communication and self-determination skills to contribute to and to decide on her care priorities, although she clearly needs support to participate fully. It was essential that the process of assessment and care planning was transparent to her and that she was enabled to make her contribution. Clients can contribute to their own care planning process in the following ways:

⌘ By giving assessment information to the nurse and checking the accuracy of assessments. Clients have the right to know what their assessment says about them.

⌘ By helping to decide on their problems and the priority of those problems. Only the client can really make these decisions.

⌘ By knowing about helping to develop and approving their care plans. The Department of Health (2001b) comments that, 'before you examine, treat or care for competent adults you must obtain their consent'. Clearly, there are difficulties in obtaining informed consent from adults who are deemed not competent but there are many ways of orienting individuals' care around their needs.

⌘ By helping to evaluate both the process and outcomes of care plans. Clients will know if they are happy with the way in which they are cared and have many ways to tell us.

If decision-making takes place in an atmosphere of true partnership then a truly person-centred and effective service can be developed that meets clients' needs as they see them. Clearly, people who have severe and complex learning disabilities will have difficulty in taking a full part in care planning processes and will need imaginative and sensitive support. We will arguably move closer to person-centred planning by using the following approaches:

⌘ Check and re-check that what we propose for the individual is really in their best interests.

⌘ Develop empathy with the individual so that we try to understand their world from their own perspective. A useful exercise when clients have no means of communication is for us to write in the first person what we think the client might want to tell us about their care. Some caution is needed, however, as we have no means of checking the accuracy of what we have written.

⌘ Use language and processes that individuals are likely to be able to understand and relate to. We may have to tailor our approach to each and every individual.

⌘ Use communication aids, visual aids, pictures, photographs, sequencing boards.

⌘ Use enhanced and extended communication skills that make optimum use of clients' communicative abilities. This may involve 'tuning in', developing sensitivity, reading body language skilfully, giving clients time and opportunity to respond.

⌘ Changing attitudes toward client involvement. What we need is a belief that involvement is not only desirable but also possible. The statement, 'oh, but James won't be able to take part' is no longer good enough. The possibilities are limited only by our imagination and skills.

This chapter has been able only briefly to explore the Ecology of Health model and its use. The model has been in development over a number of years and the ideas and concepts have evolved in discussion with practitioners and students. The model has been used in primary and secondary care sectors across the country and has been used to coordinate the care of individuals across home, day care and short-term care services. There is further material that would help practitioners in the use of the model that can be obtained by contacting the author on: john.aldridge@northampton.ac.uk

References

Brigham L (1998) Representing the lives of women with learning difficulties: ethical dilemmas in the research process. *Br J Learning Disability* **28**: 146–50

Bronfenbrenner U (1977) Toward an experimental ecology of human development. *Am Psychologist* **32**: 513–31

Bronfenbrenner U (1979) *The Ecology of Human Development: experiments by nature and design*. Harvard University Press, Cambridge

Christie M, Mellett P, eds (1986) *The Psychosomatic Approach: contemporary practice of whole-person care*. Wiley, Chichester

Department of Health (2001a) *Valuing People: A New Strategy for Learning Disability for the 21st Century*. DoH, London

Department of Health (2001b) *12 Key Points on Consent: the law in England*. DoH, London

Frost D, Taylor K (1986) This is my life. *Community Care* 7 August: 28–9

Hussain F, Racza R (1997) Life story work for people with learning disabilities. *Br J Learning Disability* **25**: 73–6

McCarthy M (1998) Interviewing people with learning disabilities about sensitive topics: a discussion of ethical issues. *Br J Learning Disability* **26**: 140–5

National Electronic Library for Health (2002) *Person Centred Planning*. National Electronic Library for Health, available online: http://minerva.minervation.com/ld/person/what.html

Nursing and Midwifery Council (2002) *Code of Professional Conduct*. NMC, London

Rolph S (1998) Ethical dilemmas in historical research with people with learning difficulties. *Br J Learning Disability* **26**: 135–9

Ryan T, Walker T (1993) *Life Story Work*. British Agencies for Adoption and Fostering, London

Waterlow JA (1991) A policy that protects. The Waterlow Pressure Sore Prevention/Treatment Policy. *Prof Nurse* Feb: 258–64

Waterlow JA (1994) *Pressure Sore Prevention Manual*. Available from Mrs JA Waterlow, Newtons, Curland, Taunton, TA3 5SG

9

Loss and bereavement

David Elliott

John thinks when we die we go to heaven and our heart turns into a star.
(Quote by a parent)

Life events such as loss and bereavement can have a profound impact on the lives of people with learning disabilities. This is supported by research, and recognised at a governmental level. Community learning disability nurses are in an ideal position to offer people support at this sensitive time in their lives. A case study was detailed highlighting how a bereaved person with learning disabilities benefited from bereavement support. The need for clinical supervision is discussed, and therapeutic outcomes noted.

During the lifetime of a person with learning disabilities, they will experience many losses including that of bereavement. These experiences are often life changing, and their impact has not always been recognised (Bonell-Pascual *et al*, 1999). How they cope and deal with them is often dependent on individual characteristics, support systems in place, and access to professional help if required (Read *et al*, 1999). Despite their impact, until fairly recently, loss and bereavement issues have received very little attention. Conboy-Hill (1992) suggests that this might be a consequence of negative Western attitudes around death and dying, and the assumption that people with disabilities will not understand what is going on at a cognitive or emotional level. In recent years this picture has started to change. Research is now being undertaken in this area, and services are attempting to address loss and bereavement needs of people with learning disabilities (Oswin, 1991; Hollins and Esterhuyzen, 1997; Read, 1996).

Loss and bereavement — a political context

Recent policy papers and Government guidelines written specifically about people with learning disabilities have highlighted the impact of loss and bereavement issues on their lives. In *The Health of the Nation: A Strategy for People with Learning Disabilities* (DoH, 1995) it states: 'Life events, such as bereavement... may therefore cause a person with learning disabilities to experience symptoms of stress reactions more readily than other people.' Similarly, in *Signposts for Success* (DoH, 1998) it states: 'People with learning disabilities may need help in coping with crisis and change such as that arising from... bereavement.' It also advocates the development of services for people with learning disabilities which would, 'help with dealing with loss, bereavement and abuse; coping with change and stress.'

Despite these positive statements, in *Once a Day* (DoH, 1999) it states that people with learning disabilities 'may be denied the opportunity to attend a family funeral or even to grieve.'

The recently published White Paper, *Valuing People: A New Strategy for Learning Disability for the 21st Century* (DoH, 2001) does not directly focus on loss and bereavement issues for people with learning disabilities. Indirectly, it states that most people with learning disabilities live with their families, and only 'leave the family home as a result of a crisis such as the illness or death of a carer' (*Ibid*, 2001). Loss issues will become particularly pertinent at this time in the person's life, as they prepare to move into residential services.

Overview of research undertaken

Research has highlighted the significant and profound affect that loss, including bereavement, has on the lives of people with learning disabilities (Oswin, 1991; Marston and Clarke, 1999). In a study by Hollins and Esterhuyzen (1997), they found that people with learning disabilities who have experienced a parental bereavement are more likely to exhibit aberrant behaviour, and an increase in psychopathology compared to a group of non-bereaved people with learning disabilities. In a follow-up study, Bonell-Pascual *et al* (1999) concluded that having a learning disability 'is a significant predictor of mental health problems following bereavement.' They also noted, 'that the response to bereavement by adults with learning disabilities is similar in type, though not in expression, to that of the general population'. The findings from these two studies mirror in part the findings from an earlier study by Emerson (1977).

According to research, a variety of interventions (both individual and group work) can be utilised to support a person following a loss, including that of bereavement (Cathcart, 1995). They include guided mourning (Kitching, 1987), a behavioural cognitive intervention (Mansdorf and Ben-David, 1986), cognitive therapy (Lindsay *et al*, 1993), bereavement counselling (Elliott, 1995) and group work (Persaud and Persaud, 1997).

In addition, when working with bereaved people with learning disabilities, research has indicated creative and imaginative approaches need to be utilised (Read *et al*, 1999). These include the use of family trees, artwork, life story work, drama, poetry and specially prepared materials (for example, Hollins and Sireling, 1989; Cathcart, 1994).

The contribution made by community learning disability nurses

The community learning disability nurse is in an ideal position to support people with learning disabilities who have experienced loss and bereavement. The support they offer will be dependent upon their qualifications and level of expertise (Elliott, 1999). They can undertake the initial loss/bereavement assessment. This will involve obtaining a loss history of the bereaved individual (number and types of loss), communication needs, the person's understanding and level of participation in events surrounding the bereavement, and an indication of how they are presently coping (O'Driscoll, 1999). Follow-up support offered by the community learning disability nurse might range from facilitating the grieving process (Read, 1999) to bereavement counselling (Elliott, 1995). The support given will be dependent upon the bereaved person's individual needs and wishes.

In addition, the community learning disability nurse can ensure that the following protective issues are implemented (*Box 9.1*). Protective factors help to ensure that the person with learning disabilities experiences positive mental health (Hardy and Bouras, 2002), and a healthy bereavement (Faulkner, 1993).

Box 9.1: Possible protective bereavement factors for people with learning disabilities

⌘ Encourage adequate nutrition and sleep (Hardy and Bouras, 2002).

⌘ Preparation before the death (if appropriate, Dowling and Hollins, 2003).

⌘ Give the person a choice whether they wish to participate in rituals associated with their bereavement, and ensure that they receive appropriate support to do so (for example, attending the funeral or memorial service) (Read, 1999).

⌘ Give consideration to the cultural and religious beliefs of the bereaved individual (Cathcart, 1995).

⌘ Make time to be with, and listen to the bereaved person with learning disabilities.

⌘ Ensure continuity in a person's life following a bereavement, avoiding any major lifestyle changes (Hollins, 1995).

⌘ Encourage the development of valuing positive relationships/support networks.

⌘ Ensure that the person accesses appropriate bereavement support if required.

Loss issues, including those of bereavement, can be highlighted and addressed in the context of a person-centred plan and health action plan. Community learning disability nurses in their role as health facilitators are in an ideal position to identify and meet these needs as delineated in *Valuing People: A New Strategy for Learning Disability for the 21st Century* (DoH, 2001).

Loss and grief

When considering offering support to people with learning disabilities who have experienced a loss including bereavement, it is important to keep in mind the types of loss they have experienced. Two types of loss they are likely to experience during their lifetime are multiple losses and successive losses (Lendrum and Symes, 1992). A multiple loss might involve losing a few close friends or the loss of one individual, for example, a parent. When a parent dies, the person with learning disabilities might have lost their main carer, best friend and confidante. Successive losses (Lendrum and Syme, 1992) occur when a person with learning disabilities moves from their parental home to residential care, possibly as a result of parental bereavement. They lose their family home, contact with friends and neighbours, and place of work or day time occupation.

Following a loss, including bereavement, a person with learning disabilities will often exhibit either one of two types of grief reactions. They are normal or uncomplicated grief reactions (for example, anger, sadness, appetite disturbance, disbelief) (Worden, 1991). Alternatively, a person will experience abnormal or complicated grief reactions (for example, chronic, exaggerated, delayed or masked grief reactions) (Worden, 1991).

The type of loss and impact upon the person with learning disabilities, will help determine the support and help they require.

Conceptual frameworks

Two theories which are useful in illuminating issues and needs of people with learning disabilities who have experienced a loss, including bereavement, are family systems theory (Rosenblatt, 1993; Jacques, 1998), and psychosocial transitional theory (Parkes, 1971a).

Family systems theory recognises the interdependency of each family member, in relation to their physical, social and emotional well being (McGoldrick and Gerson, 1985; Jacques, 1998). When a family member dies, this can have a catastrophic effect on the surviving family members, especially a person with learning disabilities. This is particularly the case if the deceased person helped to meet most of the needs of the bereaved person with learning disabilities, when they were alive (Rosenblatt, 1993).

Psychosocial transitional theory (Parkes, 1971; 1993) is a useful model to help explain bereaved people with learning disabilities reactions to their loss. According to Parkes (1971; 1993), psychosocial transitions occur over a short time span and result in a person rethinking their thoughts and beliefs about their immediate world. For example, a bereaved person with learning disabilities might wonder who is going to help them now that their mother has died, and how are they going to cope without her? In addition, the impact of a psychosocial transition endures and is not short-lived. It is associated with a great deal of distress, and can be linked to the development of mental health problems (Parkes, 1993; Rahe, 1979). For these reasons, Parkes (1993) advocates appropriate counselling and support for people who have experienced a psychosocial transition.

It is very understandable from these two perspectives why losses and bereavement have a profound effect on the emotional lives of people with learning disabilities.

A case study

The following is a case study of a person I supported, following a bereavement he had experienced. Certain biographical details have been changed in order to preserve the person's anonymity.

Biographical details

John presently lives at home with his elderly father. His mother died a couple of years ago from cancer. John's brother Tom, lives in a nearby village with his wife. John has cerebral palsy and receives a great deal of support from his father and brother Tom. He is able to make his needs known. He presently attends a day service for people with learning disabilities, twice a week. I received a request to offer John bereavement support, following a review meeting held on him, at the day service.

Undertaking the assessment

After informing John's general practitioner of the request to offer him bereavement support, I met with him and his brother Tom, at Tom's house. I informed John that I would like to offer him support following his bereavement.

He gave me his permission and consent to do so. Process consent as outlined by Read (2001) was used throughout the bereavement sessions.

I then undertook a bereavement assessment on John (see *Appendix III*, for an assessment tool), with support from Tom. The aim of the assessment was to obtain a 'snapshot' of John and his bereavement needs, and useful background information in relation to these needs. It is important to point out that the assessment undertaken was not diagnostic in nature. Areas covered by the assessment included: John's personal history; cultural/religious beliefs which may need to be taken into account; nature of the death (ie. was it a natural death, accidental death, suicide or murder [Worden, 1991]); did John participate in events surrounding the death; his present health status; what help is considered necessary; and where John is in the grieving cycle (Worden, 1991).

A plan of action

On the basis of the assessment, we developed a plan of action. It was agreed that I would undertake bereavement support, with help from Tom. I would visit John and Tom, at Tom's house, on a fortnightly basis. The framework of helping I would use would be based on Worden's (1991) task model of grief (*Box 9.2*). It would be used in a non-prescriptive way, and support would be geared to John's needs and undertaken at his pace. Built into the helping relationship, was the opportunity for John to terminate the bereavement support whenever he wished. It was envisaged that the bereavement support would last over a period of ten to fifteen sessions. In addition, it was anticipated that each session would last from half an hour to three quarters of an hour. This would be determined very much by John's wishes and needs.

Box 9.2: Worden's (1991) Task model of grief

- Accepting the reality of the loss
- Working through to the pain of grief
- Adjusting to live without the deceased
- Emotionally relocating the deceased and moving on with life

---

Focusing on John

Initially, when supporting John with help from Tom, I started to build a warm, positive and valuing relationship with him (*Figure 9.1*). I encouraged him to talk about himself, his interests and life generally.

In the following sessions we focused on significant people and places in John's life by using an ecogram and ecomap. Also sections of *My Story: A Celebration of My Life* (National Association of Bereavement Services [NABS], 1996) were used and photographs of John's family. John was encouraged to talk about his feelings toward them, and ways in which they helped him. He also mentioned his deceased mother at this time.

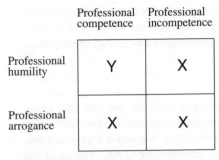

	Professional competence	Professional incompetence
Professional humility	Y	X
Professional arrogance	X	X

Figure 9.1: Qualities of an effective bereavement practitioner

Alive and death

During the following sessions we explored the concept of being alive, and death. In the case of being alive, the focus was very much on what a person can do when they are alive (ie. functional ability). For example, they can walk, talk, sleep, laugh and breathe. In the case of death, questions were based on Kane's (1979) components of the concept of death, as cited by Cathcart (1996) (*Box 9.3*). These were sensitively explored with John. John appeared to have a reasonable understanding of both these concepts.

Box 9.3: Components of the concept of death

- Realisation — that people die
- Separation — where is the deceased?
- Immobility — can a dead person move?
- Irrevocability — can a dead person come alive again, or is it a permanent state?
- Causality — how do people die?
- Dysfunctionality — what can a dead person do?
- Universality — do we all die?
- Insensitivity — can a dead person sense anything?
- Appearance — what does a dead person look like?
- Personification — how does the bereaved person see a dead person?

Source: Kane, 1979; Cathcart, 1996

Focusing on the death

In the next couple of sessions, with support from Tom, we focused on events surrounding the death of John's mother. She had died peacefully at home, and John, Tom and their father had been at her bed side. Although John did not attend the funeral, as it was not considered in his best interests to do so, John, with support from Tom, told me his story. John had very clear and vivid memories of events surrounding the death of his mother. Towards the end of the session, I narrated John's story, back to them both. The booklet *When Mother Died* (Hollins and Sireling, 1994), was used in the following session. John was encouraged to express his own thoughts and feelings in relation to the events detailed in the booklet, which he did.

Emotions

John was given an opportunity to ventilate his feelings, using specially prepared materials (Holland *et al*, 1998), during the next couple of sessions. The two feelings which we focused upon were sadness and happiness. John indicated feelings of sadness around the death of a pet dog, and the death of his mother. Memories of past holidays and birthdays were associated with feelings of happiness.

Successive losses

At this time in the bereavement support process, Tom told me that their father had been taken very ill, and had been admitted to hospital. Their father had decided that he could no longer care for John, and a residential placement was being sought. This imminent life change situation for John, highlights his powerlessness and lack of control in his destiny. I focused on these impending losses with John, during the next couple of sessions. I sensitively focused on their father's illness, and addressed an imminent move for John (a residential placement had been identified for him). I helped John focus on the positives and negatives in relation to this move. I also utilised the book *Peter's New House* (Hollins and Hutchinson, 1993) to help John reflect on his feelings regarding the move.

John's life now

Following on from these sessions, I focused on John's life now, with support from Tom. Places and people who are meaningful to John, were highlighted. In addition, recent achievements made by John were acknowledged. By focusing on the present, I was able to gauge how John was coping in relation to the sad loss of his mother. Tom, in particular, was surprised to find out how well John was coping.

Reminiscing about mother

During the next session, John was encouraged to reminisce about his mother. This was facilitated by showing me a photograph of her. Also by showing me photographs of a family holiday John, Tom and his parents went on. We focused on this holiday, and the emotions evoked by the photographs. The reminiscent session was guided by the work of Stuart (1977), and was particularly influenced by her notion of the 'pleasure' function of reminiscence.

Towards the end of the session, I told John that I would be seeing him on a couple of occasions, as we were nearing the end of the bereavement support process. I felt it was important to prepare John in a sensitive way, for the ending of my involvement with him.

John's support networks

In the next session I focused on John's support networks. Tom helped identify all the people who cared about John. Also, the input they had in John's life. It was envisaged these people would continue to be able to offer John support, even after his move from his home.

Saying goodbye

In the final session, I recapped with John the areas we had covered. I also helped him look forward to the future. Before saying goodbye to John, he said that he felt I had helped him cope with his losses, and that he had enjoyed the bereavement support he had received. Tom said he thought that John had benefited from my input. He felt that John would be able to handle future losses more effectively in the future, and that he would feel more confident supporting John through them.

Clinical supervision

It is essential that all practitioners who undertake bereavement support for a person with learning disabilities receive appropriate clinical supervision. This is because of the challenges associated with offering this support (*Box 9.4*; Worden, 1991). This supervision should be offered by a more experienced practitioner. A useful bereavement supervision model is the three function interaction model of supervision postulated by Proctor (1988). The three functions of supervision she has identified are the restorative, normative and formative functions (Proctor, 1988).

> **Box 9.4: Challenges when supporting a bereaved person with learning disabilities (Worden, 1991)**
>
> - Coping with one's own anger and frustration which originates from a personal sense of helplessness
> - Empathic preparation in being able to respond positively to the bereaved person's pain
> - Dealing with a bereaved person's discomfort
> - Awareness of own losses
> - Awareness of feared losses
> - Awareness of own mortality

The restorative function of supervision provides the practitioner a base where the feelings stirred up by grief work may be expressed, contained and reflected upon (Lendrum and Syme, 1992). In addition, during supervision, it might be recognised that a person might require a break or rest from grief work.

While the normative function is the quality control element of supervision (Faugier and Butterworth, 1992) it ensures that the practitioner is adhering to and maintaining practice that is of a sound ethical standard.

The third function identified by Proctor (1988) is the formative function. According to Faugier and Butterworth (1992) this is the educative process. It involves developing the skills, understanding and abilities of the practitioner offering bereavement support to the person with learning disabilities. This is achieved through reflection and exploration of the practitioner's work with clients in clinical supervision sessions (Faugier and Butterworth, 1992).

Conclusion

As outlined, loss issues, including bereavement, have a profound impact on the lives of people with learning disabilities. Despite this, as Wertheimer (1998) has indicated, 'we still have a long way to go in recognising that attachments and losses matter' in an emotional context as opposed to focusing on a person's functional ability. Through person-centred planning and health action plans (DoH, 2001), loss and bereavement needs can be both anticipated and identified. A plan of action can then be drawn up in collaboration with the person with learning disabilities, which can sensitively help to address these needs. The outcome of any planned intervention would be to:

- encourage the person to say a final goodbye, and allow the person to carry on living in a meaningful and positive way (Worden, 1991)
- increase the person's emotional well being and hopefully increase the person's self-esteem
- improve the quality of the person's life
- reduce ill health caused by mental illness (DoH, 1995).

By supporting the person with learning disabilities at this sensitive time in their life one is sharing their emotional pain, and helping them move on in a very positive sense. To achieve this successfully, community learning disability nurses need continually to develop and update their knowledge and skill base in this challenging and rewarding area.

References

Bonell-Pascual E, Huline-Dickens S, Hollins S *et al* (1999) Bereavement and grief in adults with learning disabilities. A follow-up study. *Br J Psychiatry* **175**: 348–50

Cathcart F (1994) *Understanding Death and Dying. Your Feelings*. The Cookley Printer Limited, Cookley, Kidderminster

Cathcart F (1995) Death and people with learning disabilities: Interventions to support clients and carers. *Br J Clin Psychol* **34**: 165–75

Cathcart F (1996) Death and people with learning disabilities: Interventions to support clients and carers (Part 1). *Bereavement Care* **15**(1): 7–9

Conboy-Hill S (1992) Grief, loss and people with learning disabilities. In: Waitman A, Conboy-Hill S, eds. *Psychotherapy and Mental Handicap*. Sage Publications Limited, London

Dent A (1996) *Bereavement care for families whose child had died suddenly and unexpectedly: A Bereavement Assessment Tool*. Bristol University, Bristol

Department of Health (1995) *The Health of the Nation. A Strategy for People with Learning Disabilities*. DoH, London

Department of Health (1998) *Signposts for Success in Commissioning and Providing Health Services for People with Learning Disabilities*. DoH, London

Department of Health (1999) *Once a day one or more people with learning disabilities are likely to be in contact with your primary health care team. How can you help them?* DoH, London

Department of Health (2001) *Valuing People: A New Strategy for Learning Disability for the 21st Century*. DoH, London

Dowling S, Hollins S (2003) Coping with bereavement: The dynamics of intervention. In: Davidson P, Prasher V, Janicki M, eds. *Mental Health, Intellectual Disabilities and the Aging Process*. Blackwell Publishing Limited, Oxford

Elliott D (1995) Helping people with learning disabilities to handle grief. *Nurs Times* 25 October 25: 26–9

Elliott D (1999) The role of the community learning disability nurse in supporting bereaved people with learning disabilities. *Lifeline* **25**: 10–12

Emerson P (1977) Covert grief reactions in mentally retarded clients. *Mental Retardation* **15**: 44–5

Faulkner M (1993) Promoting a healthy bereavement. *J Community Nurs* May: 18–22

Faugier J, Butterworth CA (1993) *Clinical Supervision: A Position Paper*. School of Nursing Studies, University of Manchester, Manchester

Hardy S, Bouras N (2002) The presentation and assessment of mental health problems in people with learning disabilities. *Learning Disability Practice* **5**(3): 33–8

Holland A, Payne A, Vickery L (1998) *Exploring Your Emotions*. British Institute of Learning Disabilities Publications, Plymouth

Hollins S (1995) Managing grief better: people with developmental disabilities. *Habilitative Mental Healthcare Newsletter* **14**(3)

Hollins S, Esterhuyzen A (1997) Bereavement and grief in adults with learning disabilities. *Br J Psychiatry* **170**: 497–501

Hollins S, Hutchinson D (1993) *Peter's New Home*. St. George's Hospital Medical School, London

Hollins S, Sireling L (1994) *When Dad Died*. St George's Medical School, London

Jacques R (1998) Families and disability in context: a systemic framework. In: Fraser W *et al*, eds. *The Care of People with Intellectual Disabilities*. Butterworth-Heinemann, Oxford

Kane B (1979) Children's concepts of death. *J Genet Psychol* **134**: 141–53

Kitching N (1987) Helping people with mental handicaps cope with bereavement. *Mental Handicap* **15**: 60–3

Lendrum S, Syme G (1992) *Gift of Tears*. Routledge, London

Lindsay W, Howells L, Pitcarthly D (1993) Cognitive therapy for depression with individuals with intellectual disabilities. *Br J Med Psychol* **66**: 135–41)

Mansdorf IJ, Ben-David N (1986) Operant and cognitive intervention to restore effective functioning following a death in a family. *Behav Ther Experimental Psychiatry* **17**: 193–6

Marston GM, Clarke D (1999) Making contact — bereavement and Asperger's Syndrome. *Ir J Psychological Med* **16**(1): 29–31

McGoldrick M, Gerson R (1985) *Genograms in Family Assessment*. Norton, New York

National Association of Bereavement Services (1996) *My Story: A Celebration of My Life*. DMP Productions, Cardiff

O'Driscoll D (1999) The six-week therapeutic assessment. In: Blackman N, ed. *Living with Loss: Helping people with learning disabilities cope with bereavement and loss*. Pavilion Publishing Limited, Brighton

Oswin M (1991) *Am I allowed to cry? A study of bereavement amongst people who have learning difficulties*. Souvenir Press Limited, London

Parkes C M (1971) Psychosocial transitions: A field for study. *Soc Sci Med* **5**: 101–15

Parkes CM (1993) Bereavement as a psychosocial transition: Processes of adaptation to change. In: Stroebe M, Stroebe W, Hansson R, eds. *Handbook of Bereavement Theory, Research and Intervention*. Cambridge University Press, Cambridge

Persaud S, Persaud M (1997) Does it hurt to die? *J Learning Disabilities for Nurs, Health and Soc Care* **1**(4): 171–5

Proctor B (1988) *Supervision: A Working Alliance* (videotape training manual). Alexia Publications, East Sussex

Rahe RH (1979) Life events, mental illness: An overview. *J Human Stress* **5**(3): 2–10

Read S (1996) How counselling services can help deal with loss and change. *Nurs Times* **92**(38): 40–1

Read S (1999) *Bereavement and People with Learning Disability*. Emap Healthcare Limited, London

Read S (1999) Creative ways of working when exploring the bereavement counselling process. In: Blackman N, ed. *Living with Loss: Helping people with learning disabilities cope with bereavement and loss*. Pavilion Publishing Limited, Brighton

Read S, Frost I, Messenger N, Oates S (1999) Bereavement counselling and support for people with a learning disability: Identifying issues and exploring possibilities. *Br J Learning Disabilities* **27**(3): 99–104

Read S (2001) A year in the life of a bereavement counselling and support service for people with learning disabilities. *Br J Learning Disabilities* **5**(1): 19–33

Rosenblatt P (1993) Grief: The social context of private feelings. In: Stroebe M, Stroebe W, Hansson R, eds. *Handbook of Bereavement Theory, Research and Intervention*. Cambridge University Press, Cambridge

Stuart M (1997) *Looking back, looking forward — reminiscence with people with learning disabilities*. Pavilion Publishing, Brighton

Wertheimer A (1998) *Attachment and loss in the lives of people with learning disabilities*. The Elfrida Society lectures, Elfrida Society, London

Worden WJ (1991) *Grief Counselling and Grief Therapy*. Tavistock/Routledge Publication, London

The following are useful world-wide web addresses:

www.nas.org.uk. (National Autistic Society)

www.learningdisabilities.org.uk. (The Foundation for People with Learning Disabilities, part of Mental Health Foundation)

www.bild.org.uk. (British Institute of Learning Disabilities)

10

Advocacy and empowerment

Steve McNally

This chapter reviews the concepts of advocacy and empowerment, and what they mean in the lives of people with learning disabilities, including implications for practitioners. Self-advocacy is considered as a route to, and expression of, empowerment. An initial theoretical overview explores the growth and influence of the concepts, particularly their potential application in achieving greater control for members of minority groups who are at risk of disadvantage in society. The policy context of empowerment and advocacy is considered. The subsequent practice section utilises original data from a research study which explored the work of self-advocacy groups for people with learning disabilities, initially through a postal survey and subsequently the conduct of interviews with self-advocacy groups. Research findings are used to illuminate professional practice. The issue of professionals supporting client self-empowerment and the challenges inherent in that process is explored. A concluding discussion of the future direction for advocacy and empowerment follows. Finally, resources for further study are included, along with editor's questions which are designed to encourage reflection and further development of empowering practice.

Advocacy

Advocacy is partly a device to influence the needs and rights of the group in favour of the needs and rights of individuals (Brandon, 1995). A basic definition of advocacy is speaking for oneself or on behalf of others. Self-advocacy, rather than advocacy by another, is regarded as the most effective form in relation to achieving a full citizenship role (Walmsley, 1993). It may be preceded by, or combined with, another type of advocacy, such as citizen advocacy (in which another person represents someone's rights and wishes as their own), but self-advocacy is ultimately the most effective kind of advocacy an individual can attain and practice in their daily life. Self-advocacy 'is, or should be, the ultimate goal of all other forms of advocacy' (Atkinson, 1999: 6). Self-advocacy is about people speaking for themselves and asserting their own rights, individually and in groups which share a common interest or face particular difficulties, eg. stigma. It has been an important and influential idea for two decades, especially in services for people with learning disabilities.

Self-advocacy

Self-advocacy is a multi-dimensional phenomenon that connects with related concepts such as autonomy, rights and choice. It can be characterised as a route to, and expression of, empowerment. It happens at different levels and in varying contexts, involving individuals, small groups or collective action by members of disadvantaged minorities. Self-advocacy is concerned with changing things in a way which is desired. Like empowerment, self-advocacy is not a simple concept. The term self-advocacy is used in two distinct contexts. 'It can refer to a process of individual development (becoming more confident and assertive), or it can refer to the process by which groups of people get together and give voice to their common concerns' (Simons, 1992: 10). Self-advocacy has played an influential role in striving to achieve rights and equality for people who are in danger of being disadvantaged or marginalised in society.

People with learning disabilities, and survivors of the mental health system are minorities associated with asserting their rights as citizens through the practice of self-advocacy. However, self-advocacy should be seen as more than a strategy for asserting rights. It seems clear that self-advocacy has become, as Atkinson (1999) has observed, a social movement with the potential to influence policy and practice. Benefits of self-advocacy may occur at an individual level, for example, gains in self-esteem, confidence, assertiveness, and self-expression. The self-advocacy movement appears to have the potential to promote individual gains in these skills (Williams and Shoultz, 1982).

The concept of self-advocacy has gained prominence in recent years. It is a device which is particularly apposite for use by people who are disadvantaged in society, or who are at risk of such disadvantage. Self-advocacy provides a strategy by means of which members of a potentially vulnerable group — for example, disabled people or users of mental health services — can redress this imbalance in society by securing their rights. Self-advocacy is associated with groups, different types with different objectives; for example, service-linked, independent. What groups have in common is the capacity to provide a supportive, empathic environment in which a person belongs and is valued. Groups offer the individual the opportunity to learn skills and to develop confidence.

People with a learning disability have described self-advocacy as 'sticking up for yourself' (Simons, 1992). Definitions of self-advocacy often refer to 'speaking up for yourself', 'standing up for your rights', 'taking action' and 'changing things' (Williams and Shoultz, 1982). The core components of self-advocacy have been identified by Clare (1990) as:

Being able to express thoughts and feelings with assertiveness if necessary; being able to make choices and decisions; having clear knowledge about rights; being able to make changes.

Any act of self-determination or choice can be seen as self-advocacy. Everyone can take part in self-advocacy at some level regardless of the severity of their disabilities (Crawley, 1988: 1). People with a severe learning disability can be and are involved in self-advocacy.

From its beginnings in Sweden in the 1960s to its growth in North America, the self-advocacy movement has developed rapidly in the UK in recent years. There is some empirical data which indicates an increase in the number of self-advocacy groups since the 1980s (Crawley, 1988; Whittaker, 1991). The number of groups in the UK was estimated at five hundred a decade ago (Simons, 1992). Subsequently, commentators have suggested that there has been a continued growth in groups numerically and in diversity of type within the past decade (Brandon, 1995; Ramcharan *et al*, 1996; Goodley, 2000).

Defining empowerment

The concepts of empowerment and autonomy are linked closely. Empowerment has several dimensions. There are questions around the extent to which it is about professionals sharing power with users. It has been suggested (Simons, 1992) that empowerment is concerned with users actively taking control.

Gibson (1991) defines empowerment as 'a social process of recognising, promoting and enhancing people's abilities to meet their own problems and mobilise the necessary resources in order to feel in control of their own life'. The concept of empowerment for service users and carers can be characterised both as a process and a goal. It is concerned with people having greater power to express their needs and to decide how these should be met (Parsloe and Stevenson, 1993). There is considerable debate in the literature on notions of empowerment and enablement and the differences between these related concepts (Jack, 1995). Another significant area of debate is the extent to which professionals and services can empower their users. The extent to which policy is being realised as practice at local and national levels is important here. People with learning disabilities from minority ethnic or cultural communities are at risk of dual discrimination (Baxter *et al*, 1990). The terms on which empowerment is offered by service providers has been identified as a major barrier for service users from these communities (Mir and Nocon, 2002).

Empowerment is easy to define in its absence (Rappaport,1984): powerlessness, real or imagined; learned helplessness; alienation; loss of a sense of control over one's life. Individuals may never have achieved power in their lives. Beresford and Croft (1993) use the following definition:

Making it possible for people to exercise power and have more control over their lives. This means having a greater voice in institutions, agencies and situations which affect them. It also means being able to share power or exercise power over someone else, as well as them exercising it over you.

Although the concept of empowerment is not well-defined, there is general agreement that it involves having a greater degree of control in one's life, including human services received. Recent legislation has been concerned with 'the empowerment of users and carers' (DoH, 1989: 4). The social model of disability (Oliver, 1996) offers a more empowering conceptual foundation than does the individual or 'personal tragedy' model which has dominated historically.

Theoretical perspectives

The policy context of empowerment

The incorporation of the European Convention on Human Rights (Human Rights Act, 1998) sends a clear egalitarian message. Article 14 states that, 'the rights and freedoms set forth in this Convention shall be secured without discrimination on any ground' (Annex — The Convention Rights: 6). While these rights had existed previously, the advantage of the Human Rights Act is that challenges can now be made in UK courts.

The recent Government White Paper *Valuing People: A New Strategy for Learning Disability for the 21st Century* (DoH, 2001) is a landmark, thirty years having passed since the previous White Paper concerned exclusively with the needs of people with a learning disability (*Better Services for the Mentally Handicapped*, 1971). It is a policy initiative with a clear emphasis on empowerment, as its declared 'key principles' of rights, independence, choice and inclusion indicate. *Valuing People* contains a Government objective of promoting more choice and control for people with learning disabilities. The document acknowledges that people currently tend to have little control in their lives; few people receive direct payments; advocacy services are inadequately developed, and that service users are often not central to the planning process (DoH, 2001: 4). *Valuing People* pledges Government funding to develop advocacy services.

The NHS and Community Care Act of 1990 emphasised the importance of representation of service users. A central policy aim of *Caring for People* (DoH, 1989) was to give people more say in the services that they use: 'promoting choice and independence underlies all the Government's proposals' (p. 4). Means and Smith (1994) cite subsequent departmental guidance for practitioners which stresses the empowerment of users and carers as the rationale for community care reforms (p. 71). Local authorities which provide social services are required to consult with service users and user organisations (Monach and Spriggs, 1994). While it has been observed that the 'consumer' role of users of health and welfare services is a myth (Shemmings and Shemmings, 1995), the voice of service users is considered crucial. This recognition is particularly significant for members of vulnerable groups.

Discussions of self-advocacy must take account of empowerment (Beresford and Croft, 1993: 85), given the close relationship between these concepts and the centrality of user and carer empowerment in recent community care legislation. Empowerment is a process which can be seen as a journey from personal needs to influencing and changing the attitudes and values, policy and practice that affect them (Croft and Beresford, 1995). It is also an outcome (Gibson, 1991). Self-advocacy can be regarded as a means of achieving or expressing empowerment. The role which professionals play in the empowerment of service users has been the subject of much debate. While some argue that they have a crucial role in the empowerment of service users (Parsloe and Stevenson, 1992), others take the view that this perspective is too comfortable — for real empowerment to occur, users have to seize power for themselves rather than depend on benign professionals to give away some of their power (Jack, 1995). There exist examples of studies which conclude that, although workers felt that they empowered users and carers through advocacy and assertiveness training, users reported frustration (Servian, 1996).

Practice case-study

This section draws on original research data collected during interviews with self-advocacy groups for people with learning disabilities. The purpose of this research was to discover how the self-advocacy movement was developing and to investigate the experience of self-advocacy for people with a learning disability (McNally, 2002).

Box 10.1: Definition of key concepts

Empowerment

Has been defined as, 'the process by which individuals, groups and/or communities become able to take control of their circumstances and achieve their own goals, thereby being able to work towards maximising the quality of their lives' (Adams, 1990: 43).

Advocacy

Exists in various forms. This is fundamentally about speaking up — for oneself (self-advocacy), with others (group or collective advocacy) and through others as in peer or citizen advocacy (Atkinson, 1999).

Self-advocacy

Speaking for yourself, standing up for your rights, making choices, being independent, taking responsibility for yourself (*People First*, 1993).

Specific objectives included: Carrying out a survey of self-advocacy groups for adults with a learning disability in a geographical region of England, and eliciting service users' views of their experience as self-advocates.

A key question posed in the survey questionnaire, 'What are the important issues for self-advocacy groups' yielded some interesting responses, including the two represented below. These have been included because they appear to capture the essence of the self-advocacy movement so effectively. The first form was completed by a self-advocate and the original spelling has been retained.

Group A

Giving your views. Being listened to. Make our own choices. Able to make our own mistakes. Improving our life to be independent. We feel when we are treated as an adult and listened to (we are)... seen as an individual to make our own decisions with or without assistant. Then we can have our own houses, relationships and jobs. **Our main thing is to be taken seriously and listened to** (author's emphasis).

Group B

Equal opportunities in all aspects of life. Respect and inclusion. Feeling good about ourselves and recognising our potential. Representing all disabled people including profoundly disabled men and women and disabled people from ethnic minorities. Linking with other civil rights movements for people who are discriminated against or disadvantaged.

Interviews with self-advocacy groups

Group interviews were conducted with members of fifteen self-advocacy groups. Groups have great potential to enhance research which focuses on people who share common concerns and experiences when members may need some support in expressing their views.

> *They allow the possibility that the discussions between members will spark off new ideas, criticism or developments.*
>
> (Dockrell, 1995: 47)

The group interview was designed as a tool for closer exploration of the phenomenon of self-advocacy and the role of the group. It built on the information collected in the survey by asking clear, mainly open questions about self-advocacy and the process and outcomes of group membership. Each of the fifteen groups interviewed had indicated in their completed survey questionnaire that they would be willing to participate further in the study. Permission was sought for tape-recording of interviews at the outset of each group interview; groups' consent was recorded on the tape.

An interview schedule was used as a framework but group members were able to say anything that they thought was relevant to self-advocacy. The researcher asked supplementary questions in order to explore themes emerging during the interviews. The questions used were mostly open. To help to generate ideas, it was necessary at times to use prompts, to pose the same question in a different way, making adjustments in the wording used according to the group giving the interview. Most of the groups, however, provided rich accounts of their experience of and views concerning self-advocacy, sometimes anticipating questions (McNally, 1999).

The purpose of the group

What is the group for?

> For service users. It's all about rights, this group... it has helped us to make choices for ourself and speaking for ourselves.

> We go and discuss it in a staff meeting and some staff don't like change.

> The group is for helping to solve things that are difficult. Our rights and what we would like to do and things like that.

> (A chair of group) I want to make things a bit more organised and stuff. We don't just talk about things we like to do things as well.

> We enjoy coming to the group and we enjoy getting involved in decision making.

> How a service should be run — not the bosses telling us how it should be run.

> We try to talk about things and we can't get anywhere.

What is self-advocacy?

> It's about speaking up for yourself and sticking up for yourself, and about how everyone's got rights.

> Speaking up for yourself. Making choices.

Do you speak up for yourself outside of the group?

You have to or otherwise you won't get anything done.

Effecting change

Effecting change is an issue for self-advocacy groups.

We have changed the name of the centre.

(Council proposing cuts in services) Things have been taken away. They weren't really bothered with us. We went to meetings but they had already made up their minds.

The two extracts above illustrate the achievement and the frustration of attempting to bring about change. The process of trying, even if the desired change is not achieved, can be a valuable learning experience.

There are a number of ways in which learning disability nurses can be involved in facilitating access to advocacy. For example: taking on the role of adviser to a self-advocacy group; helping clients to make contact with an existing group; getting involved with local citizen advocacy schemes. However, it is important that practitioners are aware of the debate surrounding professionals and advocate roles.

Advocacy and nursing

It has been noted that recent years have seen an increase in publicity for the career of the nurse as patient advocate, with a preponderance of advocacy-related literature emanating from the United States and exerting influence on nursing in Britain (Mallik, 1995). The most influential proponents of the nurse advocate role are probably Murphy and Gadow (Millette, 1989). The advocacy role has been conceptualised as enabling and supporting the client (Murphy,1979). She developed three models of advocacy in order to examine the barriers to the practice of such a role: the bureaucratic advocate; the physician advocate; and the patient advocate model. Each model is distinguished by the influence of the salient factor, eg. bureaucracy. In the client advocate model the person becomes the primary focus with all health professionals working together to attain the client's self-determined goal. According to Murphy, it is the client advocate model which is most conducive to a positive nurse-patient relationship.While all three models may be employed at different times, it is the client advocate role which is the preferred model for the professional nurse.

Gadow characterised advocacy as the philosophical foundation of nursing. She sees freedom of self-determination as the most fundamental and valuable human right (Gadow, 1979). Moreover, the nurse has a responsibility to assist the patient to achieve self-determination in the context of an egalitarian relationship (Gadow, 1980). Teasdale (1994: 94) summarises the advocacy debate thus:

The main argument in favour of advocacy by nurses is the amount of contact they have with their patients, which potentially helps them to become aware of the worries and wants of the vulnerable people in their care. Ranged against this is the argument that nurses may lack the independence and objectivity required of a true advocate.

The empowerment of service users is central to the role and mission of learning disability nurses. A Department of Health project on learning disability nursing concluded that nurses should place stronger emphasis on the support of initiatives that enable people with a learning disability to advocate for themselves and that the DoH should support initiatives which develop better information for managers and professional staff on advocacy and self-advocacy (Kay *et al*, 1995). According to Gadow (1980), the nurse is in an ideal position to relate to the patient as a unique and complex individual, and she believes this to be a precondition for advocacy. Some writers are more circumspect about nurses as advocates but acknowledge that in certain circumstances it is desirable that they should take on this role (Gates, 1995).

Conclusions

Clarity may be lacking about the extent to which advocacy roles can be assumed by professionals (Blackmore, 2001). There exists a view that learning disability nurses, for example, have an important role to play in supporting the empowerment of clients (Kay, 1995). This might involve introduction to a self-advocacy group or to an independent advocacy service. While the professional body endorses nurses taking on an advocacy role (UKCC, 1998; NMC, 2002), it has been stressed that learning disability nurses should only advocate on clients' behalf after 'careful consideration of the issues involved' (Jenkins and Northway, 2002: 11). The White Paper, *Valuing People* (DoH, 2001) emphasises the importance of advocacy in various forms. This may reflect the involvement of service users in the *Valuing People* consultation (People First *et al*, 2000). It will be interesting to see to what extent endorsement in policy is translated into practice nationally via the regional implementation teams and local partnership boards. Recent policy documents have acknowledged the importance of person-centred approaches (DoH, 2002): the challenge for policy-makers and services will be to make the philosophy a reality for the person 'in the street' who has a learning disability. Progress is evident but there is no justification for complacency on the part of any of the stakeholders involved. Dawson (2002: 26) admonishes that:

There is a danger that self-advocacy is becoming valued, accepted and expected in meetings at a certain level, but that the fundamental experience of life for people with learning difficulties is not changing.

Some have contended that self-advocacy groups have concentrated on benefits for the individual at the expense of collective political action (Hunter and Mills, 1997). Other commentators, including Bright (2000), acknowledge that until recently, the voice of the service user has not been heard but nevertheless are more sanguine about the future of the self-advocacy movement. One has to be circumspect about the future but it is encouraging to note that self-advocacy groups for and by people with learning difficulties are beginning to penetrate public consciousness as a force against discrimination (Mack, 2001). The diverse, rich nature of the movement should be supported and nurtured. Professionals and academics should not be prescriptive about what constitutes self-advocacy but need to be mindful that self-advocacy groups have the capacity to define themselves and to set their own agenda. People First London Boroughs, having recognised the trend for service users to be 'consulted' by provider and commissioning organisations, included the following clause on their policy concerning agreement to be on committees:

*We must have a **real** voice on the committee. We will not be on your committee just to make it look good.*

(People First, 1994: 16)

In order to support the empowerment of clients, nurses need to consider their own position *vis à vis* empowerment. Learning disability nurses have repeatedly been required to justify themselves (Jukes and Bollard, 2002). If one works in a bureaucratic, business-driven system in which one has little influence and consequently feels frustrated, it is likely to be difficult to sustain a positive, enthusiastic and evolving style of practice. Access to appropriate clinical nursing supervision and opportunities for professional development, including funding, will be crucial. *Valuing People* (DoH, 2001) and its emphasis on the health facilitator role offers a way forward for specialist nurse practitioners in learning disability nursing to improve health outcomes for clients. However, there exist some concerns that learning disability nurses may become restricted in their practice so that they are confined to helping people to access primary and secondary health services. While this is a crucially important aspect of practice, the role of the learning disability nurse should not become too narrow. Bearing this in mind, the health facilitator role could be seen as a springboard for our continued and developing contribution. It is imperative that learning disability nurses are involved with the well-being of people in an holistic sense. There is a significant area of practice which relates to individuals' psychological and emotional health; these domains cannot of course be separated from physical health.

There are many skills and attributes which learning disability nurses have to offer at a variety of levels from newly-registered to expert practitioner, including training primary healthcare professionals and facilitating courses for people with learning disabilities on issues such as assertiveness, or personal relationships. Facilitating a group is potentially an effective use of professional time. The facilitator can help to promote awareness of a range of issues. Group members learn from their peers, who may have encountered similar transitions or situations and have views grounded in experience. This is also a potentially rich learning experience for the facilitator. Supporting empowerment in practice, including involvement in self-advocacy in individual or group contexts, will be a key tenet of practice in learning disability nursing.

Reflective questions/salient points

❀ To what extent do you act as an advocate in your role as a nurse for people with learning disabilities?

❀ How can we enable people with multiple and profound disabilities to have greater control in their lives?

❀ Do you feel empowered as a practitioner?

❀ What access do you have to clinical supervision?

References

Adams R (1990) *Self-Help, Social Work and Empowerment*. Macmillan, Basingstoke

Atkinson D (1999) *Advocacy: A review*. Pavilion/Joseph Rowntree Foundation, Brighton

Baxter C, Poonia K, Nadirshaw Z (1990) *Double Discrimination*. King's Fund, London

Beresford P, Croft S (1993) *Citizen Involvement — a practical guide for change*. MacMillan, Basingstoke

Blackmore R (2001) Advocacy in nursing: perceptions of learning disability nurses. *J Learning Disabilities* **5**(3): 221–34

Bright A (2000) Towards a better future for the self-advocacy movement. *Community Living* April/ May: 13–15

Brandon D (1995) *Advocacy — Power to People with Disabilities*. Venture Press, Birmingham

Braye S, Preston-Shoot M (1995) *Empowering Practice in Social Care*. Open University Press, Buckingham

Chappell A (1998) Still out in the cold: People with learning difficulties and the social model of disability. In: Shakespeare T, ed. *The Disability Reader: Social Science Perspectives*. Cassell, London: 211–20

Clare M (1990) *Developing Self-advocacy Skills*. Further Education Unit, London

Crawley B (1988) *The Growing Voice: A survey of self-advocacy groups in adult training centres and hospitals*. CMH, London

Croft S, Beresford P (1995) Whose empowerment? Equalizing the competing discourses in community care. In: Jack R, ed. *Empowerment in Community Care*. Chapman and Hall, London: 59–73

Dawson P (2002) Hearing but not listening. *Learning Disability Practice* **5**(7): 26

Department of Health (1989) *Caring for People: Community Care in the Next Decade and Beyond*. HMSO, London

Department of Health (2001) *Valuing People: A New Strategy For Learning Disability for the 21st Century*. The Stationery Office, London

Department of Health (2002) *Planning with People*. The Stationery Office, London

Dockrell J (1995) Exploring users' views. In: Wilson G, ed. *Community Care: Asking the Users*. Chapman and Hall, London: 37—53

Dowson S, Whittaker A (1993) *On One Side — the role of the adviser in supporting people with learning difficulties in self-advocacy groups*. Values into Action/King's Fund Centre, London

Gadow S (1979) Advocacy, nursing and new meanings of aging. *Nurs Clin N Am* **14**(1): 81–91

Gadow S (1980) Existential advocacy: philosophical foundation of nursing. In: Spicker S, Gadow S, eds. *Nursing: Images and Ideals*. Springer, New York

Gates R (1995) *Advocacy: A Nurse's Guide*. RCN/Scutari, London

Gibson CA (1991) A concept analysis of empowerment. *J Adv Nurs* **16**(3)354–61

Goodley D (2000) *Self-advocacy in the Lives of People with Learning Difficulties*. Open University Press, Buckingham

Human Rights Act (1998) The Stationery Office, London

Hunter S, Mills L (1997) Bringing about positive change. *Community Living* July: 10–11

Jack R, ed (1995) *Empowerment in Community Care*. Chapman and Hall, London

Jenkins R, Northway R (2002) Advocacy and the learning disability nurse. *Br J Learning Disabilities* **30**: 8–12

Kay B, Rose S, Turnbull J (1995) *Continuing the Commitment – Report of the Learning Disability Nursing Project*. DoH, London

Jukes M, Bollard M (2002) Health facilitators in learning disability are important roles. *Br J Nurs* **11**(5): 297

Mack T (2001) We'll do it our way. *The Guardian* (weekend), 14 April: 21–8

Mallik M (1995) *Advocacy in Nursing: a study of the diffusion and interpretation of a concept*. Unpublished MPhil Thesis, University of Nottingham, Nottingham

Mallik M (1997) Advocacy in nursing – a review of the literature. *J Adv Nurs* **25**: 130

McNally S (2002) A survey of self-advocacy groups for people with learning disabilities in an English region. *J Learning Disabilities* **6**(2): 185–99

McNally S (1999) Professionals and user self-advocacy. In: Malin N, ed. *Professionalism, Boundaries and the Workplace*. Routledge, London: 47–64

Means R, Smith R (1994) *Community Care Policy and Practice*. Macmillan, London

Millette B (1989) *An exploration of advocacy models and the moral orientation of nurses*. Unpublished PhD thesis. University of Massachussetts, Massachusetts

Mir G, Nocon A (2002) Partnerships, advocacy and independence: service principles and the empowerment of minority ethnic people. *J Learning Disabilities* **6**(2): 153–62

Monach J, Spriggs L (1994) The consumer role. In: Malin N (1994) *Implementing Community Care*. Open University Press, Buckingham: 138–53

Murphy C (1979) Models of the nurse-patient relationship. In: Murphy C, Hunter H, eds. *Ethical Problems in the Nurse-patient Relationship*. Allyn and Bacon Inc, Boston, USA: 8–26

NHS and Community Care Act (1990) HMSO, London

Nursing and Midwifery Council (2002) *Code of professional conduct*. NMC, London

Oliver M (1996) *Understanding Disability: from theory to practice*. MacMillan, London

Parsloe P, Stevenson O (1992) *Community Care and Empowerment*. Joseph Rowntree Foundation, York

People First (1993) *Self-advocacy Starter Pack*. People First, London

People First (1994) *People First*. Spring, Edition 6

People First, Change, Speaking Up in Cambridge and Royal MENCAP (2000) *Nothing About Us Without Us – The Learning Disability Strategy: The User Group Report*. Department of Health, London

Ramcharan P, Whittell B, Thomas B, White J (1996) *The Growing Voice in Wales: People with a Learning Difficulty and Self-Advocacy in Wales*. People First NE Wales in association with the Centre for Social Policy and Research and Development, University of Wales, Bangor

Rappaport J (1984) Studies in empowerment. *Prevention in Human Services* **3**: 1–7

Servian R (1996) *Theorising Empowerment – Individual power and community care*. Policy Press, Bristol

Shemmings D, Shemmings (1995) Defining participative practice in health and welfare. In: Jack R, ed. *Empowerment in Community Care*. Chapman and Hall, London: 43–58

Simons K (1992) *Sticking up for Yourself – Self-advocacy and people with learning difficulties*. Joseph Rowntree Foundation, York

Teasdale K (1994) Advocacy and the nurse manager. *J Nurs Management* **2**: 93–7

Walmsley J (1993) 'Talking to top people': some issues relating to the citizenship of people with learning difficulties. In: Swain J, Finkelstein V, French S, Oliver M, eds. *Disabling Barriers — Enabling Environments*. Sage, London: 257–66

Whittaker A (1991) *How are self-advocacy groups developing?* King's Fund, London

Williams P, Shoultz B (1982) *We Can Speak for Ourselves*. Souvenir Press, London

Resources

The following websites may be useful to the reader:

American Association on Mental Retardation, online at: http://aamr.org

British Institute of Learning Disabilities, online at: http://www bild.org.uk

Center on Human Policy, Syracuse University, New York, online at: http://www.soeweb.syr.edu/

Human Rights Act, online at: http://www. doh.gov.uk/ human rights

European Convention on Human Rights, online at: http://www.echr.net

Joseph Rowntree Foundation, online at: http://www.jrf.org.uk

People First, online at: http://www.peoplefirst.org.uk

Self advocates' website, online at: http://www.oneforus.com

Royal College of Nursing, online at: http://www.rcn.org.uk

Training pack: Dawson P, Palmer W/East Midlands Further Education Council (1991) Self-Advocacy at Work – Training Materials. EMF, Nottingham

SELF ADVOCACY GROUPS STUDY

1) What is your group called ?
e.g. People First group,
Self-Advocacy group or
Speaking for Ourselves

2) When did the group start ?

Month ....

Year ....

3) How did the group start ?

....

....

....

....

4) Where does the group meet ?

e.g. Day centre, college, Community centre

Address ....

....

5) When do you meet ?

(e.g. every week, once a month)

Advocacy group
meetings

6) How long do your
meetings last ?

(e.g. two hours, or
one and a half hours)

7) How many members belong
to the group ?

8) What are the important
   issues for self-advocacy
   groups ? *e.g. jobs, housing,
   relationships, staff*

relationships Staff housing jobs

....

....

....

....

....

9) Please add anything else that you would like to say
   about the group. Please send any information
   you have about the group which is not private
   e.g. a brochure, leaflet
   (if you need more space you can carry
   on writing on the last sheet)

BROCHURE

....

....

....

10) Would you be interested in working with me in this
    study ? This would involve meeting me to talk about
    self-advocacy. I would be happy to come to a group
    meeting if this is OK.

	✔	YES
	✘	NO

Please tick

Please telephone me
if you have any
questions

Please return to :

Steve McNally,
Self Advocacy Groups Study ,
Isis Education Centre,
Warneford Lane,
Headington,
Oxford OX3 7JX

SPACE FOR MORE COMMENTS

....

....

....

....

....

....

....

....

*Thank you for taking the trouble
to fill in this questionnaire*

Abuse and vulnerability

Neville Parkes

This chapter is an example of a therapeutic approach undertaken by a community learning disability nurse specialist, who works with people with a learning disability and issues pertaining to sexuality.

The specific focus is upon work achieved with a man with moderate to mild learning disabilities, who reported that he was sexually abused as a child while living within a residential care setting. As a result of this abuse, he had many features of post-traumatic stress disorder (PTSD). Roy's Model of Nursing, which is based around stress-adaptation, was adopted as an appropriate theoretical framework for assessment and subsequent selection of clinical interventions employed. The range of interventions also incorporated counselling skills, which brought into focus issues around Julian's view of his own disability and masculinity.

Introduction

This chapter discusses sexual abuse with regard to people with learning disabilities, and will include a brief review of the prevalence rates of sexual abuse among this sector of the population.

The term 'survivor' is promoted as opposed to the term 'victim' because it is less likely to promote notions of helplessness for individuals who have experienced sexual abuse. The issues and consequences for the male survivor with learning disabilities will be discussed identifying some differences with female survivors. It is not the intention by any means to suggest that male survivor needs are any greater than female survivor needs. The rationale for the focus on the male survivor relates to my specific professional specialist domains of clinical practice, where the majority of work is with men with learning disabilities.

Client confidentiality will be maintained through acknowledgement of the Nursing and Midwifery Council's (NMC) *Code of Professional Conduct* (2002) where some significant details have been changed so as to protect anonymity.

Use of a case study approach

There are a variety of types of case studies, as described by Stake (1994). This chapter represents an intrinsic case study. The value for the reader is that they can consider issues highlighted by this case to their own practice, or to gain more knowledge into a particular phenomena. Assessment and methods of intervention are not intended or considered as being a prescribed package of treatment to be applied to other survivors with learning disabilities. As is common when working with people with learning disabilities, it is necessary for any practitioner to assess each person on an individual basis and tailor an interventionist approach based around such presentation of individual issues and symptomatology.

Sexual abuse and people with learning disabilities

Sexual abuse is no respecter of age, gender, financial status, race, culture, physical prowess, sexual orientation or intelligence. This provocative statement enables consideration of many issues including how vulnerable people are treated. It is a mistake to locate the vulnerability as being only a characteristic of the survivor. The factors associated with abuse are dependent upon dynamics within the environment that the survivor was in. McCarthy and Thompson (1996) argue that services for people with learning disabilities may inadvertently predispose sexual abuse. The Department of Health (1998) published *No Secrets,* which is a report that includes multi-agency guidelines which seek to develop polices and initiatives at local service levels. *No Secrets* was borne out of the recognition of the scale of abuse that people with learning disabilities have experienced. Services have a mandate to ensure that protection and abuse prevention for people with learning disabilities are major considerations in service delivery.

Determining the scale of sexual abuse of people with learning disabilities is problematic. Brown (1994) highlights that there can be many factors that prevent the reporting and recognition of sexual abuse. Factors include individuals with a learning disability, lack of knowledge of sexual matters, communication difficulties and human service workers' lack of confidence and awareness of abuse issues. Studies tend to have a lack of commonality in how they define sexual abuse combined with a variance in the populations of people with a learning disability under study. It is more appropriate to take the view that the figures do not represent a truly accurate figure; moreover, they probably reflect significant underreporting (Brown, 1994). The statistics, although limited, serve a very important function in that they reinforce the message that sexual abuse for people with learning disabilities is a reality.

Prevalence and incidence rates of sexual abuse for people with learning disabilities are variable. Turk and Brown (1993) report on the Kent study that was undertaken with the most stringent of the definitions of sexual abuse, ie. based on criminal convictions. This is the least contestable of all the studies carried out in the UK. The rates suggested by the Kent study indicate an incidence rate (new cases per year) of 0.5 per 1000 individuals. Prevalence rates of sexual abuse range from; Buchanan and Wilkins (1991) 8%, Balog *et al* (2001) 14%, to Hard and Plumb (1987) 58% in Brown (1994).

Approximately two thirds of the survivors identified by the studies were female. It is highly likely that females experience more sexual abuse than men; however, Brown (1994) suggests that one of the factors that the numbers of female victims is of such a high proportion, which may reflect issues associated with male socialisation, is the likelihood that females disclosing abuse, are more likely to be believed than males (see next section). It is possible that males are considered more (*sic*) sexual than females. Sexual violence and abuse indicators could be perceived stereotypically, as being part of normal male sexual expression. An example of how this may be manifested, could be that a man with severe learning disabilities, who is being sexually abused, as a behavioural consequence of the abuse, masturbates in inappropriate places. The masturbation is probably more likely to be viewed as being part of his 'maleness' than a sign of abuse. Another example could be a man with learning disabilities who suffers sexual abuse by his male partner. Care staff could interpret this behaviour as part of normal homosexual life rather than sexual violence, based upon personal assumptions and that the practitioner is uninformed or knowledgeable in regard to the presence of existing theory.

Services for people with learning disabilities are required by *No Secrets* to concentrate on prevention, awareness and responding to abuse; but they also need to offer support services to those whom have been abused. An issue to consider is the gender needs of both male and female survivors. To date, and from my professional exposure and experience, access to skilled workers to help people with learning disabilities who have been sexually abused is patchy and inconsistent.

Male survivors with learning disabilities

The long-term psychological and behavioural consequences for survivors of sexual abuse, with or without learning disabilities, are similar for both genders. Until recently, very little attention has been given to males as survivors of childhood sexual abuse (Rentoul and Appleboom, 1997). Yet sexual abuse against men and boys is very much a reality, as identified by a study by Coxell *et al* (1999) from a UK-based survey which identified that within the general population, 5.25% of men had experienced non-consenting sex as children and 2.35% as adults.

There are significant issues to consider that are pertinent for male survivors. Etherington (1995) discusses the role of patriarchy within society, in which a stereotyped view of masculinity is conveyed. An ideology of masculinity is perpetuated which negates vulnerability and weakness within society (Shakespeare, 1999). This is projected into prejudice against many other groups including women, disabled, black, gay and lesbian people. Etherington highlights that there are social and cultural messages that men should be strong, productive and sexually successful within heterosexual norms. Disability contravenes such cultural messages and can lead to contradictory and confusing messages for disabled men. Shakespeare (1999) highlights this by quoting one disabled man's views:

As a disabled person I'm told I'm to be meek and mild and childlike. Yet as a man I'm meant to be masterful and a leader and get angry.

Etherington states, 'The male survivor is imprisoned by patriarchy'. She argues that patriarchy views victimisation as antithetical to 'maleness'. This often leads to the person experiencing a state of cognitive dissonance. She identifies also that the male survivor is more likely than the woman survivor to remain silent or deny his abuse. This is because of the need to 'take it like a man', ie. to be strong and deny weakness. She identifies that male survivors are more likely to question their own notions of masculinity more often than female survivors would question their notions of femininity.

My view on Julian's owns notion of his masculinity was embroiled with his own expression of negative self-esteem. He viewed himself as being an unsuccessful male because of his experience of childhood sexual abuse, his lack of paid employment and his lack of a sexual relationship. These were potent indicators for him of his failure as a male. Human service workers when working with men with learning disabilities need to be sensitive to the above issues, continuously questioning their own assumptions of masculinity and be conscious not to perpetuate these values as notions of the disabled man as being an unsuccessful man.

The rationale of Roy's model of nursing

In nursing theory development, Roy's model (1976) is classified as a system's model where the human is described as a biopsychosocial being who is in constant interaction with their changing environment. For Julian, as his internal and external environment experiences change (stimuli), his needs also change, resulting in deficits and excesses in day-to-day living. To protect himself, as a result of his abuse, his physiological, and social integrity will also adapt and he will bring into play his own personal coping mechanisms to deal with these changes and satisfy his needs. Through application of Roy's model with Julian's situation, the 'environment' should also include Julian's interaction with his personal carers and supporters. The concept of stress adaptation within the application of Roy's model has also been reported by Woods and Isenberg (2001) when working with battered women who have also endured intimate abuse. Areas such as adaptation to cancer diagnosis within children has also been applied and researched relative to the adoption of Roy's model (Yeh, 2001).

Roy's model explores within the concept of adaptation the reaction to stimuli, referred to as outputs, either internal or external and is suggested by Roy to be either adaptive or ineffective. Health results when positive adaptation is achieved in protecting the integrity of the person through his ability to adapt. Adaptation is therefore defined as an ability for 'the person who is able to meet most goals of survival and growth' (Galbreath, 1990; Logan, 1990). Conversely, ineffective reactions/outputs are when the person is unable to adapt to meet these goals. In Julian's case, the role of nursing interventions is to promote positive adaptation within his daily lived experience to be able to cope positively with his past experiences of abuse

Adaptation is suggested to be processed through four adaptive modes: physiological, role function, self-concept and interdependence. This is illustrated in *Figure 11.1*, which is an interpretation of how Roy views the adaptive modes, which interact constantly within the internal and external environment. Each adaptive mode is suggested to receive: focal stimuli, which is what the person experiences; contextual stimuli, which is stimuli from the external environment; and residual stimuli, which is conceptualised through the clients views, beliefs and experiences.

In terms of assessment, Roy incorporates six steps as part of the nursing process: first level assessment; second level assessment; problem identification; goal setting; intervention; and evaluation (Roy, 1976).

First level assessment involves the assessment of client behaviours — and is the evaluation of the person's behaviour in each of the four adaptive modes: physiologic; self-concept; role-function; and interdependence.

The nurse practitioner selects areas of concern, or those maladaptive behaviours which require reinforcement. These areas are then taken into a second level assessment, where the assessment of those influencing factors are pursued and further evaluates them in terms of which determine the focal, contextual and residual stimuli which contribute to the concerns or maladaptive behaviours.

Assessment in these areas will then allow for an individualised nursing diagnosis with the formulation of goals and subsequent nursing action for both Julian and the nurse practitioner to embark upon.

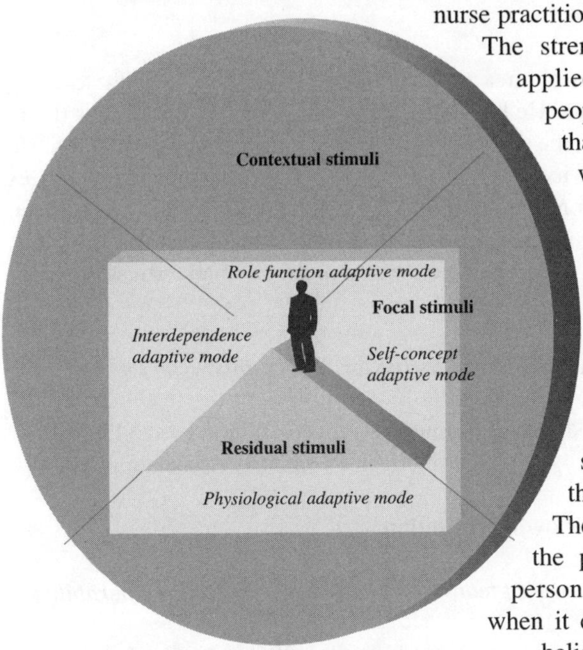

The strength of Roy's model when applied to peripatetic work with people with learning disabilities is that it is a conceptual framework which can appropriately identify the complexities of the physiological and social influences on the individual. It avoids what I refer to as the **plastic bubble approach**, when there is an over focusing on the individual without considering the wider social world that the person interacts within. The plastic bubble approach has the potential to 'pathologise' the person with a learning disability when it can be a manifestation of the belief system and behaviours of their carers. A simple example is a carer who gives a person with learning disabilities a sweet in an attempt to stop them self-injuring and as a result, the self-injuring behaviour becomes enduring. The nurse when applying Roy's model would have the potential to identify the wider perspective on these actions and beliefs of the carers, and not merely seek to over focus on the behaviours of the client.

Figure 11.1: The adaptive modes and the interactions with focal, contextual and residual stimuli

Roy's model has the potential to enable the nurse to consider the nursing actions within a multi-agency and multi-disciplinary context. It is useful for learning disability nurses in the twenty-first century as the emphasis by the Government in the White Paper, *Valuing People* (DoH, 2001), is on partnership working between agencies. It is critical for the specialist nurse to practice authoritatively with a sound appreciation of knowledge and theoretical domains for own practice when collaborating with other professionals.

The needs of survivors of sexual abuse are specific to the individual. They involve the behavioural, psychological and emotional consequences of sexual abuse and the result can be debilitating to the individual and challenging to the people who are in their social world. For a comprehensive description of the consequences of childhood sexual abuse please refer to Sanderson (1996) or Finklehor (1986). The nurse applying Roy's model can consider what behaviours and thoughts the survivor has which are ineffective and maladaptive, and consider the impact that social systems have upon the survivor. If, for example, a survivor with a learning disability became distressed at bath time due to previous abuse incidents which have caused a phobic type response, the nurse, adopting Roy's model as a framework, could identify the stimuli which influences the client and enable an approach that modified the bath time practices.

Client profile

Julian had lived prior to referral in a residential home for people with learning disabilities for a number of years. He has moderate to mild learning disabilities (there was no formal assessment of the level of his learning disabilities available). He attended learning disability services such as special education and some day services throughout his life. Shortly before the referral to myself, he reported that he had been sexually abused while a child in a care setting. He described being distressed by this. His behaviours and thoughts were characteristic of post traumatic stress disorder (PTSD), which is defined by the following:

> *Witnessing and or experiencing threats to life or severe injury to the self or significant other.*

> Ashead (2000) includes this definition by the DSM IV
> (American Psychiatric Association, 1994)

This is expanded upon by the following definition:

> *A failure to process the experience of fear reflecting either a previous vulnerability to fear or extremes of fear.*

> Foa and Kozak (1986) in McCarthy (2000)

Post traumatic stress disorder is characterised by the individual having recurring unwanted thoughts or phobic reactions often related to the past traumatic event. The symptomology that Julian experienced was in common to many sufferers of this condition: he had recurring nightmares or flashbacks, felt guilt and shame and sadness. He resorted to using alcohol in an attempt to 'blot out' (his words) his memories.

The first level assessment using Roy's model

The following (*Figures 11.2, 11.3* and *11.4*) is a graphic representation of Julian's needs as part of a first level assessment where I assessed his adaptive and ineffective coping strategies within the respective focal, contextual and residual stimuli.

The interventions identified from a second stage assessment process

In working with Julian, my aim was to promote adaptation by attempting to modify the ineffective coping strategies Julian was using.

Ineffective coping strategies used by Julian	Approaches used to develop adaptation
⌘ His internal environment including his psychological processes caused Julian to exhibit panic attacks and sleep disturbance	⌘ To educate Julian about PTSD ⌘ To utilise counselling/talking about his thoughts and feelings. Thus, desensitising him when thinking about the sexual abuse to become less inclined to panic ⌘ Use of phenothiazine medication (discuss with psychiatrist and GP)
⌘ Alcohol usage	⌘ To educate, using health education leaflets and discussion, about the problems alcohol can give. At this stage not considered problematic an it is debatable whether this is ineffective or as adaptive as Julian can be in the circumstances
⌘ Employment opportunities	⌘ To liaise and contact relevant agencies

Physiological adaptive mode	Role function adaptive mode
⌘ PTSD symptoms including flashbacks resulting in sleep disturbances and panic ⌘ Use of alcohol two–three days a week to 'blot out' his abuse memories	⌘ Resident of a home for people with learning disabilities. Takes part in helping with some jobs around the home ⌘ Attends a further education college course for basic literary skills ⌘ Has contact with family and has a positive relationship with them
Self-concept adaptive mode	**Interdependence adaptive mode**
⌘ Has a low opinion of self, this is related to his views about his abuse (see residual stimuli) ⌘ He views his learning disability negatively seeking to distance himself from other people with learning disabilities ⌘ Does not consider himself to be a successful male (see residual stimuli)	⌘ Able to undertake most daily living skill tasks competently. Able to travel independently within locality. Requires help from staff to organise himself for appointments and needs emotional support when upset with abuse memories

Figure 11.2: Focal stimuli

Description of counselling interventions

The focus on clinical work with Julian, and as a result of Roy's second stage assessment involved counselling approaches. The following is a brief outline of what was undertaken.

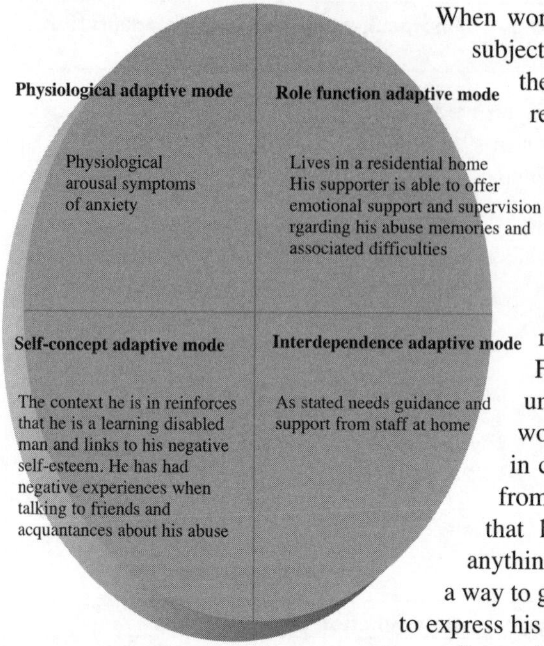

Physiological adaptive mode

Physiological arousal symptoms of anxiety

Role function adaptive mode

Lives in a residential home His supporter is able to offer emotional support and supervision rgarding his abuse memories and associated difficulties

Self-concept adaptive mode

The context he is in reinforces that he is a learning disabled man and links to his negative self-esteem. He has had negative experiences when talking to friends and acquantances about his abuse

Interdependence adaptive mode

As stated needs guidance and support from staff at home

Figure 11.3: Contextual stimuli

When working with any individual around subject matters that are distressing to them it is important to develop a relationship which they feel they can trust. An agreement was reached to which we would both adhere. This is usual in counselling/psychotherapy work (Heron, 1995; Mearns and Thorne, 1992; Egan, 1994). The reason for this was two-fold. Firstly, to ensure that he understood the parameters of the work and to emphasise that he was in control of the sessions. Key rules from the contract clearly emphasised that he did not have to talk about anything if he did not want to. It was also a way to give permission for him to be able to express his feelings safely.

I worked collaboratively with his supporter the proprietor of the residential home. This approach is similar to what Corbett *et al* (1996) describe as, 'advocate supporter roles'. She is very committed to him and supportive. He would often talk about his abuse memories to his supporter. Julian gave me his permission to discuss his reaction to the sessions with his supporter. Please note I discussed in detail what subjects I would discuss with his supporter. This was a valuable way to be able to check on progress and difficulties beyond the confines of the counselling sessions.

The therapeutic relationship is the most pivotal aspect to achieve in this type of work. To do this one needs to be able to work in an empathetic way or be able to strongly identify with the client. Mearns and Thorne (1992) state that an emotional warmth is required in the relationship with the therapist for the client to express feelings of safety. With survivors of sexual abuse, it is imperative that they feel safe with whatever type of therapist. It is churlish to think of this as 'an approach' like one would put on a metaphorical white coat.

The approach undertaken was influenced heavily by Egan's (1994) skilled helper model. The skilled helper model is a client-centred approach, which has the potential to enable valued outcomes. The process involves an eclectic use of psychotherapeutic and counselling approaches to be used within a three-stage model. The stages of the model are not separate, distinct and sequential, they can and often do overlap and are required to be repeated. The model is biased towards action rather than just being analytical or reflective, where its emphasis from the outset is based upon ownership by the client on the problem management process. The stages of the model are illustrated in *Figure 11.5*.

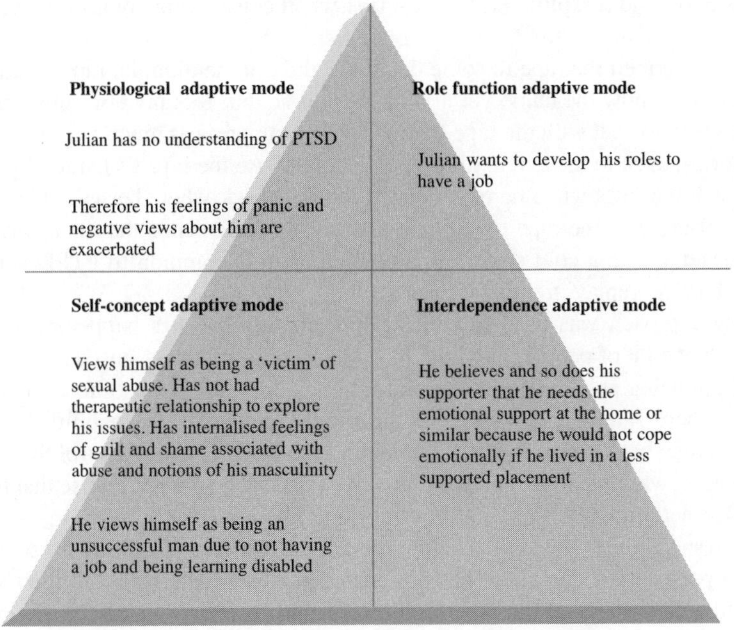

Physiological adaptive mode

Julian has no understanding of PTSD

Therefore his feelings of panic and negative views about him are exacerbated

Role function adaptive mode

Julian wants to develop his roles to have a job

Self-concept adaptive mode

Views himself as being a 'victim' of sexual abuse. Has not had therapeutic relationship to explore his issues. Has internalised feelings of guilt and shame associated with abuse and notions of his masculinity

He views himself as being an unsuccessful man due to not having a job and being learning disabled

Interdependence adaptive mode

He believes and so does his supporter that he needs the emotional support at the home or similar because he would not cope emotionally if he lived in a less supported placement

Figure 11.4: Residual stimuli

Stage one is concerned with reviewing the client's current scenario. It enables them to express what their per- spectives are upon the problems in focus. In Julian's case, it was his thoughts, feelings and memories about the abuse. The skilled helper uses empathetic type responses to explore, clarify and probe to elucidate the story. This is essential in the helping process as it enables the perspective of the client to be expressed.

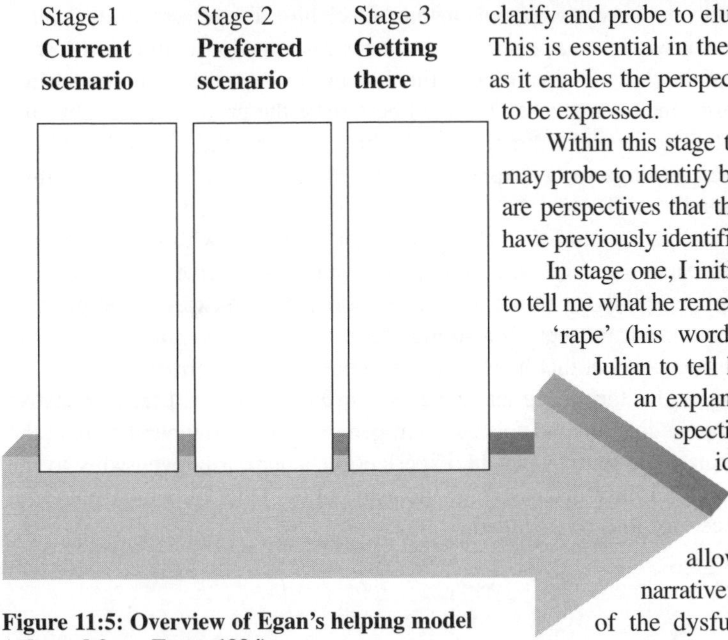

Within this stage the skilled helper may probe to identify blind spots, which are perspectives that the client may not have previously identified or considered.

In stage one, I initially asked Julian to tell me what he remembered about the 'rape' (his words). Encouraging Julian to tell his story enabled an explanation of his per- spective of the abuse identifying for example self-blame. This can allow from their narrative; an examination of the dysfunctional trauma

Stage 1 **Current scenario**	Stage 2 **Preferred scenario**	Stage 3 **Getting there**

Figure 11:5: Overview of Egan's helping model (adapted from Egan, 1994)

beliefs as Scott and Strapling (1992) describe when considering counselling survivors of PTSD.

Julian described the rape in some detail but did not mention the rapist's name. He said he did not know the name yet it is likely that he did. It is my conjecture that part of Julian's way to deal with the rape traumas was to suppress as much as possible about the memories, even to the extent of not being able to use the rapist's name. A powerful feature for Julian was when he experienced the flashback where he was able to recall the smell of urine as the rape took place in a lavatory. He stated that he always woke up frightened and in a cold sweat. This phenomenon is common to PTSD survivors, who psychically 'replay' traumatic events.

A didactic approach was used to educate him about what was happening to him. I explained that a lot of people, like him, have this type of reaction. I used a metaphor of the mind not being able to deal with painful things, like rape, so it 'throws them away into somewhere like a dark corner of the mind, sometimes the painful things like memories come back out of the dark corner and the person cannot control this.' Julian, in my opinion, was able to comprehend this. He said that he did not realise that this was a 'typical' reaction. Understanding this was quite liberating for him.

Within stage one of the skilled helper model, the therapist is looking for blindspots, which are perspectives the client has not considered as an alternative to their view of events. Julian's account of the rape highlighted that he felt to blame for the incident. Survivors of sexual abuse in some cases attach blame, inappropriately, to themselves. This is often due to the way that the perpetrator carried out the abuse (Finklehor, 1986; Sanderson, 1995; Ainscough and Toon, 1993). I challenged his schemata of self blame, or as Sanderson (1995: 176) identifies this as ' reframing', by asking him to demonstrate how physically large the 'rapist' would have been and how tall he would have been at the time of the rape. From this process, I emphasised that the difference in size and physical strength would have been considerable. I suggested that the 'rapist' would have been waiting for him and may have pre-planned to attack him. The effect was difficult to assess but I feel that he was given a perspective that he had not previously fully considered.

In stage two of the skilled helper model, the therapist enables the client to consider a preferred scenario. In Julian's case, it was to be free of the unwanted thoughts and memories and to feel better about himself. To do this I suggested to Julian that he had not allowed certain feelings to be expressed. I adapted the rhetorical letter writing approach (Ainscough and Toon, 1993). Julian was unable to do this by himself. I suggested words and phrases to him but checked that he agreed with what I wrote. I explained that the person that he was writing to would not receive the letters (see below). The letter was a way for Julian to be given a mandate to express feelings that he had not allowed himself to 'feel'. It also may have helped him to gain some power and challenge his own concept that he is helpless to one of empowerment.

I do not apologise for the strong language used in Julian's letter; I feel it conveys deep and real emotions for him and for me. I am genuinely moved when I re-read the letter and contemplate the trauma that he experienced. I hope it conveys this to the reader. Please note that I have discussed the inclusion of the letter in this chapter with Julian and he is keen for it to be included.

The rhetorical letter Julian wrote to his rapist

To the rapist

I'd like to kill you, you raped me you 43'er [refers to prison slang for a sex offender who are detained on Rule 43] you made me angry you are a fucking bastard. You wrecked my fucking life. You raped me. I want to punch you on the nose, stomach arms legs. I can smell the piss every night when I go to sleep. I feel dirty about it. I feel ashamed about it. I have been called a queer, pervert 43-er because what you did to me. I feel fucking angry still. I feel sad. I was in the wrong place wrong time. I didn't deserve [it] I am not to blame. You were stronger and bigger than me.

I was small I couldn't fight back.

Within stage two of the skilled helper model, Julian identified that he felt bored and a failure. What was identified was that he wanted to be employed. He did not feel attending day centres for people with learning disabilities was appropriate for him.

Stage three of the model involves commitment and consideration of how to achieve the preferred scenario. In Julian's case, to obtain a job involved partnership of using my role as a nurse to facilitate access to outcomes for him. The preferred scenario of being free of unwanted memories involved an ongoing re-affirmation of the work we had done, especially about his challenging his internalised beliefs of blame and shame and also challenging any responsibility he had wrongly attributed to himself for the abuse.

In seeking a job for Julian, it was fortunate to have a student nurse on placement. She was requested to make contact with as many relevant agencies as she could and this took a considerable amount of time, patience and effort. I did not have the available clinical time to do this. It became apparent, in the geographical locality, that there was a paucity of supported work schemes for people like Julian. This was further exacerbated by the likelihood of Julian's income from the Department of Social Security (DSS) benefits being reduced if he obtained paid employment. After much effort, the student nurse found Julian two voluntary jobs. Initially, Julian saw these very much as second best but, after trying them, he reacted very positively. Instead of being in bed until the early afternoon he was rising in the mornings on working days to be punctual.

Results

I worked with Julian on a fortnightly basis for about two years. Working with Julian highlighted a difficulty in obtaining a reliable baseline for his PTSD symptoms. It was difficult for him to maintain a record of his flashbacks prior to the initiation of the therapy. A rough baseline was used which indicated that he experienced at least two to four flashbacks a week. His supporter commented that during the period he was having counselling sessions, he would sometimes be quiet and withdrawn post sessions, but she commented that from her perspective they were having a positive effect by making him happier. These subjective comments were helpful and if we consider that the essence of Roy's model is to promote adaptation then, in this case, it was successful. On a recent follow up visit with Julian two years after the sessions were completed, he is still working in his voluntary job, his alcohol consumption is stable and unproblematic and he reports to having no flashbacks and no self-injurious behaviours.

There was a prescription of a phenothiazine-type medication to help with the night-time flashbacks for Julian; this was not successful, as Julian did not like the adverse effects. It was decided that in lieu of the possible interactions with his alcohol usage and the increased chance of adverse reactions, that it would be better to avoid pharmacological approaches.

Discussion

This case study has indicated that it is within the role of the specialist learning disability nurse to work with survivors of sexual abuse with a learning disability. Using Roy's model of nursing and incorporating Egan's skilled helper model, the nurse is able to be flexible and holistic in their assessment and approaches with clients.

This case study demonstrates that a nurse/worker needs to be eclectic and client focused, using a range of approaches. Egan (1994) describes the role as that of a helper, rather than being process driven where clients have to fit the therapy.

In obtaining a voluntary job for Julian, it could be argued that throughout the work I have reinforced notions of masculinity, which seeks to see men as being productive. I leave it to the reader to decide whether this work has perpetuated the stereotyped notion of masculinity or whether I have enabled a person with learning disabilities to gain a semblance of being valued through an activity that he finds enriching to his life.

Notwithstanding the above, I have demonstrated that the nurse has the potential to offer some work with survivors of sexual abuse with learning disabilities. I must finish this chapter with a series of cautionary notes:

⌘ Working with survivors of sexual abuse is not easy. It can be rewarding but it can be emotionally draining. The emotional impact upon myself from working with Julian ranged from frightened that I was 'out of my depth', feelings of sadness and anger at what he had experienced to exhilaration when we had a 'good session. Regular opportunities for reflective practice within competent clinical supervision is essential for this type of work.

⌘ It is imperative that the nurse/worker has a good working knowledge of sexual abuse, both specifically to people with learning disabilities and to the general population. This is to enable the therapist to appreciate the issues in depth so that they can consider the issues for the survivor from an informed standpoint.

⌘ The risks of the person with a learning disability becoming distressed as part of therapy needs to be fully discussed with their supporters, and contingency arrangements should be carefully considered.

⌘ Finally, the nurse/worker needs to be committed to helping the survivor with a learning disability; to be genuine and focused on helping the client. As I have stated, the most important aspect of this type work is the therapeutic relationship. If nurses/workers do not pay due seriousness to this, it conveys little respect to people who have already been damaged by others who have denigrated their humanness by their abusive acts.

Acknowledgements

I acknowledge with great humility the tremendous courage Julian showed in our work together. I am privileged to have worked with him and I am thankful for the trust he had in me. I also acknowledge the valuable role that the proprietor of the residential home had in the support towards his progress,without which Julian would not have made such positive gains. I pay due thanks to Carole Goddard who was student nurse at the time on placement with the community learning disability team for finding a voluntary job for Julian, which made an enormous positive difference to his life. Finally, I thank Mark Jukes for his patience and comments, which I found invaluable in constructing this chapter.

> ### Reflective comment
>
> Both Roy and Neuman's model consider stress-adaptation as the basis to their theories. Consider the application of this concept within your work with people with a learning disability who consistently have to adapt to new people, situations and where to live.

References

American Psychiatric Association (1994) Diagnostic and Statistical Manual of Mental Disorders. 4th edn. APA, Washington DC

Ainscough C, Toon K (1993) *Breaking Free: Help for survivors of child sexual abuse*. Sheldon Press, London

Ashead G (2000) Psychological therapies for post-traumatic stress disorder. *Br J Psychiatry* **177** (August): 144–8

Balog R, Bretherton K, Whilby S, Verney T, Graham S, Richold P *et al* (2001) Sexual abuse in children and adolescents with intellectual disability. *J Intellectual Res* **45**(3): 194–201

Brown H (1994) Establishing the incidence of abuse in services for people with learning disabilities. In: Harris J, Craft A, ed (1994) *People with Learning Disabilities at Risk of Physical or Sexual Abuse*. British Institute of Learning Disabilities, Kidderminster

Buchanan AH, Wilkins R (1991) Sexual abuse and the mentally handicapped difficulties in establishing prevalence. *Psychiatric Bull* **15**: 601–5

Corbett A, Cottis T, Morris S (1996) *Witnessing Nurturing Protesting: Therapeutic Responses to Sexual Abuse of People with Learning Disabilities*. David Fulton Publishers, London

Coxell A, King M, Mezey G, Gordon D (1999) Lifetime prevalence, characteristics and associated problems of non-consensual sex: cross section survey. *Br Med J* **318** (March): 846–50

Department of Health (1998) *No Secrets*. HMSO, London

Department of Health (2001) *Valuing People: A new strategy for learning disability for the 21st century*. DoH, London

Egan G (1994) *The Skilled Helper*. 4th edn. Brooks/Cole, California

Etherington K (1995) *Adult male survivors of childhood sexual abuse*. Pitman, London

Foa E, Kozak M (1986) Emotional processing of fear: exposure to corrective information. *Psychol Bull* **99**: 20–35. In: McCarthy J (2000) Post-traumatic stress disorder in people with learning disability. *Advances Psychiatric Treatment* **7**: 163–9

Finklehor D (1986) *Child Sexual Abuse: A sourcebook*. Sage, London

Galbreath JG (1990) Sister Callista Roy. In George JB, ed *Nursing Theories The Base for Professional Nursing Practice*. Prentice Hall, New Jersey

Hard S, Plum W (1987) Sexual abuse of persons with developmental disabilities. Unpublished manuscript cited by Brown H (1994) Establishing the incidence of abuse in services for people with learning disabilities. In: Harris J, Craft A , ed (1994) *People with Learning Disabilities at Risk of Physical or Sexual Abuse*. British Institute of Learning Disabilities, Kidderminster,

Heron J (1995) *Helping the Client: A creative practical guide*. Sage, London

Logan M (1990) The Roy adaptation model: are nursing diagnoses amenable to independent nurse functions? *J Adv Nurs* **15**: 468–70

Mearns D, Thorne B (1992) *Person-centered Counselling in Action*. Sage, London

McCarthy M,Thompson D (1996) Sexual abuse by design: an examination of the issues in learning disability services. *Disability and Society* **11**(2): 205–17

McCarthy J (2000) Post-traumatic stress disorder in people with learning disability. *Adv Psychiatr Treatment* **7**: 163–9

Nursing and Midwifery Council (2002) *Code of Professional Conduct*. NMC, London

Rentoul L, Appleboom N (1997) Understanding the psychological impact of rape and serious sexual assault of men: a literature review. *J Psychiatr Ment Health Nurs* **4**(part 4): 67–74

Roy C (1976) *An Introduction to Nursing: an adaptation model*. Cited by Galbreath JG (1990) Sister Callista Roy. In: George JB, ed (1990) *Nursing Theories: The base for professional nursing practice*. Prentice Hall, New Jersey

Sanderson C (1995) *Counselling Survivors of Child Sexual Abuse*. Jessica Kingsley, London

Scott MJ, Strapling SG (1992) *Counselling for Post-traumatic Stress Disorder*. Sage, London

Shakespeare T (1999) The sexual politics of disabled masculinity. *Sexuality Disability* **17**(part 1): 53–64

Stake RE (1994) Case studies. In: Denzin N, Lincoln S, eds *Handbook of Qualitative Research*. Sage, Montreal

Turk V, Brown H (1993) The sexual abuse of adults with learning disabilities: results of a two-year incidence survey. *Ment Handicap Research* **6**(part 3): 193–216

Woods SJ, Isenberg MA (2001) Adaptation as a mediator of intimate abuse and traumatic stress in battered women. *Nurs Sci Q* **14**(3): 215–21

Yeh CH (2001) Adaptation in children with cancer: Research with Roy's model. *Nurs Sci Q* **14**(2): 141–8

12

Participatory research

Ruth Northway

Traditionally, research has been thought of as an activity which only 'expert' researchers undertake. During the past decade this view has been challenged by disabled people who have criticised much disability research for failing to have a positive impact on the lives of disabled people (Oliver, 1993) and, as a result, participatory and emancipatory research approaches have emerged. Until relatively recently the use of such approaches within the context of learning disability research had not been widely explored. This situation is, however, beginning to change.

This chapter will provide an overview of participatory research, discuss its importance in developing learning disability nursing research and explore some of the practical implications of using such an approach. It aims both to encourage readers to develop participatory research projects and to provide them with tools to assist them in this process.

The nature and importance of participatory research

What is participatory research?

Participatory research recognises that, within society, there are some groups of people who have traditionally been marginalised and oppressed. Part of this oppression has been due to the fact that their views and opinions have not been heard, because the voices and experiences of more powerful groups have been dominant (Stoeker and Bonacich, 1992). Even the knowledge which oppressed groups have regarding their own situation, the factors which contribute to it, and what is needed if change is to happen, has not been recognised. This has meant that research has been viewed as an activity which powerful and knowledgeable people undertake and the role of oppressed groups has been one of objects or subjects of other people's study.

Participatory research seeks to change this imbalance of power both within the research process, and within wider society (Finn, 1994). One strategy used is to encourage the participation, at all stages, of the research process of groups usually excluded from research. Participation in this context is not about advising the researcher but rather it involves control over the decision-making process (Stoeker, 1999). Stoeker (1999: 850) identifies six key points at which decisions need to be taken:

- 'defining the research question,
- designing the research,
- implementing the research design,
- analysing the research data,
- reporting the research results, and
- acting on the research results.'

Participatory research also seeks to change power relations within wider society. There is an emphasis on ensuring that research is the basis for action, rather than research being an end in itself. However, it recognises that people have the ability to develop and implement their own solutions rather than having them imposed by others (Cocks and Cockram, 1995).

Participatory research is an educational process in which people learn together (Finn, 1994). Researchers may bring to the research their knowledge of the research process but other members of the research team bring experience and expertise with regard to their situation. People contribute different things to the research project but, since all contributions are equally valued and necessary, this provides the opportunity to learn from each other.

The role of the researcher within participatory research is very different. They are not the expert, but instead bring particular knowledge and skills to the research. Moreover, whereas within more traditional research approaches they are expected to be detached and unbiased, participatory research requires that they work from an explicit value base and that they are committed to bringing about change (Cocks and Cockram, 1995). This means that the researcher needs to adopt a critical and reflexive approach in which they continually reflect upon their role within the research, their wider beliefs and values, and upon their relationship with their co-researchers.

Why is it important in learning disability research?

Over the past decade the role which people with learning disabilities play in the context of research has been questioned and new research approaches have begun to emerge. Such approaches have provided the opportunity for people with learning disabilities to exercise increased choice and control in the context of research (*Figure 12.1*).

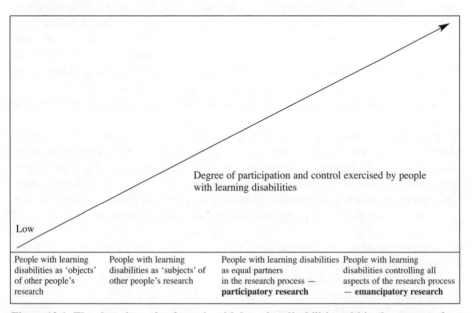

Figure 12.1: The changing role of people with learning disabilities within the context of research

Historically, people with learning disabilities have tended to be assigned a very passive role within research and they have been viewed as 'objects' or 'subjects' of other people's research. Since research has been viewed as relying upon intellectual skills it has often 'by definition' been seen as inaccessible to people with learning disabilities (Ward, 1997). Booth (1996) however, argues that it is traditional research methods which have discriminated against their active involvement because they have relied upon reading, writing and abstract reasoning. People with learning disabilities have been judged against these traditional requirements and their ability, rather than questioning the appropriateness of the research methods (Booth, 1996).

Kiernan (1999: 43) observes that research has tended to be 'research on people rather than research with people'. This has meant that while people with learning disabilities have been 'tested, counted, observed, analysed, described and frequently pathologised' (Walmsley, 2001:188), their views have seldom been sought. Indeed, it has sometimes been the case that if we wished to know their views then we have asked other people (Ramcharan and Grant, 1994; Ward and Flynn, 1994).

People with learning disabilities are a group of people whose views and knowledge have tended to be marginalised both within and without the research process. There has been pressure from both advocacy groups and Government policy to change this situation (Kiernan, 1999). For example, the recent *Valuing People* White paper (DoH, 2001) stressed the importance of person-centred planning. This approach to care planning is 'rooted in the values of shared power and self-determination' (Sanderson, 2000: 3) and hence reflects the value base of participatory research as discussed in the previous section. In recent years, some researchers have sought to develop more participatory approaches to research with people with learning disabilities (for example, Minkes *et al*, 1995; March *et al*, 1997; Williams, 1999).

There is one further point which requires some clarification. In the literature concerning participatory research and learning disabilities, readers will come across another term, namely, 'emancipatory' research. It has been suggested that sometimes the two terms seem to have the same meaning (Stalker, 1998) but for Chappell (2000) there are two key differences between the research approaches. First, she argues that emancipatory research is clearly based upon the social model of disability whereas this is seldom the case in participatory research. This position might be challenged since some participatory research studies have clearly been based on the social model (for example, Northway, 1998a; Richardson, 2000). The second difference is, she argues, that within emancipatory research disabled people control the research process. It has already been seen that participatory research does not preclude such an approach (Stoeker, 1999). The dividing line between emancipatory and participatory research is rather blurred (Walmsley, 2001) and any differences may be one of emphasis rather than differences of kind (Kiernan, 1999).

In the context of this chapter, I will continue to use the term participatory research and it is stressed that, in *Figure 12.1*, the approaches to research are viewed as a continuum rather than as clearly distinct approaches. Moreover, while there is a sense of historical development from left to right within this continuum, it should be recognised that this development has tended to be one of expanding the range of research approaches to include participatory and emancipatory research, rather than the direct substitution of one approach for another.

Why is it important in learning disability nursing?

The need to develop further learning disability nursing research has been noted (Turnbull, 1997; Parahoo *et al*, 2000). In responding to this agenda it is important that we carefully consider how best we can work with people with learning disabilities so that their views and experiences are not excluded as has previously been the case.

Participatory research has much to offer research in the field of learning disability nursing. First, it provides a framework within which we can work with people with learning disabilities to ensure that their views are central to practice, policy, and research development. Second, because participatory research requires that the researcher adopts a reflexive approach it provides a vehicle for not only reflecting upon the situation of people with learning disabilities and our role as researchers, but also makes us reflect more critically upon our wider practice (Northway, 2000a). It thus has implications outside of the research. Finally, the emphasis on action within participatory research means that it offers the potential to provide a clear link between research and practice (Northway, 2000b).

Having presented the case for participatory research within the context of learning disability nursing research it is important to consider how this agenda might be taken forward. The subsequent sections present a hypothetical case study of how such an approach might be used. The case study will be considered in two sections to highlight the issues which need to be considered before using participatory research approaches, as well as those which need to be considered during a participatory research study.

Planning a participatory research study

Case study — the beginnings of participatory research

Jane Wilson is an experienced learning disability nurse who has developed an interest in research. Recently, she has become one of the nursing representatives on a committee established within her Trust to coordinate clinical governance activities. Jane has been asked to gather information concerning the quality of the nursing service offered within the learning disability directorate.

The learning disability nursing service has set practice standards which are regularly audited. Jane is thus assured that there is some information which can be presented. However, she is also aware that clinical governance requires the involvement of patients and clients (Royal College of Nursing, 1998a) and is concerned that people with learning disabilities have not been asked directly what they think of the service provided for them. She knows that elsewhere 'satisfaction' surveys have been carried out but, during her reading, she notes that professionals and people who use health services may identify different aspects of these services as important (Oliver, 1999). She wonders how this problem can be overcome, decides to carry on reading around the subject.

Jane has not come across participatory research before but she learns that it involves people with learning disabilities at all stages of the research process and thus they, rather than nurses, would be identifying which aspects of the nursing service were important. There is not a great deal written about how you can use such an approach but, from what she reads, she finds that it can be a very time-consuming process which needs to be carefully planned.

At the next committee meeting Jane reports that she feels a participatory research approach is needed if they are really to involve people with learning disabilities in the quality development agenda within the Trust. She explains, however, that to use such an approach (and to get meaningful participation) would take time. Some members of the committee treat her suggestion with scepticism — how on earth could people with learning disabilities be actively involved in research? However, others feel that it sounds like a good idea and that the use of such an approach should be explored. Jane agrees to look more fully at how this initiative might be taken forward.

Issues in planning participatory research

Before Jane can proceed there are a number of issues that need to be considered. Three key areas will be explored: resources; identifying co-researchers; and approaching co-researchers. The term 'co-researchers' will be used here to refer to people with learning disabilities who work alongside non-disabled researchers to undertake a research project.

Resources

All research is time-consuming: the time available to undertake the study needs to be carefully considered. In Jane's situation there are a number of factors which may influence this. First, there may be deadlines imposed by the Trust: is a report required by a particular date? Second, there is the question of Jane's time. She is working in a full-time post with no dedicated time to undertake research. However, participatory research is a very time-consuming process (Northway, 1998a) and she would have an obligation to her co-researchers to devote the time required. Finally, involvement in the study would place demands upon her co-researchers who also have other commitments in their lives.

Practical issues will also have resource implications. For example, do meetings of the research group need to be in a building which is accessible to wheelchair users? Will co-researchers require transport to the meetings and/or the support of a personal assistant? Will it be necessary to produce information in a range of accessible formats? What funding is available to pay co-researchers for their times and/or travel expenses?

A final but important issue relates to who should undertake a participatory research study. The Royal College of Nursing (1998b) remind us that all nurses involved in research must ensure that they have the necessary knowledge and skills. They also highlight the need for new researchers to work under the supervision of a more experienced researcher. It is very important that any nurse who is considering undertaking a participatory research study reflects carefully upon their own level of experience and expertise and seeks support and supervision as appropriate.

Who to approach to become co-researchers?

One of the key decisions which Jane needs to take is who she should approach to work with her as co-researchers? From her reading she is aware that some people have questioned the ethics of developing research with people whose social networks are limited, if there is not an offer of continued involvement when the research ends (Booth, 1998). It might be difficult to bring together a group solely to undertake the research if she is unable to offer to work with them on a long-term basis (if this is what they want). Another approach might be to approach a self-advocacy organisation who would already have an established group identity and support mechanisms in place along with their own programme of work. However, the potential for such groups to be 'in demand', and for their own agendas to become secondary to those of other people, has been noted (Stalker, 1998).

How best to approach potential co-researchers?

Once it has been decided who to approach to act as co-researchers the question arises as to how best to make such an approach. At this stage, even though Jane is asking people to become co-researchers rather asking them to consent to be subjects of her research, she would still be asking them to give of their time and expertise. This means that the principles of informed consent should still be observed. It is important to provide information about exactly what might be involved in undertaking the research project, for this information to be given in accessible formats, and for there to be the opportunity to ask questions.

It is also important to remember that, although we may believe that we are working in a participatory way, we may be perceived differently by those we support. Richardson (1997) reminds us that, as nurses, we may be seen as part of a system which has taken power away from people with learning disabilities. It may be difficult for people to say no to us simply because of the professional role we fulfil. In such circumstances, it might be helpful to consider providing information which can be discussed by potential co-researchers before they agree to meet with us face-to-face.

Undertaking participatory research

Case study – undertaking participatory research

Having thought carefully about the issues discussed above, Jane decided to pursue a participatory research study. Since she had no real experience in this area of research she sought the support of someone working locally who had been involved before in a similar project. It was decided that they would work together to develop this research. Jane sought the support of her nursing manager who agreed that she could be allocated some time to undertake the research and who also offered an accessible meeting room for the research group to use. It was further agreed by the Trust that monies would be available to pay the travel expenses of co-researchers. Contact was also established with the speech and language therapist within the Trust who agreed to assist with the development of accessible information.

Jane thought carefully about whom she should approach to work with her on the research. Finally, she decided that it would be best to ask members of the advocacy group which had recently been formed within the Trust since they were a group which had been meeting for some time, they had an independent supporter, and they had all had contact with the nursing service. She developed a letter (using both words and pictures/symbols) setting out what she was hoping to do, the type of help she was asking for, and asking if she could meet with the group to discuss it further. The group discussed this and Jane was asked to attend their next meeting.

At this meeting Jane gave some further information about the study, such as how long she thought it might take, how often they would need to meet and what it would involve. One thing she did feel important to say, was, that while it would be possible to pay travel expenses, it would not be possible to pay for their time. She also answered a lot of questions from the group. At the end of the meeting five people said that they would like to work with her. It was agreed that they would meet again.

Following this, a series of weekly meetings were established. Initially these involved developing an understanding of research, thinking about what the research should focus on, and thinking about how the group could gather information. The key points discussed at each meeting were noted and minutes produced in accessible formats. These were then discussed at the beginning of the next meeting to make sure that everyone was in agreement with them. At times Jane found that the whole process was taking much more time than she had originally anticipated. However, she felt that it was important if participation was not to be tokenistic. She also found that she needed to review regularly her role in the research to check whether she was influencing the group unduly, or whether they were truly exercising control when it came to decision-making.

The group identified a lot of things that they felt were important about the nursing service. However, they were also aware that they only had a limited amount of time to do the research. It was therefore agreed that they would start by looking at something which everyone felt was important: the information which people with learning disabilities are given about their health and their medication.

It was decided that it would not be possible to send questionnaires out to people as some might find them difficult to fill in. However, it was agreed that they could ask people questions and everyone worked together to develop the questions that they felt were important and to practice undertaking interviews.

When it came to doing the interviews two people said that they had enjoyed practising interviews but they did not want to do them. Jane and the other co-researchers thus undertook the interviews and reported back to the whole group at the regular meetings. They talked about what they had found, what they thought of what people had told them, what they needed to put in the research report and what changes they thought the Trust needed to make.

At the end of the project a report was produced by the group. This included symbols and pictures to make it accessible. Jane and two of the co-researchers presented this to the clinical governance committee. As a result, the advocacy group were asked to work with the Trust to develop better information for people with learning disabilities.

Reflecting upon the process of undertaking participatory research

From the second part of the case study it can be seen that throughout the research Jane had to deal with some important issues. First, it was important that potential co-researchers were fully informed about what the research might entail before they made a decision to work with her. However, as the research progressed new issues arose, such as, what to research and who should be involved in gathering the data. Two people who had originally indicated that they wished to be involved in interviewing later changed their minds. There is thus a need to check constantly that co-researchers still wish to be involved, to support people in opting out of certain activities if they so wish and to be flexible. In short, there is a need to review regularly and (if necessary) renegotiate the terms of working together throughout a participatory research study (Northway, 2000b). This means that researchers need to be able to tolerate ambiguity (Finn, 1994).

Another key issue which emerged was the question of time. Even though Jane was aware that participatory research could be time-consuming, she was not prepared for what, at times, felt like a very slow process. If people are to be actively involved in all stages of the research process then it is important that they are provided with the necessary training, but this can be time-consuming (Stoeker, 1999). In addition, involving people with learning disabilities in the process of data analysis is '... time consuming and offers no easy shortcuts' (Richardson, 2002: 57). A relationship exists between the level of participation desired, the scope of the research and the time available (Northway, 1998b). In the case study, achieving participation was a prime aim and there were limits on the time available since it was necessary to report back to the committee. A decision was taken that the scope of the research should be narrowed to look at just one aspect of the service.

Conclusion

Participatory research will not be the right approach for all learning disability nursing research and not all people with learning disabilities will want to be involved in research (Northway, 2000a). However, it is important that any expansion to the research base within learning disability nursing includes the use of participatory research. Such developments would be in keeping not only with wider developments in disability research, but would also reflect the person-centred values which underpin both learning disability nursing practice and contemporary policy developments (DoH, 2001).

This chapter provides readers with an overview of the participatory research process and explores some of the practical issues which need to be considered by nurses who use such an approach. The case study might be viewed as somewhat idealistic — Jane was able to secure time and some resources to undertake the research, to find a group of people to work with throughout the research process, and her employers were receptive both to her taking this approach and to the findings of the research. Of course, in practice, things seldom work out so well but this is not peculiar to participatory research! Opportunities do exist to support people with learning disabilities if they wish to become involved in research. It is hoped that readers will have been able to identify strategies that they could use to increase participation in research.

References

Booth T (1996) Sounds of still voices: issues in the use of narrative methods with people who have learning difficulties. In: Barton L, ed. *Disability and Society: Emerging Issues and Insights*. Longman, London: 237–55

Booth W (1998) Doing research with lonely people. *Br J Learning Disabilities* **26**(4): 132–4

Chappell AL (2000) Emergence of participatory methodology in learning difficulty research; understanding the context. *Br J Learning Disabilities* **28**(1): 38–43

Cocks E, Cockram J (1995) The participatory research paradigm and intellectual disability. *Mental Handicap Res* **8**(1): 25–37

Department of Health (2001) *Valuing People. A New Strategy for Learning Disability for the 21st Century*. DoH, London

Finn JL (1994) The promise of participatory research. *J Progressive Human Services* **5**(2): 25–42

Kiernan C (1999) Participation in research by people with learning disability: origins and issues. *Br J Learning Disabilities* **27**(2): 43–7

March J, Steingold B, Justice S, Mitchell P (1997) Follow the Yellow Brick Road! People with learning difficulties as co-researchers. *Br J Learning Disabilities* **25**(2): 77–80

Minkes J, Townsley R, Weston C, Williams C (1995) Having a voice: involving people with learning difficulties in research. *Br J Learning Disabilities* **23**(3): 94–7

Northway R (1998a) *Oppression in the Lives of People with Learning Difficulties: A participatory study*. Unpublished PhD thesis, University of Bristol

Northway R (1998b) Engaging in participatory research: some personal reflections. *J Learning Disabilities Nursing, Health and Social Care* **2**(3): 144–9

Northway R (2000a) Finding out together: lessons in participatory research for the learning disability nurse. *Mental Health Care* **3**(7): 229–32

Northway R (2000b) The relevance of participatory research in developing nursing research and practice. *Nurse Researcher* **7**(4): 40–52

Oliver M (1993) Redefining disability: A challenge to research. In: Swain J, Finkelstein V, French S, Oliver M, eds. *Disabling Barriers — Enabling Environments*. Sage, London: 61–7

Oliver S (1999) Users of health services: following their agenda. In: Hood S, Mayall B, Oliver S, eds *Critical Issues in Social Research. Power and Prejudice*. Open University Press, Buckingham: 139–53

Parahoo K, Barr O, McCaughan E (2000) Research utilization and attitudes towards research among learning disability nurses in Northern Ireland. *J Adv Nurs* **31**(3): 607–13

Ramcharan P, Grant G (1994) Setting one agenda for empowering persons with a disadvantage within the research process. In: Rioux MH, Bach M, eds. *Disability is Not Measles: New Research Paradigms in Disability*. Roeher Institute, North York, Ontario: 227–44

Richardson M (1997) Participatory research methods: people with learning difficulties. *Br J Nurs* **6**(19): 1114–21

Richardson M (2000) How we live: participatory research with six people with learning difficulties. *J Adv Nurs* **32**(6): 1383–95

Richardson M (2002) Involving people in the analysis. Listening, reflecting, discounting nothing. *J Learning Disabilities* **6**(1): 47–60

Royal College of Nursing (1998a) *RCN Information: Guidance for Nurses on Clinical Governance*. RCN, London

Royal College of Nursing (1998b) *Research Ethics*. RCN, London

Sanderson H (2000) Person-centred Planning: Key features and approaches. Online at: http://www.paradigm-uk.org/ (accessed 12/12/02)

Stalker K (1998) Some ethical and methodological issues in research with people with learning difficulties. *Disability and Society* **13**(1): 5–19

Stoeker R (1999) Are academics irrelevant? Roles for scholars in participatory research. *Am Behavioural Scientist* **42**(5): 840–54

Stoeker R, Bonacich E (1992) Why participatory research? Guest Editor's Introduction. *Am Sociologist* **23**(4): 5–14

Turnbull J (1997) Learning disability nursing: a position paper. *J Learning Disabilities for Nurs, Health and Social Care* **1**(4): 186–90

Walmsley J (2001) Normalisation, emancipatory research and inclusive research in learning disability. *Disability and Society* **16**(2): 187–205

Ward L (1997) Funding for change: translating emancipatory disability research from theory to practice. In: Barnes C, Mercer G, eds. *Doing Disability Research*. The Disability Press, Leeds: 32–48

Ward L, Flynn M (1994) What matters most: disability research and empowerment. In: Rioux MH, Bach M, eds. *Disability is Not Measles: New Research Paradigms in Disability*. Roeher Institute, North York, Ontario: 29–48

Williams V (1999) Researching together. *Br J Learning Disabilities* **27**(2): 48–51

Further reading

Bashford L, Townsley R, Williams C (1995) Parallel text: making research accessible to people with intellectual disabilities. *Int J Disability, Development and Education* **42**(3): 211–20

Cupples J (2001) *Research. What it is and how to do it. An easy to read training book for people being supported to do research in the community*. Hexagon Publishing, Minehead (a resource pack and tape which can be used with people with learning disabilities who wish to become involved in research)

Useful web-sites

http://www.bris.ac.uk/Depts/NorahFry/PlainFacts/index.html
This is the web-site for the 'Plain Facts' magazine published by the Norah Fry Research Unit. 'Plain Facts' makes research findings accessible for people with learning disabilities

http://www.changepeople.co.uk/
This is the web-site of CHANGE, an organisation of disabled people. On the web-site you will find details of the picture bank which can be purchased from them. This is a useful resource when seeking to produce accessible information

Section IV:
Specialist services

13

Mental health in learning disabilities

Janet C Bailey, Veronica R Jackson

Mental health in learning disabilities

The provision of mental health services for people with learning disabilities has been contentious for many decades. The National Service Framework for Mental Health (DoH, 1999) made no mention of the need to provide services for people with learning disabilities and mental health problems. *Valuing People* (2001) the new strategy for learning disabilities, requires learning disabilities services to work closely with those implementing the Mental Health NSF to develop services to meet the needs of people with learning disabilities and mental health problems. While *Valuing People* (2001) offers much for people with learning disabilities it does not resolve this dispute, leaving much to local interpretation. The focus of this chapter is to define mental health needs in learning disabilities and through considering clinical examples, explore areas of weakness in current services, and suggest how we might improve our skills as nurses to provide the best care for people with learning disabilities experiencing mental health problems.

Introduction

Historically, people with learning disabilities who had complex needs, including mental disorders, were cared for in learning disability hospitals. All medical, psychiatric, and social care was provided within these hospitals and people with learning disabilities did not come into contact with generic services. In 1992, the Department of Health stated that, 'wherever possible, people with learning disabilities should be enabled to use ordinary health services as well as specialist assessment and treatment services' and this was re-iterated in other Government policy statements (Royal College of Psychiatrists, 1997; National Health Service Executive, 1998). In order to facilitate this process we need to look more closely at our skills for recognising symptoms of mental ill health, and supporting appropriate treatment approaches for people with learning disabilities.

What do me mean by mental health in learning disabilities?

For some time we have used the phrase 'dual diagnosis' when discussing mental Health in learning disabilities. The 'dual diagnosis' refers to the diagnosis of a learning disability with a mental health problem. This term is confusing as within mainstream mental health it is also used to describe people who misuse substances such as alcohol or drugs. Therefore, agreed consensus is use of the term mental health in learning disabilities, to be clear what it is we are discussing.

Defining mental illness in people who have learning disabilities is complicated by several issues, the most problematic of which is challenging behaviours. Challenging behaviours are the most common reason for which people with learning disabilities are referred to a consultant psychiatrist. While there is some evidence of the relationship between mental health disorders and challenging behaviours (Emerson *et al*, 1999), and a number of studies have suggested that challenging behaviours may sometimes be symptoms of, or be exacerbated by, underlying mental health disorders (Reiss and Rojahn, 1993), the determinants of challenging behaviours are poorly understood and in many cases likely to be highly complex — a combination of learned behaviour, biological, environmental, social and psychological factors, and at present, the majority of diagnostic instruments for mental health problems do not make it possible to tease out these various factors. As discussed by Moss and Lee (2001), it is hoped that more sophisticated assessment models with the power to make these complex analyses of behaviour, are developed in the future.

Prevalence of mental health problems

People with learning disabilities experience the same range of mental disorders as seen in the general population, but while in the general population it is generally indicated that the incidence of mental disorders is approximately 25%, Gibbs and Priest (1999) indicate that the incidence of mental disorders among people with learning disabilities may be three to four times more common than in the general population, together with a prevalence figure of 3% for schizophrenia which is three times the figure in the general population. Studies investigating the estimates of the number of people with a learning disability who have mental health problems vary between 10–80%.

Generally, studies which report higher rates use measures that count the full range of mental health symptoms, including the full range of personality disorders and challenging behaviours, whereas studies that report lower rates use measures that omit some of the symptoms of mental disorders. Very few studies report data that is relevant to understanding fully the discrepancy between prevalence estimates, but general discussion within much of the literature indicates that the main reasons for these variations relate to the difficulty of relying on others for observing and reporting symptoms, and uncertain status of challenging behaviours. Most worrying though is that all the literature indicates that there has been a substantial tendency to under-diagnose and inadequately treat mental health disorders for people with learning disabilities (Patel *et al*, 1993; Martin *et al*, 1997).

Why are people with learning disabilities at increased risk of developing mental disorders?

As nurses we recognise the importance of promoting mental well being. We often take for granted the ways that we have developed mechanisms and strategies for coping with exposure to fatigue, adventure, injury, risk, challenge, experimentation, failure, frustration and discouragement. A good quality of life with supportive networks, together with well-developed coping strategies, contribute to the overall quality of our lives and we are probably unaware of their influence, unless circumstances remove them from us. Most of us have had the experience of being overwhelmed in our day-to-day lives, but these networks and strategies often protect, or at least lessen the impact of mental illness if it occurs. Adults with learning disabilities are at increased risk of developing mental health disorders due to a complex interaction of social, biological, psychological factors, including underexposure to many of those experiences and networks we take for granted (*Table 13.1*).

Table 13.1: Protective factors potentially influencing the development of mental health problems and mental health disorders in individuals

Individual factors	Family factors	School context	Life events and situations	Community and cultural factors
Easy temperament	Supportive caring parent	Sense of belonging	Involvement with significant other person (partner/mentor)	Sense of connectedness
Adequate nutrition	Family harmony	Positive school climate	Availability of opportunities at critical turning points or major life transitions	Attachment to networks within the community
Attachment to family	Secure and stable family	Prosocial group	Economic security	Participation in church or other community group
Above average intelligence	Small family size	Required responsi-bility and helpfulness	Good physical health	Strong cultural identity and ethnic pride
School achievement	More than two siblings	Opportunities for some success and recognition of achievement		Access to services
Problem solving skills	Responsibility within the family	School norms against violence		Community/cultural norms against violence
Internal locus of control	Supportive relationship with other adult (for a child or adult)			
Social competence	Strong family norms and morality			
Social skills				
Good coping skills				
Optimism				
Moral beliefs				
Values				
Positive self-related cognitions				

Reproduced from: Commonwealth Department of Health and Aged Care (2000) *Promotion, Prevention and Early intervention for Mental Health — A Monograph.* Mental Health and Special Programs Branch, Canberra

While there are well documented examples of links such as high rates of Alzheimer's Disease and depression in people with Down's syndrome (Collacott *et al*, 1992,) over activity in people with Fragile X syndrome, (Murphy 1994) and over eating in people with Prader-Willi syndrome (Holland 1994), the level of learning disability is an important factor. People with severe or profound learning disabilities are likely to relate to complex neurological, genetic and other biological abnormalities. On the other hand, people with mild or moderate learning disabilities are likely to show, to a much greater extent, the impact of social risk factors.

For a child with learning disabilities the inability to keep up with other children and the experience of repeated failure at academic tasks, together with social marginalisation and stigmatisation, will interfere with the development of self-esteem. This is an established risk factor of depression, although it is true that most families continue to function well when they have a member who has a learning disability . Where family adjustment fails, or inadequate services are provided, people with learning disabilities may live in unusual restrictive circumstances, leaving them vulnerable to stress. Residential care provision often fails to provide exposure to many normal learning experiences. We see evidence of little interaction with the wider community, few friendships and no contact with family, which in turn restricts the ability to develop healthy coping strategies. Lack of knowledge and essential life skills also increase the risk of physical and sexual abuse (Brown, 1994). The development of sexuality may also be denied by care givers. This may lead to someone being diagnosed as sexually deviant when in fact they have never been given an appropriate sexual knowledge.

People who are dependent on others may be more vulnerable to the effects of loss, especially of a carer. Disturbed behaviour may follow the loss life events but carers often deny that the person with learning disabilities is aware of loss. The person with learning disabilities may be denied the opportunity to grieve. Such exclusion compounds the problem, delaying the person's understanding of the loss events and increasing the likelihood of the development of a depressive illness. People who cannot communicate well, express themselves behaviourally if they are in pain or have chronic ill health. Symptoms such as anorexia and restlessness may be caused by infections and gastrointestinal disorders. Physical and psychiatric pathology are often difficult to distinguish. Therefore, the possibility of underlying mental illness in people with newly arisen behaviour disturbance must be considered.

Just being labelled may lower self-esteem. It may also lead to exclusion from opportunities for employment and an adequate income, leisure activities, relationships, marriage, and a valued social role (*Table 13.2*).

How do we recognise mental health problems in learning disabilities

Adults with learning disabilities experience the same range of mental disorders as seen in the wider general population, but psychoses are often difficult to diagnose when individuals are unable to verbalise complex experiences, such as hearing voices. The diagnosis of organic psychoses and personality disorders is difficult in most adults with learning disabilities, as it is hard to obtain a baseline and long-term account of functioning, behaviours and symptoms. Psychoses may be misdiagnosed in adults with learning disabilities exhibiting stress-related confusion, odd behaviour, muddled speech and suspiciousness. Classic symptoms are usually present but may be difficult to identify and masked/overshadowed by atypical features, which can lead to diagnostic problems in schizophrenia and paranoid psychosis. Hysterical symptoms, pseudo-seizures, and visual hallucinations are common. Delusions are often transient and rarely systemised or interpreted.

Table 13.2: Risk factors potentially influencing the development of mental health problems and mental health disorders in individuals

Individual factors	Family factors	School context	Life events and situations	Community and cultural factors
Prenatal brain damage	Having a teenage mother	Bullying	Physical, sexual and emotional abuse	Socio-economic disadvantage
Prematurity	Having a single parent	Peer rejection	School transitions	Social or cultural discrimination
Birth injury	Absence of father in childhood	Poor attachment to school	Divorce and family break up	Isolation
Low birth weight Birth complications	Large family size	Inadequate behaviour manage	Death of a family member	Neighbourhood violence and crime
Physical and intellectual disability	Anti-social role models (in childhood)	Deviant peer group	Physical illness impairment	Population density and housing conditions
Insecure attachment in infancy	Marital discord in parents	School failure	Unemployment, homelessness	Lack of support service, including shopping, transport, recreational facilities
Low intelligence	Poor supervision and monitoring of child		Incarceration	
Difficult temperament	Low parental involvement in child's activities		Poverty/economic insecurity	
Chronic illness	Neglect in childhood		Job insecurity	
Low self-esteem	Longterm parental unemployment		Workplace accident/ injury	
Alienation	Criminality in parent		Caring for someone with an illness/disability	
Impulsivity	Harsh or inconsistent discipline		Living in a nursing home or aged care hostel	
	Social isolation		War or natural disaster	
	Experiencing rejection			
	Lack of warmth and affection			

Affective (manic-depressive) psychoses often run in families and can present as cyclical manic, depressive or mixed disorders. Disturbed activity levels, biological and social functioning often accompany irritability and signs of depression. Regression, confusion, vomiting, self-injurious behaviours may represent 'depressive equivalents'. Rapid cycles of bipolar disorder are particularly associated with learning disabilities.

Neuroses are generally under-diagnosed, especially in adults with moderate to severe learning disabilities. Reactive depression commonly follows a life event such as the loss of a significant carer, friend or pet or placement changes, but it is not often recognised. Most practitioners will have seen anxiety states develop in response to stress and environmental changes, particularly during resettlement from hospitals. Anxiety may have presented with panic attacks, agitation, low mood, pseudo-seizures, and hypochondrical, self-injurious and acting out behaviours. Although phobias tend to be over-diagnosed — a refusal to try something new may represent more general avoidance of possible failure. However, specific phobias of dogs, scissors, dirt, water or heights, for example, do occur , particularly in people with autism. The repetitive thoughts and ritualistic behaviours that are resisted and cause anxiety to those with obsessive compulsive disorder may be diagnosed as autistic features (Bouras *et al*, 2000).

There is no universal agreement among specialists as to the existence of personality disorders in adults with learning disabilities because of their different developmental process of personality due to impaired intellectual and social functioning. While personality disorders are more easily diagnosed in adults with mild and moderate learning disabilities, similar presentations in adults with severe learning disabilities are more likely to be seen as challenging behaviours.

Dementia is increasingly diagnosed as more adults with learning disabilities survive into old age. Delirium is probably under-diagnosed. Acute confusion caused by constipation, medication, infections, or epilepsy may not be noticed as it usually resolves with treatment of the underlying causes.

Assessing mental health problems

Some progress has been made in developing ways of assessing people with learning disabilities who present with mental health problems, particularly in the use of the PAS-ADD checklists and semi-structured interviews.

In order to facilitate a thorough assessment and treatment formulation we need to ensure that multidisciplinary assessment information is sought and integrated.

Moss and Lee (2001) suggest a structured format for collection of this information, such as Gardeners (1996) Multimodal model, but whatever model is adapted in practice the basic pathway for gathering information would look something like *Figure 13.1 (page 185)*.

Despite the advances in available information regarding assessing, diagnosing and treating mental health problems in people with learning disabilities, there is still limited evidence about best treatments. Teaching relaxation and social skills may help people manage their anger or anxiety. Cognitive behavioural approaches may help people manage their anxiety, depression and anger, and can help men who sexually offend. It has also been suggested that psychodynamic psychotherapy can help people who have behaviour problems, although there is sparse evidence about its effectiveness.

The following case studies highlight some of the complexities of meeting the mental needs with an individual with a learning disability and mental health problem. Including within the case studies are a 'toolbox' of the available assessment tools (*Box 13.1*) and intervention/management strategies (*Box 13.2*).

Table 13.3: Patterns of illness (comparison of prevalence figures for persons who have/do not have learning disability)

General populaton		Associated DSM IV code		Learning disabilities
Diagnostic category	Prevalence %		Prevalence%	Diagnostic category
Alcohol abuse	5.4	F10.0–10.09	0.0	Substance abuse
Drug abuse	1.7	F11.0–19.9		
Schizophrenia/ Schizophreniform	0.3	F20.0–29	6.3	Schizophrenia/ psychosis of uncertain type
Autism	0.04	F84–F84.12	3.6	Autism
Manic episode	0.1	F30, F31, F34		
Major depression disorder	3.2	F32, F33	1.7	Affective
Dysthymia	3.7	F34.1		
Phobia	5.1	F40.1, F40.2		
Panic	0.7	F40.0, F41.0	2.0	Neuroses
Obsessive/compusive	1.6	F42.0		
Anti-social personality	1.8	Not comparable	10.9	Behaviour disorders

Case study 1

Jacob, a twenty-year-old man with mild learning disability, first became involved with mental health services at the age of eighteen. He became suicidal after a period of feeling low due to his personal circumstances. His father had died a few years previously, and his relationship with his mother became strained due to her own personal difficulties. He became homeless and lived temporarily in hostel accommodation. He was uncommunicative, and did not readily express himself through words. He was guarded about his private life. He would gain the attention of others by his behaviours, his attempts to run off, taking overdoses of medication and excessive drinking of alcohol. He felt people around him would think him unintelligent, so was very guarded in the presence of others. His mother initially played a limited role; there was some denial of their relationship. So there were difficulties with getting information from carers in following the pathway for gathering information (*Figure 13.1*).

He had a current diagnosis of mild LD, personality disorder and anxiety. The initial mental health diagnosis was depression. The Mini PAS-ADD interview indicated a depressive disorder.

He had recently been discharged from mental health services, which were inadequate to meet his mental health needs at that particularly time due to his behavioural problems, ie. attention seeking, and absconding behaviours. He was eventually transferred to inpatient learning disability services. He continued to have a community nurse as his key worker who was part of the community mental health team. He was able to access services from mainstream psychiatry. This happened partly through default of the systems, but in the short term provided links of joint working between mental health and learning disabilities services.

Case Study 2

Inez is a forty-five-year-old African Caribbean woman. She has a mild learning disability, a simple (process) schizophrenia. She was referred to learning disability services and the basic pathway (*Figure 13.1*) was completed to ascertain which service would best meet her needs. Currently, joint working occurs on the part of the consultants in the two directorates, although there is no agreed local protocol.

She has been involved with mental health services on and off over a period of seventeen years. Her presentation and bizarre behaviours leads some professionals to suggest that her behaviours are due to her learning disability and not due to possible loss of social skills (she isolated herself within her home for a number of years) or mental illness.

> **Box 13.1: Assessment tools**
>
> - Aberrant behaviour checklist (ABC)
> - Camberwell assessment of need for adults with developmental and intellectual disabilities (CANDID)
> - Diagnostic assessment of the severely handicapped (DASH) II Scale
> - Learning disability version of the cardinal needs schedule (LDCNS)
> - Motivation assessment scale
> - Psychiatric assessment schedule for adults with developmental (PAS-ADD)
> - Psychopathology instrument of mentally retarded adults (PRIMRA
> - Reiss Screen for maladaptive behaviour

> **Box 13.2: Intervention/management strategies**
>
> - Assertive outreach
> - Behaviour therapy
> - Behavioural family therapy
> - Cognitive behavioural therapy
> - Coping strategies
> - Crisis intervention
> - Early intervention
> - Multi-sensory therapy
> - Occupational therapy
> - Pharmacological interventions
> - Psychotherapy (individual/group)

The assumption that the loss/ limitations of social skills was part of her learning disability, although she had no previous diagnosis of learning disability, and a recent IQ test indicated only mild learning disabilities, became the main focus of her referral. She had adequately maintained herself in the community for a number of years without substantial support from services, although she lived with certain delusional beliefs about having won a substantial amount of money, but this was not causing her great distress. This only became an issue for services when she was getting herself into financial difficulties. Interventions of managing her delusional beliefs have been used, alongside medication management in which she has been non-compliant.

Some history was gained from her daughter and the foster parents of her children but this was limited. One of the main assessment outcomes was to compare her current presentation with past episodes.

The Mini PAS-ADD interview was completed and indicated that psychosis was present.

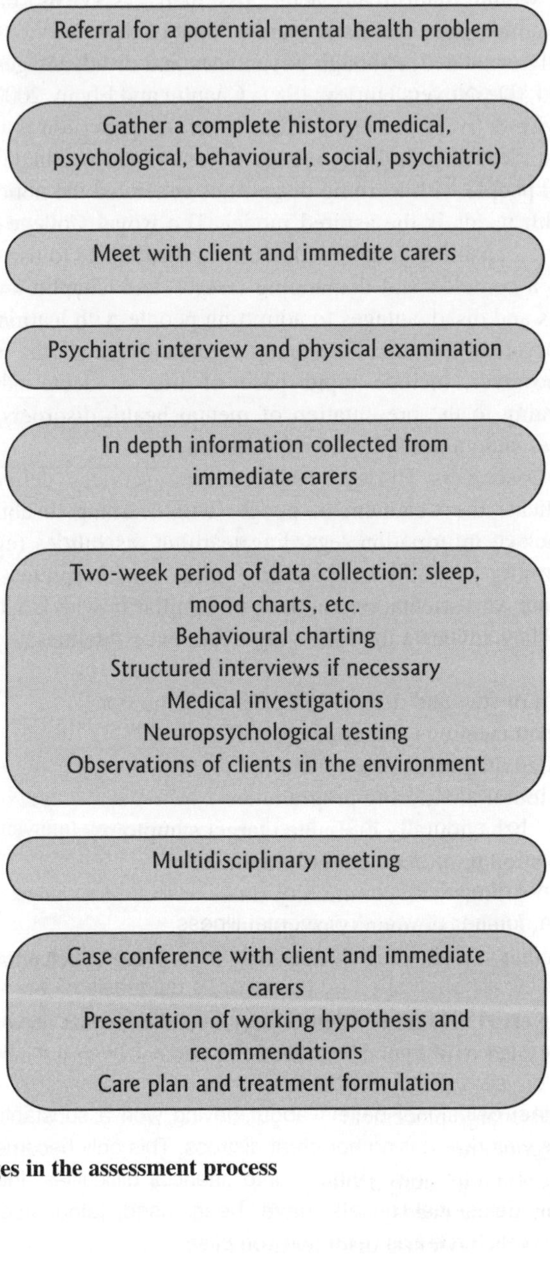

```
┌──────────────────────────────────────────────┐
│   Referral for a potential mental health problem   │
└──────────────────────────────────────────────┘

┌──────────────────────────────────────────────┐
│        Gather a complete history (medical,        │
│  psychological, behavioural, social, psychiatric)  │
└──────────────────────────────────────────────┘

┌──────────────────────────────────────────────┐
│      Meet with client and immedite carers      │
└──────────────────────────────────────────────┘

┌──────────────────────────────────────────────┐
│  Psychiatric interview and physical examination  │
└──────────────────────────────────────────────┘

┌──────────────────────────────────────────────┐
│        In depth information collected from        │
│                immediate carers                │
└──────────────────────────────────────────────┘

┌──────────────────────────────────────────────┐
│  Two-week period of data collection: sleep,      │
│             mood charts, etc.               │
│            Behavioural charting             │
│        Structured interviews if necessary       │
│            Medical investigations            │
│          Neuropsychological testing          │
│   Observations of clients in the environment    │
└──────────────────────────────────────────────┘

┌──────────────────────────────────────────────┐
│            Multidisciplinary meeting            │
└──────────────────────────────────────────────┘

┌──────────────────────────────────────────────┐
│    Case conference with client and immediate     │
│                    carers                    │
│     Presentation of working hypothesis and      │
│               recommendations               │
│      Care plan and treatment formulation      │
└──────────────────────────────────────────────┘
```

Figure 13.1: Stages in the assessment process

Models of care

While investigating how the provision of mental health in learning disabilities services is being addressed up and down the country, three main service models re-occur: mental health services within learning disabilities services, small specialist learning disabilities units within mainstream acute psychiatric services, or access within mainstream acute admission psychiatric wards. None of these services appear to have been systematically evaluated, although advantages and disadvantages of each model have been reported (DesNoyers Hurley, 1987; Chaplin and Flynn, 2000; Kwok, 2001). Each form of service delivery produces different service provision issues.

Discussion with learning disability nurses currently involved in developing mental health services for people with learning disabilities generated the notion that access to acute mental health wards is the aspired model. The Royal College of Psychiatrists (1996) agree that: '... enabling people with learning disabilities to use ordinary mental health services is a complex and demanding task...' and Chaplin and Flynn (2000) outline advantages and disadvantages to admitting people with learning disabilities to acute admission psychiatric wards. For example, reduction in stigma of local services. Disadvantages, however, include rapid pace of life on acute admission wards, difficulties in relating to the presentation of mental health disorders in people with learning disabilities and vulnerability to exploitation.

Sovner and DesNoyers Hurley (1987) outline services delivery issues that potentially complicate the treatment of people with learning disabilities in mental health settings: lack of information regarding learning disabilities (eg. normal stress responses in learning disabilities, patients being misinterpreted as psychiatric symptoms), an acute care orientation and lack of familiarity with behavioural analysis and monitoring . They advocate the following treatment guidelines:

- establish length of stay and disposition prior to admission
- set up orientation meetings for inpatient staff
- carry out detailed diagnostic assessment
- develop behavioural monitoring programmes
- develop and set behaviourally-orientated target symptoms
- develop habilitation reinforcement programmes
- set up regular meetings with community staff
- have the patient attend community programmes
- contact with medics to make drug changes only in response to behavioural changes.

Sovner and DesNoyers (1991) further outline seven conditions that need to be fulfilled in order to increase the chances of a good outcome being attained from and inpatient admission:

- guarantee of 'discharge placement'
- stable medical condition
- adequate feeding and toileting skills
- ability to communicate needs
- absence of severe behavioural disorder/autism
- specific treatment goals
- adequate provision of appropriate activity and the use of non-pharmacological treatments.

A role for the specialist practitioner?

As learning disability nurses, we have reviewed and increased our training and education to ensure that all professional carers are familiar with the presentation, care and treatment of mental illness for people with moderate/severe learning disabilities. The issue of employing primarily RN(LD)s to develop services for mental health in learning disabilities highlighted skills deficits which many services have attempted to address by seconding nurses to undertake registered nurse mental health RN(M) training.

Wallace (2002) argued that with regard to nurses with both qualifications the impact on care outcomes appears to be an unexplored area, but there is growing anecdotal evidence that those individuals with moderate to severe learning disabilities who have a mental health problem, are receiving a good service within specialist learning disability services. RN(LD)s are becoming adept at working with this group and filtering out the issues that are often masked by problem behaviours, which is often how these issues are highlighted in the first place. However, what we have are a group of people with borderline/mild learning disabilities that continue to fall through the cracks of the services.

Mental health nurses have different interactional styles with patients than RN(LD)s and such differences often lead to negative perceptions of mental health in learning disabilities, even when dual registered. Professionals and staff unaccustomed to working with adults with learning disabilities continue inappropriately to attribute signs of a mental disorder to a person's learning disability *per se,* and not giving rise to mental health needs.

Wallace (2002) asks two questions about the ability of current services to accommodate the needs of people with learning disabilities who experience a mental disorder:

⌘ What is the current appropriateness of learning disability and/or mental health services to facilitate effectively individuals with a dual diagnosis and whose responsibility is it?

⌘ What is the ability of learning disability qualified nurses to identify indicative signs related to mental illness, and current preparation of pre-registration students following the learning disability branch in mental health/illness awareness?

Valid questions, but should we be asking instead: what is the ability of mental health qualified nurses to identify the indicative signs related to mental illness and current preparation of pre-registration mental health nurses in disability awareness?

In the past, as previously said, mental health needs for people with learning disabilities were met through learning disability hospitals. Admission to hospital was almost a matter of routine. The increasing emphasis on enabling people with learning disabilities to remain in their local community, even if they have additional complex needs, has highlighted the need for specialist services for these patients.

Despite the well intentioned rhetoric of learning disability psychiatry services and general psychiatric services integrated in a local mental health service, many services have failed to agree boundaries and responsibilities. There is consensus that patients of differing abilities need differing programmes of therapy (appropriate to their verbal ability); but experience of many units up and down the country is that there is immense difficulty in arriving at a successful mix within a particular facility.

Conclusion

Learning disability services continue to take full responsibility to meet the needs of mental health in learning disabilities. People with learning disabilities, of all severities and types, with whatever mental health problem, are currently accessing comprehensive psychiatric services from within learning disability services. The development of specialist practitioners and consultant nurses in this area of practice has been very positive.

The ongoing discussion regarding access to mainstream mental health remains to be that of whether mental health in learning disabilities is a special case, or normal variant. We would argue that the advantages for people with learning disabilities being able to access a wide range of services within the specialist services, far outweigh some of the difficulties that may be encountered in accessing mainstream mental health services. The role of the specialist practitioner for mental health in learning disabilities is clearly to support mental health services practitioners in assessment, and ensuring community teams develop appropriate outreach and monitoring strategies.

References

Brown H (1994) Establishing the incidence of abuse in services for people with learning disabilities. In: Harris J, Craft A, ed. (1994) *People with Learning Disabilities at Risk of Physical or Sexual Abuse*. BILD, Kidderminster

Bouras N, Holt G, Day K, Dosen A, eds (2000) *Mental Health in Mental Retardation: The ABC for Mental Health, Primary Care and Other Professionals*. World Psychiatric Association, London

Chaplin R, Flynn A (2000) Adults with learning disabilities admitted to psychiatric wards. *Adv Psychiatric Treatment* **6**: 128–34

Collacott RA, Cooper SA, McGrother C (1992) Differential rates of psychiatric disorders in adults with Down's syndrome compared with other mentally handicapped adults. *Br J Psychiatry* **161**: 671–4

Corbett JA (1979) Psychiatric morbidity and mental retardation. In: James FE, Snaith RP, eds. *Psychiatric Illness and Mental Handicap*. Gaskell Press, London

DesNoyers Hurley A (1987) Individual psychotherapy with mentally retarded individuals: a review and call for research. *Research in Developmental Disabilities* **10**: 261–75

Department of Health (1992) *Health Services for People with Learning Disabilities*. HSG(92) HMSO, London

Department of Health (1999) *National Service Framework for Mental Health: Modern standards and service models*. HMSO, London

Department of Health (2001) *Valuing People: A New Strategy for Learning Disability for the 21st Century*. HMSO, London

Emerson E, Moss SC, Kieran CK (1999) The relationship between challenging behaviour and psychiatric disorders in people with severe learning disabilities. In: Bouras N, ed. *Psychiatric and Behavioural Disorders in Mental Retardation*. Cambridge University Press, Cambridge

Gardner WI (1996) Non Specific behavioural symptoms in persons with a dual diagnosis: a psychological model for integrating biomedical and psychosocial diagnoses and interventions. *Psychology of Mental Retardation in Developmental Disabilities* **21**: 6–11

Gibbs M, Priest HM (1999) Designing and implementing a 'dual diagnosis' module: A review of the literature and some preliminary findings. *Nurse Educ Today* **19**(5): 357–63

Holland AJ (1991) Learning disability and psychiatric/behavioural disorders: A genetic perspective. In: McGriffin P, Murray R, eds. *The New Gentics of Mental Illness*. Butterworth–Heinemann, Oxford

Kwok H (2001) Development of a specialised psychiatric service for people with learning disabilities and mental health problems: Report of a project from Kwai Chung Hospital, Hong Kong. *Br J Learning Disabilities* **29**: 22–5

Martin DM, Roy A, Wells MB (1997) Health gain through health checks: improving access to primary healthcare for people who have intellectual disability. *J Intellectual Disability Research* **41**: 401–8

Moss S, Lee P (2001) Mental Health. In: Thompson J, Pickering S, eds. *Meeting the Health Needs of People who have a Learning Disability*. Baillière Tindall, London

Murphy G (1994) Understanding challenging behaviours. In: Emerson E, McGill P, Mansell J, eds. *Severe Learning Disabilities and Challenging behaviours: designing high quality services*. Chapman and Hall, London

National Health Service Executive (NHSE) (1998) *Signposts for Success: Commissioning and providing for people with learning disabilities*. HMSO, London

Patel P, Goldberg D, Moss S (1993) Psychiatric morbidity in older people with moderate and severe learning disability: The prevalence study. *Br J Psychiatry* **163**: 481–91

Reiss S, Rojahn J (1993) Joint occurrence of depression and aggression in children and adults with mental retardation. *J Intellectual Disabilities Research* **37**: 287–94

Sovner R, DesNoyers Hurley A (1987) Guidelines for the treatment of mentally retarded persons on psychiatric inpatient units. *Psychiatric Aspects of Mental Retardation Reviews* **6**: 7–14

Sovner R, DesNoyers Hurley A (1991) Seven questions to ask when considering an acute psychiatric inpatient admission for a developmentally disabled adult. *Habilitative Mental Healthcare Newsletter* **10**: 27–30

Roy M, Clarke D, Roy A (2000) *An Introduction to Learning Disability Psychiatry*. Online at: http://www.ldbook.co.uk

Royal College of Psychiatrists (1997) *Meeting the mental health needs of people with learning disability*. Council Report CR56. Royal College of Psychiatrists, London

Wallace B (2002) Boxed in : The challenge of 'dual diagnosis'. *Learning Disability Practice* **5**: 24–6

References for *Box 13.1*

Aberrant behaviour checklist (ABC)
Aman MG, Singh NN (1986) *Aberrant Behavior Checklist Manual*. Slosson Educational Publications, East Aurora, NY
CANDID
Xenitidis K, Thornicroft G, Leeds M *et al* (2000) Reliability and validity of the CANDID: a needs assessment instrument for adults with learning disabilities and mental health problems. *Br J Psychiatry* **176**: 473–8

Diagnostic assessment of the severely handicapped (DASH) II Scale
Matson JL, Rush KS, Hamilton M, Anderson SJ, Bamburg JW, Baglio S (1999) Characteristics
of depression as assessed by Diagnostic Assessment for the Severely Handicapped-II
(DASH-II). *Research in Developmental Disabilities* **20**(4): 305–15
Learning disability version of the cardinal needs schedule (LDCNS)
Raghavan R, Marshall M, Lockwood A, Duggan L (2001) The learning disability version of
the cardinal needs schedule (LDCNS): a systematic approach to assessment needs of
people with dual diagnosis. Unpublished version (r.raghavan@bradford.ac.uk)
Motivation assessment scale
Spreat S, Connelly L (1986) Reliability analysis of the motivation assessment scale. *Am J Ment
Retardation* **100**: 528–32
Moss SC, Prosser H, Costello H, Simpson N, Patel P, Rowe S, Turner S, Hatton C (1998)
Reliability and validity of the PAS-ADD checklist for detecting disorders in adults with
intellectual disability. *J Intellectual Disability Research* **42**(2): 173–83
The Reiss Screen for malapdaptive behaviour
Sturmey P, Burgam KJ, Perkin JS (1995) The Reiss Screen for maladaptive behavior: its
reliability and internal consistencies. *J Intellectual Disability Research* **39**: 191–6

References for *Box 13.2*

Assertive outreach
Thiru S (2002) Assertive outreach. *Learning Disability Practice* **5**: 10–13
Behaviour family therapy
Falloon IRH (1988) *Handbook of Behavioural Family Therapy*. Guilford Press, New York and
London
Behaviour therapy
Emerson E (1995) *Challenging Behavior. Analysis and Intervention in People with Learning
disabilities*. Cambridge University Press, Cambridge
Cognitive behaviour therapy/coping strategies
Stenfert-Kroese B, Dagnan D, Loumidis K (1997) *Cognitive Behaviour Therapy for People
with Learning Disabilities*. Routledge, London
Early/crisis intervention
Sainbury Centre for Mental Health. Online at: http://www.scmh.org.uk
Multi sensory therapy
Baillon S, Diepan E, Prettyman R (2002) Multi-sensory therapy in psychiatric care. *Adv
Psychiatric Treatment* **8**: 444–52
Occupational therapy
Malley SM, Dattilo J, Gast D (2002) Effects of visual arts instruction on the mental health of
adults with mental retardation and mental illness. *Mental Retardation* **40**(4): 278–96
Pharmacotherapy
Reiss S, Aman MC ((1998) *Psychotropic Medications and Developmental Disabilities: The
International Consensus Handbook*. The Ohio State University Nisonger Center, USA
Psychotherapy
Beail N (1995) Outcome of psychonanalysis, psychoanalytic and psychodynamic
psychotherapy with people with intellectual disabilities: a review. *Changes* **13**: 186–91
Solution-focused brief therapy
Iveson C (2002) Solution-focused brief therapy. *Adv Psychiatric Treatment* **8**: 149–57

14

Challenging behaviour

Andy Howe

This chapter examines changes in a local service for individuals who present with challenging behaviours in the community. Local developments and practice will be reviewed in the context of national and regional trends. A case study will be presented of an individual, who presents with challenging behaviours in the community, and illustrates the types of assessment and interventions that can be applied.

The chapter concludes with a discussion on the role of the community nurse in learning disabilities and challenging behaviour in the context and expectation to work in diverse ways in care and case management.

Issues include the identification that if specialist nurses are to be invested in behaviour analysis, then a further examination into the role is required to be appraised in the light of current policies and professional dilution of learning disability nurses roles.

Introduction

Community-based teams specialising in working with individuals with a learning disability and challenging behaviour living in the community were developed in the late 1980s. It has been suggested that the provision of high-quality community-based supports should be seen as an integral component for effective intervention (Cameron *et al*, 1998). In 1989, the Behavioural Services Team (BST) in Plymouth was established by McBrien (1999), and in Clwyd the Intensive Support Team was developed by Toogood (Toogood and Bell, 1994).

By 1993, Emerson *et al* (1996) estimated that there were sixty-five teams with 450 staff, costing around £10,000,000 a year. These teams were usually comprised of multidisciplinary teams of psychologists and nurses working to a behavioural methodology for clients with severely challenging behaviour. The range of provision included; consultation, staff and carer training, service development and hands on assessment and intervention.

Concurrent with the development of these teams a debate on the use of non-aversive or aversive approaches to behaviour management was ongoing. Cullen (1996) stated that it is impossible to separate the analysis of challenging behaviour from considerations of ideology and values which influence the approach of the practitioner. In other words, the nurses' personal ideology would influence how they analyse behaviour and how they would treat it, a non-aversive versus an aversive approach.

Many teams adopt a non-aversive approach to behaviour management. A model of Applied Behavior Analysis (LaVigna and Donnellan, 1986) provided a framework that several teams, including our local behaviour support team used initially to supplement existing skills and knowledge.

Research into the effectiveness of peripatetic support teams has continued. One survey showed a perceived reduction in frequency, duration and intensity of challenging behaviour and gains in quality of life (Toogood and Bell, 1994). Later findings show that simply naming a team as specialist makes little difference to outcomes.

A core of specialist competencies is necessary and the quality of mainstream services may need to be developed through a broader training strategy (Lowe and Felce, 1996). A national survey (Emerson *et al*, 1996) showed a perceived success rate for 13% of local need and cases were closed due to a reduction in challenging behaviour for only 36% of cases, and concluded by suggesting that achieving significant and sustained outcomes for clients is likely to be difficult without quality mainstream services, clear operating procedures, effective management and skilled performance in the assessment and treatment of challenging behaviour. The need for an emphasis on achieving quality standards in mainstream services was highlighted again by Lowe *et al* (1996) as a way of enabling specialist support service to be more effective.

Behaviour services teams were designed to take assessment and intervention out to the client (McBrien, 1999) rather than clients attending an assessment centre where the variables governing behaviour would be significantly altered. The types of assessment and interventions used in our behaviour support team followed an applied behaviour analysis model of assessment, analysis and intervention, adapted from the format described by LaVigna and Donnellan (1986). Three levels of assessment were used:

- a brief consultation with recommendations
- a full assessment and analysis report
- support from the service by providing staff training.

Table 14. 1 details a range of assessment techniques from which elements are used for each client according to need.

A specialist behavioural practitioner would possibly adopt the following sequence (numbered in Table 14.1) when concluding a level 1 assessment:

1. Screening
2. Direct observations
3. ABC Charts

If this process was not productive, that is, not seeing any challenging behaviours, or direct staff were unable to write clear ABC charts, the practitioner would then proceed to:

4. Event recording charts (for days of the week, code whether any new behaviours occur or not).
5. This should be enough for a level 1 assessment, having an idea of the functioning behaviour or whether in fact it is a staff attitude issue (bias or prejudice against the person with a learning disability). You should then be able to ascertain whether it is a challenging behaviour or a staff training/attitude issue.

If a challenging behaviour, for straightforward cases this would lead to a brief set of recommendations with limited support. If more complex, then a level 2 assessment would be conducted which would lead into the following methods:

1. Screening

2. Direct observations
4. event recording charts
3. ABC charts

At this point I would avoid 5 (Motivational questionnaires) part of a level 2 assessment as they tend to be unreliable. Then proceed to:

6. Completion of the behaviour assessment guide

In *Table 14.1* analogue assessment is identified, but is a provocative form of assessment with behaviour analysts as it presents with an ethical dilemma and forces the client into a situation where they demonstrate the function of the behaviour.

On completion of the assessment, the behaviour analyst analyses the information and comes up with a hypothesis relative to the function of the behaviour and proceeds to write up a report with recommendations.

As a result of the analysis, the report would include all observations and outcomes and be formulated as identified in *Table 14.1* under sections 7, 8, 9, 10 and 11 to the service. (These instruments and assessments are obviously specialised and extremely detailed. A glossary of terms can be found at: www.coedu.usf.edu/abaglossary/main.asp and in Kazdin, 2002.

Table 14.1: Assessment and intervention techniques

Process	Description	Function
New referral	Allocation	First visit
1. Screening visit	Prioritisation	Taken on or referred elsewhere
Behaviour interview	Structured interview to determine the facts as far as , possible, including outcome wanted	Initial indication of which the target behaviours may be and what type of assessment and intervention to use
2. Direct observations (see below)	Choice of techniques according to need (see below)	May sample certain times or make a composite day by sampling different hours over several days or weeks. The presence of an observer can alter the observed behaviour
2. Continuous observations	Recording in writing all that occurs in the environment with and around the individual for a set time period	Helps to determine if the behaviours actually occur and helps to write a description of the target behaviours. Provides initial data for analysis
2. Momentary time sampling (by hand or using Psion hand-held computer programme)	A period of observation recording if the behaviour targeted occurs at the last moment of each interval	Provides data for analysis or baseline of behaviour
2. Tally count	Sports tally counter used for target behaviour	Useful for high frequency discrete counting, makes some noise that may distract
2. Duration recording	Recording the amount of time by stopwatch that the target behaviour occurs in a set time	Provides data for analysis or baseline of behaviour

Table 14.1: cont.

Process	Description	Function
4. Event recording forms	Staff complete forms	Reliability an issue, can be used for finding a baseline of behaviour frequency and times when behaviour occurs
3. ABC charts	Staff record the antecedent, behaviour and consequences along with other variables	Variable reliability depends on staff motivation and accuracy, need to be completed soon after an incident
5. Motivational questionnaires	Various types available, several staff are interviewed to determine what they perceive as the behaviour function	Can be unreliable, but sometimes with low frequency behaviour that cannot be easily seen directly may be necessary
Video recording	Recorded and viewed later in combination with a method, as above	Need consent, data protection issues arise. Can be a distraction to clients and alter behaviour, shows a limited field of view if stationary
Computerised multi-variable recording (Obswin)	Palm top computer pre-programmed with likely relevant variables, one key stroke to record brief events or ongoing conditions	Requires skill, useful for high frequency behaviours, computer analysis of results
6. Completion of the behaviour assessment guide (Willis, LaVigna et al, 1989)	Working through all relevant sections of the guide for the individual including the history and reinforcement sections	To complete in full takes about forty hours. Helps ensure that vital pieces of information are not missed
Analysis of data **(Pivotal role of practitioner)**	Identifying patterns in data that indicate a causal relationship that explains the function of each target behaviour. A report writing structure can help to direct this process	Generates a hypothesis based on evidence and increases the likelihood of targeting intervention accurately. Proof of the behaviour function may be possible with analogue assessment, if ethical
Report writing to set format	A structured report following a standard format, for example LaVigna and Donnellan (1986)	Provides a structure that helps check you have all the information you need and formats your intervention to include a range of elements
Intervention strategies be (see below)	A broad range of recommendations to ameliorate the targeted challenging behaviours	May have cost implications and difficult for services to implement without support
7. Environmental changes	Changes to the physical, social and organisational environment that will reduce the likelihood of the target behaviours	May be easily implemented and require little further effort from carers
8. Positive programmes	A range of skill development recommendations in areas indicated in the assessment to increase coping and functional skills	Not so easily implemented, requires time and effort, not often given a high priority by staff

Table 14.1: cont.

Process	Description	Function
9. Direct treatment	Use of reinforcement schedules and stimulus control programmes to reduce the frequency or severity of the target behaviour	Often seen as old fashioned behaviour modification and can be resisted by staff
10. Reactive management	Methods for dealing with the target behaviour when it occurs, used until other methods take effect	Often popular, gives staff approved coping strategies, can limit incentive to use other's strategies
11. Staff training	Training targeted to areas identified during assessment	Popular with staff, immediate changes in staff attitude can occur, slow to alter practice
Support with implementation	Initial introduction of the recommendations by team members that demonstrate that the interventions work	Proves interventions work and allows for small changes to be quickly made. When support is withdrawn staff teams can feel unsupported

Members of behaviour analysis teams range in diversity of experiences, from those who are well recognised practitioners who publish authoritatively in this area to those teams who are of less status in terms of development and experience. Representatives from these teams regularly meet in the north west region of England to share ideas and network experiences in an informal way.

From sharing practices, applied behaviour analysis remained the core aim of assessment in teams, but more expedient approaches and methods were being adopted by some teams. This is a trend observed from the meetings and is not referenced in any research identified in this chapter.

Table 14.2 gives a summary from a recent workshop and is a compilation of the views expressed by those members attending.

From the late 1990s and from successive meetings of this group, there were reports of behaviour teams discontinuing or merging into existing community learning disability team services. An example of this is a team set up in 1993 that has now merged with their local psychology service and has moved from a behavioural analysis approach to a more cognitively behavioural model (Simpson *et al*, 1997).

As service priorities changed locally the behaviour support team was disbanded and over a period of time there was a gradual reduction in team members. The remaining members moved into the community learning disability nursing team, continuing to have a challenging behaviour caseload. This community nursing team was then split into two geographical areas as joint community learning disability teams, coterminous with local authority boundaries working with social work colleagues and managed by social work team leaders.

Table 14.2: Overview of assessment preferences

Assessment and intervention tools used	Benefits	Limitations
The behaviour assessment guide (Willis, LaVigna et al, 1989)	Good, can use whole or selected key parts	Long format. Includes jargon
Interviews and notes	Useful for low rate behaviours	Needs to be conducted soon after incidents
Momentary time sampling (MTS). Recording the last moment of an interval and recording the behaviour	Easy to use. Can be used to evaluate intervention effectiveness	Not useful with low rate behaviours
Video recording	Can be watched repeatedly to clarify what occurred	Consent and data protection issues need addressing
ABC charts systematically recording antecedents behaviour and consequences	Useful for analysis	Varies with quality of completion
Motivational assessment scale (questionnaire)	Indicates staff view	Indicates staff view
Aide to functional analysis (questionnaire)	Indicates staff view	Indicates staff view
Psion MTS (momentary time sampling)	Good, now used less frequently	
Obswin palm top observation programme. Can record multiple variables	Good for high rate behaviour Analysis by computer. Good in classrooms	Time to set up and pratice necessary. Expensive
Review of records and history	Checks for accuracy of anecdotal evidence, can explode myths	Takes time
Good day bad day graph	Gives staff a visual record	
Reinforcement list (by carer or client)	Quicker than an inventory	
Reinforcement sampling. Client selects presented items	Provide choices to sample as reinforcers	
Analogue assessment (experimental method to test for behaviour function)	Good if adapted to create experiences for the client and then use MTS	Emphasis on the reduction of rather than generation of target behaviour
Self-recording	Useful for able clients	
Clinical intuition	Test by trying method with MTS, check the validity	Use with caution
Report writing	Provides a framework for thinking through issues and asking questions	
Graphs	Useful visual representation	
Statistical analysis	Useful with sufficient data	Data needs to be accurate
Single case design abab format.	Test hypothesis for complex cases and proof of intervention effectiveness	

Local practices for working as a nurse in challenging behaviours have changed and now include:

- community care assessments often looking for health funding for packages of care
- assessment and advice on minimising the likelihood and impact of challenging behaviours: including writing/helping to write reactive management plans for challenging behaviours
- working with adults recently moved from children's services, assessing and advising on ways of working with them in adult services
- requests to teach staff physical intervention techniques
- assessment and recommendations adopting a much shortened version of the behaviour support teams original methodology
- health screening in support of health action plans.

Practice case study

Charlie is a twenty-eight-year-old who has a mild learning disability, lives alone, as part of supported living, in a house rented from a housing association which has twenty-two hours support per week from paid carers plus support from family.

Charlie has a range of self-care skills but has recently become more dependent upon carers. Charlie has a range of challenging behaviours and was referred when carers kept leaving due to Charlie's behaviour towards them. Management strategies for Charlie were requested to allow the service to continue. At screening, Charlie's behaviour was reported and observed to include swearing, personal abusiveness to care staff, ignoring care staff, refusing to work with care staff, demanding care staff to do domestic work and being out when care staff arrived. The assessment methods used and interventions developed are recorded in *Table 14.3*.

Evaluation

This case study is an example of a case that uses some of the skills previously used within a behaviour support team. The study does not give an ideal example of an intervention, at the time of writing it was one of the few referred cases where these skills and methods were relevant.

The initial request was for management strategies for Charlie to allow a service to continue. To date, this has been successful as a service is still provided and there are a series of guidelines for carers to follow. This continuation of the service is in part due to the repertoire of interventions applied, but is also due to the continuing work of the care manager in finding and working with a more robust care provider, that is one which can match service provision which includes a high quality of staff

For the outcomes so far achieved and future work see *Table 14.4*.

Table 14.3: Assessment methods and interventions

Assessment methods used	Behaviours reported
Review of written records	• Personal verbal abuse to carers
Initial interview with case manager	• Swearing/verbal abuse in public places towards carers
Initial interview with carers	• Ignoring carers to play computer games.
Follow up interviews with carers	• Insufficient money for purchases leading to verbal abuse
Follow up interviews with case manager	• Running off when out
Anecdotal evidence from carers at case meetings	• Threats to carers
	• Out or not answering the door when carers arrive
	• Throwing objects at carers

	Interactional style with Charlie
Interraction profile interview with the case manager and carer and write up	Information gathered to complete the first version of an Interactional Profile (Burchess 1991), this sent out to those working with Charlie, providing information on the most successful ways working with Charlie.

	Analysis of recording
Event recording charts	36% of time no problems 50% of times out when a carer arrived 100% of occasions rude when other people were there and when the carer arrived 6% of the time out when other people were visiting

	Analysis of ABC charts
ABC charts	• Being out behaviour may be a coping strategy for needing to have a carer
	• Leaving a calling card when Charlie is out on arrival has a short-term effect to increase being in behaviour for up to two future visits
	• Charlie prefers support from certain people not paid carers
	• Charlie is verbally abusive to carers when others are in the house, this may be a way of coping with the emotions involved with having to settle for a less preferred carer, or a learned behaviour reinforced
	• When the preferred other has left Charlie often becomes pleasant to the less preferred carer
	• The arrival of a paid carer signals to Charlie the pending loss of mother or brother for a period of time
	• Charlie may have learned to keep mother or brother for longer by having an emotional outburst or rudeness to the carer, which may be maintained by intermittent reinforcement
	• Reactions to Charlie's behaviour are inconsistent and include punishment, reward, reprimand, attention and demand removal
	• The computer is a self-stimulating reinforcer
	• Givien some space Charlie can cope with the emotions of needing/having a carer, and allows satiation with the computer game

Table 14.3 cont.

	Analysis of ABC Charts contin.
	• Unresolved issue with the family often concerning money or buying items is a warning sign that a challenging behaviour may occur
	• Charlie's behaviour is intermittently reinforced with purchases
Interventions	**Interventions**
Calling cards and calling card protocol	• Agreed to call charlie by phone 15–20 minutes prior to the start of a shift, on arrival knock and wait 5 minutes for access then enter if the door is open. If the property is locked and access is not possible a pre--printed calling card is posted through the door after writing on it the time of the next shift
Interaction profile	**Interaction profile questions asked when interviewing carers**
To ensure consistent work with Charlie minimising the likelihood of a challenging behaviour	• What activities or tasks could/can your service user do?
	• How complex should/can tasks be?
	• Are there any activities that should be avoided?
	• When doing activities does it make a difference how close you are? How?
	• Does physical contact help or make things worse? What type?
	• Does eye contact or the way you face make a difference?
	• Does the way you speak make a difference? How?
	• Is there any topic of conversation that helps? Should you be quiet?
	• When giving instructions or advice about an activity how complex should instructions be?
	• What is the best way to make sure of success? Prompts? What type? Demonstrations?
	• How quickly are new skills learnt?
	• Do any aides, adaptations or positioning help?
	• What is the best way to introduce an activity?
	• What preparation needs to be done before you start? Do you ask encourage or tell the person to do the activity?
	• How do you explain how much the person is expected to do, too little or too much?
	• What is the best way to end an activity?
	• What rewards should be used and how?
	• What should be done for doing part of the task? How can you avoid reinforceing inappropriate behaviour?
Agreement on acceptable behaviour	• At a joint meeting with Charlie, it was agreed that physical aggression to carers, verbal abuse towards carers and continuing playing on computer when carers arrived to work were not acceptable behaviours. Charlie accepted these agreements

Table 14.3 cont.	
Information sheet	• An information sheet on who does what activity and how much spending money is available was agreed at a follow-up meeting. Copies for all involved were printed and laminated to remove confusion or dispute
Individual reactive management plan	**Interventions**
For each of the behaviours a protocol for intervention has been written, using the framework on the right, based on local policy	• Target behaviour • Triggers • Warning signs • Behaviour chain • Non-physical intervention • Breakaway techniques • Personal consideration prior to physical intervention • Principles and values to be considered prior to physical intervention • Physical intervention • Staffing requirements • Staff training
Discussion with consultant psychiatrist	• Carers had related concerns that recent medication changes had made Charlie have increased mood swings, medication reviewed
Further assessment and analysis to be undertaken	• Using continuous observation, pro-forma tick box for targeted behaviours and ABC charts in situ
Direct observations of Charlie's behaviour in various settings	• Observation of social interaction between Charlie and carers to include frequency of praise, criticism, demand and assistance
Completion of a reinforcement inventory	• To determine the most effective reinforcers to use with schedules of reinforcement
Further data collection by care staff	• Using ABC forms and event recording forms for further analysis and comparison with baseline

The likelihood of enduring success in maintaining support is reduced due to limited co-operation from Charlie who has the ability to live alone with twenty-two hours of care support and support from family and friends. The case manager employed by social services is under pressure not to increase the amount of support provided, with an expectation of no significant change until there is a service breakdown possibly requiring intervention under the Mental Health Act (1995).

Further applications/relevance

Thorough behaviour assessment, analysis and intervention is extremely time-consuming and expensive, as can be gained from briefly reviewing the above case. Research into the efficacy of behaviour support teams (Emerson *et al*, 1996) has shown that perceived success rates by teams are low, and that the percentage of demand served is also low. The requirements for successful work go beyond the skills of the specialist

Table 14.4: Case study outcomes

Outcomes	Details of outcome
Continuation of service provision	• Support is available for 80% of the hours in the care plan. Negotiations for the other 20% ongoing
Guidelines in place to minimise the likelihood of incidents and to manage them when they occur	Guidelines and training to support staff in place for the following: • personal verbal abuse to carers • swearing/verbal abuse in public places towards carers • ignoring carers to play computer games • insufficient money for purchases leading to verbal abuse • running off when out • threats to carers • out or not answering the door when carers arrive to work with her • throwing objects at carers
An initial hypothesis of function has been formed	These hypotheses need testing by trialling interventions and measuring their effect using MTS or other recording methods (see *Table 14.1*). The hypothesis of function being 'to gain access to preferred carers and purchase of goods'.
Outcomes not yet achieved	
Further assessment	See *Table 14.3*
Assessment and intervention report	A letter to the referrer including assessment details and recommendations, with sections on environmental changes,positive programs, direct treatment, reactive management and staff training
Environmental changes 24-hour	Continued use of the interactional profile, investigation into the availability of other support mechanism, such as support
Teach coping skills	Relaxation training, anger management and problem-solving skills, as part of the positive programming section of broader recommendations. repeated offer of a referral to psychology for the above and counselling
Direct treatment	The introduction of reinforcement schedules for the absence of target behaviours, using reinforcements based on a reinforcement inventory. This to include methods of fading reinforcement over time
Reactive management	See *Table 14.3*
Carer training	See *Table 14.3*

team and need to include quality and capacity of mainstream services, clarity of team operating procedures and effective management of the consultancy process. However, if a team can prevent admissions they can become cost effective:

> *For example, the cost of a six-week admission to the specialist residential facility operated by the service would have exceeded the annual cost of the specialist peripatetic support by around 100%.*

Allen and Lowe, 1995

The intervention techniques used in the above case study are appropriate for a wide range of referrals. Implementation is often limited by the staff team's ability to respond. From personal experience, most services are keen to make environmental changes to reduce the likelihood of challenging behaviour, to have a strategy in place for managing behaviour and to receive staff training; however, positive programmes, such as teaching coping strategies for clients and direct treatment strategies such as reinforcement schedules are less popular and can be resisted by staff teams that have many other demands on their time. The extent of technical jargon and complexity of some tools for assessment/intervention are also a limitation when working with less skilled or experienced staff teams.

Methods used by specialist teams and, in particular, methods of functional analysis are not fully researched. Toogood and Timlin (1996) state that functional assessment increases the likelihood of selecting a successful treatment. When comparing methods of functional assessment they suggest that multiple assessment formats would benefit from analysis of their combined reliability. Repp (1994) in Toogood and Timlin (1996) suggested a sequence of developing a hypothesis, for example, by interview and rating scale, confirming the hypothesis by direct observation and testing the hypothesis by experimental analysis of assessment-based hypotheses, or trying intervention strategies. Whitaker and Hirst (2002) argue that functional analysis is not enough and that correlations between behaviours and other variables could be tested using a trial intervention that is carefully evaluated, as the analysis is speculative.

Local experience shows an increased demand from providers to provide training to their staff teams in understanding challenging behaviour, physical interventions and writing reactive management plans. The Department of Health and Department for Education and Skills (2002) have published *Guidance for Restrictive Physical Intervention* under the *Valuing People* ethos of inclusion, which refers to the British Institute of Learning Disabilities (BILD) *Code of Practice for Trainers in Physical Intervention* (2001) and the standards that are expected.

The white paper, *Valuing People* (2001) refers to developing specialist local service for people with challenging behaviour, stressing that local services have to develop the competencies needed to provide treatment and support within the local area. The BILD *Code of Practice* (2001) and the *Guidance for Restrictive Physical Intervention* (2002) emphasise the need for a broader proactive approach of prevention of challenging behaviours as an essential part of training in and using physical intervention.

The relevance and area of application for the skills and techniques illustrated above has become difficult for purchasers of services to evaluate. Now, with research showing limited efficacy of teams and methodology, new directions through *Valuing People* (2001) and *Guidance for Restrictive Physical Intervention* (2002) mean that the development and continuation of intensive/expensive peripatetic teams could easily become a lower priority.

Conclusion

This chapter has identified a range of assessments which would be undertaken by some behaviour service/intensive support teams. A brief review of the research into the development and efficacy of such teams, with some factors that may have lead to a decrease in the number of teams, culminating in a drift away from longer assessments or engagement by some teams.

In local services the changes in team structure have led to the replacement of a behaviour support team by two joint community learning disability teams, which include nurses experienced in behaviour analysis.

The adoption of a case study has demonstrated how these skills have been applied and shows a dilution of the intensive methods used by those following the applied behaviour analysis model, set against the background of the varied roles within the joint team.

The changes locally seem to relate to the results of the research: low perceived and measured success rates and increasing evidence that quality mainstream services and skilled performance by teams were two essential components of successful services. McBrien (1999) discussed the possibility that in the future there would be no need for a specialist team, which is highly labour intensive. These factors have made it far more difficult to maintain a strong enough argument to maintain an expensive local service.

Joint working and collaboration between health and social services in learning disability and the ethos within *Valuing People* (DoH, 2001) on social inclusion are a priority. Local implementation of *Valuing People* is built on the Joint Investment Plan (Giraud-Saunders and Grieg, 2001) that prioritises transition into adult life, good health, more choice, control and fulfilling lives.

Valuing People (2001), when referring to challenging behaviour, stresses the need for a full medical assessment, supports the efficacy of modern behavioural approaches, and puts an onus on disability partnership boards to ensure that local services develop the competencies needed to provide treatment and support within local services. How this is interpreted locally will be determined by commissioners' and providers' willingness to invest in supporting people with learning disabilities who present with challenging behaviours, which will ultimately effect the shape of future services.

Locally, a significant amount of time has been spent on developing policy and training on the prevention and management of violence and aggression. This has followed on from the two linked documents, the BILD *Code of Practice for Trainers in the Use of Physical Intervention* ((2001) and the *Guidance for Restrictive Physical Intervention* (2002). This will lead to increased training of staff in the use of physical intervention and will become an additional role for at least one member of the joint team.

The research into methodologies of behaviour analysis is ongoing, often pointing to the need for more research, for example, Whitaker and Hirst (2002). The level of competence required to analyse behaviour and develop appropriate interventions is one factor that can lead to successful or unsuccessful intervention. According to Kiernan (1997), 'organisations working under the general auspices of the then Department of Health and Social Security (HMSO 1980)' had decided 'that the training of specialist behaviour analysts to work with people with intellectual disability and challenging behaviour was a high priority' and continued to say that the Royal College of Nursing developed the English National Board Course 705 to help address this need, and that the target group of professionals for this qualification are nurses.

This course provides the core skills necessary to analyse behaviour and develop appropriate intervention strategies. In the absence of a framework within which to work, it is important that these skills are practised and maintained. One mechanism to help maintain competence is clinical supervision, where the relationship between theory, skills and practice is pursued.

The skills of behaviour analysis are appropriately employed by nurses. At present, locally, it is necessary to be involved with addressing some of the management and professional issues around challenging behaviour. This includes increasing the skill level of mainstream services through teaching staff teams about behavioural methodology, appropriate prevention and the management of violence and aggression.

There can be no doubt that from the behavioural literature, the implementation of behavioural procedures can influence and demonstrate a reduction in challenging behaviours. Emerson (2002), in the support of people with learning disabilities who demonstrate challenging behaviour, asks the following questions: What proportion of people with particular forms of challenging behaviour is likely to benefit from behavioural intervention? And, what resource requirements would be associated with providing behavioural supports to that segment of the population?

Answers to both these questions means investing in those nurses with skills in behaviour analysis.

References, resources and www addresses

Allen D, Lowe K (1995) Providing intensive community support to people with learning disabilities and challenging behaviour: A preliminary analysis of outcomes and costs. *J Intellectual Disability Res* **39**(1): 67–81

British Institute of Learning Disabilities (2001) *Code of Practice for Trainers in the Use of Physical Interventions*. BILD, Kidderminster, Worcestershire.

Burgess I (1991) *Who Needs Help with Challenging Behaviour?* British Institute of Learning Disability, Kidderminster, Worcestershire

Cameron MJ, Maguire RW, Maquire M (1998) Lifeway influences on challenging behaviours. In: Luiselli JK, Cameron MJ, eds. *Antecedent Control: Innovative approaches to behavioural support*. Paul H Brookes, Baltimore: 273–88

Cullen C (1996) Challenging Behaviour and Intellectual Disability: Assessment, analysis and treatment. *Br J Clin Psychol* **35**: 153–6

Department of Health (2001) *Valuing People: A new Strategy for People with a Learning Disability for the 21st Century*. HMSO, London

Department of Health (2001) *Joint Investment Plans — A Learning Disability Workbook*. DoH, London

Department of Health (2002) *Guidance for Restrictive Physical Interventions. How to provide safe services for people with learning disabilities and autistic disorders*. DoH, London

Emerson E (2002) *Challenging Behaviour — Analysis and intervention in people with severe intellectual disabilities*. 2nd edn. Cambridge University Press, Cambridge

Emerson E, Forrest J, Cambridge P, Mansell J (1996) Community support teams for people with learning disabilities and challenging behaviours: Results of a national survey. *J Ment Health* **5**(4): 395–406

Kazdin AE (2000) *Behaviour Modification in Applied Settings*. 6th edn. Wadsworth Publishing

Kiernan C (1997) Future directions. In: Jones RSP, Earys CB, eds. *Challenging Behaviour and Intellectual Disability: A Psychological Perspective*. British Institute of Learning Disabilities, Plymouth

LaVigna GW, Donnellan AM (1986) *Alternatives to Punishment: Solving behaviour problems with non-aversive strategies*. Irvington Publishers Ltd, USA

Lowe K, Felce D, Blackman D (1996) Challenging behaviour: the effectiveness of specialist support teams. *J Intellectual Disability Research* **40** part 4: 336–47

Lowe K, Felce D (1996) Challenging behaviour services: How effective are they? *Clinical Psychology Forum* **93** July: 20–3

McBrien J (1999) The behavioural services team for people with learning disabilities. In: Emerson E McGill P, Mansell J, eds. *Severe Learning Disabilities and Challenging Behaviours: Designing high quality services*. Stanley Thomas (Publishers Ltd), Cheltenham: 203–4

Repp AC (1994) Comments on functional analysis procedures for school-based behavior problems. *J Appl Behav Analysis* **27**: 409–11

Simpson K, Campbell M, Ord P, Fairhurst A (1997) A brief report on the Wolverhampton intensive support service (ISS): A retrospective and prospective summary. *J Learning Disabilities for Nurs Health and Social Care* **1**(4): 196–9

Toogood S, Bell A (1994) Meeting the challenge in Clwyd: The intensive support team. *Br J Learning Disabilities* **22**: 46–52

Toogood S, Timlin K (1996) *A Comparison of Methods used in the Functional Assessment of Challenging Behaviour*. The Mental Health Foundation, UK

Whitaker S, Hirst D (2002) Correlation analysis of challenging behaviours. *Br J Learning Disabilities* **30**: 28–31

Willis TJ, LaVigna GW, Donnellan AM (1989) *Behaviour Assessment Guide*. California Institute for Applied Behaviour Analysis, Los Angeles. Online at: http://www.rnld.co.uk/cb.html

15

A nursing role in commissioning forensic services?

Bernard Natale

What constitutes a nursing role in modern learning disability services has always been difficult to define, and that is clearly the case in my current role, which involves commissioning services for people with learning disabilities. I work in a joint health and social services commissioning team where roles and skills merge. What seems evident is that the nursing role should not be limited by internal or external stereotypes. Nursing skills are wide ranging and transfer into various settings.

The function of the commissioning service and my role within it can be divided loosely into three main areas. Firstly, specifying service requirements; secondly, the development of local community-based services for people who are currently placed out of the area; and thirdly, the monitoring of services. This is in line with the Audit Commission's definition:

> *Commissioning is the process of specifying, securing and monitoring services to meet individual needs both in the short and the long term. As such, it covers what might be viewed as a more strategic approach to shaping the market for care to meet future needs.*
>
> Audit Commission, 1997

For the purpose of this chapter, I will use a fictitious case study to examine the service development role. The chapter will also look at the rationale for commissioning this service, the tendering process, the contract, and finally the monitoring mechanisms. The focus will be on developing a forensic service in Manchester for a man who has been placed in a long-stay hospital in the North West of England for more than ten years. The individual described has committed serious offences but complies with the hospital regime. He goes out on regular community outings under strict escort. His current staff team believe that he will require strict supervision for the foreseeable future. The hospital where he currently resides was formerly a long-stay hospital for people with learning disabilities and is now a forensic assessment and treatment facility for people with learning disabilities and associated disabilities. Among the individuals placed in this service are people who have committed the following offences: violent and destructive behaviour; indecent assault; indecent assault on a minor; arson; physical assault, and manslaughter. Some of the people placed in the forensic service have very mild learning disabilities and are unlikely to meet the eligibility criteria for community learning disability services.

One aim for commissioners is to keep forensic beds to a minimum and to defend against this type of service becoming a growth area. There is a great demand placed on these beds, and to comply with current philosophy, hospital admissions should be for assessment and treatment and not for long-term support. In order to ensure that waiting lists are not going to lengthen considerably, it is the responsibility of commissioners to ensure that when individuals are ready to be discharged, services are readily available to meet their needs. These services need to be of a high standard incorporating an emphasis on quality and best value. In relation to local authorities, the Department of the Environment, Transport and the Regions (DETR) Circular 10/99 focuses on the responsibility for ensuring continuing improvement when commissioning services, while at the same time having regard for, economy, efficiency, and effectiveness.

A review of health and social services for mentally disordered offenders (The Reed Report, 1992) made the following recommendations regarding service design.

⌘ The service should be designed with a focus on quality of care, and proper attention to the needs of the individual.
⌘ The service should be in the community rather than in an institutional setting, wherever possible.
⌘ There should be no greater security than is justified by the degree of danger the individual presents to themselves and others.
⌘ The service should be designed to maximise rehabilitation and enhance the individual's chances of sustaining an independent life.
⌘ The service should be as close as possible to their homes and families.

Case study specification

Paul is thirty-five years old. His index offence was inappropriate sexual behaviour with a minor. He has lived in a secure residential setting for twelve years. On occasions when he has had limited free time he has assaulted males. He is considered to be a high risk to vulnerable males, and children. His own personal history is one of living in a home where he was on several occasions sexually abused. He has not responded to treatment and appears to have very little insight into his behaviour and its effects on others. He is compliant with strict staff supervision in his current environment, and accepts this level of supervision on community outings and holidays.

Paul has a diagnosed bi-polar condition and during periods of severe depression he has displayed suicidal tendencies. On one occasion he placed a plastic bag over his head and tried to suffocate himself. On another occasion he attempted to cut his wrists.

There are a number of additional factors in relation to Paul that commissioners would expect prospective provider agencies to consider when submitting a tender for the project.

1. He has a speech impediment and a hearing impediment and will require continued input from a speech and language therapist following his move to a community setting.
2. He will require structured work activities, which will need to be in place prior to him moving to a community setting. He particularly enjoys cookery and kitchen work.
3. He has good social skills.
4. He requires minimal support with household activities.
5. He enjoys sport and should be given the opportunity to watch and participate in sporting activities.
6. He accepts that he will be supervised at all times and has been compliant with the requests of the current service provider in the hospital setting and on community outings.
7. He is currently on Section 3 of the Mental Health Act (1983) and will require a registered setting when he is placed in the community. He will also require the support of a responsible medical officer (RMO).

8. He will require community learning disability team (CLDT) support. It will be for the CLDT, based on the current support he receives, to decide on who will be the most appropriate team members to work with Paul. In addition to speech and language therapy, it is likely to be a combination of community nursing and psychology input.
9. He will require ongoing care management support.

The following information regarding risk management strategies will also be included when the service is put out to tender.

Risks

- There is a risk of suicide. Paul is at extreme risk during periods of mental deterioration. This can be managed by having experienced staff around him who can monitor his extreme mood swings.
- He is vulnerable sexually. Problems are more likely to occur if Paul is living with people who are intellectually more able than he is and who are predatory sexually. This can be managed by placing him with appropriate peers, and having twenty-four-hour supervision from experienced staff.
- There is a very high risk of him sexually assaulting others. This is more likely to occur if Paul is placed with less able people and not closely supervised. He will require twenty-four-hour support. The service should have a very clear structure with guidelines clearly highlighting what is and what is not acceptable behaviour.

Commissioning rationale

There are a number of reasons to commission a service for Paul. Firstly, it is believed that he can be supported in a community-based service. Secondly, a move into the community will free up a place for a more high risk offender. Thirdly, it is considered that he could be supported more economically in a community placement, or, at least, the commissioners would exercise more economic control over the contract. Fourthly, he is likely to become increasingly vulnerable in his present setting because the people who are currently being placed in the setting are generally far more able than those people placed in this type of service a decade ago.

   The national strategy for people with learning disabilities is set out in the White Paper, *Valuing People* (2001). As highlighted in the Secure Learning Disability Services Plan (North West Secure Commissioning Team, 2001) the paper does not directly refer to secure services or comment on those who come into contact with the criminal justice system. The general philosophy remains the same and is outlined in *Valuing People, — Legal and Civil Rights*:

> *All public services will treat people with learning disabilities as individuals with respect for their dignity, and challenge discrimination on all grounds, including disability. People with learning disabilities will also receive the full protection of the law when necessary.*

Someone who comes into contact with the criminal justice system and is placed in a secure facility, should have the opportunity to return to the community when they have participated in a programme of treatment.

Most of the individuals who are resident in the hospital where Paul is placed are considered to have borderline learning disabilities. In a number of instances, individuals have transferred from the prison service, where it was considered their learning disability was severe enough for them to be unable to participate in treatment programmes. Some individuals have transferred from secure hospitals, other individuals have been placed in the hospital forensic service as an alternative to prison. People moving from this type of forensic service into a community setting will, generally, fall into one of three categories. Firstly, there are individuals who will require minimal support in relation to their learning disabilities. The service design will be more likely to focus on helping the person to settle into the community, and supporting them with financial matters, employment, relationships, and understanding their rights within the community. A major concern is allowing the individuals the degree of independence they are capable of, while at the same time managing the risk of re-offending. Secondly, there are individuals who have similar needs to our first example but who require a higher level of support in relation to their learning disabilities. They may also require continual support in relation to offending behaviour. Thirdly, there are some people who may not respond to treatment programmes, who may have little insight into their offending behaviour but who are compliant. Someone fitting into this category could be placed into the community with a very strict regime that would require that they are escorted at all times. In order to work within the framework of the law, it is important to have the facility to place someone fitting into this category on a Mental Health Act Section rather than assuming that they will permanently comply. In all instances where serious offenders are placed in community settings it is important to assess the need for involving additional support from the police and the probation service. This would be particularly true in cases where the person has committed serious sexual offences or other offences.

Tendering

Prior to advertising the tender, the commissioners will have carried out detailed assessment work in conjunction with the current forensic service provider. The type of service required will have been clearly defined and a service specification formulated. Although this exercise has focused on one individual, it should be stressed that when an individual is suited to living in a group setting rather than an individual setting, the tendering process may involve providing information on a number of individuals.

In order to have realistic timescales, consideration needs to be given to all areas where delays are likely to occur. With this in mind, accommodation and funding need to be high on the planning agenda. Prior to tendering, the service will need to be costed in detail and a minimum and a maximum costing band agreed.

As the commissioners are also responsible for overseeing the contract with the local community learning disability team, it important to calculate a cost of this additional service. In some instances this will be minimal, but in others, with people who have complex needs, this could involve an extensive use of clinical services. Although the contract price will not increase or decrease as people move into or out of the service, it is important for commissioners to have a general gauge on the changing needs of the population and increased demands on the service.

With all this information available the service will be advertised. The tendering process will ensure that confidentiality is maintained at all times.

When service plans and costings have been submitted, service providers who come within the assumed costing framework, ie. not above or below the agreed costing band will be shortlisted. The key areas to look for at this stage are:

- Does the provider have a good track record in the provision of this type of service, or equivalent service provision?
- Can the service provider deliver the service within the agreed acceptable timescale?
- Is the organisation financially viable? A financial audit would need to be carried out on organisations that are not already accredited.

Regular planning meetings with the existing service provider and liaison with the agreed housing provider will be ongoing at this stage. Meetings will be approximately once each month but will adapt to meet the needs of a developing situation.

The following list outlines the work required when an agreement has been reached to place someone in a community setting. In some instances, the order may change slightly, for example, contact with the housing association may be concurrent with contact with the care provider; in others, property may be available from an existing source.

1. Liaise with a housing provider.
2. Ongoing work on properties will continue until the property is ready for occupancy.
3. Decide on where to advertise the tender and put the service out to open tender, or liaise among existing accredited service providers and limit the tender to these agencies.
4. Agree an interview panel and interview process. In addition to health and social services staff, the interview panel should include a housing representative and stakeholder representation from a parent or relative of someone with a learning disability. The interview process requires that a service specification is developed and the provider agency is measured against the service specification criteria.
5. When the care provider has been appointed, meet with both the care provider and housing provider.
6. Arrangements will need to be made for the provider to meet the person requiring the service. Ongoing assessment work by the provider agency should then commence.
7. Planning meetings involving the commissioners, the existing service provider and the future service provider will commence. This will be a continuation of person-centred meetings with a greater focus on a move to a new agency in a community setting. They will take place as deemed necessary by all those involved.
8. The community learning disability team in the area where the individual is about to move will be contacted several months prior to a move taking place and appropriate referrals will be made to the team.
9. Clinical specialists who are currently involved in work with the individual, will be asked to write reports on the client and to liaise with and pass on information to future clinical support services.
10. A discharge date will be arranged.
11. The service provider will have staff in post well in advance of the discharge date to enable them to work with the client and to set up the service. This will include,

for example, setting up day activities, educational activities, liaising with other health components, GPs, and dentists. It will also involve dealing with financial matters, like setting up a bank account and arranging benefits.

12. A pre-discharge meeting will be arranged where all issues will be finalised. This will involve checking that all the issues highlighted above have been arranged. The psychiatrist will have liaised with colleagues in the receiving district and issues around the individual's Mental Health Act status, and securing RMO cover will have been agreed. Arrangements for transferring the individual will be agreed. In some instances, arrangements may be made for hospital staff to work alongside the new staff for a period of time to ensure a smooth transition.

13. A discharge meeting will be organised to formalise the issues highlighted in 12 above and a post-discharge meeting will be arranged.

14. At the post-discharge meeting, approximately two months following discharge, issues regarding the move and the current service provision can be assessed and reviewed.

This type of service is somewhat different from the social care services that have developed, in particular, over the last two decades. Although the service philosophy is person-centred, it also incorporates an equal emphasis on managing the risk of re-offending. A point worth mentioning is that there is currently a lack of experienced service providers in community forensic services. This also extends to a lack of experienced clinicians in the field.

Contract

⌘ The contract will clearly define the service requirements. This includes specifying who the service is for and the staff support required to run the service.

⌘ It will insist that commissioners must be informed prior to any changes in clientele.

⌘ It will ensure that an adequate monitoring system is in place for any new referrals.

⌘ It will insist that the service providers have appropriate policies and procedures in place.

⌘ It will insist that the providers participate in quality monitoring and contract monitoring exercises.

⌘ It will outline a method of dealing with disputes.

⌘ It will clearly detail the requirements if either party wishes to terminate the agreement.

⌘ It will clearly outline standard requirements in relation to service delivery.

Monitoring mechanisms

When the individual is finally transferred to a community setting a number of mechanisms need to be in place to ensure that the individual receives a service that adheres to recognised quality standards. The service will also be required to have internal quality mechanisms.

The commissioning team will have three mechanisms in place in addition to the contract. Firstly, a regular contract monitoring process. Secondly, the commissioners will carry out quality assessments of the service. These will take place at least once every five years using the Manchester Quality Assessment Monitoring Tool (1998). This exercise will take approximately three weeks to carry out. A report will be submitted after approximately six weeks. The findings will be reviewed after six months and a final review will take place after twelve months. Finally, a link person from commissioning will liaise with each agency. The link person will be available to look at new proposals or at any problems the organisation may be encountering. In addition, the link person will arrange visits to individual facilities. These visits will act as less formal monitoring exercises.

Contract monitoring

Regular meetings are necessary to monitor any problems that may arise with the contract. Commissioners need to be aware of any changes that may affect the contract, and to ensure that the provider formally reports any serious offences, accidents, or injuries in relation to the individuals who are supported in the service, or in relation to staff who are responsible for providing support.

Prior to the meeting, the provider completes a contract monitoring form. This will be the basis for discussion at the meeting. In addition, any other issues relating to the contract are discussed.

From a commissioner's perspective, information on the following issues is likely to be required in relation to the contract:

1. Has the service provider experienced any problems receiving payments?
2. Have there been any changes to the management structure?
3. Have there been any changes to the staffing structure?
4. Has the service used any agency staff (on how many occasions and under what circumstances)?
5. Have there been any relevant criminal, civil, or professional offences against any members of the management team or staff? This would include the manager being prosecuted under the Registered Homes Act or any nurses in the service being debarred from practice as a nurse.
6. Has there been any unlawful racial discrimination?
7. Has there been any formal investigation by the Racial Equality Commission in respect of alleged unlawful discrimination?
8. Have there been any offences under the Health and Safety at Work Act (1974)?
9. Have there been any offences under the Food Safety Act (1990) or Food Safety (General Food Hygiene) Regulations (1995)?
10. Has there been any change of circumstances in relation to the people using the service. Has anyone moved into or out of the service?
11. Have there been any changes to the premises?
12. Details will be required of all accidents and incidents relating to health and safety, food hygiene and manual handling.
13. Have there been any allegations of abuse?

Information in relation to serious incidents, accidents, allegations of abuse, and any offences will be reported to commissioners immediately. Commissioners will also be consulted prior to anyone moving into or out of the service.

Quality assessment

The Manchester quality monitoring exercise requires two people to work together on assessing the service. This is to ensure greater objectivity around areas of subjectivity. The exercise is usually carried out by two staff from the commissioning team but, on occasions, staff from the community learning disability teams have also worked on quality monitoring exercises. The assessment tool looks at the following areas:

⌘ Management and administration: including policies and procedures, health and safety issues, staff development and support, and the general management of the service.
⌘ The physical setting: the inspection of the interior and exterior of the building.
⌘ The management of the household: this section is concerned with the day-to-day management of the house, including financial management.
⌘ The social environment: this section looks at what resources are used in relation to work and leisure, and educational activities. It also looks at friendships, relationships, and family contact.
⌘ The developmental environment: this section is concerned with person-centred planning, and general support issues.

An additional part of the exercise involves sending out questionnaires to all the people who have some involvement in the individual's life, including: the individuals using the service; their parents and/or relatives who have close contact with the individuals; staff; volunteers; and care managers.

The information is then fed back to service managers and the service is expected to draw up an action plan to look at areas which need to improve. Any areas of concern will need to be dealt with as a matter of urgency.

In addition to monitoring the quality of the service, data from the exercise is used to measure different service providers and to inform the commissioning team about the strengths and qualities of provider agencies.

Another part of the commissioning role is creating a level playing field for all provider agencies, be they statutory public services, independent or voluntary sector services. The standards and expectations must be focused on the needs of people with a learning disability and not on the organisation providing the service. Having assessed the expertise of service providers it is the role of commissioners to match the individual to a service best equipped to provide the appropriate support. It is essential that commissioners maintain an up-to-date database on the learning disability population, and the agencies that provide specialist services.

The commissioning framework is circular rather than linear and the work carried out on monitoring exercises should not only help to inform the team about current services, but should also help to shape future services.

Summary

I have outlined the role of a nurse commissioner working in learning disability services. Although many of the skills used in the commissioning process are not exclusive to nursing, I feel the broad understanding of learning disability services, and the skills acquired as a nurse are an excellent foundation for individuals who wish to pursue this particular type of work. Registered learning disability nurses are equipped to work with individuals who have various needs, including physical, emotional and behavioural needs. The training that nurses get in skills assessment, and behavioural assessment, is vitally important in understanding the issues when service planning with regard to risk, compatibility, and providing appropriate support. A good working knowledge of the Mental Health Act, and an understanding of the roles of other clinical staff and where their roles fit in is also important.

By looking at commissioning in relation to our case study we have not only focused on the service development process, but have also reflected more closely on a specific type of work currently being carried out by commissioners in learning disability services. In addition, we have looked at a wider range of commissioning responsibilities. This work involves monitoring area placements, and assessing the needs of individuals placed in these services. It includes the planning and development of future services. It requires that commissioners have the necessary skills to negotiate with agencies and appoint suitable providers. The process needs to be co-ordinated to ensure a smooth transition between institutional and community providers, including a transfer of knowledge between clinical support staff. When services are established in the community they need to be closely monitored. The services should be of high quality but should also offer value for money. The commissioning process is circular and the information acquired is used to inform future service planning.

All of the work described is within the remit of my present role as a clinical nurse specialist within a joint commissioning team. This all-encompassing role is a reflection of professional backgrounds merging in a pool of skills, knowledge, and resources.

References

Audit Commission (1997) *Take your Choice*. Audit Commission, London

Department of the Environment, Transport and the Regions (1999) Local Government Act 1999: Part 1 — Best Value (circular 10/99). DETR, London

Department of Health (2001) *Valuing People: A New Strategy for Learning Disability for the 21st Century*. DoH, London

Food Safety Act (1990). HMSO, London

Food Safety (General Food Hygiene) Regulations (1995). HMSO, London

Health and Safety at Work Act (1974). HMSO, London

Mental Health Act (1993). HMSO, London

North West Secure Commissioning Team (2001) Strategic Overview and Issues Paper — Secure Learning Disability Services Plan, 2001

Quality Assessment for People with Learning Disabilities, April 1998 MANCOR-RST, Revised June 2001

Registered Homes Act (1984). HMSO, London

Review of Health and Social Services for Mentally Disordered Offenders and others with similar needs (Reed Report) (1992). HMSO, London

16

Forensics

Mark Alison

This chapter concerns forensic nursing in learning disabilities. It deals with various models of practice that have relevance in the care of the mentally disordered offender (MDO) and traces some of the developments that have led to the current practice situation. It is written from a practitioner's perspective, and attempts to consider issues that are relevant to forensic nursing practice. In particular, it takes the role of the community forensic nurse to explore further the various skills and knowledge base for contemporary practice. The focus of the chapter will be around key areas of the community forensic nurse's role, including; risk assessment and management, case formulation, and therapeutic interventions. Following an exploration of these key areas a case study will be used to illustrate how these skills may be practically applied.

Policy overview

There have been several reports and Government guidance that has influenced the provision for mentally disordered offenders over the last decade.

The Reed Report (1994) made several recommendations and set out some guiding principles for the provision of mentally disordered offenders (MDOs). These included caring for mentally disordered offenders:

- with regard to the quality of care and proper attention to the needs of individuals
- as far as possible in the community, rather than in institutional settings
- under conditions of no greater security than is justified by the degree of danger they present to themselves or to others.
- in such a way as to maximise rehabilitation and their chances of sustaining an independent life
- as near as possible to their own homes or families if they have them.

It established features of a high quality service, which were:

- multi-agency and multi-professional working
- a diversion from the criminal justice system
- a range of provisions, from community support to high security.

The report also made specific recommendations about the provision for learning disabilities and autism groups. These included:

1. Provision based on the assessment of need, as an aim of medium secure arrangements.
2. The care programme arrangements be extended to offenders with learning disabilities leaving hospital or prison.

3. Staff training in the needs of people with learning disabilities wherever they have contact with such clients (especially police, probation, magistrates, etc).
4. Court diversion schemes developed for learning disabled offenders (LDOs).
5. Planning for the longer term needs and recognising the implications of failure to respond to future needs.
6. Requirement for skilled nurses to be employed to work with LDOs.
7. Development of a core therapy service.
8. Priority for research on learning disability offending.

A number of other documents have also influenced the provision of services for mentally disordered offenders.

Signposts for Success (DoH, 1998) made specific reference to the various models of service provision for LDOs that can be employed successfully.

Without good community-based services there is an inevitable breakdown in community placements (*Figure 16.1*). It also makes the distinction that LDOs are different from other MDOs both in the nature and origins of their offending behaviour and in their treatment needs (DoH, 1998).

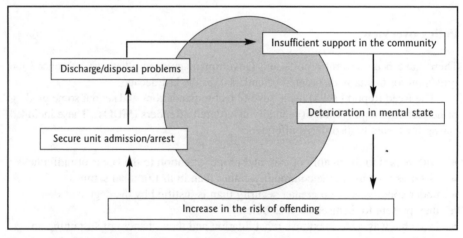

Figure 16.1: The breakdown in community placements

Valuing People (2001) outlines as part of its principles, the need for specialist learning disability services that are locally based. In addition, it suggests that some people with learning disabilities will require intensive healthcare support through specialist community services, because of their complex disabilities or challenges which they place on services. It emphasises the philosophy of ordinary living principles of independence, choice, inclusion and civil rights, with the aim to provide services in the least restrictive environment .

The traditional service for learning disabled offenders has been hospital-based but there are a wide range of services for this client group, which cover a range of needs (*Table 16.1*).

Of these, the intensive health care support model is the most significant feature to emerge over the last decade, especially the proliferation of independent sector provision for high risk offenders.

These vary in model design but are based on similar principles of relational and environmental security to reduce the risk of re-offending. Typically, they may use high staffing levels in small group homes with minimal security, or they may use higher degrees of physical security with corresponding lower staffing levels.

While we have these good practice guidelines for the disposal of mentally disordered offenders, there is uncertainty about the response of the criminal justice system and the type of

Table 16.1: The range of services and support for forensic clients
⌘ High security hospitals
⌘ Regional secure units
⌘ High dependency/local secure units
⌘ Acute/intensive care — locked provision
⌘ Supported accommodation — twenty-four hours, staffed
⌘ Community support — community forensic team, etc
⌘ Informal support — family, friends, etc

disposal a criminal is likely to receive because of the adversarial nature of our justice system. We cannot say with any great degree of accuracy what the likely outcome of a trial might be. The relationship between forensics, behavioural disturbance and the degree of learning disability further complicates matters when trying to gauge what the likely response of the courts will be . The type of sentence a person receives can vary quite considerably. Criminal responsibility in the country is defined by determining that the accused commited the act and, in so doing, showed pre-determined intent. This latter point is crucial in determining the guilt and appropriate sentence/disposal of someone with a mental disorder. If it can be shown that the person's mental disorder had an effect on their behaviour at the time of the offence, then this will have a bearing on the type of sentence they will receive. It often requires a psychiatrist to assist the court in determining the correct sentence, which may move the emphasis of the sentence away from punishment and towards treatment or, indeed, may involve a combination of the two. This is why we often find convictions that include an element of compulsory treatment as part of the sentence. A typical sentence might be a community rehabilitation order for a crime like indecent assault, with conditions attached so that the person has to attend a sex offender treatment programme. We cannot be certain that a judge or magistrate will follow recommendations of the psychiatrist. Uncertainty and ambiguity are features of the sentencing of offenders. This means planning and provision are often at the mercy of the courts decision-making process. This does much to undermine good practice because service providers are never sure until the last moment what the outcome of a trial will be. Nevertheless, practitioners do tend to predict the outcome of trials and have guidelines for practice and their interventions with clients.

Good practice

There are a number of good practice models that could be useful in shaping the role of the community forensic nurse. These can be divided into those that guide practice and those that guide professional development.

There is little published research on the most effective community forensic approach, but there have been several support models that could be seen as meeting the needs of forensic clients. Commonly identified core themes can be summed up in the assertive outreach model which requires:

- developing a therapeutic relationship with the client
- the use of therapeutic interventions
- a highly flexible and creative practitioner
- addressing expressed needs of the client
- being involved in the day-to-day life of the client.

While this is a mental health model, it has found its uses in the field of learning disabilities, especially with dual diagnosis clients (Porter and Sangha, 2002).

A similar process can be seen in the emphasis on using the care programme approach (1991). It was designed to provide a network of care in the community for those leaving hospital or as new patients, but was soon adopted as good practice for prisoners leaving prison as well as learning disabled clients with additional mental health problems. Its essential elements are:

- systematic assessment of health and social care needs
- a care plan that is agreed by the multidisciplinary team
- identified keyworker who keeps in close contact with the client
- regular review of clients needs and the delivery of care
- risk assessment and consideration of client for the supervision register.

Other mental health models that may give guidance to forensic practice include the intensive case management models for violent mentally ill people (Dvoskin and Steadman, 1994). Again, an emphasis is placed on gaining compliance of the client through building a trusting relationship with the worker and working in the client's home environment, and building idiosyncratic partnerships with other service providers such as probation, the criminal justice system, police, etc.

The main aim of these models is crisis prevention and management, reflected in the crisis prevention and management service model (see Lowe and Felce. 1996) which identified three levels to this work. These include:

⌘ Level 1: Crisis prevention through improved monitoring, staff training and service development.
⌘ Level 2: Additional support directly to services to prevent a potential crisis from worsening.
⌘ Level 3: Additional support to individuals and use of temporary accommodation when required.

While these approaches are addressing slightly different issues, ie. mental health, violence, and challenging behaviour, there is considerable overlap with the provision for LDOs in the community. Therefore, the best practice elements for community forensics would probably include the following:

- supervision of client
- intervention to prevent deterioration of mental health
- a philosophy of ordinary life principles in the least restrictive environment
- care management
- supplementing existing generic resources

- interventions to address offending clients
- working in a highly flexible, innovative manner
- good working relationships with the criminal justice system.

Skills of the community forensic nurse

The skills of the forensic nurse are pivotal in determining the outcome for learning disabled offenders. This is about effective responses to the specific needs of mentally disordered offenders.

One feature of working with mentally disordered offenders is recognising to whom the nurse is primarily responsible. This raises the issue of public safety and the individual's right to self-determination with the forensic team striving to create a safe balance between the two. Traditionally, nurses are primarily responsible for the care that they provide to the client with whom they are working. When working with offenders, it could be argued that the main outcome that all forensic services are aiming for is public protection. The forensic nurse has to consider the individual's needs and the impact of their offending on person's immediately at risk, and then the implications for this behaviour on the wider public. This can only be achieved by determining what risks are involved in a client's offending, who is at risk and how dangerous and serious this is. Being skilled in risk assessment is a primary competency for the forensic nurse. This is closely associated with the ability to formulate a care plan that deals with the risks a client presents. An integral part of this process is risk management, key features including:

- early identification of mental disturbance
- prioritising care for the most serious and dangerous offenders
- an action plan for all elements of life outside of the formal care setting
- encouraging a stable life with support if necessary
- facilitating employment/training, education, and meaningful activities
- developing strong social and community ties
- additional help with mental health problems
- support to tackle offending.

Risk assessment

Risk assessment is a continuous process to gather information. This information needs to be shared between the relevant organisations. Individuals need to take account of the 'best interests' principle, ie. confidentiality may sometimes need to be breached for the greater good. The purpose of collating the maximum amount of data possible is to increase the potential for predicting accurately, the likelihood of the perceived danger occurring. Brooks (1984) suggests the following framework for studying dangerousness:

1. The nature of the harm involved.
2. Its magnitude.
3. Its imminence.

4. Its frequency.
5. The likelihood or unlikelihood that will occur.
6. Situational circumstances and conditions that alter the likelihood of harm occurring.
7. Balancing between the alleged harm on one hand and the nature of society's interests on the other.

By taking responsibility for assessment and management of risk the forensic nurse requires the ability to make sound judgements about the level of risk posed and how best to deal with this. One such tool for assessing risk is the risk assessment and management audit system (RAMAS) developed by O'Rourke *et al* (1994). It assesses risk according to four domains. These are:

- dangerousness
- mental instability
- self-harm
- vulnerability.

Whatever tool is used for assessing risk, the best practice principles covered in the Reed Report (1994), can provide us with some guidance. These include assessments of risk being undertaken on a multidisciplinary basis and follow up should usually form part of the care plan and the care programme. Agencies providing a service need to develop and observe clear guidelines for risk assessment and staff should be trained accordingly.

The nurse may also be active in the treatment part of someone's community rehabilitation order. This can include liaison or supervision of the client in the community and reporting untoward or 'near miss' incidents to the supervising probation officer. In the case of sex offenders' treatment programmes, protocols may be in place for the nurse to follow up work done in the classroom, by assisting the offender to apply the skills and knowledge to everyday situations. An example of this might be an offender who is attracted to young children who is practising recognising the thoughts that lead them to offend. The nurse can identify with the client those high risk situations in a week when the offender is in danger of acting on these thoughts, such as seeing children walking to school or playing in the park. By the client having an alternative behavioural repertoire for this risk, the nurse can assist to reinforce the skills learnt in the classroom such as through role play and modelling. By linking in with the treatment programme the nurse can give valuable feedback on the client's progress based on information that is gleaned from observation of the client in their everyday surroundings.

The nurse also has to be mindful of those factors which can undermine successful risk assessment and management. In learning disability nursing we are often reliant on third parties for information about a client's offending history. Caution should be exercised when information is given verbally which cannot be cross-referenced from other sources. This is because a number of factors may be introduced into the assessment process that can reduce its accuracy. One issue highlighted by Robertson and Clegg (2002) is staff minimising the importance of the risks involved. Another factor is family denying or minimising the client's past history of offences out of a sense of loyalty to their relative. One has to be mindful of these potential biases in the risk assessment process and attempt to gain information from as many sources as possible.

Case formulation

The idiosyncratic nature of a client's offending means few, if any, standardised treatment approaches can make sense of the behaviour and its motives without first understanding more about the client and their background. This requires the need to describe in detail both the internal events and the environmental influences, both past and present, which led up to the offending. However, how this information is interpreted, and what emphasis is placed on its importance, means that practitioners may all hold differing views about the causes of the offence, and how to deal with it. This is partly because professional disciplines operate from differing paradigms, and different professionals within a given discipline may favour a particular theoretical perspective, especially in terms of how to treat the offending behaviour. Some common ground needs to be found in order for the multi-disciplinary team to agree on treatment goals and objectives. This is often made difficult when the review of clients' care seldom addresses the issue of gaining a shared understanding.

A traditional approach to this problem is case formulation. Tarrier and Calam (2002) suggest:

It involves the elicitation of appropriate information and the application and integrity of a body of theoretical psychological knowledge to a specific clinical problem in order to understand the origins, development and maintenance of that problem. Its purpose is both to provide an accurate overview and explanation of the patient's problems that is open to verification through hypothesis testing; and to arrive collaboratively with the patient at a useful understanding of their problem that is meaningful to them.

One particular body of knowledge that has found increasing application in the field of forensics has been the use of cognitive behaviour therapy. It stands up to the rigours of case formulation because it is open to testing and validation.

Cognitive behaviour therapy and dialectical behaviour therapy

Cognitive behaviour therapy (CBT) is a set of empirically grounded clinical interventions that are carried out by clinicians who seek to operate as scientist-practitioners (Salkovskis, 2002).

The principle defining theory of CBT is that it makes the assumption that psychological problems are caused by cognitive distortions which influence our emotions and behaviours. It relies upon the therapeutic relationship fostered between the therapist and the client to address the problems these irrational beliefs cause. 'People with learning disabilities are a heterogeneous group whose mental health needs can often be complex' (Hardy and Bouras, 2002) and therefore require appropriate therapeutic interventions to deal with problems when they arise. Stenfert *et al* (1997) have reported on the use of CBT with clients who have a learning disability, while others have reported widely on its use in the treatment of sex offenders (eg. Lindsay *et al*, 1998). There is also a substantial amount of published research on the use of anger management with CBT as its main framework (eg. Rose *et al*, 2000).

An emerging area is the use of dialectical behaviour therapy (DBT) with people who have personality disorders (Linehan, 1987). This has found particular relevance to women who self-harm and have a borderline personality disorder. There has been reported use of DBT with women in a special hospital (Low *et al*, 2001). Both CBT and DBT have been highlighted as good practice approaches in the field of forensics by the national standards for general adults services in psychiatric intensive care units (PICUs) and low secure environments (DoH, 2002). Both of these approaches are useful for making sense of the clients' offending in general and because each is a goal-orientated, collaborative approach, offering the forensic nurse a way of working with the client on their problems. Also, being practical and concrete, they give a good basis to a nurse's intervention, ie. offering a rationale and structure for day-to-day work because the nurse and client are both active in the solution to the offender's problems. It also recognises the offender as having other problems apart from their offending and, indeed, other psychological problems may well be at work in the causes of offending.

By utilising the case formulation model, the nurse can use CBT to explain the links between a person's thought processes and their offending as well as any other psychological problems they may be experiencing. These issues will now be explored further using a case study.

Case study

Joan is a young woman with learning disabilities. In addition, she also has a diagnosis of personality disorder. She has previous admissions to hospital with bouts of depression and deliberate self-harm. She has disclosed that she was sexually abused as a child by her father. She is now living in a flat in the community having been discharged from a secure unit. Joan was previously held under section 37 of the Mental Health Act 1983 for a serious sexual offence against a child.

Just recently she has been displaying unpredictable violent behaviour, which has culminated in a serious assault on a member of staff at a day centre. She was arrested and detained in a police station. While there, an appropriate adult was called from social services to attend during her interview. She was charged with grievous bodily harm and held in custody until her court appearance the next day. Joan is seen by the court diversion nurse who screens Joan for mental health problems and her degree of learning disability. At her court appearance the magistrates consider Joan for bail but no placement can be found at such short notice and the court consider Joan too much of a risk to the public for her to return to the community. When she arrives at prison she is placed on the vulnerable prisoners' wing and a buddy system is used to match Joan up with a trusted prisoner who will befriend Joan and watch out for her.

Despite these safeguards, Joan attempts to self-harm by cutting her arms which results in her transfer to the prison hospital wing where she remains for the rest of her remand. The community forensic nurse visits Joan regularly, and co-ordinates her discharge plan.

Joan is given a trial date and she is asked to submit her plea. At the hearing she pleads guilty to the lesser charge of actual body harm. The probation service and psychiatrist both file reports with the court which make recommendations about the sentencing of Joan.

She is given a two-year community rehabilitation order with psychiatric conditions attached. These include the attendance for anger management sessions as part of the input from the community forensic team. Using the care programme approach, a care plan is designed for Joan. This care plan includes contingency planning if Joan refuses to comply with the conditions of her rehabilitation order. These include admission to hospital if necessary. Joan is assigned a key worker from the forensic team and she is risk assessed with regards to self-harm, her danger to others and her vulnerability to neglect and abuse. Consequently, it is decided to place Joan on the supervision register, and to use guardianship under the Mental Health Act 1983 in order gain compliance with the plan and to place Joan in a group home run by an independent provider.

The forensic nurse commences anger management sessions with Joan. In addition, the nurse applies the theories of dialectical behaviour therapy when dealing with Joan's suicidal ideation and self-harm.This includes dealing with emotional recognition and validation, distress tolerance, and problem solving. For this work, the nurse utilises clinical supervision provided by a clinical psychologist.

The probation officer sees Joan every two weeks and liaises with the nurse about Joan's compliance with the care plan. A case formulation meeting is held shortly after discharge where the full MDT are present. They agree on some clinical indicators which may show when Joan is becoming mentally unstable . These include isolation, and rumination, with consequent bouts of deliberate self-harm and unpredictable outbursts of violence. The community forensic nurse chairs the meeting and draws together a case formulation which makes the connection between Joan's previous traumatic experiences and her offending (*Figure 16. 2*). This forms the basis for future interventions with Joan and the various stakeholders use the formulation map to make sense of her behaviour. Subsequent reviews of care adjust the map accordingly and changes in the hypotheses are explored which ultimately reflect in the changes to interventions and the management of Joan's care.

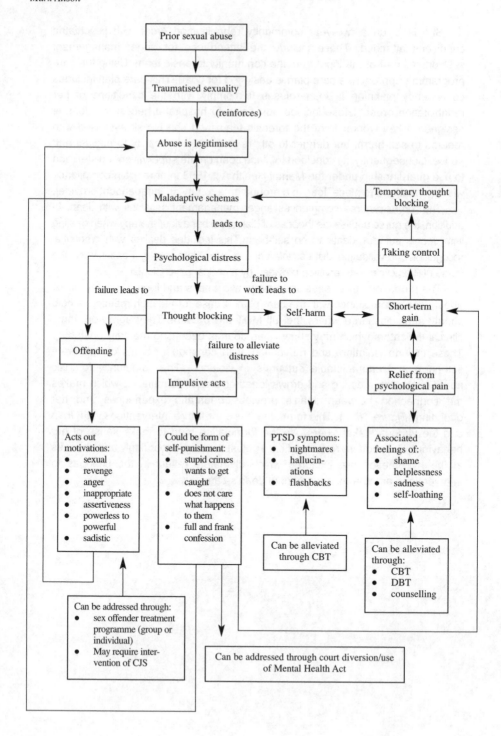

Figure 16.2: A case formulation map of sexual abuse, its effect on offending and potential areas for intervention

Conclusion

This chapter has explored forensics as one of the specialist fields to which a learning disability nurse can make a contribution. It is hoped to have demonstrated the type of skills necessary to practice at a higher level with this client group. These skills form part of the practitioner's role and are open to scrutiny because they are evidence-based interventions, although not specific to learning disabilities. The 'borrowing' of different theoretical and skill bases from other disciplines, such as mental health, is necessary because this particular client group present with so many challenges and we have not yet built our own evidence base to deal with all of these. When developing the skills to meet these challenges, the nurse has to consider what the defining areas of complexity are that are unmet by existing provision, then seek to acquire the theoretical knowledge which underpins any given skill. An integral part of this is the ability to adapt to novel situations and flourish. This requires a good grounding in generic skills so that the practitioner has a sound base from which to specialise. This chapter has dealt with forensics as an issue which a community nurse has to deal with, not as a forensic practitioner dealing with the issue of community. This is because local knowledge of services, building and supporting local networks, forging local alliances and good working relationships, are the building blocks of good practice. Likewise, for any specialist practitioner, the expert cannot function effectively in isolation and without being part of the team. The chapter has emphasised the multidisciplinary nature of forensic work and shown the contribution of the nurse. It also demonstrates how nurses can specialise to improve their role and function within the team and, in so doing, reinforce their clinical credibility.

References

Brooks AD (1984) Defining the dangerousness of the mentally ill: Involuntary civil commitment . In: Craft M, Craft A, eds. *Mentally Abnormal Offenders*. Balliere Tindall, London

Department of Health (1991) *The Care Programme Approach*. DoH, London

Department of Health (1998) *Signposts for Success in Commissioning and Providing Health Services for People with Learning Disabilities*. DoH, London

Department of Health (2002) *Mental Health Policy Implementation Guide. National Minimum Standards for General Adult Services in Psychiatric Intensive Care Units (PICU) and Low Secure Environment*. DoH, London

Department of Health (2001) *Valuing People. A New Strategy for Learning disability for the 21st Century*. DoH, London

Dvoskin JA, Steadman HJ (1994) Using intensive case management to reduce violence by mentally ill persons in the community. *Hospital and Community Psychiatry* **45**(7): 679–84

Hardy S, Bouras N (2002) The presentation and assessment of mental health problems in people with learning disabilities. *Learning Disability Practice* **5**(3): 33–8

Home Office and Department of Health (1994) *Reviewing health and social services for mentally disordered offenders and others requiring similar services, Volume 7: People with learning disabilities (mental Handicap) or with autism*. HMSO, London

Linehan MM (1987) Dialectical behaviour therapy. A cognitive approach to parasuicide. *J Personality Disorders* **1**: 328–33

Lindsay WR, Neilson C, Smith AHW *et al* (1998) The treatment of six men with learning disability convicted of sex offences with children. *Br J Clin Psychol* **37**: 83–98

Low G, Jones D, Duggan C, Power M, Macleod A (2001) The treatment of deliberate self-harm in borderline personality disorders using dialectical behaviour therapy. A pilot study in a high security hospital. *Behav Cognitive Psychother* **29**: 85–92

Lowe K, Felce D (1996) Challenging Behaviour in the community. In: Gale E, ed. *Challenging Behaviour: What We Know*. Mental Health Foundation, London

O'Rourke M *et al* (1994) *RAMAS For Interagency Casework*. FCPU Factsheet, Forensic Clinical Psychology Unit, Guildford, Surrey. See: http://www.RAMAS. co.uk

Porter I, Sangha J (2002) Reaching out. *Learning Disability Practice* **5**(6): 18–21

Robertson J, Clegg J (2002) Dilemmas in the community: Risk management of sexually offensive behaviour. *Br J Learning Disabilities* **30**: 171–5

Rose J, West C, Clifford D (2000) Group interventions for anger in people with intellectual disabilities. *Research in Developmental Disabilities* **21**: 171–81

Salkovskis PM (2002) Empirically grounded clinical interventions: Cognitive — behavioural therapy progresses through a multi-dimensional approach to clinical science. *Behav Cognitive Psychother* **30**(1): 3–9

Stenfert Kroese B, Dagnan D, Louimidis K (1997) *Cognitive Behaviour Therapy for People with Learning Disabilities*. Routledge, London

Tarrier N, Calam R (2002) New developments in cognitive behavioural case formulation epidemiological, systemic and social context: An integrative approach. *Behav Cognitive Psychother* **30**(3): 311–28

17

Multi-sensory impairment

Rachael Skinner

For a considerable period of time evidence has shown that the incidence of hearing and sight problems in the population of individuals with learning disabilities far exceeds that for the general population (McCulloch *et al*, 1996; Aitchison *et al*, 1990; Yeates *et al*, 1995; Evenhuis, 1995). Despite this, there continues to be inconsistent recognition of the significance of these issues, both in relation to the degree of need and in services willingness to provide sufficient support. There has also been overwhelming evidence that, in general, people with learning disabilities experience barriers to access the services that they require in order that these needs be recognised (Band, 1998; Department of Health 1999). This chapter aims to introduce the reader to some of the issues that exist and, more importantly, suggest what nurses can and should do to support individuals with whom they come into contact. The chapter will begin by highlighting some of the most significant evidence in relation to incidence. Consideration will then be given to potential implications of unrecognised sensory impairment. A case study will be used to highlight some of these issues and also give consideration to aspects related to the accessibility of health services and the need for an intra-disciplinary approach. Further applications will be discussed, including the need to incorporate hearing and sight screening assessments into protocols and pathways for other areas of specialist healthcare for people with learning disabilities.

Theoretical overview

Incidence and prevalence of sensory impairment

The incidence and prevalence of hearing and sight difficulties among the population of individuals with learning disabilities far exceeds that which is experienced within the general population.

For hearing impairment the scope of reported figures varies widely, and is largely influenced by definitions of what constitutes a sufficient level of functional loss and whether data relating to impairment was gathered using subjective and objective testing methods or the sole use of subjective opinions gathered from carers (Lavis, Roy and Cullen, 1997).

Authors report on incidence rates as low as 5% (Kerr, Fraser and Felce, 1996) and as high as 73% in specific high risk groups, such as those individuals with Down's syndrome (Lavis, Roy and Cullen, 1997). Between 1988 and 1992 the South East Thames Regional Health Authority funded a project to investigate the hearing status of approximately 500 individuals with learning disabilities. This study found that 39.6% of individuals had hearing loss (Yeates, 1989). The study was replicated from an initial study of 100 people. Reports were finalised from samples of 100, then 300, then 500 people and were consistent in reflecting a hearing loss incidence of between 38% and 40% (Yeates, 1989; 1991; 1992).

Specific groups of individuals with learning disabilities are known to experience increased incidence of hearing loss. Individuals with Down's syndrome are more likely to develop hearing loss as a consequence of untreated middle ear disorders (Brooks *et al*, 1972) and age-related hearing loss which occurs at a much younger age (from thirty years of age as opposed to fifty years of age) (Buchanan, 1990). The incidence of impacted ear wax is excessive among the population of people with learning disabilities and may account for some degree of conductive hearing loss for those who have persistent problems (Crandell and Roeser, 1993). Other conditions which may be associated with learning disabilities are also related to increased prevalence. The incidence of hearing loss among a population of individuals with autism far exceeds that experienced within the general population and is not accounted for by the addition of developmental delay (Rosenhall *et al*, 1999).

As for reported figures for the incidence of hearing loss, visual impairment among the population of individuals with learning disabilities far exceeds that which is experienced in the general population. Evidence suggests that two hundred times more children with learning disabilities are blind than children without additional developmental delay (Kwok *et al*, 1996). In the adult population, the percentage of adults with learning disabilities who have significantly poor sight even after the issue of corrective lenses, is over ten times that experienced in the general population (20% compared to 1.5%) (Warburg, 1994).

A number of studies suggest that the incidence of impaired vision including the need for corrective lenses is approximately 60% (Woodhouse *et al*, 2000; Aitchison *et al*, 1990). Approximately 50% of adults with learning disabilities require corrective lenses for refractive errors (Aitchison *et al*, 1990). However, the percentage of individuals who are prescribed or consistently wear glasses in the right context is far less than this (Aitchison *et al*, 1990).

There are a number of groups of individuals for whom the incidence of visual problems exceeds that which is experienced within the wider learning disability population. This includes, for instance, individuals with congenital Rubella (Warburg, 1986) and Down's syndrome (Woodhouse *et al*, 2000). Individuals with the most severe and profound disabilities experience progressively more visual problems (Woodhouse *et al*, 2000) and are also more likely to experience the types of conditions which are not amenable to corrective treatment (McCulloch *et al*, 1996). The population of individuals with learning disabilities develop the range of age-related sight problems which are experienced within the general population; however, the incidence of these types of visual impairment is again excessive within the learning disabled group (Evenhuis, 1995).

The significance of unrecognised sensory impairment

The effect of a single sensory impairment which occurs in addition to existing learning disabilities is not purely additive but cumulative. For an individual who already has difficulties in processing information, the effects of an impairment which distorts available information further hinders an individual's ability to learn.

The implications of unrecognised hearing or sight loss for any individual can be astounding. Historically, individuals' abilities have been seriously underestimated. Kropka (1979) noted that individuals with hearing loss and learning disabilities represent a 'hidden minority'. Other authors support the notion that deafness is often an invisible disability (Denmark, 1978) and this may in part account for the degree to which loss continues to go unrecognised for so many individuals.

Williams (1982) supports how limited speech, as a consequence of deafness, can mask cognitive ability and hence communication difficulties may be wrongly attributed to developmental delay. The study undertaken by Kropka in 1979 reported that a significant number of individuals were living in institutions in the South West who had measured IQs within limits accepted as 'normal' intelligence, but had been misplaced as a result of having profound hearing loss. This then led Williams (1982) to speculate that there must be significant numbers of people around the country who were profoundly deaf, whose communication needs were continuing to be unrecognised and whose quality of life had been significantly impaired as a result of low expectation.

There is no question that the presence of hearing loss can influence the acquisition of verbal language (Lederberg, 1993). When hearing loss is recognised, alternative methods of communication may be taught and used to facilitate language and meaningful communication development. If left unrecognised, hearing loss is likely to influence an individual's abilities to develop accessible language, a component in achieving social and emotional wellbeing (Monteiro and Critchley, 1994). In the general population, delayed or reduced verbal language development is usually constrained to those with the most severe or profound hearing loss (Bishop and Mogford, 1988). For those individuals who have additional problems in processing information, even mild levels of hearing loss, or fluctuating loss as a consequence of recurrent middle ear health problems, can result in significant difficulties in understanding, receiving and reproducing verbal language (Hamilton and Owrid, 1974; Klein and Rapin, 1993). Opportunities to learn and expand knowledge are compromised (Denmark, 1994) and hence the implications are complex and not to be underestimated. Poor language and communication development are highly influential components in establishing self-esteem and-confidence (Montanini-Manfredi, 1993). There are additional implications for relationship development. Where a society exists that perpetuates prejudice and stigma for individuals with learning disabilities, the additional hurdles for community living that may occur as a consequence of recognised hearing loss can feel overwhelming.

The use of the human voice to draw focus from others is often learnt unintentionally early in an individual's development. Where the power of vocalisation goes unrecognised by an individual with hearing impairment, or the individual has not developed a repertoire of visual holding skills, less appropriate means of attracting and holding attention may develop that are likely to further marginalise individuals from their peers and other significant people in their lives (Leonhardt, 1990). Sensory deprivation is reported as being a potential contributory factor in the development of self-stimulatory behaviours (Warren, 1986).

For some individuals, this stereotypical behaviour can become so frequent or consuming that it further goes on to become self-injurious (Leonhardt, 1990). Self-injurious behaviours for some individuals are believed to be functional and develop as a response to communication deficits or changes in an individual's ability to communicate effectively (Nottestad and Linaker, 2001). Where communication difficulties are highly prevalent among the population of individuals with sensory impairments, it may be deduced that self-injurious behaviours may too be over-represented.

Table 17.1: Summary of the potential implications of hearing impairment when it occurs in addition to learning disabilities

Implications of hearing impairment	Implications of unrecognised hearing impairment with learning disabilities	Potentially leads to...
Difficulties in acquiring and interpreting speech	Poor language development attributed to learning disability	Communicative attempts not recognised
Need to access alternative modes for communicating	Alternative modes of communication not taught or used as a basis for language	Influence on ability to form and maintain relationships, develop self-esteem and emotional security
Isolation in addition to difficulties in anticipating events outside of immediate vision	Impaired social skill development, fewer attachments and difficulties in developing concepts	Growing insecurities about how the world operates. Development of behaviours in attempt to enforce order and routine to establish security

General behaviour problems and more formal psychiatric disorders are reported to be more common among children who are blind, visually impaired or present with multiple disabilities, including visual impairment (Jan *et al*, 1977). This may not be surprising considering the major component that vision plays in aspects of usual development.

Table 17.2: Summary of the potential implications of visual impairment when it occurs in addition to learning disabilities

Implications of visual impairment	Implications of unrecognised visual impairment with learning disabilities	Potentially leads to...
Available information is distorted	Difficulties in making sense of available information	Development further hindered, may appear more 'learning disabled' than actual potential
Difficulties in acquiring and using non-verbal skills used in communication	Difficulties in developing conventional methods for initiating and maintaining communicative events	Development of unconventional behaviours to command and maintain attention or contact
Difficulties in sustaining motivation to search, reach or move	Increased probability of additional motor delays	Isolation in both a physical and and then emotional sense
Initial difficulties in motivation to relate outside of self	Poor development of understanding outside of themselves	Development of self-stimulatory behaviours that may progress to become self-injurious

Not only does vision contribute to the development of independent movement and other gross and fine motor skills (Sonksen, 1996), but also stimulates motivation and an incentive to investigate or confirm hypotheses about the world around us (Fazzi *et al*, 1992). Vision and visual skills also play an important role in the development toward intentional communication in sighted individuals. Differences in the presentation of behaviour which is otherwise representative of these skills may lead communication partners to feel rejected when there are perceptions that communication is unreciprocated (Mills, 1993). This has the potential to influence interaction and the frequency of communicative attempts made by others (Ware, 1996).

In addition to difficulties in accessing aspects of the visual world, loss of vision may also influence the individual's ability to access information through other senses. Hearing, although present from before birth, matures through a series of stages (as defined by Gleason, 1984). This development in part relies upon the use of vision to attach meaning to particular stimuli in order that individuals can develop to differentiate and discriminate between sounds. Without vision sounds may appear meaningless and, if overwhelmed by meaningless sound, individuals may choose to 'tune out' or inhibit responses (Hanson *et al*, 1992). In addition, the locating of objects and developing orientation by sound may take longer to learn, though these are significant skills required for those with visual impairment. Many children develop satisfactorily despite these factors, though others may remain apparently locked in a world of isolation (Cass, 1998).

Many authors have commented on similarities between the descriptors of behaviours seen in visually impaired children and those sighted children with autism (Cass, 1998). The exact relationship between autism and visual impairment is a complex one. Studies have attempted to clarify common causative factors that may account for the high prevalence of autistic-like behaviours among the population of individuals with visual impairment, though none have so far conclusively been able to determine whether environmental considerations are crucial or whether a common neurological pathology (which is common in particular causes of significant visual impairment) has the most influence (see, for example, studies cited in Cass, 1998). Difficulties remain in the differentiation of indicators of usual development for those with visual impairment and those who go on to develop autism. This is in part due to the limited studies available on the subject, given the relatively small sample sizes of children with visual impairment without additional disabilities, but also the fact that some behaviours presented by those with autism are not very different to those presented as part of 'usual' development for individuals with visual impairment.

Problems exist in the assessment of mental state for both blind and hearing impaired individuals (Kitson and Thacker, 2000; Critchley *et al*, 1981). Given some of the difficulties that may be encountered when attempting accurate mental state assessment for individuals with learning disabilities (Reid, 1994) the combination of disabilities is likely to present compounded difficulties for professionals. When comparing possible behavioural indicators of both depressive illness and acquired visual impairment, it is possible to identify how diagnostic overshadowing may occur.

> Diagnostic overshadowing is a major problem whereby behaviours are automatically attributed to the person's learning disability. In these instances, issues such as mental health needs or progressive hearing or sight loss are overlooked.

A study by Marston *et al* (1997) describes signs of depression in people with learning disability. It states that social isolation, increased self-injury or aggression that is defensive in nature, loss of interest in the surrounding environment and irritable mood are some of the more common signs. Leonhardt (1990) in a report to the *Journal of Visual Impairment and Blindness* uses these same indicators to describe some of the behaviours seen in visually impaired individuals who present with stereotypical mannerisms.

What is certainly evident is that there is a crucial need for services to be available that can identify sensory impairments that occur in combination with learning disabilities; and for there to be sufficient support for individuals, their families and carers to facilitate person-centred care that is appropriate to need.

There has been overwhelming support in the literature concerning the need for specialist assessment services, but despite this many areas of the country do not have this provision or services are not sufficiently funded. Where services do not exist, the possible consequences for individuals with unrecognised needs can only be imagined. The following case study highlights the advantages for individuals when services are able to recognise need and act accordingly.

Case study

Sam is a fifty-seven-year-old gentleman with moderate learning disabilities. He currently lives with two other gentlemen in a terraced home in an inner city area. Sam has always enjoyed a reasonable level of independence. He requires assistance in managing finances and particular household tasks but has always been proud of his appearance and able to take care of personal care needs when his mental state is good.

Sam first experienced an episode of depressive illness approximately twenty years ago. Sam has been prescribed medication to maintain a stable mood and is generally compliant with his medication regime.

Sam's general health is good. He has had the opportunity to have hearing assessments at key stages of his adulthood, the frequency of which has increased since he turned fifty years of age.

Sam's carers recognise the importance of accessing regular sight tests. Carers know that good vision is not only required for reading and driving! They are aware that there are other rewards in life that require good vision and also that sight tests include important eye health checks. Approximately eight years ago, lenticular changes were noted at a routine optometry visit. Sam was supported to access a local optometry branch and has been seen by the same optometrist at each visit. This has allowed Sam to develop trust in the optometrist and allowed the optometrist to monitor progressive changes in the opacities developing in the lens of Sam's eyes.

Eighteen months ago Sam had a fall. Carers did not witness the fall and so were unable to identify why it had happened. Over the following weeks Sam's behaviour changed. He began to show less interest in his usual activities. He no longer wished to take the short walk to the local shop every morning. He became less sociable and carers noted that he would often not respond to attempts to involve him in conversation. When he did engage in conversation he would not give eye contact.

Not only was Sam unwilling to leave his home, he was also becoming reluctant to move around his home. He spent long periods of time in his bedroom. When encouraged to leave his room he walked with a small shuffling gait and his head bent low. Sam began to eat less food at meal times and drink much less (Sam had always enjoyed having his own pot of tea and jug of milk on a tray at mealtimes). Carers became increasingly concerned about Sam and a multi-disciplinary team meeting was arranged. Sam's current situation was discussed and a decision was made to review his anti-depressant medication. In addition, the identification of lenticular changes were discussed and a referral was made to the specialist sensory impairment team within the learning disability services, to review Sam's current level of visual functioning and identify if anything more could be done for him.

Sam was seen by the specialist nurse who heads the team, who undertook to identify how Sam was using his vision and what circumstances allowed him to optimise his visual abilities. The assessment unearthed some worrying findings. Sam was not able to identify any objects placed on a table which were of low contrast to their background. This included such things as a white cup on a white table cloth, cutlery with narrow steel handles on a patterned tablecloth. Sam was completely unable to identify any object at floor level when he was in a standing position. In addition, Sam was not able to identify objects moving into his visual field until they were virtually in the centre of his vision. Sam was immediately referred for an ophthalmic consultation. A copy of Sam's functional assessment was included along with the referral letter. From the functional assessment information the ophthalmic team were able to identify that in order to assess Sam's visual acuity (his ability to see detail) an appointment would need to be made with a low vision practitioner who was skilled in using specific test material that was suitable to Sam's level of ability. Following an ophthalmic examination, Sam was identified as having glaucoma. It was too late to regain the areas of visual field loss that had occurred but treatment was prescribed to prevent any further deterioration. Past optometry prescriptions were found and there was no evidence that important checks for eye pressure had been conducted. Staff had not been aware that this type of test was available. Despite Sam having reasonable verbal language he had not been given the opportunity at optometry visits to talk about the changes he knew were occurring with his vision.

Following ophthalmic intervention, Sam was revisited by the specialist nurse from the sensory impairment team. A workshop was arranged to involve staff in completing an environmental assessment (*Figure 17.1*). Together, the specialist nurse and Sam's care team were able to recognise areas of the home that were poorly lit, provided too much glare or unshielded light, and areas where contrast between doors and walls, furniture and floor was low and acted further to disable Sam in attempts to move around with independence. Sam was able to suggest colours that he was better able to see and went out to purchase a new teapot and tray. A fluid level indicator was provided by a rehabilitation officer for visually impaired people. With a little initial support to rebuild confidence Sam was again able to pour his own tea at meal times. The rehabilitation officer had little knowledge or experience of working with individuals with learning disabilities, but had valuable skills in teaching mobility skills. A collaborative approach was agreed between the rehabilitation officer and the specialist nurse and, together with Sam and the care team, a programme of intervention was agreed to support him, initially with appropriate sighted guiding, but working toward developing independent cane work.

Hearing was then screened and age-related hearing loss was diagnosed. A referral to ENT was made and again a copy of the assessment of Sam's functional hearing and the implications of his hearing loss on his everyday ability was included. Sam's level of hearing loss was within the limits whereby hearing aids may not routinely be prescribed. Because the ENT specialist had available information of the impact of Sam's hearing loss on a functional level, it was agreed that an aid would be prescribed. Once in receipt of his hearing aid, significant support was required in order that Sam was able to feel that he could benefit from its use. Staff training was made available to enable staff to clean and maintain Sam's aid correctly and support Sam in becoming increasingly competent at being responsible for cleaning and checking his aid himself.

Twelve months on Sam is happy. He requires some help in areas of self-care but with the aid of an appropriate environment he moves around his home independently. He pours his own tea at meal times and is enabled to eat independently by using utensils and crockery that are well contrasted against a plain coloured table mat.

Sam is well on the way to using a red and white striped cane (to indicate hearing and sight loss) and is working toward a short independent route to and from the local shop.

Towards an integrated service

The importance of early identification of sight and hearing problems cannot be overemphasised. Individuals with learning disabilities are both at greater risk of hearing and sight problems and at greater risk of misdiagnosis or lack of recognition due to the complexities of testing and diagnostic overshadowing.

There is a need for consistency across the country to provide appropriate assessment and rehabilitation services for people with learning disabilities and additional hearing and/or sight loss. This need has long been recognised but many areas continue to fail individuals with learning disabilities by not recognising issues related to the difficulties experienced in accessing audiology, ENT, optometry and ophthalmic services. Professionals who work in these departments are often unaware of the additional needs presented by individuals with learning disabilities (McMillan and Buckley, 1995). When attempting to access health care this knowledge and consequential attitude formation can play a major part (McConkey and Truesdale, 2000). It is here that the specialist nurse can develop a vital role.

Education and training for generic workers, as well as workers within the learning disability field, is essential. The specialist nurse cannot hope to know all there is to know about their specialist field, but they do need to have available a network of knowledge: a range of professional and knowledgeable individuals who can be accessed. Despite the specific tools available to test visual acuity for individuals with severe and profound needs, not all practitioners are aware of their existence, or know how to use them. Providing an optometrist with the contact details of other optometrists who have developed specific skills to work with individuals with more complex needs, may be all that is required to facilitate practice development for one practitioner.

The function of making links between, and with other professionals is another essential component of a specialist nurse's role. The network of services for people with learning disabilities and other specialist services that meet the needs of people with sensory loss is so wide that there is a need for collaborative links to be made. In the past, these links have been too often informal, based on 'friendly' agreements between learning disability service providers and considerate colleagues in acute healthcare settings. Unfortunately, what sometimes occurred was that when the colleague left that particular service the link collapsed. Models of service are now being established that are based on formal links that form concrete foundations for collaboration. These models of service are specifically financed through the formulation of business plans and often take considerable time to get agreed upon and up and running.

Integrated care pathways in other areas of care have proved to be valuable in developing collaborative approaches where different disciplines, sometimes at different levels of care provision, are required to work together to provide seamless services (de Luc 2000).

Within learning disability services, integrated care pathways are beginning to flourish and early indications point to their success in achieving improved health outcomes where there is necessity for intra-disciplinary working to occur (Ahmad *et al*, 2002). Learning disability nurses are actively involved in the development of newly established pathways and, in the case of hearing impairment and learning disability, our team in North Warwickshire lead a pilot site for an integrated care pathway. It is hoped that this pathway will form the basis for the development of formal collaborative links between local services. The pathway will be formally evaluated in the near future and further plans have been made to establish closer links with primary healthcare teams to improve access to ear health treatments for adults with learning disabilities within a defined geographical area.

Within an integrated care pathway for the assessment of hearing or visual impairment, the specialist nurse can provide the essential link between clinical information and the day-to-day practicalities of a sensory loss. The way that a particular sight or hearing condition manifests itself for any individual will vary according to a range of extrinsic and intrinsic features. For instance, for sight conditions, factors such as available cognition, environmental considerations, time and degree of onset as well as clinical features, such as acuity and visual fields, will have an impact on a person's ability to use their vision. The provision of assessment data which details this individual ability to use vision is an important consideration when clinicians are making clinical judgements. Many of the individuals with whom we work will have great difficulty in giving accurate details of their functional vision and carers are often relied upon to provide this. In some services, specialist nurses have developed functional assessment skills to provide detailed accounts of how the environment impacts upon a person's ability to perform daily tasks and what circumstances are required to maximise a person's vision. Functional assessments are not only invaluable to contribute toward assessment, but also give carers and individuals practical solutions for maximising hearing and vision and reducing disabling barriers to living. In our service this component of provision has been one of the most valuable. We have received positive feedback from carers, individuals, learning disability professionals and acute healthcare colleagues. In addition to this, for some individuals who have had extreme difficulties with accessing acute services due to anxiety-related behaviour, functional assessments have provided the only available information regarding the person's sight or hearing. It is essential that work continues to achieve access to clinical assessment for all individuals. Functional assessment can only detect difficulties in sight or hearing once they have occurred. It does not provide the information required for the early detection and treatment of conditions before they manifest in clinical symptoms.

Given the degree of diagnostic overlay between hearing impairment/sight loss and other conditions associated with learning disabilities, there is a need for the screening for hearing and sight problems to form part of other pathways, eg dementia care and assessment, general health assessment, sequences for planning intervention for people with 'challenging behaviour'.

People with learning disabilities are able to benefit from medical science and improved lifestyles in the same way as you or I are able, and an increasing number of services are required to provide appropriate care services for older adults with learning disabilities. With increasing age comes age-related sensory loss.

There is likely in the future to be an increasing number of individuals with learning disabilities who develop dual sensory impairments as a result of the effects of age on sensory systems. Services and roles need to develop that provide sufficient and appropriate support to the developmental needs of adults with learning disabilities, but also have specific expertise in areas related to hearing and/or sight loss. Liaison and co-ordination are required, particularly when supporting individuals with complex combinations of need. Learning disability nurses are ideally placed to be able to take on such roles.

References

Ahmad F, Bissaker S, de Luc K, Pitts J, Brady S, Dunn L, Roy A (2002) Partnership for developing quality care pathway initiative for people with learning disabilities. Part1: Development. *J Integrated Care Pathways* **6**: 9–12

Aitchison C, Easty DL, Jancar J (1990) Eye abnormalities in the mentally handicapped. *J Ment Deficiency Res* **34**: 41–8

Band R (1998) *The NHS — Health for all?* Mencap, London

Bishop DVM, Mogford K, eds (1988) *Language Development in Exceptional Circumstances*. Churchill Livingston, Edinburgh

Bishop DVM, Mogford K, eds (1993) *Language Development in Exceptional Circumstances*. 2nd edn. Lawrence Erlbaum Associates, Hove

Brooks DN, Wooley H, Kanjilal GC (1972) Hearing loss and middle ear disorders in patients with Down's syndrome (Mongolism). *J Ment Deficiency Res* **16**(21): 21–9

Buchanan LH (1990) Early onset of presbyacusis in Down's Syndrome. *Scandinavian Audiology* **19**: 103–10

Cass H (1998) Visual impairment and autism. *Autism* **2**(2): 117–38

Crandell CC, Roeser RJ (1993) Incidence of excessive/impacted cerumen in individuals with mental retardation: A longitudinal investigation. *Am J Ment Retardation* **97**(5): 568–74

Critchley EMR, Denmark JC, Warren F, Wilson KA (1981) Hallucinatory experiences of prelingually profound deaf schizophrenics. *Br J Psychiatry* **138**: 30–2

de Luc K (2000) Care pathways: an evaluation of their effectiveness. *J Adv Nurs* **32**: 458–96

Denmark JC (1978) Early profound deafness and mental retardation. *Br J Ment Subnormality* **24**: 1–9

Denmark J (1994) *Deafness and Mental Health*. Jessica Kingsley Publishers, London

Department of Health (1999) *Once-a-Day*. Health Service Circular/107. DoH, London

Evenhuis HMC (1995) Medical aspects of aging in a population with intellectual disability: Visual impairment. *J Intellectual Disability Res* **39**(1): 19–25

Fazzi DL, Kirk SA, Pearce RS, Pogrund RL, Wolfe S (1992) Social focus: Developing socio-emotional, play and self-help skills in young blind and visually impaired children. In: Fazzi DL, Lampert JS, Pogrund RL, eds. *Early Focus: Working with young blind and visually impaired children and their families*. American Foundation for the Blind, New York

Gleason D (1984) Auditory assessment of visually impaired preschoolers: A team effort. *Education of the Visually Handicapped* **16**(3): 102–13

Hamilton P, Owrid L (1974) Comparisons of hearing impairment and socio-cultural disadvantages in relation to verbal retardation. *Br J Audiology* **8**: 27–32

Hanson NH, Finello KM, Kekelis L (1992) Cognitive focus: Developing cognition, concept and language in young blind and visually impaired children. In: Pogrund RL, Fazzi DL, Lampert JS, eds. *Early Focus: Working with young blind and visually impaired children and their families*. American Foundation for the Blind, New York

Jan JE, Freeman RD, Scott EP (1977) *Visual Impairment in Children and Adolescents*. Grune and Stratton, New York

Kerr M, Fraser W, Felce D (1996) Primary health care for people with learning disabilities: A keynote review. *Br J Learning Disabilities* **24**: 2–8

Kitson N, Thacker A (2000) Adult psychiatry. In: Hindley P, Kitson N, eds. *Mental Health and Deafness*. Whurr Publishers, London: 25–98

Klein SK, Rapin I (1993) Intermittent conductive hearing loss and language development. In: Bishop D, Mogford K, eds. *Language Development in Exceptional Circumstances*. Lawrence Erlbaum Associates, Hove

Kropka BI (1979) *A study of the deaf and partially hearing population in the mental handicap hospitals of Devon*. A report to the Royal National Institute for the Deaf (RNID), London.

Kropka BI, Williams C (1986) The epidemiology of hearing impairment in people with a mental handicap. In: Ellis D, ed. *Sensory Impairments in Mentally Handicapped People*. Croom Helm, London: 35–60

Lavis D, Roy A, Cullen P (1997) Identification of hearing impairment in people with a learning disability: From questioning to testing. *Br J Learning Disabilities* **25**: 100–5

Lederberg A (1993) The impact of deafness on the mother-child and peer relationships. In: Marschark M, Clark M, eds. P*sychological Perspectives on Deafness*. Lawrence Erlbaum Associates, Hove

Leonhardt M (1990) Stereotypes: A preliminary report on mannerisms and blindisms. *J Visual Impairment and Blindness* 216–18

Marston GW, Perry DW, Roy A (1997) Manifestations of depression in people with intellectual disability. *J Intellectual Disability Res* **41**: 476–80

McConkey R, Truesdale M (2000) Reactions of nurses and therapists in mainstream health services to contact with people who have learning disabilities. *J Adv Nurs* **32**(1): 158–63

McCulloch DL, Sludden PA, McKeown K, Kerr A (1996) Vision care requirements among intellectually disabled adults: a residence-based pilot study. *J Intellectual Disability Res* **40**: 140–50

McMillan J, Buckley R (1995) Nursing Standard Nurse 95 Awards: Caring for special clients. *Nurs Standard* **10**(2): 20–2

Mills A (1993) Visual handicap. In: Bishop D, Mogford K, eds. *Language Development in Exceptional Circumstances*. 2nd edn. Lawrence Erlbaum Associates, Hove

Montanini-Manfredi M (1993) The emotional development of deaf children. In: Marschark M, Clark M, eds. *Psychological Perspectives on Deafness*. Lawrence Erlbaum Associates, Hove

Monteiro B, Critchley E (1994) Deafness and communication. In: Critchley E, ed. *The Neurological Boundaries of Reality*. Farrand Press, London

Nottestad JA, Linaker OM (2001) Self-injurious behaviour before and after deinstitutionalization. *J Intellectual Disability Res* **45**(2): 121–9

Reid AH (1994) Psychiatry and learning disability. *Br J Psychiatry* **164**: 613–18

Rosenhall U, Nordin V, Sandstrom M, Ahlsen G, Gillberg C (1999) Autism and hearing loss. *J Autism and Developmental Disorders* **29**(5): 349–57

Sonksen PM (1996) Recognition and management of visual impairment. In: Rosenblum L, ed. *Clinical Paediatrics: Diagnosis and management of neurological disabilities in childhood*. Balliere Tindall, London: 451–66

Warburg M (1986) Medical and Ophthalmological Aspects of Visual Impairment in Mentally Handicapped People. In: Ellis D, ed. *Sensory Impairments in Mentally Handicapped People*. Croom Helm, London

Warburg M (1994) Visual impairment among people with developmental delay. *J Intellectual Disability Res* **38**: 423–32

Ware J (1996) *Creating a responsive environment — For people with profound and multiple needs*. David Fulton Publishers, London

Warren DH (1986) *Blindness and Early Childhood Development*. American Foundation for the Blind, California.

Williams C (1982) Deaf not daft, the deaf in mental subnormality hospitals. *Special Education: Forward Trends* **9**(2): 26–8

Woodhouse JM, Griffiths C, Gedling A (2000) The prevalence of ocular defects and the provision of eye care in adults with learning disabilities living in the community. *Ophthal Physiol Opt* **20**(2): 79–89

Yeates S (1989) Hearing in people with mental handicap: A review of 100 adults. *Mental Handicap* **17**: 33–7

Yeates S (1991) Hearing loss in adults with learning disabilities. *Br Med J* **353**: 427–8

Yeates S (1992) Have they got a hearing loss? A follow-up study of hearing in people with mental handicaps. *Mental Handicap* **20**: 126

Yeates S (1995) The incidence and importance of hearing loss in people with severe learning disability: The evolution of a service. *Br J Learning Disabilities* **23**

Other useful reading and resources

Aitken S, Buultjens M (1992) *Vision for doing — Assessing functional vision of learners who are multiply disabled*. Moray House Publishers, Edinburgh

Aitken S, Long L (1998) Hearing loss in people with learning disabilities. *Tizard Learning Disability Review* **3**(2): 29–32

Bradley H, Snow B (1994) *Making Sense of the World*. 2nd edn. Sense

Murdoch H (1994) 'He can hear when he wants to!' Assessment of hearing function for people with learning difficulties. *Br J Learning Disabilities* **22**: 85–9

Tobin M (1994) *Assessing Visually Handicapped People — An Introduction to Test Procedures*. David Fulton Publishers, London

The RNIB produce a range of very useful and accessible fact sheets which can be located on their website: http://www.rnib.org.uk

In addition to this, the RNIB support the running of a number of special interest groups for professionals and workers who specialise in the field of hearing or sight impairment with adults with learning disabilities. Details of membership and group meetings can be accessed by contacting:

> Hearing Impairment and Learning Disability Group
> Laura Waite, RNIB
> Tel: 0151 298 3236
> e-mail: laura.waite@rnib.org.uk

> Visual Impairment and Learning Disability Group
> Gill Levy, RNIB
> Tel: 0208 438 9121
> e-mail: gill.levy@rnib.org.uk

Example of Sam's environmental assessment

Sight condition:

- Bilateral dense cataracts
- Glaucoma and resulting visual field loss

Visual function summary:

- Unable to view any low contrast items
- Only able to view items in central vision
- Vision obscured by glare
- Requires good overall level of light
- Sam is 'confused' by shadows and sometimes interprets them as objects

Sam also has a moderate hearing loss.

Area to be developed	Action plan	Who responsible
Walls	High contrast is required between walls, doors and door handles. Most rooms are ok but Sam's bedroom has stripped wallpaper. 1. Paint Sam's bedroom walls in a plain, light matt colour. 2. Put a square of yellow onto each door to highlight the area of the handle.	
Floors	The team need to ensure that floor surfaces are safe as Sam is unable to identify hazards in his path. Sam **must** keep his downstairs bedroom. 1. Remove the mat from the kitchen area. 2. Never leave the washing basket on the floor in the corridor when putting away laundry. 3. Find an alternative storage area for the wheelchair that is not within one of the regular routes that Sam takes within his home.	
Lighting	A good level of even light is required with some focused lighting around areas where Sam requires it for near tasks (ie. meals). All areas of glare need to be eliminated. 1. Change the lightshade in Sam's bedroom to one which disperses light evenly and does not leave shadows in areas of the room. 2. Purchase higher watt bulbs for all main living areas, hallway, corridor and Sam's room. 3. Purchase light shades for those light fittings that are currently 'bare'. 4. Purchase a desk lamp with extendable arm to enable light to be focused down on specific areas (this will be particularly helpful at mealtimes). 5. Put net curtains in rooms that do not currently have them (to reduce glare from sunlight). 6. Fit an additional blind to the dining room window. Sam has to face this window directly as he walks into the dining area. The blind should be closed just before he walks into the room and then be opened once he is seated to allow natural light to shine down from behind him onto the table.	
Contrast	High contrast is required for all items that are used by Sam. He has stated that he sees red on a yellow background and dark blue on a white background most clearly. 1. Purchase red teapot and yellow tray. 2. Always use plain, pale tablecloths. 3. Purchase some dark blue plates, a bright blue mug, and cutlery with dark blue handles.	

Area to be developed	Action plan	Who responsible
Furniture	The sideboard in the dining room is in Sam's path from the doorway to his chair. 1. It should be moved to the other side of the room as it is not easily visible. 2. All furniture should remain in its place. Please do not move items around and remember to replace after cleaning under them. If changes need to be made be sure to consult with Sam and provide 'sighted guiding' around the changes for a number of days. 3. Sam has agreed that his armchair would be better placed to the right of the doorway as he enters the lounge area. 4. Purchase a pale throw to place over the chair and a red cushion to place on the seat. This cushion should also have a distinctive texture.	
Landmarks	Sam's level of hearing loss means that he is unable to access auditory landmarks that give him clues as to where he is in the home (ie. the sound of the wall clock in the hall area). 1. Tactile symbols should be placed on doors to enable Sam to understand the function of the room he is approaching. Work with Sam to decide on 'symbols' to identify each room. 2. Secure each symbol to a wooden plack which should then be secured to each door. 3. To enable Sam to access the symbols (and to avoid Sam walking into a half-opened door) always ensure that doors that are not in immediate use are kept closed. 4. Develop particular smells for specific rooms (check with Sam that he is not adverse to the smell chosen). Use smells that are easily replicable (very specific fragrances have a habit of being discontinued from sale at some point).	

Signature and name printed of all those 'responsible' in the plan:	Signature of home manager (if appropriate):
•••••••••••••••••••••••••••••••••••••• •••••••••••••••••••••••••••••••••••••• •••••••••••••••••••••••••••••••••••••• •••••••••••••••••••••••••••••••••• •••••••••••••••••••••••••••••••••••• ••••••••••••••••••••••••••••••••••	•••••••••••••••••••••••••••••••••••••• •••••••••••••••••••••••••••••••••••• Date of review:•••••••••••••••••••••••• Copies of plan forwarded to: ••••••••••••••••••••••••••••••••••••••

The role of the specialist sensory team

The core team consists of a specialist nurse and two advisor/assistant posts. Strong links are maintained with other specialist teams, namely psychology, communication therapy, occupational therapy, physiotherapy and consultant psychiatrists.

Assessment

Functional assessment skills have been developed to provide the following:

- ⌘ Clarify the extent of residual hearing or vision for individuals with known impairment.
- ⌘ Clarify the contribution of known hearing or visual impairments to current behaviour presentations (or to contribute toward differential diagnosis).
- ⌘ Identify previously unrecognised hearing or visual problems. The use of functional assessments have been particularly useful for individuals who would have extreme difficulties in tolerating clinical test procedures.
- ⌘ To provide ENT and ophthalmic clinicians with a detailed picture of the person's use of their hearing or vision to inform clinical judgement.

Advice and support

- ⌘ To advise on the nature of appropriate living, working and leisure environments for people with sight conditions or hearing impairment.
- ⌘ To advise on the nature of accessible learning and leisure activities.
- ⌘ To support the clinical assessment process for those who need to access ongoing assessment or treatment for sight or hearing conditions. This may include desensitisation or familiarisation techniques for particular procedures/tests and user accessible information to support the process of informed consent.
- ⌘ Contribute toward the development of effective communication regimes for individuals with hearing or sight impairment.
- ⌘ Monitor the initial use of prescribed aids (mainly glasses or hearing aids) and advise on routines to help individuals develop tolerance to aids, thus establish most effective use.

Education and training

In addition to having strong links with higher education, the following is a list of the most commonly requested or presented training.

- ⌘ Awareness of hearing impairment/visual impairment for workers in the field of learning disability.
- ⌘ Awareness of issues related to learning disability and hearing/visual impairment for a wider range of health and social care workers.

⌘ Aspects of mobility including sighted guiding, wheelchair guiding, empowering independent mobility by supporting individuals to learn trailing and other personal safety skills for use when moving around.

⌘ The use and maintenance of hearing aids. This includes cleaning, checking power, general troubleshooting and where to go for help.

⌘ Workshops to support teams to assess the suitability of environments for individuals with hearing/sight impairments. These workshops are never delivered before general awareness sessions and it is usual for them to follow a functional assessment of a person that lives, works or otherwise engages within the environment under consideration.

⌘ Developing functional assessment skills. These are most often delivered to other professional groups, although direct care workers are encouraged to develop skills to inform baseline and ongoing assessment as their day-to-day contact puts them in an ideal position to do so.

Networking and liaison

A significant role of the team is to establish increasingly formal collaborative links with mainstream providers of services to individuals with hearing and/or sight loss. This includes all professional groups, departments and individuals detailed below.

In addition, practice development is enhanced through membership of national special interest groups (see 'Resources').

Hearing impairment workers	Visual impairment workers
Audiologist	Local optomotrists and local optical
ENT nurse	committee
ENT consultant surgeon	Orthoptist
Specialist speech and language	Low vision specialists
therapist	Consultant ophthalmic surgeon
Hearing therapist	Rehabilitation officers
Specialist social work team (hearing	Mobility officers
impairment)	Specialist social work team (visual
Local deaf community	impairment)
Local association for deaf people	Local association for blind people
and other voluntary sector	and other voluntary sector
organisations	organisations

Epilepsy and learning disability

Catherine C Doherty

Overview of epilepsy

Epilepsy in the twenty-first century continues to be a fear ridden, socially unacceptable, stigmatised disease in the eyes of the majority. This remains unchanged from the earliest reference to epilepsy 4000 years ago in the Babylonian Code of Hammurabi (Brodie *et al*, 2001). It is often associated with convulsive 'fits' or seizures, mental illness and an inability to function as a member of society. All these myths are untrue, epilepsy is more complex than just seizures. It is not a mental illness, although mental health problems may exist and it certainly does not make the individual less of a person within society.

This chapter does not aim to inform the reader of epilepsy classifications, assessment, tests, diagnosis, treatment or how to live with epilepsy and learning disability; the literature on these issues is vast and numerous. The focus of this chapter is to highlight the role of the specialist epilepsy nurse and the contemporary issues in relation to people with the dual diagnosis of epilepsy and learning disability.

This will be illustrated by a case-study scenario and the significance of a newly developed hand-held document *Current Epilepsy Health Record*, (*Appendix IV*), to support the individual. The evolution of the document (*Appendix IV*) is to address the salient issue of communication and poor record keeping, addressed in The National Sentinel Clinical Audit (Hanna *et al*, 2002). The significance of the document is to alleviate unnecessary hospital admissions, drug changes and investigations, improve communication across the domains of primary, secondary and tertiary care.

The definition of epilepsy according to Gestault (1973) is:

A chronic brain disorder of various aetiologies characterized by recurrent seizures, due to excessive discharge of nerve tissue.

Epilepsy is the propensity to have either a single or re-occurring seizure that is unprovoked.

Epilepsy is the most common neurological condition in the United Kingdom, affecting one in one hundred and thirty of the general population, equating to 380,000 people (Department of Health, 2001a). It is known that this figure dramatically increases in the learning disability population. Lhatoo and Sander (2001) advise of figures in relation to children, and Lund (1985) with regard to adults (*Table 18.1*).

Epilepsy is often associated with some genetic disorders, for example, Angleman syndrome, Fragile X syndrome. Webb *et al* (1991) advises a 62% risk of developing epileptic seizures in Tuberous Sclerosis.

Epilepsy in learning disability leads to an 'increase in social disadvantage through double stigma or over protection' (Zaagman, 1998). These issues are pertinent for this

Table 18.1: Epilepsy incidence in learning disability population

Disability	Lhatoo and Sanders, 2001 %	Lund 1985 %
Mild	6	4
Moderate	–	7
Severe	24	12
Profound	50	28

Table 18.2: Relevant issues

Prevalence of learning disability

4 per 1000 people have severe learning disability

210,000 people will have severe and profound disability

65,000 children and young people

120,000 adults of working age

25,000 older people

25 per 1000 population of people with mild/moderate disability — equating to 1.2 million people in England (DoH, 2001b: 15–16)

Increased risk of epilepsy within the learning disability populus (see *Table 18.1*)

Epilepsy due to poverty/low income (Waldman *et al*, 2000)

client group as they affect quality of life for the individual. *Table 18.2* identifies relevant issues, including lifestyle and prevalence of learning disability, demonstrating how people with a learning disability have an increased ratio of being diagnosed with epilepsy.

Epilepsy services should be delivered with accuracy, continuity and diligence. However, services are frequently described as fragmented, poorly directed, with a lack of communication between primary and secondary care, and a reluctance from some general practitioners to deliver care to people with epilepsy (Ridsdale, 2000; Thomas, 2000; Department of Health, 2001a).

There have been five reports advising on epilepsy care since 1953 (Chief Medical Officer 2001a), including *Epilepsy Task Force* (1999), Clinical Standards Advisory Group (1999) — *Services for Patients with Epilepsy*. Parallel to these, Department of Health documents for learning disability services corroborate a change to service delivery in respect of epilepsy management. These documents include: *Health of the Nation* (1995, p. 15); *Signposts for Success* (1998a, p. 10); *Once a Day* (1999, p. 23); *Valuing People* (2001b, p. 101), however the metamorphosis to date has not succeeded in improving care delivery.

Morbidity and mortality increase for people with the dual diagnosis of epilepsy and learning disability (Graydon, 2000), as do hospital admissions (Branford, 1998). With the recent National Sentinel Clinical Audit of Epilepsy (Hanna *et al*, 2002) reporting 1000 deaths per annum from epilepsy and 500 sudden unexpected deaths in epilepsy (SUDEP), management of this chronic condition has to improve. This includes tackling social inequalities contributing to an increase in epilepsy, learning disability, poor health care and premature deaths (Waldman *et al*, 2000p; Department of Health, 2001b; Department of Health, 1998b). The annual report of the Chief Medical Officer (2001a), reiterates that epilepsy care is not satisfactory:

Understanding of the illness amongst health professionals is not high and the problem is not addressed by health services with the same commitment as is given to other chronic diseases like diabetes mellitus.

People with a dual diagnosis of epilepsy and learning disability could receive a very poor and marginalised service in relation to the management of their diagnosis. As the evidence indicates, the healthcare needs of people with a learning disability are not met by general practitioners (Mencap Report, 1997; Kerr, 1998; Stanley, 1999) and epilepsy services are poor (Thapar *et al*, 1998; Hannah and Brodie, 1998). People with this diagnosis have the same right to access and receive quality services as the general population.

Discrepancies exist as to who is best placed to provide epilepsy services, primary, secondary or tertiary care. Ridsdale *et al* (1996) concluded that patients preferred to receive epilepsy care within primary care. Chappell and Smithson (1998) surmised in their general population study that people's preference lay in the secondary care arena. Macdonald *et al* (2000) supported Ridsdale conclusions, but did recommend 'about 30% of people with epilepsy require continuous access to specialist epilepsy services'.

Given this conflicting information and the complexities of delivering appropriate health care to a person with a dual diagnosis of epilepsy and learning disabilities, who is the best professional(s) to support and work in collaboration with the individual presenting with epilepsy and learning disability? The idea of a specialist epilepsy nurse within the learning disabilities service, co-ordinating care across the domains of primary, secondary and tertiary services, could resolve some of the difficulties in managing people's epilepsy who also have a learning disability (Graydon, 2000; Loughran and O'Brien, 2001).

Specialist epilepsy nursing

The specialism of epilepsy nursing is an ideology that has failed to materialise nationally within learning disability and neurology services. Specific areas of the country have developed the good practice of specialist epilepsy nurse within learning disabilities adult and children services. The role of the specialist epilepsy nurse has been supported by Epilepsy Task force (1999), Clinical Standards Advisory Group (1999), National Sentinel Clinical Audit of Epilepsy (Hanna *et al*, 2002; Meads *et al*, 2001; Wallace *et al*, 1997) but to date their recommendations merely remain as that. Through the National Service Framework for Epilepsy (due for publication in 2005), the disparity of employing specialist epilepsy nurses may be alleviated. Until fruition of the framework (2005), practitioners will continue to provide services to this client group, improving standards and tackling the stigma of this often life-long condition.

The specialist community learning disability nurse who has additional epilepsy qualifications will have the skills and knowledge to engage in this critical role of specialist epilepsy nurse. The development of the specialist nurse in this area, will promote improved clinical practice, better outcomes for the individual and be a support/knowledgeable resource for the multi-disciplinary team, through evidence-based practice.

The specialist practitioner in learning disabilities and epilepsy engages in tackling the contemporary issues associated with this dual diagnosis for the individual, family and carer. To improve services the contemporary issues highlighted in *Table 18.3* (listed alphabetically) must be considered.

Table 18.3: Contemporary issues

Age related needs: children's needs, the transition between children and adult services and the elderly.

Assessment: including nursing assessment, Epilepsy Outcome Scale, Espie *et al* (1998), Seizure Checklist (Source – North West Epilepsy Forum, 2002; Seizure Severity Scale; O'Donoghue *et al*, 1996).

Audit – regularly review and audit services to ensure a first class service

Cognition- linked to quality of life and medication.

Communication – a paramount and key issue.

With multi-disciplinary workers involved in an individual's care across the domains of primary, secondary and tertiary care communication is vital. The specialist epilepsy nurse has a pivotal role in co-ordinating care, to improve the quality of life for the individual.

Consent – in relation to taking medication. Referring to the document *Seeking Consent, working with people with learning disabilities* (Department of Health, 2001c).

Diagnosis and Classification – in accordance with the definitions from the International league Against Epilepsy 1981 (Chadwick, 2001).

Education and Training – to inform and teach the community in relation to learning disability and epilepsy. This will include families, carers, professionals, schools, employment settings, adult education centres, day services, residential and nursing homes.

Fast-track treatment — develop service through links with accident and emergency department and primary care.

Gender specific/related issues – female issues include sexual development, menstrual cycle/catamenial epilepsy, fertility, contraception, pre-conceptual counselling, pregnancy, medication, menopause and care of children (Crawford, 2001: 375–82). Male issues include — sexual development, fertility and medication.

General Information – including legal issues, aspects of epilepsy, associations, support groups, alleviate misconceptions.

Medication — including side-effects, quality of life, gender issues, anti-epileptic medication, rescue medication.

Mortality and Morbidity — addressing the work of Branford *et al* (1998), Hanna *et al* (2002).

Non-epileptic attack disorder — addressing issues associated with this disorder.

Nurse Prescribing- anti-epileptic drugs although not on the nurses prescribing formulae to date, the issue is currently being debated. Titration of medication, offering advice to medical staff.

Review Care and Services — holistic plans and protocols to be reviewed regularly, including medication and risk assessments.

Risk assessment linked to quality of life issues — social and psychosocial issues. Addressing the work of Kokkonen *et al* (1997), Baribeault (1996), Baker (2001), Baker *et al* (1997).

Specialist nurse-led clinics — the question being are they of value? These clinics enhance service delivery including better communication between client and nurse, leading to improved outcomes for the client.

Status epilepticus — including rescue medication and the most appropriate route for administration.

SUDEP — addressing the recommendations of the National Sentinel Clinical Audit of Epilepsy — Related Death (Hanna *et al*, 2002).

Surgery — not to be dismissed for this client group, including vagal nerve stimulation. Baker (2001) and Hanna and Brodie (1998).

Treatment and care plans — plans need to be specific, indicating treatment and addressing issues pertinent to the individual (Kerr, 2001).

The specialist epilepsy nurse within learning disabilities could orchestrate and develop the role in the following domains, as listed in *Table 18.4*. These have been compared to the key characteristics of the Higher Award English National Board (1995), which identify roles and tasks of the specialist nurse practitioner. Some characteristics run concurrently throughout the specialist epilepsy nurse role, including the utilisation of research to improve care delivery.

The specialist practitioner must have the skills and knowledge to function at this advanced level, including the ability to work 'intuitively' (Kelly, 1996; Gateley, 1992), to tackle the issues confronted on a daily basis. To participate in this professional role, the specialist epilepsy nurse for people with this dual diagnosis must remain with the fraternity of the National Health Service, continuing to develop the rudimentary role of clinical practitioner. The Health Services Act 2001 (DoH, 2001d) has enabled the transference of registered nurses for people with learning disabilities to further social inclusion and health, promoting the dilution of clinical skills. As nurses engage in care management, the health needs of clients may become neglected, this is supported by Messent and Caan (2000) who advise that nurses are 'addressing aspects of social care'.

Case study

Mary aged nineteen years, has a mild learning disability. She was twelve years of age when her epilepsy was diagnosed. Mary currently lives at home with her parents and brother. She is seen regularly by a consultant paediatrician who manages her epilepsy, although this is under review. Her diagnosis is that of tonic clonic seizures and juvenile myoclonic epilepsy. After several years of uncontrolled seizures and variations to drug regimes, Mary's current medication of sodium valproate, lamotrigine and clobazam is controlling the seizures with good effect. She has in the past been admitted to hospital due to her epilepsy.

Mary is due to leave school in the next four months and the management of her care is to be transferred to adult services, including day services, further education, short breaks, community nursing and consultant psychiatrist in learning disabilities. However, the debate has arisen as to who should manage Mary's epilepsy, neurology services, a consultant psychiatrist or both specialists. All of these issues will add stress to Mary's life, a trigger factor that has increased seizure activity.

Issues for consideration in managing Mary's epilepsy at this critical time of her life include:

- transition from child to adult services
- who is the most appropriate clinician to manage Mary's epilepsy
- stress indicators, support required from the multidisciplinary team to reduce seizure activity
- communication in the transferring of services to ensure key and vital information is not lost
- polypharmacy, an issue to be considered in the future, but not immediately, due to the changes in Mary's life
- gender-specific issues, including catamenial epilepsy, contraception, polycystic ovaries and possible pregnancy in the future
- appropriate risk assessment and protocols to manage Mary's epilepsy.

If Mary were to receive a hand-held client record (see below), information in relation to her epilepsy from paediatrics service would be readily available for her first appointment in adult services.

Table 18.4: Specialist epilepsy nurse in learning disability roles

Specialist epilepsy nurse	Key characteristics of specialist nurse (ENB 1995)
Specialist nursing care including nursing assessments, risk assessments Establish and implement treatment plans Counselling, addressing all issues including, quality of life and gender specific needs for the individual Resource for client, family, carer and professionals	Clinical skills — having a broader understanding and specialist skills and knowledge
The development of protocols/ care plans	Quality of care — evaluate care as an ongoing process
Specialist nurse-led clinics	Accountability — demonstrating professional accountability utilising skills and knowledge in varying environments
Invest and improve epilepsy services through leadership	Management of change — manage and improve service through initiating and facilitating change to improve quality of care
Educate professionals, clients and carers supporting appropriately Networking with colleagues in the independent sector, supporting and developing their skills and expertise in this specialist field	Staff development — to develop and teach staff and others appropriately
Be a 'clinical advocate' (Baribeault, 1996)	Innovation — to act professionally and appropriately to support the individual ensuring their needs are met
Collaborate and liaise across the domains of primary, secondary and tertiary care Co-ordinate services	Teamwork — to ensure via teamwork and through role change as required, clients treatment and care plans are adhered to
Monitor drugs treatments	Health promotion — engage in strategies to ensure effective treatment. Appropriate use of health promotion policies to contribute to the individual's welfare
Domiciliary visits	Resource management — acting appropriately for the benefit of the individual through allocation and management of resources effectively

Current Epilepsy Health Record (*Appendix IV*)

People need to be part of the process in managing their condition. Not only through complying with drug regimes and medical tests, but also by taking responsibility for information and records, as this will support continuity and stability in managing the individual's condition. The development of a hand-held client record, would improve care, abolish repetitive questioning (Hart, 2002) and encourage collaboration between the individual and services (Fischbach *et al*, 1980).

The aim of the hand-held client record is five-fold, as outlined in *Table 18.5*.

Proposed benefits of the document are illustrated in *Table 18.6*.

Table 18.5: Aim of the document
⌘ To allow for emergency care/treatment to be administered at the onset of a seizure.
⌘ To ensure continuity of care and aid communication across the multidisciplinary team, including the accident and emergency department.
⌘ To ensure any possible admissions to hospital due to a seizure via the accident and emergency department will **not** result in a change to drug regimes (unless absolutely necessary) or unnecessary tests, eg. bloods, scans.
⌘ Support the sub-objective 5.1 of *Valuing People* (DoH, 2001b: p125) to 'reduce the health inequalities experienced by people with a learning disability'.
⌘ Support the transition from children's services to adult services.

Table 18.6: Proposed benefits of the document
⌘ Improved communication.
⌘ Ensure collaborative working of the multi-disciplinary team across the domains of primary, secondary and tertiary care.
⌘ Accurate and up-to-date information available at all appointments.
⌘ Reduce inequality in healthcare delivery for people with learning disabilities and epilepsy.
⌘ Due to available information treatment/care plans would be precise, supporting improved care and improved quality of life.

Client hand-held records have not been a customary practice in the field of epilepsy as it has been in other areas eg obstetrics, midwifery, oncology and mental health services (Kirkham, 1997; McCann, 1998; Warner *et al*, 2000; Henderson, 2002). One study in the area of hand-held records and epilepsy, Thapar *et al* (2002), recorded inconclusive findings, but favourable results:

⌘ Improved recording of key clinical information in patient records.
⌘ Most doctors felt the 'cards' to be useful.
⌘ 'Card' needed to be used in a more patient-centred manner.
⌘ Patients forgot to bring their cards.
⌘ GPs were too busy to use the 'card'.
⌘ Shown to improve epilepsy care (personal communication within the study).

It must be noted that people with severe learning disability were excluded from the study. To introduce hand-held records to people with a learning disability and epilepsy may evoke the same difficulties as this general population study. When introducing hand-held client records into a service, ethical issues must be considered. These issues would include confidentiality, consent and loss of records. If hand-held client records are not a customary practice within the reader's service, a multi-disciplinary approach or an application to the local ethics committee should be considered. This approach would ensure that it is in the client's best interest to engage in the practice. Anecdotal evidence, from epilepsy clinics for people with a learning disability demonstrates, clients/carers present seizure-recording charts on a regular basis. Allowing people with this dual diagnosis to take responsibility for information is a positive step, encouraging autonomy and control for the individual.

Should the onset of a seizure occur, often the immediate reaction of the public is either to ignore the person or call an ambulance. The introduction of this hand-held record for people with epilepsy and learning disabilities may support neither of these actions occurring unless the latter is required. The aim being that the person with epilepsy who does not require assistance in everyday life events, eg. shopping and socialising, will carry the hand-held record allowing people to give assistance, should they have a seizure, by reading the 'emergency plan' and act accordingly.

According to Ryan *et al* (1998), 'epilepsy is one of the commonest neurological conditions presenting at the accident and emergency department'. This is corroborated by Laville (1998). It is therefore important that people presenting at the accident and emergency department with epilepsy and learning disability have up-to-date and accurate information in their possession. Ryan *et al*'s (1998) study reiterates the importance of accurate information being available in relation to a person's epilepsy state.

The initial information recorded in the *Current Epilepsy Health Record* relates to the following areas:

Personal details	(Appendix IV pages 325, 326)
Medical information	(Appendix IV page 326)
Professionals involved	(Appendix IV page 327)
Diagnosis of Epilepsy	(Appendix IV page 327)

All clinicians caring for an individual require this information. Ryan *et al* (1998) and Gruman *et al* (1998), verify this by advising that information relating to history was often unrecorded and that the ability to have patient's progress notes to hand would be an asset. Basic details of the client would trigger medical notes within the accident and emergency department, allowing access to vital information.

The language used and methods of interpreting and communicating all need to be established in order for staff to communicate with the individual. Non-verbal communication could be interpreted as the patient remaining in a seizure state.

Religion and ethnicity are areas of people's lives that require consideration. There are 1000 known deaths from epilepsy per annum. Given this information, hospital staff need to be aware of spiritual needs (Laukhauf and Werner, 1998) as people with epilepsy may die when admitted to hospital. Customs and practice of people's religion and culture should be observed.

Drug calculations regularly necessitate height and weight data, particularly for children. Paediatric epilepsy syndromes including West and Lennox-Gestaut, often present with between 100–300 seizures per day (Robinson and Guerrini, 2001: 79). This high incident of seizure activity frequently requires hospital admission via the accident and emergency department, hence the necessity of this information.

Blood groups, allergies and rescue medication (as required due to status epilepticus) are vital details to ensure that clients do not deteriorate if admitted to hospital. This information can support clinicians when prescribing medication.

Having the knowledge of professionals/specialists involved in a client's care package (*Appendix IV, page 326, 329*) will help to provide continuity of care, collaboration and allow for the multi-disciplinary team to communicate. Through this collaboration, health gain may be achieved, improving the person's quality of life and reducing morbidity rates.

Diagnosis of epilepsy *(Appendix IV)*, including seizure type and syndrome, is essential knowledge in order for physicians and nurses to ensure accurate treatment, realistic risk assessments and care plans. All seizures should be diagnosed using the criteria of the International League Against Epilepsy 1981 as described by Chadwick (2001: 7–12). This will ensure continuity in treatment plans including anti-convulsant therapy.

Current medication (*Appendix IV, page 328*) will inform the multidisciplinary team or staff at the accident and emergency department of the up-to-date prescription. Current prescription information will ensure that new drugs prescribed will not contra-indicate. This information will allow drug dosages to be titrated to control seizures and reduce polypharmacy. The ultimate aim and optimum solution for people is mono-therapy in order to reduce 'cognitive impairment and side-effects' (Carvill *et al*, 1999).

Previous anti-convulsant medication prescribed, (*Appendix IV, page 328*) are key facts, which those prescribing medication require knowledge of. The reason for discontinuing the medication is critical as this may influence future prescriptions. Drug information is crucial if people are having their epilepsy managed across the boundaries of primary and secondary care, a favourable result in Chappell and Smithson's (1998) study.

Rescue medication and alternative therapies (*Appendix IV, page 329*), although not pertinent to every individual are essential to some. Rescue medication can be administered via three routes. Therefore, it is important that the prescription is legible and accurate, stating medication, route and dose, critical information on admission to hospital. The important issue of when someone goes into status epilepticus is to stabilise the person, not to take action (if you are appropriately trained) could result in intellectual impairment, motor paralysis or death (Dodson *et al*, 1992).

Alternative therapies need to be monitored with accuracy, as this type of therapy like some drug therapies can increase seizure activity. The ketogenic diet is an established treatment for intractable seizures in children (Freeman *et al*, cited in Casey *et al*, 1999). It is important that the child's height, weight and present health state are all known in order to determine an optimal ketogenic diet, ensuring 'adequate nutrition for growth and development' (Casey *et al*, 1999).

Seizure management	(Appendix IV page 330)
Seizure checklist	(Appendix IV pages 330, 331)
Epilepsy record	(Appendix IV page 332)

This information will determine a person's seizure type and syndrome and ultimate drug regime. Seizure checklist and management information will assist carers to manage a person through the three stages of a seizure, pre-ictal, ictal and post-ictal. Accurately recording the time of a person's seizure will determine their drug regime and ensure optimum anti-convulsant levels and reduction in seizures. These forms within the document will assist parents and unqualified staff to manage and support the individual and ensure accurate up-to-date information is available when attending appointments (key information according to Kerr and Bowley, 2001 and Hannah and Brodie, 1998).

Precipitating factors (*Appendix IV, page 333*) are pivotal; this information will allow the individual, carers and the multi-disciplinary team to plan care. Including lifestyle issues, triggers, medication and non-compliance of medication. If triggers are managed, a reduction in seizures can occur improving quality of life and reducing mortality and morbidity for the individual.

Blood tests	(Appendix IV page 333)
Drug level investigations	(Appendix IV page 334)
Investigations (eg. scans)	(Appendix IV page 334)
Epilepsy surgery	(Appendix IV page 335)
Hospital admissions due to epilepsy	(Appendix IV page 336)

Investigations, surgery and hospital admissions have a two-fold effect:

1. Trauma for the individual.
2. Additional costs to the service.

Medical procedures are often traumatic for individuals, especially for the learning disabled person who may not have an understanding as to why a certain procedure or test is being undertaken. Professionals must consider the necessity of any investigation prior to requesting it. The value of blood tests and scheduled drug level monitoring require careful consideration, they are often performed without necessity (Carvill *et al*, 1999; Ryan *et al*, 1998; Hannah and Brodie, 1998).

Electroencephalography and other scans can all play an important role in the diagnosis and management of a person's epilepsy. However, performing such investigations can be fraught with difficulties, and does not always help in the management of epilepsy (Hannah and Brodie, 1998; Carvill *et al*, 1999). Epilepsy surgery in the learning disability population is not a regular occurrence due to a risk of 'cognitive deterioration after surgery' (Hannah and Brodie, 1998). Surgery should not be dismissed for this client group. Anecdotally, vagal nerve stimulation has now shown to be successful in people with learning disabilities.

Nursing workload in the accident and emergency department increases due to hospital admissions for people with epilepsy with little, if any, gain to the individual (Ryan *et al*, 1998).

Repetitive and unnecessary investigations, due to the lack of communication contribute to demanding budgets within the NHS. Comprehensive information within the document (*Appendix IV*) would be accessible to the multidisciplinary team, including staff in accident and emergency. This would enable a reduction in accident and emergency visits, non-repetition of tests and investigations, hospital admissions which may activate depression (Kaye *et al*, 2000) and paramedic involvement. Ryan *et al* (1998) reported that, '90% of patients were brought to the hospital in ambulances'. This would benefit both client and the service. Alleviating stress to the client with epilepsy can only be positive, as a diagnosis of depression and anxiety can cause complications for people with epilepsy (Piazzini and Canger, 2001). It is paramount that people with epilepsy and learning disability are not admitted to hospital unless it is absolutely necessary, in order to reduce the risk of depression and anxiety which may increase seizure activity. With a health authority district spending £600 million per annum in direct costs (Cockerell *et al*, 1994, cited in Laville, 1998) epilepsy care is expensive.

> Risk assessment (Appendix IV page 336)
> Care plan (Appendix IV page 337)

This information will assist the multi-disciplinary team, the client, their family/carer to plan care, minimise risk and reduce morbidity (supporting Gruman *et al*, 1998 who recommends, 'collaboratively drafted care plans for each patient with seizures').

> Information/advice given (Appendix IV page 335)
> Comments/questions (Appendix IV page 337)

These areas are important within such a document for professionals to record advice that they have given to an individual enabling the person to retain the information. For example, information may include; first aid, drug titration, preconception and pregnancy advice. Chappell and Smithson (1998) revealed 'only one third of women could recall receiving pre-conception advice and nearly 80% of people could not recall first aid having been discussed'. For people with learning disabilities, writing or depicting information will aid their memory.

A comments/question page will allow clients/carers to make notes which can then be used as an aid memoir at appointments, giving the individual an opportunity to be actively involved in their care and treatment plan.

The specialist epilepsy nurse, in collaboration with the client and main carer, would update the document accordingly, supporting continuity of care. Each professional requesting and receiving information should endorse the hand-held record, ensuring accurate records.

The *Current Epilepsy Health Record* demonstrates how communication and inconsistencies across the interface of primary, secondary and tertiary care could be enhanced, improving services for people with epilepsy and learning disabilities.

The document has the potential to improve people's quality of life. *Table 18.7* outlines the possible benefits.

This document would be of value to clients, professionals and service delivery, and supports Ryan *et al*'s (1998) conclusion that, 'improvements in the quality of documentation might be achieved by the introduction of a structured proforma'.

Summary of the nurse's role

This chapter has highlighted the role and value of the specialist epilepsy nurse for people with the dual diagnosis of epilepsy and learning disability.

Table 18.8 illustrates the key aspects of this significant role in supporting people with epilepsy and learning disability

Table 18.7: Potential benefits of the document

- ⌘ Alleviate stress/anxiety in relation to unnecessary investigations for the client
- ⌘ Ensure a collaborative treatment/care plan is developed, and is accessible to the multidisciplinary team
- ⌘ Improve communication among the multidisciplinary team across the interface of primary, secondary and tertiary care
- ⌘ Improve the quality of life of clients
- ⌘ Reduce morbidity rates
- ⌘ Reduce mortality rates
- ⌘ Reduce hospital admissions
- ⌘ Improve health gain for the clients
- ⌘ Reduce costs
- ⌘ Engage clients in taking some responsibility for their own health

Table 18.8: Role of the specialist epilepsy nurse

- ⌘ Communicate effectively to improve care to the individual
- ⌘ Co-ordinating care across the domains of primary, secondary and tertiary care
- ⌘ Collaborative working with the multi-disciplinary team, clients and carer
- ⌘ Develop appropriate care plans and strategies through accurate assessments, diagnosis and treatment plans to improve the individual's quality of life
- ⌘ Teacher and educator to client, carer and the wider community
- ⌘ Resource for client, family, carers and professionals
- ⌘ To be a key individual in driving forward change through leadership, to improve service delivery which will have a positive and lasting effect on the individual and their carers

Conclusion

The ultimate goal when supporting an individual with epilepsy and learning disability is to improve their 'quality of life'.

Although inclusion of people with learning disabilities into mainstream acute hospital services is the ideal when treating a person with epilepsy, the service they often receive is poor and negative and does not improve their quality of life. Delivery of care may be enhanced in the future with the introduction of health facilitators (DoH, 2001b: 63) who will have a key role in teaching and educating professionals within secondary care in how to support and treat people with learning disabilities.

The specialist epilepsy nurse in learning disabilities has a primary role to support and improve standards of care to this client group, who are often doubly stigmatised.

Key developments of specialist epilepsy nurses in learning disabilities and the introduction of the *Current Epilepsy Health Record*, should improve service delivery and outcomes for this client group. *Table 18.9* outlines recommendations, that need to be actioned in order to benefit clients, carers, professionals and service delivery.

The *Current Epilepsy Health Record* does not replace assessments, care pathways, or other documentation used in planning an individual's care. It is designed as a hand-held record for the individual; ensuring that he/she has the most up-to-date and accurate information in his/her possession when visiting the various members of the multi-disciplinary team involved in their treatment, aiding communication and reducing unnecessary tests, investigation and hospital admissions.

This document is currently being produced on CD-Rom format in conjunction with a pharmaceutical company in order that professionals can access and utilise it.

It is planned that it will be audited in the future. A grant has been sought from the pharmaceutical company (producing the document on CD Rom format) to fund the audit.

Table 18.9: Recommendations

⌘ Introduce the *Current Epilepsy Health Record* into service delivery, for people with the diagnosis of epilepsy and learning disability

⌘ Assessment and treatment of epilepsy should be multidisciplinary, based across the boundaries of primary, secondary and tertiary care where appropriate, requiring action immediately

⌘ Appropriate and functional documentation is required to ensure continuity of care across the three domains of care. Introduction of the *Current Epilepsy Health Record* would support this

⌘ Effective communication within service delivery, the *Current Epilepsy Health Record* would help in achieving this goal

⌘ The inclusion of the hand-held client record will support a system-based approach to managing care, reducing the need for unnecessary tests, changes in drug regimes and hospital admission

⌘ Training and promotion of the *Current Epilepsy Health Record* will have to be undertaken with clients, carers and professionals within the three domains of care, including accident and emergency staff

⌘ Education of professionals in respect of epilepsy services and care is required to improve the quality of life of people with this dual diagnosis

⌘ To deliver evidence-based practice, promoted by the National Institute of Clinical Excellence (NICE)

⌘ Specialist epilepsy nurses undertake key tasks in improving service delivery and quality linked to clinical governance

⌘ Specialist epilepsy nurses to work collaboratively to co-ordinate care in order to improve the individual's 'quality of life'

References

Baker GA (2001) Psychological and neuro-psychological assessment before and after surgery for epilepsy. Implications for the management of learning disabled people. *Epilepsia* **42** (suppl 1): 41–3

Baker GA, Jacoby A, Buck D, Stalgis C, Monnet D (1997) Quality of life of people with epilepsy: A European study. *Epilepsia* **38**(3): 353–62

Baribeault JJ (1996) Clinical advocacy for persons with epilepsy and mental retardation living in community based programs. *J Neurosci Nurs* **28**(6): 359–72

Branford D, Bhaumik S, Duncan F (1998) Epilepsy in adults with learning disabilities. *Seizure* **7**: 473–77

Brodie MJ, Aldenkamp AP, Arroyo S, Avanzini G, deBoer HM, Boon PA *et al* (2001) *European White Paper on Epilepsy*. Eucare, Belgium

Carvill S, Clarke D, Cassidy G (1999) The management of epilepsy in a hospital for people with a learning disability. *Seizure* **8**: 175–80

Casey CJ, McGrogan J, Pillas D, Pyzik P, Freeman J, Vining EPG (1999) The implementation and maintenance of the ketogenic diet in children. *J Neurosci Nurs* **31**(5): 294–302

Chadwick DW (2001) Classification of seizures. In: Duncan JS, Sisodiva SM, Small JE, eds. *Epilepsy 2001 from Science to Patients*. 8th edn. Burleigh Press Ltd, Bristol: 7–12

Chappell B, Smithson WH (1998) Patient views on primary care services for epilepsy and areas where additional professional knowledge would be welcome. *Seizure* **7**: 447–57

Clinical Standards Advisory Group (1999) *Services for Patients with Epilepsy*. Clinical Standards Advisory Group, United Kingdom

Cockerell OC, Hart YM, Sander J, Shorvon SD (1994) cited in Laville L (1998) Switching the management of epilepsy to primary care. *Nurs Times* **94**(19): 52–3

Crawford P (2001) Epilepsy and women. In: Duncan JS, Sisodna SM, Smalls JE, eds. *Epilepsy 2001 from Science to Patients*. 8th edn. Burleigh Press Ltd, Bristol

Department of Health (1995) *The Health of the Nation: A Strategy for People with Learning Disabilities*. DoH, London

Department of Health (1998a) *Signposts for Success in Commissioning and Providing Health Services for People with Learning Disabilities*. DoH, London

Department of Health (1998b) Acheson report. Independent Inquiry into Inequalities in Health Report. HMSO, London

Department of Health (1999) *Once a Day*. DoH, London

Department of Health (2001a) Annual Report of the Chief Medical Officer 2001. On line at: http://www.doh.gov.uk/cmo on 14.04.2002

Department of Health (2001b) *Valuing People: A New Strategy for Learning Disability for the 21st Century*. DoH, London

Department of Health (2001c) *Seeking Consent Working with People with Learning Disabilities*. DoH, London

Department of Health (2001d) Health and Social Care Act. HMSO, London. Online at: http://www.hmso.gov.uk/acts 18/06/02

Dodson WE, Leppik IE, Slovis CM (1992) Status epilepticus. *Patient Care* **26**(18):100–10

English National Board for Nursing, Midwifery and Health Visiting (1995) 10 Key Characteristics of the Higher Award In University of Central England Community Health Nursing Degree Handbook. UCE, Birmingham

Epilepsy task force (1999) *Specification for Epilepsy Services*. Glaxo Wellcome

Espie CA, Paul A, Graham M, Sterrick M, Foley J, McGarvey C (1998) The Epilepsy Outcome Scale: The development of a measure for use with carers of people with epilepsy plus intellectual disability. *J Intellectual Disability Res* **42**(1): 90–06

Fischbach RL, Sionelo A, Needle A, Delbanco T (1980) The patient and practitioner as co-authors of the medical record. *Patient Counselling and Health Education*. First Quarter: 1–5

Freeman JM, Kelly MT, Freeman JB (1996) cited in Casey JC, McGrogaan J, Pillas D, Pyzik P, Freeman J, Vining EPG (1999) The implementation and maintenance of the ketogenic diet in children. *J Neuroscience Nurs* **31**(5): 294–30

Gateley EP (1992) From novice to expert: the use of intuitive knowledge as a basis for district nurse education. Nurse Educ Today 12: 81–7

Gestault H (1973) *Dictionary of Epilepsy*. World Health Organization, Geneva

Graydon M (2000) Do learning disability services need epilepsy specialist nurses? *Seizure* **9**: 294–6

Gruman J, Vonkorff M, Reynolds J, Wagner EH(1998) Organizing health care for people with seizures and epilepsy. *J Ambulatory Care Management* **21**(2): 1–17

Hannah JA, Brodie MJ (1998) Epilepsy and learning disabilities – a challenge for the next millennium? *Seizure* **7**: 3–13

Hanna NJ, Black M, Sander JWS, Smithson WH, Appleton T, Brown S, Fish DR (2002) *The National Sentinel Clinical Audit of Epilepsy — Related Death: Epilepsy — Death in the Shadows*. The Stationery Office, London

Hart JT (2002) Continuity would be achieved with patient held records. *Br Med J* **324**: 51 (letter)

Henderson C, Laugharne R (2002) Patient held clinical information for people with psychotic illnesses (Cochrane Review) In: *The Cochrane Library* Issue 1 2002. Oxford: Update Software downloaded 30.04.2002

Kaye J, Morton J, Bowcutt M, Maupin D (2000) Depression: The forgotten diagnosis among hospitalised adults. *J Neuroscience Nurs* **32**(1): 7–16

Kelly A (1996) The concept of the specialist community nurse. *J Adv Nurs* **24**: 42–52

Kerr M (1998) Primary health care and health gain for people with a learning disability. *Tizard Learning Disability Review* **3**(4) 6–14

Kerr M, Bowley C (2001) Multidisciplinary and multi-agency contributions to care for those with learning disability who have epilepsy. *Epilepsia* **42**(suppl 1): 55–6

Kerr M and members of the working group of the International Association of the Scientific Study of Intellectual Disability (2001) Clinical guidelines for the management of the scientific study of intellectual disability. *Seizure* **10**: 401–9

Kirkham M (1997) Client held notes — a Talisman or a Truly Shared Resource? *Modern Midwife* **7**(3): 15–17

Kokkonen J, Kokkonen ER, Saukkonen AL, Pennanen P (1997) Psychosocial outcome of young adults with epilepsy in childhood. *J Neurology, Neurosurgery and Psychiatry* **62**(3): 265–8

Laukhuf G, Werner H (1998) Spirituality: The missing link. *J Neuroscience Nurs* **30**(1): 60–7

Laville L (1998) Switching the management of epilepsy to primary care. *Nurs Times* **94**(19): 52–3

Lhatoo SD, Sander WAS (2001) The epidemiology of epilepsy and learning disability. *Epilepsia* **42** (suppl 1): 6–9

Loughran S, O'Brien D (2001) The developing role of learning disability nurses in epilepsy. *Epilepsy Care* **1**(3): 6–8

Lund J (1985) Epilepsy and psychatric disorder in the mentally retarded adult. *Acta Psychiatr Scand* **72**: 557–62

Macdonald D, Torrance N, Wood S, Womersley J (2000) General practice-based nurse specialists taking a lead in improving the care of people with epilepsy. *Seizure* **9**: 31–5

McCann C (1998) Communication in cancer care: Introducing patient-held records. *Int J Palliative Nurs* **4**(5): 222–9

Meads C, Bradley P, Burls A (2001) *The Effectiveness of Specific Epilepsy Services*. West Midlands Health Technology Assessment Course, Birmingham

MENCAP (1997) *Prescriptions for Change*. Mencap, London

Messant P, Caan W (2000) Learning disabilities nurses must stay linked to the NHS. *Br J Nurs* **9**(19): 2062

North West Learning Disability Epilepsy Forum (2002) *Seizure Checklist*. In: Nursing Epilepsy Assessment Document, unpublished

O'Donoghue MF, Duncan JS, Sander JWAS (1996) The National Hospital Seizure Severity Scale. A further development of the Chalfont Severity Scale. *Epilepsia* **37**(6): 563–71

Piazzini A, Canger R (2001) Depression and anxiety in patients with epilepsy. *Epilepsia* **42** (suppl 1): 29–31

Ridsdale L (2000) The effect of specially trained epilepsy nurses in primary care: A review. *Seizure* **9**: 43–6

Ridsdale L, Robins D, Fitzgerald A, Jeffery S, McGee L (1996) Epilepsy monitoring and advice recorded. GPs' views, current practice and patients' preferences. *Br J Gen Pract* **46**: 11–14

Robinson RO, Guerrini R (2001) Severe paediatric epilepsy syndromes. In: Duncan JS, Sisodiva SM, Smalls JE, eds. *Epilepsy 2001. From Science to Patients*. 8th edn. Burleigh Press Ltd, Bristol

Ryan J, Nash S, Lyndon J (1998) Epilepsy in the accident and emergency department — Developing a code of safe practice for adult patients. *J Accid Emerg Med* **15**: 237–43

Stanley R (1999) Supporting the person with learning disability to access primary care. *Learning Disability Practice* **2**(3): 30–3

Thapar A, Jacoby A, Richens A, Russell I, Roberts C, Porter E *et al* (2002) A pragmatic randomised controlled trial of a prompt reminder card in the care of people with epilepsy. *Br J Gen Pract* **52**: 93–8

Thapar AK, Stott NCH, Richens A, Kerr M (1998) Attitudes of GPs to the care of people with epilepsy. *Fam Pract* **15**(5): 437–42

Thomas M (2000) New directions for care. *Nurs Times* **96**(19): 39

Waldman HB, Swerdloff M, Perlman SP (2000) Children with mental retardation and epilepsy. Demographics and general concerns. *J Dentistry for Children* **67**(4): 268–74

Wallace H, Shorvon SD, Hopkins O'Donoghue M (1997) *Adults with poorly controlled epilepsy*. Royal College of Physicians, London

Warner JP, King M, Blizard R, McClenana Z, Tang S (2000) Patient-held shared care records for individuals with mental illness. *Br J Psychiatry* **177**: 319–24

Webb DW, Fryer AE, Osborne JP (1991) On the incidence of fits and mental retardation in tuberous sclerosis. *J Med Genetics* **28**(6): 395–7

Zaagman P (1998) Epilepsy and learning disability nursing — the case for expert knowledge. *J Assoc Practitioners in Learning Disability* **15**(1): 4–9

Section V:
Further dimensions of
learning disability nursing practice

19

Reflective practice and clinical supervision

Rosemary Brown

There are very few research studies reporting on the use of clinical supervision and reflective practice in learning disability nursing. Malin (2000) evaluated clinical supervision in community homes and teams serving adults with learning disabilities and reported that clinical supervision is still not widely recognised and practised by learning disability nurses. He questioned that there was possibly confusion over what it is, stating that 'some nurses... have heard of the term but are unfamiliar with it'.

This chapter focuses on how in one community trust, clinical supervision and reflective practice for learning disability nurses works very well. It describes two case studies highlighting how the use of reflective practice in the clinical supervision session can be used as a tool to develop self-awareness, critical analysis and problem solving.

Introduction

Clinical supervision and reflective practice is not specifically designed for use within learning disability nursing, it is a concept that has been encouraged to become an inherent and a 'cultural norm' within the whole sphere of nursing and medicine.

Its roots lie in the psychotherapeutic arena, writers of humanistic theory (Rogers, 1969) and andragogical theory (Knowles, 1985) believe that learning and developing are achieved in a trusting and non-threatening environment, which involves the self, feelings and intellect. Knowles (1985) states that:

Adults become ready to learn when they experience a need to know or do something in order to be able to perform more effectively in some aspect of their lives.

Clinical supervision brings practitioners and skilled supervisors together to 'reflect' on practice. Supervision and reflection aims to identify solutions to problems, improve practice, relate theory to practice and practice to theory and increase understanding of professional and organisational issues.

Butterworth and Faugier (1992) define supervision as, 'an exchange between practising professionals to enable the development of professional skills'. They further define (1992) clinical supervision as a process that promotes personal and professional development within a supportive relationship that is formed between equals.

Clinical supervision was endorsed by the UKCC (1995) who produced a position statement proposing that clinical supervision would enable practitioners to maintain and promote standards of care by encouraging continuous professional development; that it would ensure safe and effective practice and that it should be a practice-focused professional relationship.

Vision for the Future (DoH, 1993: target 10) identified the need for nurses to be supported in developing their clinical practice, and suggests that clinical supervision should be an important process to provide this support. This has been further endorsed in *Making a Difference* (DOH, 1999), whereby the Government has clearly set the agenda for nursing ensuring that the profession was in the vanguard of clinical developments. Even though *Making a Difference* is part of the clinical governance agenda, there is a clear linkage between clinical supervision and the clinical governance agenda, which focuses on improving practice, supporting staff and promoting lifelong learning.

In 1994, the Allitt enquiry highlighted concerns about the supervision of safe and accountable practice, and the Department of Health (1994) reviewed the literature by Butterworth and Faugier (1992) which states that clinical supervision can help to sustain and develop practice. Moores (1994), in a letter to all the professional bodies, stated that the concept of clinical supervision is 'fundamental to safeguarding standards and the development of professional expertise'. The UKCC's *Code of Conduct* (1992) and the *Scope of Professional Practice* (1993) placed the responsibility of standards of practice in the hands of each qualified practitioner. However, Moores (1994) stated that 'the profession's leaders and others must recognise this accountability by ensuring that sufficient support, information and supervision is available to practitioners'. This can be further endorsed by clinical governance in that all trusts and practice areas should have now identified that clinical governance ensures that there are mechanisms in place to:

- address quality issues, such as dealing with clinical incidents/risks and complaints
- setting practice standards
- benchmarking standards of practice and auditing practice
- improving practice and care for service users and in particular
- supporting staff and promoting lifelong learning (McSherry, 2002).

The clinical supervision processes and clinical governance, although not the same, are an integral part of the quality agenda.

A sample of research studies

Berg *et al* (1994) and Hallberg and Norberg (1993) carried out research in psychogeriatric hospitals and from their findings supported that clinical supervision was an effective support system. Berg *et al* (1993) state 'that systematic clinical supervision and individually planned care encouraged nurses to reflect emotionally and cognitively on their provision of nursing care'.

In 1997, Butterworth *et al* published an evaluation study entitled *It is good to talk*. Overall the study could not categorically state in quantitative terms that clinical supervision has a clear benefit for nurses. However, 70% of the participants receiving clinical supervision were positive about the experience. Butterworth *et al* (1997) discuss the 'feel good factor' when professionals receive clinical supervision.

Brocklehurst (1997) carried out a quantitative quasi-experimental research in the West Midlands regarding the effectiveness of clinical supervision and stated that, when measured quantitatively, 'it is without context and therefore loses meaning and value'.

Powell (1989) focused her research on reflective practice in nursing and supports its use, but indicates that nurses are not particularly skilled at reflecting. Fish *et al*'s (1989) study supported these findings. Schon (1987), Boyd and Fales (1983) and

Titchen and Binnie (1995) have all reported the positive aspects of reflective practice.

Johns (1993) utilised a case study approach, and used reflection and supervision to observe how the skills associated with primary nursing could be learnt. He discusses the developmental processes of reflective practice and supervision and offers these as a method to enable both supervisor and supervisee to grow into effective practitioners that are unique and meaningful. Johns (1994) suggests that the analysis of everyday practice provides the organisation with valid subjective feedback, enables theory to be appropriately juxtaposed with practice and identifies and focuses elements of everyday practice.

Why do learning disability nurses need clinical supervision?

It has been highlighted for many years that staff working in the field of learning disabilities are subject to high levels of stress. Bromley and Emerson (1995) showed that unpredictability, hopelessness and inability to understand clients' behaviours were significantly greater stressors than the person injuring him/herself or others. Staff in learning disability services spend a great deal of time in intense interaction with others. Stress can arise from this intense involvement and chronic stress can lead to burnout (Caton *et al*, 1988). Therefore the requirement for clinical supervision is greater.

Since the closure of long-stay hospitals, many practitioners now work in comparative isolation, both professionally and geographically. Learning disability nurses are working in a variety of settings and have been required to transfer and develop their skills into community-based services. They are expected to work as autonomous, highly skilled independent practitioners, often 'facility independent' (Cullen, 1991). The flattening of management structures has meant that G and H grade staff have had to take on more clinical and managerial responsibilities.

The contract culture has deemed purchasers and providers of health and social care to be more specific and explicit in their requirements. What they can purchase and provide is becoming more reliant on evidence-based practice and measurable outcomes of care.

Community learning disability nurses have been used to working in multi-disciplinary teams, their casework often involves long-term therapeutic working, directly with clients and their carers. This can often be stressful with too few resources to draw upon.

The development of collaborative working, using within it structured models of supervision can only empower learning disability nurses to share ideas and evidence leading to best practice.

In 1996, the author's place of work was an NHS trust. This trust developed a clinical supervision strategy, through a practitioner-led forum, consisting of learning disability nurses, district nurses, practice nurses and health visitors. Clinical supervision was redefined 'as a structured formal exchange between professionals leading to enhanced practice and professional development through supportive reflection' (First Community Health NHS Trust, 1997).

The strategy was agreed and implemented in 1997, the clinical supervision framework addressed issues such as:

- frequency of sessions
- location
- confidentiality

- conduct/ground rules
- documentation of sessions
- identification and selection of potential supervisors
- characteristics and skills of supervisors
- education and development of supervisors.

Further collaboration between the NHS trust and the local university enabled the development of an ENB accredited course to train prospective supervisors. It appears from the literature available that other NHS trusts developed varying clinical supervision strategies according to the needs of the trust.

The application of clinical supervision and reflective practice in learning disability nursing

It has been found by Titchen and Binnie (1995) in their action research study, that the facilitation of professional growth and learning in the practice setting requires something different than the traditional hierarchical approach that often only concentrates on errors, omissions and reprimands when the nurse has done something wrong. Within clinical supervision, the supervisee is helped in discussion with the supervisor to progress by being challenged and helped to think in new ways. Titchen and Binnie (1995) utilised Johns and Butcher's (1993) work that focused on learning through supervision. Johns (1992, 1993, 1994), in particular his reflective model, concentrates on a holistic model of care, asking a set of questions that enable the supervisee to question their thoughts, feelings and to analyse the lived experience enabling a development of self-awareness, of psychological and physical needs and to plan future care or indeed a conscious response if the problem arose again. In comparison, Gibbs (1988) uses a cyclical reflective cycle, suggesting that reflection is an ongoing process. Both of these models ask a similar set of questions allowing for the supervisee to explore theory to practice and practice to theory. Proctor's three stage interactive model (1986) allows for further structure to be included in the supervision sessions.

The particular models lend themselves to learning disability nursing due to the long term, often stressful and in-depth nature of the work. As previously stated, learning disability nurses work in a variety of settings and are required to have a broad skill base underpinned by a humanistic and valuing approach (Rogers, 1969; DoH, 2001). They are involved with a broad spectrum of people who are complex, challenging and vulnerable. Working with this group of people can often produce negative feedback from staff, as emotions and stress levels are high. Nurses require time to reflect and analyse their thoughts and feelings so that they are able to remain positive and objective in their work.

Through reflection by using a structured model, issues become clearer to the supervisee. A skilled supervisor is able to help a supervisee reflect, theorise, evaluate and direct their own learning. The supervisor is also able to guide the supervisee towards knowledge that they may need to acquire in order for them to gain further understanding of the needs of their client group.

Reflecting on practice can also enable a supervisee to gain a broader understanding around clinical issues, local and national policies and procedures, legal and

Government legislation all related to their client group.

The domains of practice of learning disability nurses can broadly be outlined as the ongoing use of a holistic approach to care, often in partnership with other key stakeholders; the facilitation of health care to all age groups, including those that have a forensic history, dual diagnosis, epilepsy, complex and enduring medical and psychological difficulties, and those that are vulnerable and open to abuse. Within these groups a range of therapeutic interventions will be utilised. Due to their diverse roles, learning disability nurses may have responsibility for care management, primary care, specialist health care, user engagement and empowerment. This requires the use of good networking skills with other professionals and the general public as well as the effective management of time, resource and caseloads. Greig (1999) acknowledges the skills of the learning disability nurse and argues that the changing policy and legislative environment requires new ways of applying these skills. The knowledge and skills of the learning disability nurse are as important today as they have ever been and clinical supervision and reflective practice is an effective arena within which to develop and clarify those skills. Sams (1996) and Bishop (1994) both state that spending time getting the supervision process right is vital, as it ultimately determines the success of clinical supervision. If the process is not effectively established, supervisee and client outcomes disappear from view.

Facilitating supervision: a case study approach using reflective practice

A useful tool for establishing a supervision relationship can be the use of learning style questionnaires, for example, Kolb and Fry's (1975) learning styles questionnaire, to ascertain the preferred learning style of the supervisee, for instance, whether they are activists, reflectors, theorists, pragmatists or a mixture of these learning styles.

The roots of reflection lie in experiential learning developed by the work of Kolb and Fry (1975) into their experiential learning cycle, and individual learning styles. In this particular case, the clinical supervision sessions had developed over a period of approximately six months. The supervisor was supervising a nurse who had recently moved from working in a residential unit to community learning disability nursing. She was experiencing the change as rewarding but frustrating. It was established that the supervisee had an activist learning style and was used to 'hands on working'. The supervisee was experiencing problems with one particular family that she had been referred. When she asked the mother to carry out instructions regarding her daughter's behaviour, the mother was not doing so. This was resulting in no behaviour change for the daughter, a mother that was still saying she could not cope, and a frustrated and confused community nurse.

In this instance, the supervisor was able to draw on her own prior knowledge of nursing models and draw parallels between clinical supervision and the client/ practitioner relationship as stated in Playle and Mullarkey (1998). Peplau (1988), in her orientation phase, suggests that 'seeking assistance on the basis of a need, felt but poorly understood, is often the first step in a dynamic learning experience from which a constructive next step in personal/social growth can occur'. The supervisor was also able to empathise with the supervisee as she had herself experienced this frustration as a practitioner.

The supervisee had begun to establish the boundaries of supervision and gain the confidence necessary to share clinical experiences together with associated emotions, strengths and weaknesses.

During this initial phase of the supervisee 'telling her story', the supervisor used basic counselling skills, such as active listening, continued eye contact and a relaxed and open posture. The supervisor should be aware of her own behaviour, such as not interrupting inappropriately or unconsciously making the supervisee feel uncomfortable or inadequate. Clarification of the issues continued throughout the sessions. Peplau (1988) describes this as the identification phase whereby the supervisee gets the feeling that they know what the situation can offer and respond to individuals who can offer the help needed.

Orientation
Focus on the processes: engaging, establishing boundaries: identifying needs, setting the context

Resolution
Focus on the processes: working towards and experiencing a health ending

Peplau's (1988) four stages of interpersonal relationships — which can parallel the stages of development within a supervisory relationship

Identification
Focus on the processes: increasing awareness of the value and function of supervision, aspects of power and control

Exploitation
Focus on the processes, learning self-direction, exploration and challenge

Underpinning the supervision sessions, the supervisor was using an 'eclectic approach' of both Gibbs' (1988) 'Reflective Cycle' and Johns' (1993) model for structured reflection, which have been found by Wolverson (2000) to be particularly useful in the area of learning disability nursing. Both of these models enable the supervisee to describe what has happened, how they thought and felt and to evaluate what was good and bad about the experience. They offer the opportunity for the supervisor and supervisee to analyse the situation, reach a conclusion and form an action plan in case the same situation arises again.

By using the reflective models of Gibbs (1988; *Figure 19.1*) and Johns (1993; *Figure 19.2*), the supervisee was enabled to see the situation from a different perspective. She stated that, when she had worked in the residential setting, she had been very prescriptive and staff had carried out tasks that she had asked them to do, often without question. She stated that she was learning that she needed to become more facilitative and more self-aware, working with clients and carers required this less directive approach in order to nurture change.

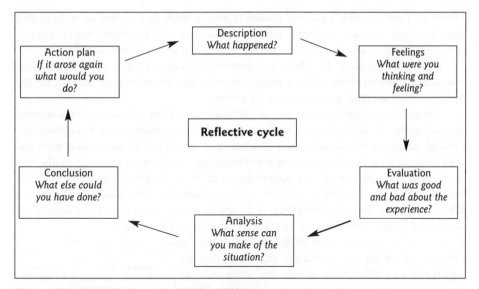

Figure 19.1: The reflective cycle (Gibbs, 1988)

Phenomenon	• Describe the experience
Causal	• What essential factors contributed to this experience?
Context	• What are the significant background factors to this experience?
Reflection	• What was I trying to achieve?
	• Why did I intervene as I did?
	• What were the consequences of my actions for:
	– myself
	– the client/patient/family
	– the people with whom I work
	• How did I feel about this experience when it was happening?
	• How did the client feel about it?
	• How do I know how the client felt about it?
	• What factors/knowledge influenced my decisions and actions?
Alternative actions	• What other choices did I have?
	• What would be the consequences of those other choices?
Learning	• How do I now feel about this experience?
	• Could I have dealt better with the situation?
	• What knowledge have I gained from the experience
	• What further knowledge do I need to gain in order to deal with this situation or a similar one in the future?

Figure 19.2: Model for structured reflection (adapted from Johns, 1993)

This is illustrated further by the work of Schon (1987) who outlined a reflection practitioner model and suggested that reflection occurs 'in action' as well as 'on action'. Schon (1987) also argued that professionals face unique and complex situations in their everyday practice, which are not solved by conventional academic knowledge alone. Wolverson (2000) states that the role of the learning disability nurse requires complex reasoning skills and consequently the need to find opportunities to reflect on their practice. Learning disability nurses work in a variety of settings and have to adapt to many differing roles, the diversity of these roles makes clinical supervision and reflective practice an even more important 'cultural norm'.

Rooted throughout the clinical supervision process is Proctor's three stage interactive model (1986). In this particular situation, the supervisor was using the formative and restorative functions of the model.

The formative function is concerned with the supervisor and supervisee assessing in partnership the strengths and needs of the supervisee, enabling them to formulate clinical strategies to develop their practice and identify alternative strategies and interventions to widen their clinical knowledge base and improve clinical skills. The restorative component is the supportive function. This element is concerned with the identification of emotional growth through self-awareness. The supervisor facilitates this through the use of counselling skills enabling the supervisee to acknowledge negative feelings and personal stresses aroused by their work situation. This is the element of supervision where basic counselling skills are essential in order that the supervisor can effectively enable the supervisee to become a more competent practitioner. These functions can be used parallel to the reflective models.

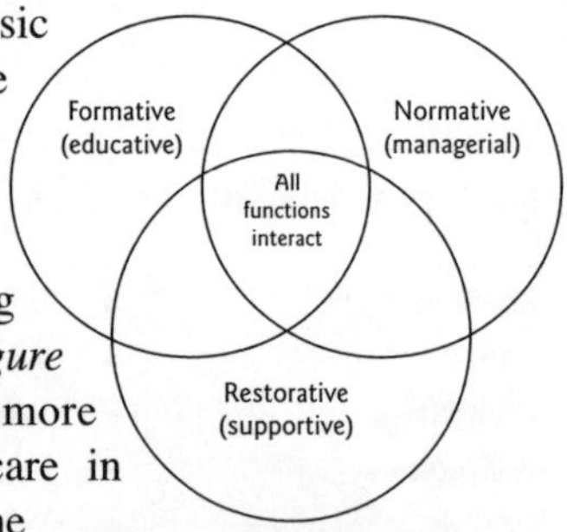

During this period of clinical supervision, using reflective models and Proctor's three-stage model (*Figure 19.3*), the supervisee was enabled to become more enlightened, increase her responsibility, plan her care in partnership with the carer, learn new skills and become more self-aware, enabling her to adapt her own behaviour depending upon whom she was visiting. The supervisor was enabled to develop her own use of reflective models in her practice and deal with situations in a positive way after they had been analysed.

Figure 19.3: Proctor's three-stage interactive model

Facilitating supervision: a second case study approach

The following case study illustrates supervision sessions in an established supervisory relationship. Chambers and Cutcliffe (2001) state that, 'clinical supervision involves the creation and maintenance of an interpersonal relationship'. The supervision sessions focused on issues raised by the supervisee with regard to a situation she had found herself in during visits to a family whose child had a learning disability and terminal illness. The supervisee expressed concerns about the commitment she had given to this family and how she had felt 'drawn in' by the family, as were other professionals involved during this difficult time. The supervisee was present when the child died, and had shared some of the grief that the family had experienced. The supervisee explained how throughout this clinical experience her manager had continually reminded her not to become too involved. The manager's prescriptive stance had been based on her own experience of a similar case. The supervisee therefore had felt compelled to distance herself from the family and to remain in control of her emotions. However, she had allowed herself to become deeply involved with the family and expressed that she felt guilty because of this, as she believed she was going against her manager's wishes and did not know if she was right to be so involved.

In these particular supervision sessions, the supervisor used Gibbs' (1988) reflective cycle and these sessions were rooted in the formative and restorative functions of Proctor's (1986) clinical supervision model. Due to the nature of the problem that the supervisee was bringing to the sessions, the supervisor decided to use her knowledge of John Heron's (1975) six category intervention analysis (*Figure 19.4*) during communication between the supervisee and herself in an attempt to enable the supervisee to move on. The supervisor did not want to be authoritative and prescriptive in this instance, as she wanted the supervisee to be enabled to explore and release her own personal feelings regarding the case, in an attempt to facilitate a self-awareness on the part of the supervisee, therefore, encouraging professional growth. The supervisor decided to utilise the three categories of the facilitative dimension of John Heron's (1975) model, in the hope that the supervisee could be helped to resolve her dilemma and move on.

Initially taking a cathartic stance the supervisee was helped to explore and release the emotions that she had felt during her experience of caring for the dying child. The supervisor continued using the catalytic category of Heron's (1975) model enabling the supervisee to be reflective and encouraging self-directed problem solving. The supervisor used supportive intervention to affirm the worth and value of the supervisee, as well as adopting Rogers' (1951) approach of showing 'unconditional positive regard' in turn leading the supervisee and focusing on areas of competence and acknowledging the interface between personal and professional experience. The supervisee was enabled to move on with her practice leaving behind feelings of anger, frustration and guilt.

Authoritative interventions		
Prescriptive	•	Supervisor explicitly directs the supervisee by giving advice or direction
Informative	•	Supervisor intends to provide information, to instruct the supervisee
Confrontative	•	Supervisor challenges the beliefs or behaviour of the supervisee. Such confrontation does not imply aggression, invites the supervisee to consider some aspect of their work or themselves that was not previously acknowledged
Facilitative interventions		
Cathartic	•	Supervisor attempts to help the supervisee move on through the expression of thoughts or emotions previously acknowledged or unexpressed
Catalytic	•	Interventions are focused on helping the supervisee become increasingly self-directed and reflective
Supportive	•	Supervisor attempts to reinforce the confidence of the supervisee through focusing on their areas of competence and attending to what they did well

Figure 19.4: John Heron's six category intervention analysis

The previous case study was again from a learning disability nurse receiving clinical supervision. As Wolverson (2000) states, the length of the relationship between the learning disability nurse and client is often longer and more in-depth than the relationship in other areas of nursing. Learning disability nurses are frequently drawn into dilemmas about acting in the client's best interests and situations are made more complex because the nurse often has to work through parents and carers. The requirement for clinical supervision and the opportunity to reflect objectively on practice is paramount, so that learning disability nurse practitioners do not end up colluding with families and are enabled to maximise the health potential of the client in a structured and holistic way.

The two previously highlighted case studies attempt to relate theory to practice and practice to theory. It should be noted that the clinical supervision sessions were as defined previously, 'a structured formal exchange between professionals leading to enhanced practice and professional development through supportive reflection' (First Community Health NHS Trust, 1977).

As stated by the UKCC (1995), clinical supervision is not a managerial control system. It is not the exercise of managerial responsibility or managerial supervision, a system of individual performance review or hierarchical in nature. It has been found in practice that the supervisor is usually a more skilled practitioner than the supervisee.

This is further endorsed by Cooke (2002) who states that if learning disability nurses are to achieve the same status as other community practitioner groups, then their managers must ensure the education of their workforce. Within the diverse roles of the learning disability nurse, who works in social services settings, the NHS, private sector, education sector and voluntary sectors make up a huge percentage of the caseload, therefore, the challenge for supervisors is individually tailored supervision in a range of settings, utilising the models described previously. Practitioners are increasingly expected to account for their professional judgements in order to be recognised as autonomous and accountable. With the introduction of clinical supervision and the wider agenda of clinical governance, clinical authority is moving from a hierarchical stance towards more professional structures.

Conclusion

In order for nurses to be recognised as autonomous and accountable, they need to develop the skills required to be reflective (Atkins and Murphy, 1993). These are the ability to become self-aware, describe situations, critically analyse, synthesise and evaluate. Conversely, Boud and Walker (1993) stated that barriers to reflecting on practice successfully were a lack of self-awareness, resistance to change, lack of time, lack of noticing skills, past negative experiences, hostile or impoverished environments, presuppositions about what may be possible and others' expectations of one's behaviour.

Clinical supervision using reflective practice provides an excellent environment to develop reflective practice skills: guided by the supervisor, the supervisee is challenged to think in alternative and different ways. Burnard (1995) states that through this process of clarification and critical development, nurses can develop the ability to trust their own judgement and accept their own ideas as valid, while respecting and appreciating others' points of view.

Boyd and Fales (1983) describe reflection as:

The process of internally examining and exploring an issue of concern, triggered by an experience, which creates and clarifies meaning in terms of self, and which results in a changed perspective.

Butcher (1995) described the benefits that clinical supervision can bring to practice and states that supervisees should be prepared to examine their work, beliefs and attitudes in depth to raise awareness of areas needing development. In the specialist and diverse arena of learning disability nursing, the ability to reflect on practice skilfully and critically, with the aid of a skilled supervisor and structured models can bring many benefits in promoting person-centred practice and maintaining and articulating the uniqueness of the role (Wolverson, 2000). This is supported by Powell (1989) who stated in her research that nurses are not particularly skilled at reflecting, especially at more complex levels and need appropriate support and guidance while they learn the process from an appropriate role model.

Newall (1994) discusses that reflective practice is unproven in its efficiency to achieve significant improvement in terms of patient outcomes. We therefore return to the premise that reflective practice is a process of learning through experience where outcomes can be monitored in terms of practitioners' actions and the description of experiences over time will demonstrate how patient outcomes have been developed. If we relate this statement back to learning disabilities services, client outcomes would require a longitudinal approach, as any outcomes would need to encompass a wider holistic viewpoint, acknowledging the many variables.

Using reflection as a tool for critical self-assessment, reflection can enable practitioners to evaluate and develop their professional practice.

Lifelong learning and quality improvement can only be achieved by providing staff with the resources, support and time to reflect on their experiences and practices. Investing in the development of a clinical supervision framework will ensure that individuals, teams and the organisation can develop and reflect to improve their practice, both singularly and organisationally.

References

Atkins S, Murphy K (1993) Reflection: A review of literature. *J Adv Nurs* **18**: 1188–92

Berg A, Hansson UW, Hallberg IR (1994) Nurses creativity, tedium and burnout during one year of clinical supervision and implementation of individually planned nursing care comparisons between a ward for severely demented patients and similar control ward. *J Adv Nurs* **20**(4): 742–9

Bishop C (1994) Clinical supervision for an accountable profession. *Nurs Times* **90**(39): 35–7

Boud D, Keogh R, Walker D (1985) *Reflection Turning Experience into Learning*. Kegan Page, London

Boyd EM, Fales AW (1983) Reflective learning; Key to learning from experience. *J Humanistic Psychology* **23**(2): 99–117

Brocklehurst N (1997) *Reviewing the evidence: Lessons for the profession*. Abstracts from Clinical Supervision and Mentorship. The University of Manchester, unpublished

Bromley J, Emerson E (1995) Beliefs and emotional reactions of care staff working with people with challenging behaviour. *J Intellectual Disability Res* **39**(4): 341–52

Burnard P (1995) *Learning Human Skills: An experiential and reflective guide for nurses.* 3rd edn. Butterworth, Oxford

Butcher K (1995) Taking notes. *Nurs Times* **91**(26): 33

Butterworth T, Faugier J (1992) *Clinical Supervision and Mentorship in Nursing.* Chapman and Hall, London

Butterworth T, Carson J, White E, Jeacock J, Clements A, Bishop V (1997) *It is Good to Talk, An Evaluation study in England and Scotland. Clinical Supervision and Mentorship.* University of Manchester, Manchester

Caton DJ *et al* (1988) Burnout and stress among employees at a state institution for mentally retarded persons. *AmJ Ment Retardation* **93**(3): 34–9

Chambers M, Cutcliffe JR (2001) The dynamics and processes of 'ending' in clinical supervision. *Br J Nurs* **10**(21): 1403–11

Cooke P (2002) Community learning disability nursing. In: Canham J, Bennet J, eds. *Mentorship in Community Nursing: Challenges and opportunities.* Blackwell Science Ltd, Oxford

Department of Health (1991) *Caring for People: The Implications for Mental Handicap Nursing.* The Cullen Report, DoH, London

Department of Health (1993) *A Vision for the Future. The Nursing Midwifery and Health Visiting Contribution to Health.* HMSO, London

Department of Health (1999) *Making a Difference.* HMSO, London

Department of Health (1994) *National Health Service Management Executive Working in Partnership.* HMSO, London

Department of Health (2001) *Valuing People. A New Strategy for Learning Disability for the 21st Century.* HMSO, London

Fish D, Twinn S, Purr B (1989) *How to Enable Learning through Professional Practice.* West London Institute of Higher Education, London

First Community Health NHS Trust (1996) *Framework for Clinical Supervision.* unpublished, Stafford

Gibbs G (1988) *Learning by Doing: A guide to teaching and learning methods.* Further Education Unit, Oxford Polytechnic, Oxford

Greig R (1999) *Beyond the community learning disability team?* A discussion paper by the community care development centre, King's College, London

Hallberg IR, Norberg A (1993) Strain among nurses and their emotional reactions during one year of systematic clinical supervision combined with the implementation of individualized care in dementia nursing. *J Adv Nurs* **18**: 1860–75

Heron J (1975) *Six Category Intervention Analysis.* Human Potential Research Project, University of Surrey

Johns CC (1992) Continuity of psychological aspects of care. *J Clin Nurs* **1**(3): 113–14

Johns CC (1993) Professional supervision. *J Nurs Management* **1**: 9–18

Johns CC (1994) The growth of management connoisseurship through reflective practice. *J Nurs Management* **2**: 253–60

Kolb D, Fry R (1975) Towards an applied theory of experiential learning? In: Cooper CL, ed. *Theories of Group Processes.* John Wiley and Sons Ltd, London

Knowles M (1985) *Andragogy in Action. Applying modern principles of adult education.* Joseey Bass, San Francisco

Malin N (2000) Evaluating clinical supervision in community homes and teams serving adults with learning disabilities. *J Adv Nurs* **31**(3): 548–57

Moores Y (1994) *Clinical Supervision for the Nursing and Health Visiting Professions.* Department of Health, London

Newall R (1994) Reflection: Art, science or pseudo science. *Nurs Educ Today* **14**: 79–81

McSherry R (2002) Clinical supervision and clinical governance. *Nurs Times* **98**(23)

Playle JF, Mullarkey K (1998) Parallel processes in clinical supervision; enhancing learning and providing support. *Nurse Educ Today* **18**: 558–66

Peplau H (1988) *Interpersonal Relations in Nursing*. 2nd edn. GTE Putman, New York

Powell JH (1989) The reflective practitioner in nursing. *J Adv Nurs* **14**: 824–32

Proctor B (1986) Supervision: a cooperative exercise in accountability. In: Hawkins P, Shohet R, eds. *Supervision in the Helping Professions*. Open University Press, Milton Keynes

Rogers CR (1951) *Client-centred Therapy. Its Current Practice, Implications and Theory*. Constable, London

Rogers C (1969) *Freedom to Learn*. Merril, Ohio

Sams D (1996) Clinical supervision: an oasis for practice. *Br J Community Health Nurs* **1**(2): 87–91

Schon (1987) *The Reflective Practitioner. How Professionals Think in Action*. Jossey Bass, San Francisco

Titchen A, Binnie A (1995) The art of clinical supervision. *J Clin Nurs* **4**: 327–34

United Kingdom Central Council for Nursing, Midwifery and Health Visiting (1993) *The Scope of Professional Practice*. UKCC, London

United Kingdom Central Council for Nursing, Midwifery and Health Visiting (1992) *Code of Professional Conduct*. UKCC, London

United Kingdom Central Council for Nursing, Midwifery and Health Visiting (1995) Registrars Letter 4/1995 Annexe 1. Position Statement on Clinical Supervision for Nursing and Health Visiting. UKCC, London

Wolverson M (2000) On reflection. *Learning Disability Practice* **3**(2)

The consultant nurse in learning disability and clinical governance

Caron Thomas

In his speech at the 1998 Nurse Awards the Prime Minister, Tony Blair, first suggested the introduction of nurse consultant posts within the NHS. There was a clear intention for these roles to have the same status in nursing as medical consultants in their field (Alderman and Lipley, 2001). However, it could be argued that the origins of the role can actually be traced back further than this, and that the global health agenda, ie. Europe and farther afield, has greatly influenced the development of nursing roles within the United Kingdom.

Following the Second World War, the first World Health Assembly (WHA, 1948) passed a resolution stating the need to establish nursing roles which would enable the most appropriate use of nursing services across member states. Over forty years later, in 1994, the publication of the *Heathrow Debate* (Department of health [DoH], 1994) identified the need to develop nursing roles, including added expertise and research, offering highly proficient care, training, and advice to colleagues. But it was not until 1997 that extensive consultation was put forward on the developments for new nursing roles in, *The New NHS — modern, dependable* (DoH, 1997). In 1999, the national strategy, *The NHS Plan* (DoH, 1999) was launched, identifying a target of having 1,000 nurse, midwife, and health visitor consultants in post by 2004. This was underpinned by the *Making a Difference* strategy for nurses, midwives, and health visitors (DoH, 1999).

The framework for the role of the nurse consultant was first set out in *Making a Difference*. The document identified that nurses, midwives, and health visitors were seen as critical to the success of the Government's plan to modernise health and social services. Behind this lay the aim of building career pathways in nurse leadership and change management within the clinical setting (Rowden, 1999), to retain senior and experienced nurses who may otherwise have left clinical practice.

The nurse consultant was identified as being at the forefront of the modernisation agenda in nursing in the United Kingdom, providing leadership and management of change in clinical care, improving quality and services. It could be argued that the role was developed out of necessity, in that a national shortage of GPs has made it necessary to expand the roles of other professions to fill the gaps in skills shortages (Farmer, 1998), including the roles of nurses and allied health professionals such as physiotherapists and speech and language therapists.

The role of the nurse consultant

Role ambiguity surrounds the nurse consultant. Certainly the proliferation of titles in nursing has caused confusion, not only within the profession, but also with other professions, carers and clients alike. Also, some nurses have developed the scope of their roles and some clinical nurse specialists may find it hard to differentiate between their role and that of a nurse consultant (Castledine, 1998). As a result, conflict may occur (Pennington, 2000) which would need careful and skilful handling, as it is important that nurse consultants are viewed very much as part of a team, rather than a stand alone, elitist group. Indeed, service users and carers may also have difficulty in understanding the differences in nursing roles. This will be just one of the many challenges facing nurse consultants in their career, to influence the patient's or client's perspective of this role in relation to better outcomes of care.

Nurse consultant practice is grounded in both the biomedical and social sciences. At the core of nursing practice is a personal interface or relationship with the client, whereby aspects of mental, physical, or spiritual health are not separated out from each other. Each one impacts on the other, and the complexities of care needs are unravelled skilfully through a combination of knowledge, skills and experience, in a way that is acceptable to the client, and safeguards their wellbeing. Arguably, it is the depth and breadth of the role that separates it out from other nursing roles.

The nurse consultant role is not about being a physician's assistant, a role that came to prominence in the United States during and after the Vietnam war due to a shortage of physicians (Torn, 1995). Indeed, it is difficult to draw a parallel in the United Kingdom with an equivalent role in the United States. It may be that nursing roles reflect the cultural values and norms of the population served, and the needs of people within the United Kingdom are met by a different type of practitioner (Manley, 1997).

Controversy still surrounds the nurse consultant role, and role ambiguity could be a complicating factor for some practitioners. For example, Woods (1999) described the advanced nurse practitioner role [ANP] as being remarkably similar to that of the nurse consultant and Berragan (1998) argued that consultancy was a sub-role for most practitioners in nursing anyway. Earlier, in 1994, the UKCC had outlined advanced practice as:

Adjusting the boundaries for the development of future practice, pioneering and developing new roles responsive to changing needs and, with advancing clinical practice, research and education, to enrich professional practice as a whole.

This description does appear to be a forerunner for the role of the nurse consultant. However, there seems to be a general consensus concerning the academic background of the nurse consultant, and that is the requirement to be working at masters' level, widely interpreted as having a masters' degree in a subject related to clinical practice.

Four core functions of the nurse consultant's role have been identified (DoH, 1999c), which should assist in emphasising and clarifying the domains of practice:

- expert practice, a minimum 50% of time working with patients, clients or communities
- professional leadership and consultancy
- education, training, and development
- research and evaluation.

These four core functions are not carried out exclusively. Rather, any one or the other of the roles may dominate according to the particular situation. Equally, other situations may require a combination of some or all of the four roles. Such is the flexibility of approach required by the nurse consultant.

Expert practice

Being able to see the broader aspects of healthcare provision is essential for the nurse consultant. This requires both strategic vision and objectivity in interpreting the wider picture. The context of this is understanding the political aspects to care provision, putting policy into practice, and contributing to the development of health and social care policy. Also, recognising the emerging themes from practice, developing strategies at local, regional and national level, and taking a long term view of care needs (Berragan, 1998). The evidence base to support nursing practice is drawn from systematic and rigorous approaches to care, personal experience, national policy, and research. The emphasis on this has been reinforced through clinical governance and the creation of the National Institute for Clinical Effectiveness (NICE), and the inspectoral role of the Commission for Health Improvement (CHI), which is to become the Commission for Health Audit and Inspection.

Health promotion, health education, and disease prevention form the basis of nursing practice. As an expert practitioner the nurse consultant will examine these issues on several levels; from a public health perspective, looking at population needs and trends, from a local community perspective, and the individual client perspective. The nurse consultant will be instrumental in devising strategy and policy to meet the needs of local client population.

For example, in the context of older people, this means understanding the health needs of the ageing population and applying the standards identified in the Older People's National Service Framework (DoH, 2001). This will involve leading on and developing care pathways which can be utilised across the whole economy of care, influencing and changing care practices whereby clients benefit from a consistent approach utilised by all people involved in the delivery of a particular aspect of care (Ellis and Johnson. 1999). The use of care pathways as an evidence base for clinical practice can be used to influence the contracting process with commissioners. The effectiveness of these care pathways can be measured through audit and contract monitoring mechanisms, to ensure that:

- the client benefits from care based on a sound evidence base
- commissioners are monitoring services in the provision of care in a more meaningful way, in terms of expected outcomes from each stage of the care pathway process.

This may also involve research and education of carers, other professionals as well as clients. In essence, the nurse consultant will have strategic vision to pick up emerging themes of practice related to client need, as well as applying the evidence base available for good practice. Nursing practice is concerned with social policies and political decisions that may affect the health of those who are being cared for, which forms part of the public health agenda. Credibility with colleagues is a requisite tool in the toolbox of the nurse consultant in order to undertake the complexity of care required in this role, directly or indirectly. This requires knowledge and experience of the health needs of the local population, with an emphasis on health promotion and maintenance, disease prevention, and diagnosis of acute and chronic diseases, in order to effect change in care and service delivery.

Professional leadership and consultancy

The nurse consultant will act as a clinical supervisor, mentor, and clinical leader. Leadership is fundamentally about engaging others as partners in developing and achieving a shared vision. Leadership also involves the ability to mobilise or influence the actions of others. The leadership role of the nurse consultant cannot be underestimated, and different situations may require different types of leadership (Goleman, 2000). In order to improve client outcomes across the whole population, the nurse consultant will need to work with and through other people to achieve the aims of care; acting as a change agent who initiates or brings about planned change (Helvie, 1998). These two roles are interrelated, according to Helvie, who argued that to bring about change one must influence and mobilise behaviour. In order to carry out the leadership role effectively in the multi-faceted arena of care provision, the nurse consultant has to understand the impact of political, economic, environmental, social, and cultural forces which influence health care. The nurse consultant will navigate their way through these to bring about change and reform, taking people along with them to achieve a given objective.

There is no one leadership style which should be adopted above all others, although transformational leadership is thought to be an effective model in creating change and having a major impact on organisations. Transformational leadership involves:

- developing a shared vision
- inspiring and communicating
- valuing others
- challenging and stimulating
- developing trust
- enabling.

(Kouzes and Posner, 1987; Stoner and Freeman, 1992; Manley, 1997)

Skills such as conflict resolution and negotiation coupled with the ability to articulate the issues in hand are also essential to bring about lasting change, this is further expanded on by Halligan and Donaldson (2001) who stated that:

> *Good leadership empowers teamwork, creates an open and questioning culture, ensures that both the ethos and day-to-day delivery of clinical governance remain an integral part of every clinical service.*

A practical demonstration of the leadership role of the nurse consultant is through clinical supervision, which has been identified as being valuable in the development of professional expertise and delivery of quality care (Arvidsson *et al*, 2001). Effective clinical supervision and reflective practice helps both the practitioner and the client, in that practice dilemmas are identified, and often resolved, to the satisfaction of the practitioner and for the benefit of the client. The nurse consultant offers a vast range of knowledge and skill at all levels, from the political overview of a situation, critical analysis skills, to expert practice in relation to the health needs of individuals. Feedback from supervisees who receive clinical supervision from the author indicates that there is a clear feeling of stress reduction following such sessions (Butterworth and Faugier, 1992).

The issue of clinical supervision for nurse consultants can be problematic, in that this needs to be carried out by someone who understands the scope and breadth of the role. Some nurse consultants are supervised by medical colleagues, but from whom do they receive professional advice and guidance? In order for clinical supervision to be effective in resolving difficult issues, the nurse consultant will need to access a supervisor with the appropriate knowledge and skill base.

Education and development

Lifelong learning, it could be argued, could have the biggest single impact on the clinical governance agenda within the health service. A well prepared workforce in terms of education, training and development opportunities related to clinical practices, will help to ensure that the standard of care delivery will be improved, enhancing the safety and well being of the client.

There are two aspects to training and development for nurse consultants: personal developmental needs; and the requirement to be involved in education, training, and development within their role. The nurse consultant is expected to be educated to masters level, with a view to undertaking doctorate level study (Manley, 1997). Although this is not a pre-requisite for the post, there is an expectation that the nurse consultant will research and add to the body of knowledge on a given subject. It would certainly assist in maintaining academic credibility in the educational arena, but should not be used to put pressure on practitioners. There should be a clear need for the research to be undertaken locally, coupled with the willingness of the nurse consultant to undertake doctorate level study, with clearly defined support from the organisation for this to take place.

There will be clear links to higher education establishments, the nurse consultant will be involved in the delivery of teaching programmes, curriculum design, and the application of theory to practice. Understanding and applying research and audit to clinical practice is an essential component of the role, although the role is so multi-faceted that there may be a danger of the nurse consultant becoming embroiled in full-time research, although equally, the nurse consultant may be drawn into full-time education.

Involvement in local, regional, and national networks is an important aspect of the educational and development role through sharing good practice, disseminating information, and commenting on national policy.

Research and evaluation

Research and audit activity help to inform nursing practice and the findings are used to make changes in direct care to the client or to the environment in which care takes place. The nurse consultant has a role to play in following up these activities to ensure that action plans are carried out based on the most effective ways of working, which requires collaboration with service managers and practitioners alike to make changes. The nurse consultant is required to have knowledge of research methodologies and experience in undertaking research to inform clinical practice, as well as initiating research activity when required. However, this also involves extensive reading and access to information in order for sound advice and guidance to be given to others based on the most up-to-date information available. Critical appraisal skills are essential for the appraisal of evidence by the nurse consultant, in order to assess its validity and reliability for practice (Sackett *et al*, 1998). For these activities to be carried out effectively, a realistic time allocation is needed.

Workforce issues

In 1994, the World Health Organization (WHO) put forward the view that the existing situation of nursing and medicine as separate occupations may change. Health organisations need to consider the workforce issues related to the needs of the local population. The 'Heathrow Debate' (1994) was pivotal in considering these issues in preparation for health service needs in the twenty-first century, whereby the need for healthcare reform and redistribution of tasks between nurses and others was discussed, and the relevance of this to the concept of 'substitution', defined as:

The continual regrouping of resources across and within care settings, to exploit the best and least costly solutions in the face of changing needs and demands.

The redistribution of tasks between healthcare professionals is a key component in the development of future health care services. In this, the nurse consultant clearly forms part of the political picture. The nurse consultant will be required to take the lead in developing flexible approaches to the delivery of health care, and recognition that the trend towards a blurring of professional boundaries requires collaborative approaches, but not necessarily the dissolution of a distinct professional identity (Warner *et al*, 1998).

However, as these roles are still evolving, and the target of 1,000 nursing, midwifery, and health visiting consultants still to be met by 2004, it is difficult to evaluate the impact that these roles have on the local healthcare economies.

The role of the nurse consultant in learning disabilities

The field of learning disabilities care encompasses a wide spectrum of needs, from people with profound and multiple learning and physical disabilities, people with mild or moderate learning disabilities, to people detained under the provisions of the Mental Health Act 1983. These needs have been reflected in the way that nurse consultant roles in learning disabilities have been developed within the United Kingdom, with a firm emphasis on the needs of local populations, taking into account epidemiological information regarding the incidence and prevalence of conditions and particular health needs.

The nurse consultant working with primary care services is involved with working with primary care teams to improve access to health services, educating teams with regard to the specific and complex health needs of people with learning disabilities, and working alongside colleagues in providing nurse-led clinics, to ensure that the physical health needs of the individual are met and equally importantly, followed up. The nurse consultant will be available for advice with regard to the individual needs of people with learning disabilities, as well as being involved with the development of local strategies affecting the delivery of health care with primary care trusts and more specifically, professional executive committees (PECs).

The nurse consultant working with people with learning disabilities and mental illness, or dual diagnosis, will be involved in leading and developing nursing practice in the assessment and treatment of people with these needs. The nurse consultant in forensic health care works within the special hospitals, working closely with prisons in assessing needs, and treatment and rehabilitation programmes for people detained under the Mental Health Act 1983.

With all of these roles, the same core functions will be carried out as identified earlier in the text, but specifically raising awareness of the needs of people with learning disabilities, whatever the context. This list is not exhaustive, but what seems to be becoming clear is the versatility of the learning disabilities nurse and the application of knowledge and skills in care provision for people with learning disabilities with a wide variation of needs.

To demonstrate this point, the author's role as a nurse consultant is to work closely with primary care teams to ensure that health needs are met, with a remit for health promotion, health surveillance, and health education, and bridging the gap between primary and secondary care services through involvement in the development of health facilitator roles (DoH, 2001a) The author led a West Midlands Regional project (Thomas *et al*, 2002) which examined how health facilitator roles have been developed within the West Midlands, and the development of a resource pack to aid those involved in improving access and quality of care for people with learning disabilities in primary and secondary care.

It is widely acknowledged that people with learning disabilities are more prone to health problems than the rest of the population (Martin *et al*,1997; DoH, 2001a). The nurse consultant has a key role to play in tackling the health inequality issues experienced by people with learning disabilities through raising awareness of these issues, in particular, with general practitioners. These inequalities have been well documented (DoH, 1998; 1999), including accessing mainstream services, as well as not being treated for conditions such as diabetes, coronary heart disease, not receiving screening for cancer, thyroid problems, etc. These issues were highlighted again in the White Paper, *Valuing People: A New Strategy for Learning disability in the 21st Century* (DoH, 2001a).

In order to influence changes in care for people with learning disabilities, the author as a nurse consultant has to utilise epidemiological knowledge of health within the local population, as well as national trends, Government policy, European influences on health care, and World Health Organization guidance. The broader understanding of health in the political and social context is essential in providing the best evidence for care for individual people. This knowledge is then married up to knowledge and skills related to the needs of people with learning disabilities. One such example is epilepsy, a condition which affects 2–3% of the general population, and approximately 30% of all people with learning disabilities (DoH, 1998; 1999d; 2001a).

Nurse prescribing (National Prescribing Centre, 2001) offers the author, the opportunity to 'close the loop' with regard to the health experiences of people with learning disabilities. Providing advice and guidance with regard to medication and its' side-effects is a key aspect of the author's role, as well as negotiating with nursing teams in relation to the development of nurse prescribing within community learning disabilities teams, specifically concerning epilepsy and mental health needs. This involves the identification of the benefits of learning disabilities nurses prescribing for particular conditions prevalent in the learning disabled population, and presenting this to people with learning disabilities and their families, healthcare teams, and healthcare organisations, such as primary care trusts and specialist care trusts. Formal preparation for the prescribing role will take place through the universities, and the author has been actively involved in leading this initiative within her organisation.

Supplementary prescribing, in particular in chronic disease management, will assist in improving the quality of life of a person with a learning disability in that they will have formed a therapeutic relationship with the nurse around their medical condition, and within agreed plans of care with the wider care team, can have adjustments made to medication regimes without having to wait for an outpatients appointment with a consultant psychiatrist. Medication can be monitored much more closely, and with a fast track back to the primary prescriber, a doctor, if there are any concerns raised. It could be argued that this may appear to be a return to a medical model of care, but actually supplementary prescribing can enhance the client's health experience within the social context, with less emphasis on the demand for medical services, and more at the point of delivery of care, ie. in the home, in a more timely, accessible way.

Networking is a key function of the author's leadership role, and as current Chair of the West Midlands Learning Disabilities Nursing Network the author is involved in ensuring the dissemination of good practice and sharing of information regarding innovations in care for people with learning disabilities and their carers. The networking function is carried out at a national level with other nurse consultants in learning disabilities nursing, and with other networking groups.

Clinical governance

During the 1990s, the NHS prepared itself to move into the twenty-first century through working to a modernisation agenda which placed the patient or client at the centre of all its activities.

The concept of clinical governance was the mechanism identified to influence the quality of health care delivery in all settings, and was first identified within Government policy in the White Paper, *The New NHS— modern, dependable* (DoH, 1997), and subsequently in a further publication *A First Class Service: Quality in the New NHS* (DoH, 1998).

Clinical governance was defined as follows:

A framework through which NHS organisations are accountable for continually improving the quality of their services and safeguarding high standards of care by creating an environment in which excellence in clinical care will flourish.
(Scally and Donaldson, 1999)

In terms of clinical practice, clinical governance offers NHS organisations and nurses, midwives, and health visitors a powerful means of addressing unacceptable variations in standards of care (DoH, 1999b).

The accountability aspect of clinical governance cannot be underestimated. This includes organisational, or corporate accountability, as well as individual accountability through self-regulation. The United Kingdom Central Council for Nurses, Midwives, and Health Visitors (UKCC, 2001) stated that professional self-regulation enhances clinical governance as it requires practitioners to monitor their own conduct and practice using three guiding principles; promoting good practice, preventing poor practice, and intervening in unacceptable practice.

The UKCC went on to add that, 'professional self-regulation and clinical governance are inextricably linked, underpinning safe, high quality patient care.'

Monitoring and developing that care at individual and organisational level are essential components of the process, and this is integral to the author's work as a nurse consultant through quality improvement programmes. The advent of the evidence-based medicine movement in the early 1990s catapulted the implementation agenda to the forefront of both Government and professional agendas (Foundation of Nursing Studies, 2001). Aspects of evidence-based practice, one of the basic building blocks of clinical governance, have been described in the Culyer Report (DoH, 1994) and by Sackett *et al* (1998), whereby the structure and funding of the NHS were addressed, as were training in critical appraisal skills to effect change in clinical behaviours, and therefore, clinical outcomes.

This does not happen in isolation. Collaborative working on an inter-agency basis is essential for nurses to influence health and social care, especially in the care of people with learning disabilities. This is a group of people whose healthcare needs are consistently not met, despite several informative documents disseminated from the Department of Health over the last few years, including, *Signposts for Success* (DoH, 1998), *Once a Day* (DoH, 1999d), and more recently the White Paper, *Valuing People* (DoH, 2001a; Thomas *et al*, 2002). In order to collaborate effectively in meeting the health needs of people with learning disabilities, key stakeholders have to be engaged and influenced to ensure sustainable strategies for health gain are in place. The nurse consultant can play an invaluable role here, through working with primary care trusts and acute hospitals, presenting evidence, working alongside other practitioners, applying theory to practice and acting as a role model, and engaging in multi disciplinary research and evaluation. Partnership boards also take an active role in the work of local learning disability (DoH, 2001a), taking a lead role in health initiatives which ensure that people with learning disabilities have access to the same standards of care as the general population, such as those identified in the National Service Frameworks, for example, the National Framework for Older People (DoH, 2001b).

National health service healthcare reforms form part of a social contract which, in turn, forms the rationale behind clinical governance (Neuberger, 1999). This social contract involves the service user playing an active role in their care. Service user and carer involvement means acting always in the best interests of patients or clients. However, working in a person-centred way has presented some challenges to nurses. Society has become more litigious, with service users being more aware of their rights through the introduction of *The Patient's Charter* (DoH, 1991; 1992); arguably, the first Bill of Rights for people accessing health services, and later, the Human Rights Act (1998). Equally, those who access NHS services feel that they will receive good quality care and that they will remain safe when they do so. In order for people with learning disabilities to take an active role in their care, they must first of all have their needs understood by those providing healthcare services. In the same way that other service user groups are consulted on their health care experiences, people with learning disabilities have the right to be consulted in such a way that is meaningful to them, taking into account the way people communicate, and whether they feel more comfortable being consulted individually, with an advocate, or within a focus group. It is essential that services are flexible enough to ensure that service user experiences are positive, and that any negative experiences are highlighted and acted upon. These are key issues that the author grapples with when engaging organisations in planning and meeting the needs of people with learning disabilities.

Better public awareness has demanded a robust course of action from the statutory agencies. In the NHS, that response has been delivered in the guise of the Clinical Governance agenda. Services are required to respond to complaints more effectively, to act to prevent reoccurrence of problems, and to assess risks to the individual and the NHS organisation more efficiently.

Clinical risk is a key element of clinical governance, and one of the key elements of nursing practice that is regularly consulted on. The nurse consultant has a significant role to play regarding clinical risk, both in assessing individual risks to clients, and in addressing areas of risk through policy, procedures and protocols. Continually monitoring the nursing practice issues around risk to the clients, picking out the emerging themes of practice, and moving the boundaries of practice forward, feature constantly on the landscape for the nurse consultant, as do ethical and legal issues.

Although the nurse consultant may not be a legal expert, they have to have an awareness of the legal frameworks of practice, and the ethical principles of respect for autonomy, justice, beneficence and non-maleficence (Beauchamp and Childress, 1989).

One of the most contentious issues in learning disabilities practice is the issue of consent. In the context of consent to medical treatment, the issue of capacity is paramount. It is usually assumed that a person has the capacity to consent unless proven otherwise, but where it is considered that a person does not have the capacity to consent , in other words they do not understand the nature or effects of a decision, a decision can be made in their 'best interests'. Issues of ethics and morality regularly cloud the delivery of nursing care, especially when these issues may appear to clash with legal requirements or local policy.

Ethical and legal issues are also raised around moving the boundaries of nursing practice forward, treading new ground, challenging the status quo of practice. All of these issues bring with them questions about the wisdom of challenging current nursing practice, risk taking, and ensuring the safety of the client at all times. The nurse consultant will not have all the answers to ethical dilemmas presented to themselves or their colleagues, but what can be offered is a view based on extensive nursing practice, knowledge of resolutions to other ethical dilemmas, and a sounding board during clinical supervision for practitioners.

Clinical governance also involves the preparation, training, education, and support for staff to carry out their roles effectively. There are several challenges in relation to the role of nurse consultant, these include:

- isolation
- lack of understanding of the role by colleagues and others
- support from the organisation

- moving the boundaries of practice forward, which requires an increase in professional autonomy and power.

Support from the organisation is crucial to making these roles work; the complexities of the role need to be understood in order for the role to develop to its full potential.

Conclusion

Despite the rhetoric, controversy, and cynicism related to the development of nurse consultant posts, it could be argued that the role of the nurse consultant is synonymous with the principles of clinical governance, as the four core functions of the nurse consultant are also recognised within the core components of clinical governance. Both have been identified as key concepts in the NHS modernisation agenda for nurses, midwives, and health visitors.

The core functions of the author as a nurse consultant have been underpinned by extensive experience in the care of people with learning disabilities. This has facilitated the development of expert practice with people with learning disabilities and their carers, along with Master's level education and the application of theory to practice. Professional leadership and consultancy is a feature of the author's practice at local, regional, and national level, continually widening the circle of influence and raising awareness of the needs of people with learning disabilities through networking activities, representation on pro active groups, and leading on initiatives.

As an educator, the author regularly exercises this function within the higher education setting, at undergraduate and postgraduate level, as well as within the organisation. This has led to an appointment to honorary lecturer status, actively influencing the knowledge and awareness of a wide variety of people involved in the care of people with learning disabilities, and assists in improving the standards of care provision, and arguably, safer care. The evidence base for the author's practice is constantly evaluated through research, audit, and updating knowledge of the evidence available, and disseminating this to others, raising the awareness of people with learning disabilities of effective health care to meet their needs.

These core functions of the nurse consultant in learning disabilities work within the clinical governance framework, make access to effective health care a reality for people with learning disabilities through influencing the policy and practice agendas at local, regional, and national levels.

As health care within the United Kingdom moves on, the nurse consultant will be at the forefront of change, constantly striving to improve services and promoting the safety and wellbeing of the public. As nurses grow and become more confident in these challenging roles, it is envisaged that the nurse consultant could prove to be extremely influential in shaping organisational culture (Manley, 2000). This will help to ensure that the client remains at the focus of all activity, achieving better outcomes of care, and consequently achieving effective clinical governance.

References

Alderman C, Lipley N (2001) Set for success. *Nurs Standard* **15**(23): 17–21

Arvidsson B, Lofgren H, Fridlund B (2001) Psychiatric nurses' conceptions of how a group supervision programme in nursing care influences their professional competence: A four-year follow up study. *J Nurs Management* **9**: 161–71

Berragan E (1998) Consultancy in nursing: Roles and opportunities. *J Clin Nurs* **7**(2): 139–43

Beauchamp TL, Childress JF (1989) *Principles of Biomedical Ethics*. 3rd edn. Oxford University Press, Oxford

Butterworth T, Faugier J (1992) *Clinical Supervision and Mentorship in Nursing*. Chapman and Hall, London

Castledine G (1998) The role of the clinical nurse consultant. *Br J Nurs* **7**(17): 1054

Department of Health (1983) *The Mental Health Act 1983*. The Stationery Office, London

Department of Health (1991) *The Patients Charter: Raising the Standard*. HMSO, London

Department of Health (1992) *The Health of the Nation: A Strategy for Health in England*. HMSO, London

Department of Health (1994) *The Challenges for Nursing and Midwifery in the 21st century*. (The Heathrow Debate 1993) DoH, London

Department of Health (1994) *Supporting Research and Development in the NHS: A Report for the Minister for Health by Research and Development Taskforce*. Chaired by Professor Anthony Culyer, HMSO, London

Department of Health (1997) *The New NHS — modern, dependable*. HMSO, London

Department of Health (1998) *A First Class Service: Quality in the new NHS*. DoH, London

Department of Health (1998) *Signposts for Success in Commissioning and Providing Health Services for People with Learning Disabilities*. NHS Executive, London

Department of Health (1999d) *Once A Day*. NHS Executive, London

Department of Health (1999a) *The NHS Plan: A plan for investment, a plan for reform*. HMSO, London

Department of Health (1999b) *Making a Difference: Strengthening the Nursing, Midwifery, and Health Visiting Contribution to Health and Health Care*. DoH, London

Department of Health (1999c) *Nurse, Midwife, and Health Visitor Consultants — Establishing Posts and Making Appointments*. (HSC1999/217) HMSO, London

Department of Health (2001a) *Valuing People: A New Strategy for Learning Disabilities for the 21st Century*. DoH, London

Department of Health (2001b) *National Service Framework for Older People*. DoH, London

Ellis BW, Johnson S (1999) The care pathway: A tool to enhance clinical governance. *Clin Performance Qual Health Care* **7**(3)

Farmer B, cited in Castledine G (1998) The role of the clinical nurse consultant. *Br J Nurs* **7**(17): 1054

Foundation of Nursing Studies (2001) *Taking Action; Moving towards evidence-based practice*. Foundation of Nursing Studies, London.

Goleman D (2000) *Leadership that gets results*. Harvard Business Review on Point, March–April 2000: 78–90 (Product no 4487)

Halligan A, Donaldson L (2001) *Br Med J* **322** 9 June: 1413–7). Cited in: The NHS Confederation (2002) Leadership Strategy and Clinical Governance. *Nexus background Briefings: Managerial* **4**. The NHS Confederation, Jarrow

Helvie Carl O (1998) *Advanced Practice Nursing in the Community*. Sage Publications Inc, California

Human Rights Act (1998) The Stationary Office, London

Kouzes JM, Postner BZ (1987) *The Leadership Challenge*. Jossey-Bass, San Fransisco

Manley K (1997) A conceptual framework for advanced practice: an action research project operationalising an advanced practitioner/consultant nurse role. *J Clin Nurs* **6**(3): 179–90

Manley K (2000) Organisational culture and consultant nurses: Part 1 Organisational culture. *Nurs Standard* **14**(36): 34–8

Martin DM, Roy A, Wells MB, Lewis J (1997) Health gain through screening — users' and carers' perspectives of health care: Developing primary health care services for people with an intellectual disability. *J Intellectual and Developmental Disability* **22**(4): 241–9

National Prescribing Centre (2001) *Maintaining Competency in Prescribing: An Outline Framework to help Nurse Prescribers.* 1st edn. NHS National Prescribing Centre, Liverpool

Neuberger J (1999) Viewpoint: The patients' perspective on clinical governance. *Br J Clin Governance* **4**(2): 40–2

Pennington (2000) Nurse consultant: Could or should it be you? *J Diabetes Nurs* **4**(5): 136–9

Rowden R (1999) Leading from the front. *Nurs Times* **95**(42): 35

Sackett DL, Richardson WS, Rosenberg W, Haynes RB (1998) *Evidence-based Medicine: How to Practice and Teach EBM.* Churchill Livingstone, Edinburgh

Scally G, Donaldson L (1999) Clinical governance and the drive for quality improvement. *Br Med J* **317**: 61–5

Stoner JAF, Freeman RE (1992) *Management.* 5th edn. Prentice Hall Inc, New Jersey

Thomas C, Corbett J, Prior M, Robson R (2002) *West Midlands Regional Learning Disability Project 2002: A Resource Pack for Health Facilitators.* M&M Publishing, Cheshire.

Torn A (1995) Can a mental health nurse be a nurse practitioner? *Nurs Standard* **11**(2): 39–44

United Kingdom Central Council for Nursing, Midwifery and Health Visiting (1994) *The Future of Professional Practice — The Council's Standards for Education and Practice Following Registration.* UKCC, London

United Kingdom Central Council for Nursing, Midwifery and Health Visiting (2001) *Professional self-regulation and clinical governance: protecting the public through professional standards.* UKCC, London

Warner M, Longley M, Gould E, Picek A (1998) *Healthcare Futures 2010* (commissioned by the UKCC Education Commission). Welsh Institute for Health and Social Care, Pontypridd

Woods LP (1999) The contingent nature of advanced nursing practice. *J Adv Nurs* **30**(1): 121–8

World Health Assembly (1948) Cited in: Warner M, Longley M, Gould E, Picek A (1998) *Healthcare Futures 2010* (commissioned by the UKCC Education Commission) Welsh Institute for Health and Social Care, Pontypridd

World Health Organization (1994) *Nursing Beyond the Year 2000: A report of a WHO study group.* Technical report series no 842. WHO, Geneva

Joint practitioners in health and social care

Noel Fagan, Tim Plant

Since the mid 1970s we have seen a sustained attempt on the part of practitioners in the fields of nursing and social work to work more collaboratively in the provision of services to people with learning disabilities and their families. One consequence of this has been the emergence of a small but significant number of pre-registration programmes leading to joint qualifications in learning disability nursing and a diploma in social work. The intention of this chapter is to analyse the historical background of this development in professional education, to consider the potential advantages for users of services of this more integrated approach and to evaluate the implications for practitioners working in learning disability services.

Development and historical context

Although the emergence of joint programmes did not take place until the early 1990s, the origins of their development lies some twenty years before that. The often-cited Briggs Committee report (DHSS, 1972) made an explicit request for the emergence of, 'a new caring profession for the mentally handicapped'. A more detailed set of proposals for the reform of professional education in this field was produced by the subsequent Jay Committee report (DHSS, 1979) which opted, with some dissent expressed, for the responsibility for residential staff training to be placed with the Central Council for Education and Training in Social Work (CCETSW).

Such a proposition proved highly unpopular among nurses in the field and the Government proved unwilling to pursue such a radical option. Instead, the General Nursing Council (GNC) and CCETSW were encouraged to explore possibilities in shared in-service and post-qualifying initiatives, and the newly created English National Board (ENB) produced a revised nursing curriculum for learning disability students in 1982 which was widely accepted as a significant break from a medicalised view of learning disability and adopting a much more social model of care.

The late 1980s witnessed a continuing interest on the part of both the ENB and CCETSW to shared educational initiatives with the creation of a joint working party in 1986 briefed to promote shared learning opportunities in the field of learning disabilities, culminating in a jointly sponsored conference in 1989 (ENB/CCETSW 1989).

The development of radical proposals for the reform of both nurse and social worker education was also having an influence on the possibilities for shared learning in this specialism, notably the development of the Diploma in Social Work (DipSW) by CCETSW in 1989 and the acceptance by the Government of the United Kingdom Central Council's (UKCC, 1986) *Project 2000* proposals for nurse education reform in 1988.

Further progress toward the creation of joint qualifying courses was delayed as a consequence of a moratorium placed on new developments by the ENB in 1993, following a Department of Health convened Consensus Conference (Elliot-Cannon and

Harbinson, 1995). The outcome of the conference was a proposal that the traditional learning disability branch programme be superseded by increased emphasis on learning disabilities in all *Project 2000* courses and the establishment of a post-registration course in learning disabilities. Following a period of wide consultation, the Department of Health (1994) rejected the recommendation and the moratorium was lifted. In retrospect, it seems clear that the subsequent development of joint qualifying programmes was a clear response to the perceived threat to the continuation of a learning disability specialism within nursing. It is important that this major development in the preparation of professionals working with people who have learning disabilities is seen not solely as a reactive measure to a perceived professional threat, but as a positive development that more closely reflects the needs and aspirations of users and carers.

A rationale for joint programmes

As practitioners in the field of learning disabilities, we are fortunate to be seeking to develop and enhance our service provision at an important historical period. The opportunities presented to us by a raft of policy and legislative initiatives are significant. Within the wider social policy environment, the need for a more integrated and cohesive response from practitioners to the needs of users and carers is more important than ever and jointly qualified practitioners are better placed than most to seize these new possibilities.

The challenge of ensuring the fullest possible participation of people who have learning disabilities in identifying and meeting their health and social care needs, is one of the most significant that faces learning disability practitioners. When Whitehead (1987) referred to 'the health divide', she could easily have been commenting on the gulf in social and health status and access to health and social care that exists between the general population and those who have a learning disability. The focus of this discussion will be on the possible strategies available to those who support learning disabled people in attaining and sustaining maximum health and social well-being, especially in the domains of information needs, user participation in decision making and social and organisational policy development.

Determining the extent of unmet health and social need in the learning disabled population is problematic for a number of reasons. *Signposts for Success* (DoH, 1998) and *Once a Day* (DoH, 1999), indicate four complex phenomena which underpin this confusion (*Table 21.1*).

Health of the Nation: A Strategy for People with Learning Disabilities (1995) painted a broad picture of systematic health inequality and called for user specific initiatives to address the anomaly. Additional evidence has emerged, usually from small-scale studies, of the associated health needs of people with learning disabilities and the disadvantage they experience in accessing primary health care services (Rodgers, 1993; Turner, 1996; Allan, 1999). One such study (Hunt *et al*, 2001), highlighted the poor health status of day centre members to whom a basic drop-in health screening service was offered. Of the thirty-five people screened: twelve (34%) were obese; eight (23%) were constipated; five (14%) had a mental health problem; and sixteen (46%) had impacted ear wax.

This familiar pattern of low level, unrecognised health concern among people with a learning disability poses a number of challenges. Firstly, how to make available to users and carers, information that is accessible. Secondly, how to facilitate wider user involvement in health promoting activity and, thirdly, what implications will this have for service organisation and delivery.

Table 21.1: The interaction between complex phenomena which collectively contribute to the systematic disadvantage experienced by people with learning disabilities in accessing high quality health and social care services

Phenomena	Manifestation
Aetiology	Underlying biological factors associated with learning disability too often assumed to be responsible for additional physical and psychological health concerns. Risks failing to consider general health screening and poor access to preventative health and social care
Marginalisation	Economic and social inequalities experienced by people with learning disabilities may contribute to higher morbidity rates in this population
Misinterpretation	Straightforward signs and symptoms of ill health may be missed as a result of communication deficits or obscured by behavioural problems
Discrimination	Inequality of access to health and welfare services, common to devalued groups, may be amplified by a lack of awareness or ability on the part of professionals to engage with learning disabled people

In addition to the Department of Health documents cited earlier; *Health of the Nation: A Strategy for People with Learning Disabilities* (1995), *Signposts for Success in Commissioning and Providing Health Services for People with Learning Disabilities* (1998) and *Once a Day* (1999), we have seen the establishment of the Disability Rights Commission following The Disability Rights Act (1995) and the recent publication of a Government White Paper, *Valuing People: A New Strategy for Learning Disability in the 21st Century* (2001).

Each of these documents recognise the need for significant improvements in the manner in which the specific health and social care needs of people with learning disabilities are identified and addressed, both by specialist learning disability practitioners and by generic health and welfare service providers. In particular, the White Paper, *Valuing People*, sets specific goals and deadlines for the provision of more accessible and relevant healthcare services for people with learning disability. The Paper's key actions for health include:

* Action to reduce health inequalities, including the possibility of an enquiry into preventable mortality amongst the learning disabled community.
* Action to challenge discrimination, especially those from ethnic minorities who often face double discrimination.
* Health facilitators identified for people with learning disabilities by Spring 2003.
* All people with learning disabilities to be registered with a GP by June 2004.
* All people with a learning disability to have a health action plan by June 2005.

⌘ The NHS to ensure that all mainstream services are accessible to people with a learning disability.

⌘ The establishment of a learning disability development fund focusing, initially, on services for people with severe challenging behaviour.

⌘ To ensure that the National Service Framework for Mental Health brings benefit to people with learning disabilities.

⌘ A new role for specialist learning disability services, making the most of existing health expertise.

Though highlighting, in particular, the objectives specifically related to health, it is clear that few, if any of these initiatives can be achieved without a degree of inter-agency and inter-professional collaboration unprecedented in the history of services for this client group or, indeed, any other. Given the ambitious and complex nature of the objectives of the White Paper, and the general move toward greater integration of service provision across the social welfare arena, the case for jointly qualified practitioners, drawing on the skills, knowledge and values of both nursing and social work, becomes clearer in principle. However, there remain important issues of the feasibility of producing practitioners equipped to operate across traditional professional boundaries and the implications for professional practice in this specialism.

Professionalism or territorialism?

The debate about the role of joint qualifying programmes must also take place against the background of the long-standing existence of the community learning disability team (CLDT) in the various guises it has taken over the years, ranging from formal but separately managed alliances between health and social service providers, through to fully integrated, jointly managed partnerships. Since the mid-1970s the CLDT has formed the backbone of domiciliary services for people with learning disabilities and their carers (Brown, Flynn and Wistow, 1992) and have provided the forum within which practitioners of nursing and social work have operated together. Despite this extensive practical experience of joint working, there remain significant concerns (O'Byrne, 1994) about the erosion or diminution of professional competence and identity. Clearly, the development of joint qualifying programmes could well be viewed as a further challenge to professional integrity.

The nature of professional identity and the process of occupational socialisation has long been recognised (Merton, 1957; Friedson, 1970; Mauksch and Styles, 1982). Though agreeing that such a process is inevitable in securing the acquisition of appropriate key professional norms, beliefs and values, some theorists (Durkheim, 1947; Merton, 1968) have also highlighted possible restraining influences upon professional development that can result from a rigid adherence to professional identity and a culture of exclusivity. These tendencies towards protectionism are particularly prevalent when a professional group perceive itself to be threatened by external factors, such as a changing policy context, alterations in patterns of service delivery, or, as in this case, a shift in programmes of professional education.

The inherent dangers to any professional group of stagnation and professional isolation include rigid occupational norms that can become detached from the needs of users and service providers. Rather than dismiss such concerns as backward looking and outmoded, it is critical that we consider the origins of professional conservatism and seek mechanisms or means by which professional groups can evolve and emerge in new forms without compromising standards of service.

Common phenomena associated with all professional groups that will be familiar to all those who have worked in a multi-disciplinary environment are:

⌘ Tribalism — expressions of resistance, conflict and sometimes grief which appear in settings when the professional boundaries of a group appear to be under threat.
⌘ Territorialism — a negative stance with elements of retreat to traditional norms and a rejection of change. It is important to note that this response may indeed be a legitimate lament for betrayed traditions.
⌘ Boundary constructs — provide professionals with a sense of identity 'within' a group. These are felt to be crucial for a sense of meaningfulness and attachment to the group.

Each of these phenomena will have both positive and negative consequences for individuals and groups. It is only when these natural characteristics of professional groups become a drag on professional development and personal growth that individuals, groups and the services they provide become less relevant and in danger of a kind of professional dystrophy.

It is, however, important not to be totally unsympathetic to professionals who feel threatened by change which can be likened to a bereavement process resulting from the loss of a group culture. Participants in a change process can often recognise the rationale and even the logic of change but are left feeling undermined and less valued without being able to articulate the reason. It is critical that these feelings are both recognised and accepted rather than dismissed, and that change agents respond to genuine concerns of practitioners.

The key to supporting practitioners through the change process lies in the identification of shared values, which in turn underpin professional beliefs and patterns of practice norms. Whereas in the past it could be argued that the values underpinning nursing and social work were not always complementary, there is a case to be made that the key principles outlined in *Valuing People* (DoH, 2001) make explicit a value base around which core professional groups can unify and, indeed, present the basis on which to build a new professional culture. The principles of **rights, independence, choice and inclusion** (DoH, 2001) should be the determining value base upon which all practitioners in this specialism construct their professional identity, relationships with colleagues and users of services, and in so doing secure the ambitious goals outlined in the White Paper.

Theory into practice

A key challenge to the successful implementation of joint qualifying programmes and joint practice is the effective integration of theoretical perspectives from traditionally diverse curricula and cultures and the degree to which this 'new' knowledge can be incorporated into the practice environment.

The following case study demonstrates how traditional service patterns and cultures can often fail, or act against the interests of service users, particularly those with complex needs, and how a more integrated nursing and social work knowledge base can be utilised to create imaginative interventions.

I first met Jason when he was thirty-one. I had been working in the team for nine months by then, but was already familiar with his name. I was employed as a community learning disability nurse, in my second post since qualifying from a joint nursing and social work programme. Jason would be, almost routinely, referred to services when his physical and mental health deteriorated to crisis point. He, or his family, would eventually reject support and the pattern would repeat. In this way, he became well known within local learning disability services. He was viewed sympathetically, indeed paternalistically, by all who came into contact with him. On this most recent occasion, he was referred to social services after seeking attention via the local A&E department. He had ceased taking his medication and was not eating properly. He had been living in a shared flat, with minimal support, and had taken to sleeping rough on occasions. His social worker was in the process of arranging a suitable placement and had asked the nursing team to look into his health needs. Initially, a student on the joint programme, who was involved in the referral noted references in his case file to his sexualised behaviour towards children and raised her concerns with me.

A more in depth review of nursing, medical and social work files revealed a quite different view of Jason. I noted that various professionals had documented their concerns about his sexual conduct toward children and his own sexual experiences, and was alarmed that despite this there had been no systematic assessment, risk management or other strategies put in place. Further contact with his social worker proved unfruitful as this colleague did not perceive the problem and was not supportive of my proposed intervention. Within a week, a further allegation was made of indecent assault against a child, the police were involved, but the child's parents did not wish to prosecute. This event hastened a new assessment and planning for a more suitable environment for Jason, who was eventually placed in a private care home. Within a few weeks things started to look up, he had gained weight and was taking his medication, and plans were made for a possible supported work scheme. During this period, I sought guidance from health and social services child protection teams who suggested a forensic risk assessment. This assessment confirmed that initial concerns were justified and that the term paedophile could be used to describe Jason.

By this time, however, he had begun, as in the past, to be drawn back into the family home and the placement broke down. I arranged a multi-disciplinary meeting and we agreed to refer Jason to a regional medium secure unit while we looked for local support options. Given his risk of seriously offending against children, the lack of suitable local care and treatment and limited residential options, Jason was subsequently placed outside the area.

At the time of these events, nurses and social workers were in separate teams. Individuals' needs were viewed as suitable for either nursing or social work input. Nurses had viewed investigations of abuse as being an activity in which social workers took the lead. For me, as a jointly qualified practitioner although employed as a nurse, the traditional boundaries between social worker and nurse do not exist. I did not think 'that's a social workers job' even though I was made to feel that I was treading on the social worker's toes. When I reviewed Jason's file, I was struck by the fact that no one had taken an overview, and how health and social services had failed to respond to the issues. My training on the joint programme stressed the need for multi-disciplinary working and working across professional boundaries to meet the needs of the individual rather than those of the professionals. We also had comprehensive input on abuse and child protection. As a nurse, I had a clear Code of Conduct, knowledge of professional accountability, risk assessment and continuing professional development. In this case, I was able to draw on nursing and social work skills and knowledge bases, and approached the work with Jason in a different way to either my nursing or social work colleagues. I gained an appreciation of Jason as a vulnerable adult who was also an abuser; the value base I developed during my joint programme helping me to stay focused on his needs in both respects.

Jason is currently receiving better care and treatment in the medium secure unit than he has enjoyed for a long time. I now work in a fully integrated health and social services learning disability team that is committed to finding local solutions for individual needs. Jason will eventually be returning to his home area and when he does, I hope that we will be able to support him to achieve finally the sort of life he deserves.

In addition to highlighting cultural barriers that commonly exist, even within integrated nursing and social work teams, the case study also raises issues about the origins and veracity of professional knowledge. Understanding the nature of professional knowledge, or epistemology, is an important task as the relationship between knowledge and action is critical within practice disciplines, such as nursing and social work. Sources of professional knowledge utilised by practitioners originate from a wide range of experiences, from everyday encounters through to formal academic or research activity. Robinson and Vaughan (1992) suggest three sources of knowledge, frequently called upon by practitioners, shaping their practice:

- tenacity — 'I know because it has always been like that'
- authority/expertise — derived from literature and professional debate
- *a priori* — 'knowledge that stands to reason or the product of logical deduction'.

Robinson and Vaughan (1992) suggest that though traditional sources of knowledge remain widely used by practitioners, there is clearly an absence of empirical knowledge gleaned through academic study and research, a problem experienced by many in practice-oriented disciplines. Recent years have seen an attempt by practitioners and academics to close this gap through the development of theoretical frameworks or models to guide professional practice (Tierney, 1998).

Though models themselves are not generally seen as constituting professional knowledge, supporters argue that they do represent a conceptual framework within which professional knowledge, experience and expertise can be utilised and evaluated.

The question of the relationship of models to practice is an important one, and underlies much of the more recent criticism of the impact of conceptual frameworks on practice. Tierney (1998) cites Cash (1990) who suggests that theoretical models became so generally defined that actual practice loses its identity. The level of abstraction of models, seen as essential by authors and proponents, is viewed with suspicion and even hostility by increasing numbers of practitioners who can view them as 'armchair theorising', unconnected with the 'real world' of practice (*Chapter 1, page 13*).

e developing criticism of the 'models industry' has in turn seen attempts, certainly within nursing, to develop a firmer, empirically-based science of nursing. Edwards (1999) suggests two attractions of such an endeavour. Firstly, the status of science itself and secondly, the belief that the status enjoyed by the sciences flows from the successes of the scientific method. Edwards (1999) intimates that the goal of a developed science of nursing is closely allied with securing professional status and credibility for nursing. Edwards (1999) expresses doubts about the possibilities for a true science of nursing, given the problems in obtaining a clear consensus in determining 'good' nursing practice and how scientific methodologies could be constructed to ratify practice in such diverse circumstances. He also highlights the difficulty, not usually encountered in the natural sciences, of recognising, and showing regard to, the subjective experience of the recipients of professional interventions in determining their effectiveness.

Supporters of a science of nursing such as Weiss (1995) dismiss such criticisms and argue that what is being sought are not universal laws, but rather reasonable predictions which can provide practitioners with expectations of human responses under certain conditions of health and illness.

In highlighting these various forms and sources of professional knowledge, it may appear that they are in some sense contradictory. On reflection, it becomes clearer that in relation to the knowledge base of professional practice, it is common for practitioners to draw upon any or all of these sources, and as Robinson and Vaughan (1992) pointed out, a characteristic of advanced professional practice is the ability to select and utilise appropriately from a range of knowledge sources. This blending of forms of professional knowledge is characterised by Robinson (1992) as occupational knowledge. She argues that occupational knowledge is not a scientific body of knowledge but rather includes:

⌘ Everyday theories current in ordinary life. This includes not only knowledge widely shared within a general culture or community, but would also be representative of Robinson and Vaughan's (1992) 'tenacious knowledge' and some aspects of '*a priori*' knowledge.
⌘ Theories derived from basic scientific disciplines whether that be 'hard' empirical evidence or 'soft' inferential data.
⌘ Occupational theories produced by practitioners represent the most interesting, and potentially most important source of new information in the corpus of professional knowledge. This particular source has the potential to create meaningful practice knowledge, originating as it does from practice itself, and providing the opportunity for practitioners to influence theory when the reverse has generally been the case.

Robinson's (1992) suggestion is that rather than relying predominantly on one form or other of knowledge, whether it is conceptual, empirical or everyday experience, practice-based professions necessarily draw upon all relevant sources of information.

The case study clearly outlines the way in which a range of sources were called upon to respond to the particular needs of the service user and highlights how a willingness to utilise concepts, skills and knowledge from the repertoires of nursing and social work can lead to a creative synthesis. This represents the emergence of a new form of occupational knowledge as proposed by Robinson (1992), and has significant implications for the emergence of joint practitioners. It suggests that a mechanism does exist whereby the new opportunities for multi-disciplinary working and professional education can provide and produce new sources of knowledge. This new knowledge source need not be bound by concepts of a homogeneous nursing or social work culture, but one that can more accurately reflect the heterogeneous nature of evolving knowledge, skills and values, which are more closely aligned to the needs of people with learning disabilities. The continuing need to validate and re-validate the knowledge base of practitioners in this specialism must also give fuller recognition to the information that lies, generally unrecognised, in the daily experience of those with learning disabilities and their carers. The conventional assumption is that professional influence lies in the possession (and protection) of a unique and inaccessible body of knowledge. The experience of preparing practitioners, competent to meet both the health and social needs of people with learning disabilities, poses a challenge to that received wisdom. It suggests that in reality, the strength of joint practice lies not in protecting narrowly defined professional boundaries, but a willingness to question traditional practices and to seek professional knowledge from a wide range of sources. The strength of joint practice relies upon a commitment to view its knowledge base as changing, not fixed, as developing, not static, as uncertain rather than certain and as inclusive rather than exclusive.

References

Allan E (1999) Learning disability: Promoting health equality in the community. *Nurs Standard* **13**(4): 32–7

Brown S, Flynn M, Wistow G (1992) *Back to the Future: joint work for people with learning disabilities*. National Development Team, London and the Nuffield Institute for Health Services Studies, Leeds

Central Council for Education and Training in Social Work (1989a) *Paper 30: Requirements and Regulations for the Diploma in Social Work*. CCETSW, London

Department of Health (1994) Letter from Yvonne Moores, Chief Nursing Officer: The Future of Learning Disability/Mental Handicap Nursing. CNO PL(94) 7

Department of Health (1995) *The Health of the Nation: A Strategy for People with Learning Disabilities*. DoH, London

Department of Health (1998) *Signposts for Success in Commissioning and Providing Health Services for People with Learning Disabilities*. HMSO, London

Department of Health (1999) *Once a Day*. HMSO, London

Department of Health (2001) *Valuing People: A New Strategy for Learning Disability for the 21st Century*. HMSO, London

Department of Health and Social Security (1971) *Better Services for the Mentally Handicapped*. Cmnd 4683. HMSO, London

Department of Health and Social Security (1972) *Report of the Committee on Nursing (Briggs Report)* Cmnd 5115. HMSO, London

Department of Health and Social Security (1979) *Report of the Committee of Enquiry into Mental Handicap Nursing and Care (Jay Report)*. Cmnd 7468. HMSO, London

Durkheim E (1947) *The Division of Labour in Society*. The Free Press, New York

Edwards S (1999) The idea of nursing science. *J Adv Nurs* **29**(3): 563–9

Elliott-Cannon C, Harbinson S (1995) *Building a Partnership: Co-operation to promote shared learning in the field of learning disability*. ENB/CCETSW, London

English National Board (1995) *Joint Validation Procedure for Pre-registration/Qualifying Programmes: a partnership between professional bodies*. Circular 1995/09/gb

Friedson E (1970) *Profession of Medicine: a study of the sociology of applied knowledge*. Dodd, Mead, New York

Hunt C, Hunt G, Wakefield S (2001) Community nurse learning disabilities: a case study of the use of an evidence-based screening tool to identify and meet health needs of people with learning disabilities. *J Learning Disabilities* **5**(1): 9–18

Mauksch I, Styles R (1982) From nurse to nurse educator: the socialisation of nurses into the faculty role. In: Henderson M, ed. *Recent Advances in Nursing 4 — Nursing Education*. Churchill Livingstone, Edinburgh

Merton R (1957) *The Student Physician*. Harvard University Press, Cambridge, Mass

Merton R (1968) *Social Theory and Social Structure*. The Free Press, New York

O'Byrne L (1994) Learning disability nursing: Shared learning should be encouraged (editorial). *Br J Nurs* **3**(15): 752

Robinson K, Vaughan B (1992) *Knowledge for Nursing Practice*. Butterworth-Heinemann, Oxford

Robinson K (1992) Knowledge and practice of working in the community. In: Luker K, Orr L, eds. *Health Visiting: Towards community health nursing*. 2nd edn. Blackwell, London

Rodgers J (1993) Primary health care provision for people with learning difficulties. *Health and Social Care* **2**: 11–17

Tierney A (1998) Nursing models: extant or extinct? *J Adv Nurs* **28**(1): 77–85

Turner S (1996) Promoting healthy lifestyles for people with learning disabilities: A survey of provider organisations. *Br J Learning Disabilities* **24**: 138–44

United Kingdom Central Council for Nursing, Midwifery and Health Visiting (1986) *Project 2000: A New Preparation for Practice*. UKCC, London

Weiss S (1995) Contemporary empiricism. In: Omery A, Kasper C, Page G, eds. *In Search of Nursing Science*. Sage Publications, California

Whitehead M (1987) *Inequalities in Health: The health divide*. Routledge, London

Appendix I

Bullock Indicator Scale

Life events

Here is a list of life events. If the person has gone through any of these in the past year, please tick the box next to the event. If none of these events have happened, please tick the box at the end of the page.

- ☐ Death of a first degree relative (child, spouse, brother or sister)
- ☐ Death of a close friend, carer or other relative
- ☐ Serious illness or injury
- ☐ Serous illness of close relative, friend or carer
- ☐ Move of house or residence
- ☐ Break up of steady relationship (a girlfriend or boyfriend)
- ☐ Separation or divorce
- ☐ Alcohol problem
- ☐ Drug problem
- ☐ Serious problem with a parent, close friend, carer, neighbour or relative
- ☐ Unemployed/seeking work for more than one month
- ☐ Retirement from work
- ☐ Something valuable lost or stolen
- ☐ Problems with police or other authority
- ☐ Major financial crisis
- ☐ Sexual problem

- ☐ Any other event or change of routine which may have caused distress to the individual (Please describe briefly)

....
....
....

- ☐ Or, none of the above

Source: Moss S (2002) *The Mini Pas-add*. Pavilion Press, Brighton

Bullock Indicator Scale

Date: ....

Client code: ....   Age: ....

Please rate by circling: 1 = Nothing abnormal detected (NAD)
2 = Moderate
3 = Severe

	Clinical	NAD	Moderate	Severe	Score
1	Mood changes	1	2	3	
2	Depressed	1	2	3	
3	Anxious	1	2	3	
4	Weepiness	1	2	3	
5	Confusion/memory loss	1	2	3	
6	Panic attacks	1	2	3	
7	Disturbed sleep	1	2	3	
8	Loss of energy	1	2	3	
9	Reduced/loss of energy	1	2	3	
				TOTAL SCORE:	

A score of   1 to 9 = Nothing abnormal detected (NAD)
9 to 18 = Moderate
18 to 27 = Severe

Scoring — Outcome criteria — Psychological

Score	Outcome	Action
1 to 9	NAD	Nothing abnormal detected
9 to 18	Moderate	Indicating to reassess in 3, 6, 9, 12 months. Evidence to: ❖ Place monitoring format in ❖ Reassess using PASS AD, Becks assessment ❖ Utilise findings to justify recommendations ❖ ? antidepressants — change in life
18 to 27	Severe	• Recommend seek GP advice and recommend medication • Secure individual management plan to support the individual

Bullock Indicator Scale — climacteric

Date: ....

Client code: ....   Age: ....

Please rate by circling: 1 = Nothing abnormal detected (NAD)
2 = Moderate
3 = Severe

Clinical	NAD	Moderate	Severe	Score
1 Hot flushes	1	2	3	
2 Tiredness	1	2	3	
3 Headaches	1	2	3	
4 Aching joints	1	2	3	
5 Digestive discomfort	1	2	3	
6 Vaginal dryness	1	2	3	
7 Mitchurition	1	2	3	
8 Menstruation	None = 0 Regular = 1 Irregular = 2			
9 Menstrual flow	NAD = 1 Other = 2 Heavy = 3			
10 Menstrual loss	Number of days			
TOTAL SCORE:				

A score of   1 to 9 = Nothing abnormal detected (NAD)
9 to 18 = Moderate
18 to 27 = Severe

Scoring — Outcome criteria — Climacteric

Score	Outcome	Action
1 to 9	NAD	Nothing abnormal detected
9 to 18	Moderate	• Indicating letter to reassess 3, 6, 9, 12 months • Monitoring format • Liaise GP? Trial of hormone replacement therapy (HRT)
18 to 27	Severe	• Contact — liaise GP re HRT • Justification and evidence for invasive test — ie. LH, FSH, thyroid blood test

Appendix II

South Staffordshire Healthcare NHS Trust Health screening checklist and personal health record

Personal details

Name: .... DOB: ....

Address: ....

.... Postcode: ....

GP name:.. Telephone: ....

Address: ....

.... Postcode: ....

Background information/family history

Has anyone in your family had any of the following? (If yes, please state relationship)

Heart Problems   [   ] Yes   [   ]   No
Diabetes   [   ] Yes   [   ]   No
Asthma   [   ] Yes   [   ]   No
Stroke   [   ] Yes   [   ]   No
Cancer   [   ] Yes   [   ]   No
Osteoporosis   [   ] Yes   [   ]   No
Sickle cell disorder   [   ] Yes   [   ]   No
How has your learning disability been described?
Are you currently receiving any medical treatment?
Do you have any allergies?
Do you drink alcohol?   [   ] Yes   [   ]   No _____ per week
Do you smoke?   [   ] Yes   [   ]   No _____ per day
In a typical week, what do you do?
In a typical week, what exercise do you get?

Stressors

Have you suffered any significant life events/stressors over the last 12 months?
(Please tick boxes which apply)
Death of a first degree relative (a parent, child, spouse, brother or sister)   [   ]
Death of a close family friend, carer or relative   [   ]
Serious illness or injury   [   ]
Serious illness of close relative, carer or relative   [   ]

Move to house or residence [ ]
Break up of a steady relationship (a girlfriend or boyfriend) [ ]
Separation or divorce [ ]
Alcohol problem [ ]
Drug problem [ ]
Serious problem with close friend, carer, neighbour or relative [ ]
Unemployed/seeking work for more than one month [ ]
Retirement from work [ ]
Laid off or sacked from work [ ]
Something valuable lost or stolen [ ]
Problems with police or other authority [ ]
Major financial crisis [ ]
Sexual problem [ ]
Any other event or change of routine which may have caused distress
to the individual [ ]

Assessment section

In the following assessment sections please tick the box which most accurately applies to the client you are assessing — using the comments boxes to record additional information.

1	**Skin assessment section**	
A	The client's skin condition is good with an absence of any difficulties? This includes; clean, well hydrated skin, healthy coloured skin, no broken skin.	
B	The client has some problems with their skin condition? This may include; the presence of rashes, irritation or itching, neglecting personal hygiene, the presence of any moles or other distinguishing marks.	
C	The client has known problems with their skin condition? This may include; damaged or broken skin, chronic or longstanding skin conditions or significant personal hygiene problems.	

Comments on the above:

2	**Scalp and hair condition**	

A	The client has good scalp and hair condition — with an absence of difficulties? ie. clean scalp, well-groomed hair.	
B	The client has some noticeable scalp and hair problems? This may include; dandruff, oily scalp, very greasy or unwashed hair.	
C	The client has known problems with their skin condition? This may include; damaged or broken skin, chronic or longstanding skin conditions or significant personal hygiene problems.	

Comments/action:

3	**Ears and hearing**	

A	The clients ears and hearing needs are being met? ie. ears are clean and free from external wax, can hear sounds/spoken words without difficulty.	
B	The client has some noticeable hearing difficulties? This may include: wax present on one/both ears, client's behaviour may indicate a hearing problem.	
C	The client has obvious ear/hearing problems? This may include; balance problems, impacted or excess ear wax, lesions present in either ear.	

Comments/action:

Date of last hearing examination:

Does the client use a hearing aid?
(If yes, comment on its use and condition)

4	**Condition of teeth/oral hygiene**	

| | The client has good condition of teeth and oral hygiene with an absence of any difficulties? This may include; clean, well-aligned teeth, regular dental checks/treatment, a good level of oral hygiene. | |
| A | | |

| | The client has noticeable problems with teeth/oral hygiene? This may include; difficulty chewing, eating or drinking, poor standard of teeth care/oral hygiene. | |
| B | | |

| | The client has more obvious teeth/oral hygiene difficulties? This may include; dribbling excessively, suffering from halitosis, frequent mouth sores/ulcers, painful/sensitive teeth. | |
| C | | |

Comments/action: Date of last examination:

Does the client have any teeth?
(Give details)

Does the client wear dentures?

Dentist name: --

Address: ---

--- Postcode: ---------------------

Telephone: ---------------------------

5	Eyes/eyesight	
A	The client is meeting eye/eyesight needs well? This may include; eyes appear to have healthy membranes, client can see well with/without glasses, has regular eye tests.	
B	The client has some difficulties with eyes/eyesight needs? This may include; obvious opacity of the eyes, observable difficulties with vision, unable to shift gaze from one object to another, any behaviour which suggests a problem with vision.	
C	The client has obvious difficulties with eye/eyesight needs? This may include; discomfort of eyelids/eyelashes, bumping into objects, recurrent problems, ie. dry eyes, styes, known eye disorders, ie. strabismus, conjunctivitis.	

Comments/action:

Is there any known family history of glaucoma?
(Give details)

Date of last eyesight test?

Name of ophthalmic practitioner: ....

Address: ....

....

.... Postcode: ....

Telephone: ....

| 6 | **Continence and elimination** | |

| | The client's continence and elimination needs are being met? This may include; regular urine output, regular bowel motion, urine looks and smells normal. | |

| B | The client has some difficulties with their continence and elimination needs? This may include; incontinence by day or night, pattern of continence has changed recently, client suffers from constipation or lose stools, suffers frequent discomfort that may originate in digestive system/bowel. | |

| C | The client has obvious difficulties with eye/eyesight needs? This may include; discomfort of eyelids/eyelashes, bumping into objects, recurrent problems, ie. dry eyes, styes, known eye disorders, ie. strabismus, conjunctivitis. | |

Urine analysis test
(Using labsticks, measure and record data from analysis)

Glucose =   Ketones =   Protein =   Blood =   Nitrates =   Leucocytes =   pH =   Spec. gravity =

Comments/action:

| 7 | **Circulation and breathing** | |

| A | The client's circulation and breathing needs are being met? This may include; respiration pattern is regular and rhythmical, client takes some form of regular exercise. | |

| B | The client has some difficulties with their circulation and breathing needs? This may include; showing signs of cyanosis, a troublesome cough, difficulties in breathing. | |

| C | The client has obvious difficulties with circulation and breathing needs? This may include; signs of finger clubbing, signs of oedema, known congenital, circulatory or respiratory disorders. | |

		Pulse	Resp	BP
Please record pulse, breathing and blood pressure at rest				

Comments/action:

8	**Condition of nails (hands)**	

	The client has good condition of nails (hands)? ie. clean, well-formed nails/well-manicured nails.	
A	The client has some difficulties in maintaining the condition of nails (hands)? This may include; noticeable irregularities in growth of nails, inflammation of nails and/or of the bed in which they rest.	
B	The client has obvious difficulties with the condition of their nails (hands)? This may include; overgrown or brittle nails, spoon-shaped or concave nails, any observable nail changes.	

Comments/action:

9	**Condition of feet and toe nails**	

	Are the client's feet and toe nail care needs well met? This includes; feet in a clean, healthy condition, no hard skin present, well-manicured toe nails.	
A	The client has some difficulties in meeting their feet and toe nail needs? This includes; fitting shoes, signs of itching or discomfort, skin problems on feet or toes, problems in relation to shape of feet.	
B	The client has obvious difficulties meeting their feet and toe nail care needs? This includes; toe nails misshapen or abnormal, pain present in feet, known chronic foot condition, hard skin or lesions on feet, circulation problems to feet.	

Comments/action:

Is a chiropodist involved in the client's foot care
(Give details)

10	**Communication**	

	The client's communication needs are well met in all situations?	
	The client's communication needs are met in familiar settings?	
	The client's communication needs require assessment and advice?	

Comment:

Are carers aware of ways in which the client communicates?

Are carers aware of the most appropriate ways to communicate with the client?

11	**Sexuality: female**	

	Menstruation: The client's menstruation needs are being met? This includes; a regular menstrual cycle, normal blood loss during menstruation, client able to cope with self-care during menstruation.	
	The client has some difficulties with their menstruation needs? This includes; some irregularity of periods, irregular monthly cycle, client requires some assistance in meeting menstruation needs.	
	The client has obvious difficulties with her menstruation needs? This includes; excessive blood loss during menstruation, physical or psychological problems experienced during menstruation, frequent or periodic itching or discomfort of anus, perineum or genitals.	

Does the client have regular cervical smear tests?   YES/NO
(Please give details)

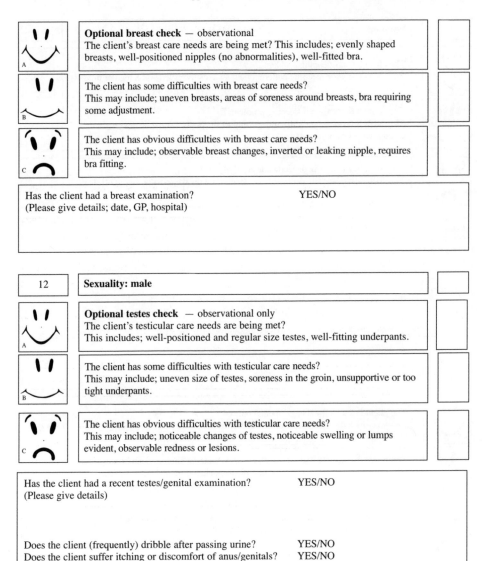

Optional breast check — observational
The client's breast care needs are being met? This includes; evenly shaped breasts, well-positioned nipples (no abnormalities), well-fitted bra.

A

The client has some difficulties with breast care needs?
This may include; uneven breasts, areas of soreness around breasts, bra requiring some adjustment.

B

The client has obvious difficulties with breast care needs?
This may include; observable breast changes, inverted or leaking nipple, requires bra fitting.

C

Has the client had a breast examination?   YES/NO
(Please give details; date, GP, hospital)

| 12 | **Sexuality: male** | |

Optional testes check — observational only
The client's testicular care needs are being met?
This includes; well-positioned and regular size testes, well-fitting underpants.

A

The client has some difficulties with testicular care needs?
This may include; uneven size of testes, soreness in the groin, unsupportive or too tight underpants.

B

The client has obvious difficulties with testicular care needs?
This may include; noticeable changes of testes, noticeable swelling or lumps evident, observable redness or lesions.

C

Has the client had a recent testes/genital examination?   YES/NO
(Please give details)

Does the client (frequently) dribble after passing urine?   YES/NO
Does the client suffer itching or discomfort of anus/genitals?   YES/NO

13	**Sleeping**	

A	The client has no sleeping problems? This includes; good sleeping pattern, client awakes refreshed – at a regular time.	
B	The client has occasional sleeping problems? This includes; occasional difficulty getting to sleep, occasional restless nights, client oversleeps occasionally.	
C	The client has a disturbed sleep pattern? This includes; disturbed sleep pattern, client often awake most of the night, sleeps during day time.	

Does the client use night sedation to assist sleep?   YES/NO
(Please give details)

Comments

14	**Mental well being**	

A	The client has a well-balanced mental outlook? This may include; suffers few or no headaches.	
B	The client displays symptoms which could indicate an altered mental state? This may include; periodic headaches, displays altered mental state, suffers emotional distress.	
C	The client has obvious difficulties with meeting their mental health needs? This may include; frequent headaches, irrational fear or anxieties, obsessional behaviour, irrational mood swings.	

Does the client see a psychiatrist?   YES/NO
(Please give details: name, location, etc)

Comments:

| 15 | **Epilepsy — (if the client does not suffer from epilepsy, move on to next section)** | |

| | The client's epilepsy is well-controlled?
This includes; accurate record of seizures, regular blood tests (if medication requires this). | |
| A | | |

| | The client has some difficulties in meeting their epilepsy care needs?
This includes; any change in frequency or pattern of seizures, recording of seizures spasmodic or incomplete, client/carer aware of side-effects of medication. | |
| B | | |

| | The client has obvious difficulties in meeting their epilepsy care needs?
Frequency and severity of seizures, client may be suffering possible side-effects of medication, blood tests to monitor anticonvulsant levels rarely carried out. | |
| C | | |

Does the client see a neurologist?   YES/NO
(Please give details)

Comments:

| 16 | **Medication** |

Current medication	Dosage

Date of last review of medication:

Name of doctor who conducted the review:

17	**Mobility**	

	The client is fully mobile? This includes no problems experienced with fine or gross motor movement.	
A		

	The client has occasional difficulties with mobility? This may include; person requiring assistance when involved in activities, client has poor posture.	
B		

	The client has difficulties with mobility? This may include; the client suffering from a degenerative condition, ie. arthritis, irregular involuntary movements, evidence of muscle wastage, client in pain when moving body parts.	
C		

Comments:

18	**Any other health issues — please comment on any issues not previously detailed**

19	**Weight/body measurements**

Weight _____ kg   Height _____ cm

Waist measurement _____ cm

Total body mass index   _____

Which BMI range is the client in   _____

What was the client's weight one year ago?

Has the client had an unintentional weight gain of more than 2 kg in the last year?

Has the client had an unintentional weight loss of more than 2 kg in the last year?

Comments:

20	**Nutrition (food groups)**	**Yes**	**No**	**Don't know**

Does the client eat the following types of food everyday?

Bread or cereals or potatoes or rice or pasta (at every meal)

Fruit or vegetable (3–5 portions a day)

Milk or yoghourt (2 pint milk or equivalent)

Meat or fish or eggs or cheese or beans (2 servings daily)

Fluids (at least 8 cups a day)

Does the client nearly always finish a meal?

Comments on the above:

Is the client on any special diet? (Please give details)

Is the client taking any nutritional supplements? (Please give details)

NB. If any 'No' or 'Don't knows' are ticked, a nutrition care plan is required to address the problem identified or referral to dietician or speech and language therapist via GP.

21	**Nutrition-related problems**

Please tick box to indicate if any of the following exist:

Does the client suffer any problems with swallowing? ☐

Does the client suffer problems with chewing food? ☐

Does the client suffer with small or poor appetite? ☐

Is the client unable to eat meals independently? ☐

Any other nutrition-related problem specify below

Comments on the above:

NB. If any boxes are ticked a nutrition care plan is required to address the problems identified, or referral to dietician or speech and language therapist via GP.

Personal Health Record

<u>**This record belongs to:**</u>

Name: _____

Address: _____

_____

_____ Postcode: _____

DoB:_____

A	😊	My good areas	

	🙂	Areas I need to consider improving	

A	☹	Areas in which I need to take action	
	Problem identified		Action taken

Signed: _____ Nurse assessor

Date: _____

I have had my Personal health record explained to me and understand that the issues raised would enable me to meet my healthcare needs.

Signed: _____ Client

Date: _____

I have had _____ Personal health record explained to me and understand that the issues raised would enable them to meet their own healthcare needs more effectively.

Signed: _____ Relative/carer

Date: _____

Date of next health screen: _____

Appendix III

Bereavement assessment tool for people with learning disabilities

Name: ....

Address: ....

DoB: ....

Main carer/key worker: ....

Date commenced: ....

Bereavement details: ....

Deceased's name: ....

Relationship to the bereaved person with learning disabilities: ....

When did the death occur? ....

Professional offering support (for example, GP, psychiatrist, social worker, occupational therapist)

```
┌──────────────────────────────────────────────────────────────────┐
│                                                                    │
│                                                                    │
│                                                                    │
└──────────────────────────────────────────────────────────────────┘
```

Medication prescribed (if applicable)

```
┌──────────────────────────────────────────────────────────────────┐
│                                                                    │
│                                                                    │
│                                                                    │
└──────────────────────────────────────────────────────────────────┘
```

Personal issues: Factors that may impact upon the bereaved person with learning disabilities (for example, complex health needs, autism, profound and multiple learning disabilities)

```
┌──────────────────────────────────────────────────────────────────┐
│                                                                    │
│                                                                    │
│                                                                    │
└──────────────────────────────────────────────────────────────────┘
```

Health (questions one might ask: Does the bereaved person with learning disabilities usually experience good health? Has there been any recent noticeable change in their health status?)

```
┌──────────────────────────────────────────────────────────────────┐
│                                                                    │
│                                                                    │
│                                                                    │
└──────────────────────────────────────────────────────────────────┘
```

Family composition/significant people (questions to ask: Nature of the relationship of the bereaved person with learning disabilities with family members/significant people) Cultural/religious beliefs (questions to ask: Are there any cultural and religious beliefs which need to be taken into account?)

```


```

Communication issues (questions to ask: Can the person make their needs known? Do they require support when communicating?)

```


```

Past losses (questions to ask: Has the person with learning disabilities experienced any other significant losses? How did they cope?)

```


```

Nature of the relationship between the person and the deceased (questions to ask: How close was the person to the deceased? How often did they see each other?)

```


```

About the death (questions to ask: How did the person find out about the death? Was the person present when the death occurred? What were the circumstances of the person's death? For example, natural, expected, sudden, untimely, after illness, etc)

```


```

After the death (questions to ask: Did the person visit the Chapel of Rest?)

```


```

The day of the funeral (questions to ask: Did the person attend the funeral? how did they cope before, during and after the funeral?)

```
┌────────────────────────────────────────────────────────┐
│                                                        │
│                                                        │
│                                                        │
└────────────────────────────────────────────────────────┘
```

How do you think that the person with learning disabilities has coped with their bereavement?

```
┌────────────────────────────────────────────────────────┐
│                                                        │
│                                                        │
│                                                        │
└────────────────────────────────────────────────────────┘
```

How does the bereaved person with learning disabilities feel they have coped with their bereavement?

```
┌────────────────────────────────────────────────────────┐
│                                                        │
│                                                        │
│                                                        │
└────────────────────────────────────────────────────────┘
```

What support does the bereaved person with learning disabilities require?

```
┌────────────────────────────────────────────────────────┐
│                                                        │
│                                                        │
│                                                        │
└────────────────────────────────────────────────────────┘
```

Social support system (for example, immediate and extended family, friends, acquaintances)

```
┌────────────────────────────────────────────────────────┐
│                                                        │
│                                                        │
│                                                        │
└────────────────────────────────────────────────────────┘
```

Other loss issues

Has the bereaved person with learning disabilities life changed dramatically following the bereavement? (questions to ask: have they moved house, entered residential care, changed day occupation?)

```
┌────────────────────────────────────────────────────────┐
│                                                        │
│                                                        │
│                                                        │
└────────────────────────────────────────────────────────┘
```

Where is the person in the grief cycle?

Does the person:

	Yes	No
Accept the reality of the loss?	☐	☐
Experience and express the pain of grief?	☐	☐

Has the person:

Adjusted to life without the deceased?	☐	☐

Is the person able to:

Withdraw the emotional energy invested in the deceased and move on with life?	☐	☐

(Worden, 1991; after Dent, 1996)

Appendix IV

Current Epilepsy Health Record

Foreword

Epilepsy is the commonest neurological condition affecting one in 130 of the general population (Department of Health, 2001). This figure increases dramatically in the learning disability populous, with up to 50% in people with profound learning disabilities (Lhatoo and Sander, 2001) with a large percentage experiencing refractory seizures. Due to the high incidence of epilepsy, there is an increase in morbidity and mortality rates.

Hospital admissions and unnecessary repeated investigations often occur in relation to people with epilepsy and learning disabilities (Branford *et al*, 1998; Carvill *et al*, 1999).

There are often numerous professionals involved in the management of an individual's epilepsy. This can lead to repeated tests, duplication of records in different locations, which are often inaccessible.

This booklet allows for all epilepsy information to be kept together, enabling professionals to have access to all necessary data and allows for continuity, which is often lacking in epilepsy services (Hannah and Brodie, 1998).

The booklet should always be carried by the individual with epilepsy, to ensure appropriate action should they have a seizure and that all information is readily available at appointments.

This booklet will hopefully lead to an improved lifestyle for the person with epilepsy. Helping to monitor medication, daily routines and minimise precipitating factors as supported by the Department of Health Document *Valuing People* (2001).

Catherine Doherty RNMH
Prof. Dip in Epilepsy
BSc (Hons) Community Health Nursing
November 2002

Index

Contents

Emergency plan

I have epilepsy and experience the
following types of seizures:

1.

2.

3.

If you should find me in a seizure, please take the following steps:

1. Make sure I am safe — remove any dangers
2. Do not move me unless I am in danger ~ then place me to the floor,
   clearing all furniture
3. Do **NOT** put anything in my mouth
4. Try to put me on my side (in the recovery position)
5. Hold my head or place a cushion underneath it
6. Talk to me
7. Allow me to come out of my seizure
8. If I do not come around after .... minutes, please call an ambulance
   or administer rescue medication if you are able to do so (record medication
   given)
9. After I come out of my seizure, place me in the recovery position
10. Please contact my next of kin/main carer
11. Please wipe away any mucus
12. Please time my seizure and observe seizure type
13. Advise either my carer or paramedic staff of the seizure type and time
14. **DO NOT PANIC**

Personal details

Name: ....Date of birth: .... Male/female

Address:...

....

....

Telephone number: ....

Next of kin: ....

Relationship: ....Contact no:....................

Main carer (if applicable): ....

Address of main carer:...

....

Personal details cont

First language: ....

Method of communication: ....

Interpreter required: ....

Religion: ....Practising   Yes/NO

Ethnicity: ....

Height: ....

Weight: ....

Medical information

Blood group:...

Known allergies..

Rescue medication required: Yes/No

General practitioner name: ....Telephone no: ....

Address: ....

....

Specialist involved in epilepsy management: ....

Type of specialism: ....

Address of specialist: ....

Telephone no. of specialist: ....

Address where main case notes held re management of epilepsy:

....

....

Telephone no. where case notes held: ....

Professionals involved in my care

The following people help me to manage my epilepsy:

Name	Position	Workplace telephone no.	Frequency of appointments
1			
2			
3			
4			
5			
6			

Diagnosis of epilepsy

I had my first seizure at the age of: ....

Diagnosis of epilepsy was confirmed on: ....

Seizure type and syndrome currently diagnoses:

1	
2	
3	
4	

Current medication
This includes all medication

Medication	Dose and schedule	Preparation	Date Initiated	Reason for medication	Side-effects experienced

Previous anti-convulsant medication prescribed

Medication	Doses and schedule	Date discontinued	Reason for discontinuation

Rescue medication

Medication	Preparation	Dose and schedule	Date Initiated	Reason for medication

At times I may go into status epilepticus (recurrent seizures)

If I do not come out of a seizure state after ....minutes, I need the above medication

The medication has to be administed **orally/rectally/nasal**

Alternative therapies

The following alternative therapy regimes can help to control my epilepsy

Ketogenic diet   yes/no   see attached diet sheet

Acupuncture   yes/no

Other therapies   yes/no

Medication	Preparation	Dose and schedule	Date Initiated	Reason for medication

Seizure management

Type of seizure

Before the seizure

Precipitating factors	
Warnings	

During the seizure

Seizure description	

After the seizure

Seizure recovery period	

Action taken

Sometimes I require rescue medication	

Seizure checklist

Pre-seizure	Y	N	N/A	Comments
Aura — taste/smell/nausea/tingling				
Associated with stress				
Behaviour change				
Mood change				
Sleep — pattern change				
Lethargy				
Constipation				
Associated with menstruation				
Illness				
Automatims				
Vocalisation				
Scream/cry/laughing				

Seizure checklist cont

During seizure	Y	N	N/A	Comments
Loses consciousness				
Remains conscious				
Cyanosis				
Face pale				
Face flushed				
Staring on onset				
Eye movement/deviation				
Do they fall				
Atonic (floppy)				
Tonic (rigid)				
Rhythmic jerking				
Brief spasms				
Incontinence				
Automatisms				
Behaviour problems				

After seizure	Y	N	N/A	Comments
Is the person confused?				
Does the person sleep?				
Aggression				
Automatisms				
Headache				
Amnesia				
Paralysis				
Mood alteration				

Seizure type	Jan	Feb	March	April	May	Jun	July	Aug	Sept	Oct	Nov	Dec

Rescue medication	Jan	Feb	March	April	May	Jun	July	Aug	Sept	Oct	Nov	Dec

Epilepsy record

Month................

	1	2	3	4	5	6	7	8	9	10	11	12	13	14	15	16	17	18	19	20	21	22	23	24	25	26	27	28	29	30	31
1 am																															
2 am																															
3 am																															
4 am																															
5 am																															
6 am																															
7 am																															
8 am																															
9 am																															
10 am																															
11 am																															
12																															
1 pm																															
2 pm																															
3 pm																															
4 pm																															
5 pm																															
6 pm																															
7 pm																															
8 pm																															
9 pm																															
10 pm																															
11pm																															
12																															

Precipitating factors

I have epilepsy, my seizures may be triggered by the following factors:

Triggers	Yes/No	Comments
Alcohol		
Boredom		
Constipation		
Lack of sleep		
Menstruation/menopause		
Missed meals		
Non-compliance of medication		
Photosensitivity		
Stress		
Illness		
Excitement		
Other issues, eg. food		

Blood tests

Please complete when undertaking blood tests in relation to epilepsy management:

Type of test	Date of test	Date tests received	Results/comments	Signature
Full blood count				
Urea and electrolytes				
Thyroid function test				
Amylase				
Other				

Drug level investigations

Please complete when undertaking investigations in relation to anti-epileptic drugs

Drug name	Date of test	Date tests received	Results/comments	Signature

Investigations

Type of test	Date of test	Date tests received	Results/comments	Signature
EEG				
Sleep derived EEG				
Ambulatory EEG				
MRI				
CAT scan				
Video telemetry				
PET scan				
Angiogram				

Epilepsy surgery

I have had the following surgery in relation to my epilepsy:

Type of surgery	Date	Hospital	Responsible medical officer	Comments

I currently have a vagal nerve stimulator fitted: .... Yes/No

(Source: Midlands Focus in Epilepsy and Learning Disabilties, 2002)

Information given

Information	Date	Comment by client	Staff member signature

Hospital admissions related to epilepsy

Please complete for **epilepsy** related
hospital admissions only

Date	Name of hospital	Reason for admission	Comments	Date of discharge

Risk assessment

Subject: ....

Name: ....

Person completing: ....

Home/respite/day care/travel: ....

Risk factors	H/M/L	Risk reducers	Resource implications	1/2/3	Date	Comments

Key	H ~ high	1 ~ easily achievable
	M ~ medium	2 ~ achievable with time/resource
	L ~ low	3 ~ not achievable ~ beyond limitations

Epilepsy care plan

My needs	How can this be achieved	Person responsible	How will we know if this is working	Expected outcome	Date of review

Signed   Designation   Date

Comments/questions

This section has been left blank in order for you to write down any questions you may wish to ask the doctor/nurse at your next appointment

References

Branford D, Bhaumik S, Duncan F (1998) Epilepsy in adults with learning disabilities. *Seizure* **7**(6): 473–7

Carvill S, Clarke D, Cassidy G (1999) The management of epilepsy in a hospital for people with a learning disability. *Seizure* **8**(3): 175–80

Department of Health (2001) *Valuing People: A New Strategy for Learning Disability for the 21st Century*. Department of Health, London

Epilepsy task force (1999) *Specification for Epilepsy Services*. Glaxo Wellcome

Field (2000) *Milands Focus in Epilepsy and Learning disabilties. Risk assessment.* Unpublished

Hannah JA, Brodie MJ (1998) Epilepsy and learning disabilities — a challenge for the next millennium? *Seizure* **7**: 3–13

Lhatoo SD, Sander JWAS (2001) The epidemiology of epilepsy and learning disability. *Epilepsia* **42**(supp.1)